Community Organizers
and Social Planners

OTHER PUBLICATIONS IN THE Community Organization Series
SPONSORED BY THE COUNCIL ON SOCIAL WORK EDUCATION (CSWE)

ARNOLD GURIN, Community Organization Curriculum in Graduate
Social Work Education: Report and Recommendations,
published by CSWE.

ARNOLD GURIN AND ROBERT PERLMAN, Community Organization
and Social Planning, *copublished by CSWE and*
John Wiley and Sons, Inc.

JACK ROTHMAN AND WYATT JONES, A New Look at Field
Instruction: Education for Application of Practice Skills in
Community Organization and Social Planning, *copublished by*
CSWE and Association Press.

DEBORAH GOLDEN, ARNULF M. PINS, AND WYATT JONES, Students in
Schools of Social Work: A Study of Characteristics and Factors
Affecting Career Choice and Practice Concentration,
published by CSWE.

Community Organizers and Social Planners

A VOLUME OF CASE AND ILLUSTRATIVE MATERIALS

Joan Levin Ecklein, *Boston State College*

Armand Lauffer, *School of Social Work*

The University of Michigan

Published Jointly by

John Wiley & Sons, Inc., *New York • London • Sydney • Toronto*

and Council on Social Work Education, *New York, N.Y.*

Library of Congress Catalogue Card Number: 75-171912

ISBN 0-471-22980-6

Printed in the United States of America.

10 9 8 7 6 5

Foreword

This volume, along with several other publications, is the result of a three-year comprehensive study of the community-organization curriculum in graduate social work education sponsored by the Council on Social Work Education (CSWE).

This book contains a number of case studies depicting problems and projects handled by professionals involved in community organization and social planning. Community organizers and social planners are found in social work and in other professions. Their tasks are important, complex and, at times, thankless. They need special knowledge and skill and require educational preparation. A key purpose of this volume is to provide current, relevant, and useful teaching material for formal educational and agency in-service training programs to prepare staff with competence in community organization and social planning.

Case and illustrative materials in this volume show community organizers and social planners at work in various settings. The inclusion of certain issues does not mean that the problems mentioned and the practices involved in solving them are the only ones or the favored ones. These issues are the problems of society today—problems with which workers must deal—and some methods by which they were handled. Only a small sampling of the problems extant and the approaches to their resolution can be included here. Some readers will know of other and more pressing problems and of different approaches.

Other publications resulting from this community-organization curriculum study include an overview, *Community Organization Curriculum in Graduate Social Work Education: Report and Recommendations,* by Arnold Gurin; a textbook, *Community Organization and Social Planning,* by Arnold Gurin and Robert Perlman (copublished by CSWE and John Wiley and Sons); *A New Look at Field Instruction: Education for Application of Practice Skills in Community Organization and Social Planning,* by Jack Rothman and Wyatt Jones (copublished by CSWE and Association Press); and *Students in Schools of Social Work: A Study of Characteristics and Factors Affecting Career Choice and Practice Concentration,* by Deborah Golden, Arnulf M. Pins, and Wyatt Jones (published by CSWE).

Publication of the findings of the community-organization curriculum development project occurs at a significant time in the history of higher education and social work education. Major social problems facing our nation underscore the critical need for personnel with competence in community organization and social planning.

The findings, recommendations, and new resources produced by the Community Organization Curriculum Development Project should be of value to faculty, students, and practitioners in social work and other professions. This volume is particularly useful in conjunction with the textbook, *Community Organization and Social Planning,* but it can also be used independently. Some of the materials also have been issued separately and are available from CSWE.

CSWE and the field of community organization and social planning are grateful to Joan Ecklein and Armand Lauffer for preparing this volume; to Arnold Gurin for his able and creative leadership of the total project; and to the other members of the project staff and the advisory committee for their many contributions.

Thanks are expressed to the Office of Juvenile Delinquency and Youth Development, Social and Rehabilitation Service, Department of Health, Education, and Welfare, whose grant made this project possible.

July 1970

ARNULF M. PINS
Executive Director CSWE

Contents

vii

Community Organizers and Social Planners

1

Community Organizers and Social Planners

INTRODUCTION TO THE BOOK

The day is short, and the work is great. It is not your duty to complete the work, but neither are you free to desist from it. PERKE AVOT, *The Ethics of the Fathers*

This is a book about people who intervene in the lives of others and who tamper with the goals and machinery of society. It is a book about a new occupational grouping of people who meddle, organize, and plan with and on behalf of others. It is a book about, for, and by community organizers and social planners. Their activities are not entirely new. Their professionalization, however, is a recent phenomenon.

As professional problem solvers, these men and women deal with the results of institutional imbalances that combine to distribute resources and opportunities inequitably. Specializing in new methods to influence the direction of social change, community organizers and social planners may be found practicing in such professions as medicine, law, public health, city planning, education, and social work. They have much in common with organizers and planners in social movements, labor, and industry. Yet they strive to develop identities of their own and to extend the mandates of their professions.

These developments have been especially rapid in social work, a profession that bases its mandate on competence to deal with the problems of dependency, deviance, and disenfranchisement. Social work, from its inception, has given priority to the tasks of identifying social and human needs, devising proposed solutions, and undertaking ameliorative programs. It has not always been successful. As the case illustrations in this volume demonstrate, organizers and planners, whatever their background,

1

are hard put to document either their failures or their successes. Since they are operating with rudimentary skills, little practice theory, and fragmentary knowledge in the field of practice of unknown complexity, it is surprising that they are successful at all.

THE CONTENT AND ORGANIZATION OF THIS BOOK

We examine particulars in order to make generalizations possible. This is a casebook. Its format departs somewhat from other casebooks used in professional education. Public and business administration cases, for example, are generally presented as dilemmas on which administrators must act. Law-school cases involve decisions that have been handed down, upon which precedents have been set. Cases used in medical schools are more likely to illustrate a particular clinical syndrome. Schools of social work use cases that depict the process by which a social worker intervenes on a client's behalf, and explore the interaction between practitioner and client or client system.

We use each of these approaches. What distinguishes this volume is that nearly all of our case materials are presented in the first person. Organizers and planners speak for themselves. At times we record their descriptions or analyses of complex intervention processes. At other times we abstract a short vignette or statement of principle that illustrates a point or a practice style. Our objective is to depict how community organizers and social planners do their work. This work is frequently spectacular and inspirational. Sometimes it is depressing and insipid. We include illustrations of good and bad performance in order to make this volume as close to the realities of practice as possible.

Cases and illustrative materials may be 1 page long, or 20 pages long. We have avoided uniform lengths in order to present only material that is useful for learning and teaching purposes. The book is divided into two sections: Part I, which deals with the activities of community organizers; and Part II, which presents comparable materials on social planners. Each section begins with a conceptual chapter that puts the work of organizers or planners into the perspective that informs the entire volume. When combined with short introductions to the cases in each of the subsequent chapters, the two conceptual chapters will enable the reader to focus on the central issues presented.

ORIGIN OF THE CASE MATERIALS; ACKNOWLEDGMENTS

All of these materials were gathered by the staff of the Council on Social Work Education's Community Organization Curriculum Development

Project, from 1965 through 1969. Interviews were conducted by the authors and their colleagues on the project, Arnold Gurin, Wyatt Jones, and Robert Perlman, or by a Massachusetts contract research firm, the Cambridge Center for the Study of Behavioral Science. These interviews were not initially conducted with a casebook in mind. Our original concern was to bypass the overly abstract or ideologically biased literature on community organization in order to recommend curriculum content to schools of social work. By going directly to the source—by interviewing the practitioners "on-the-line"—we hoped to learn more about the real "stuff" of which practice is made.[1] We learned a great deal. The decision to transform our interviews into case materials for instructional purposes was made after continual urgings by our colleagues in graduate schools of social work, in the field, and in other professional schools, who called our attention to the need for new and up-to-date teaching materials.

In a number of cases, we abstracted reports by other authors, or asked colleagues with access to interesting materials to record them for inclusion in this book.

In many of our cases, names and localities are disguised for the protection of the individuals involved. In some instances, we may have transposed a setting from a Community Action Board to a Model Cities Administration, or from a Western city to an Eastern community. In several cases, we brought incidents together that were originally related to us by more than one practitioner. In other cases, we present one practitioner's observations in more than one place. This is done in order to make the book more readable, and to make each case more distinctive or useful for learning purposes. In every case, however, we kept the opinions, chronologies, and insights intact in the way they were presented to us. To the extent possible, we recorded the words and language of the practitioner whom we interviewed. We think the authenticity of this volume will be readily apparent.

No book is written by its authors alone. We owe many debts to the scholars and theoreticians whose works preceded ours. In particular, we owe an intellectual debt of great magnitude to Ronald Warren. The content, form, and conceptual format of this book is as much the product of our colleagues, Arnold Gurin, Wyatt C. Jones, and Robert Perlman as it is our own. We spent three exciting, informative, and difficult years together as staff members of the Community Organization Curriculum Development Project. Sponsored by the Council on Social Work Education (CSWE) located at Brandeis University and funded by the Federal

---

[1] See the appendix for an interview guide useful to those who may wish to gather additional case materials.

Office of Juvenile Delinquency and Adult Crime, the Project staff might have been subjected to numerous pressures. We were not.

The support from OJD was adequate to complete the task. Arnulf M. Pins, Executive Director of the CSWE, gave us continued encouragement despite the controversies he knew our work would engender. Charles I. Schottland, dean of the Florence Heller Graduate School for Advanced Studies in Social Welfare and now president of Brandeis University, made it possible for us to work together as a staff despite our other academic commitments. Arnold Gurin's leadership lent integrity and coherence to the project.

It is hard to measure how much we owe to our spouses, David Ecklein and Rickie Lauffer. Rickie read and proofed the semifinal and final drafts. David suffered his wife's absence on more than one field trip. The unsung heroines of the book are our secretaries. Betty Jean Akbarian at Brandeis sorted out and typed our rough field notes. Katie Lee at Berkeley typed the semifinal manuscript, working into the late hours and on weekends for an entire summer. Lynn Phillips began a new job at the University of Michigan with the chore of completing the final draft.

But most of all, we are indebted to the organizers and planners whose work and whose lives make up the pages of this book. Some are social workers, many are not. All of them have contributed to the re-making of America in the 1960s. Without their work and that of those who follow, this book would have neither meaning nor substance.

CONCEPTUAL FRAMEWORK

The conceptual scheme that informs this volume was developed by the staff of the Curriculum Project. We will summarize it briefly in this chapter and expand on it subsequently.

Organizers, as we have observed them, direct their activities at modifying the behavior of people in their roles as citizens, consumers, members, or functionaries of organizations. *Planners* direct their activities towards the modification, elimination, or creation of policies, programs, services, or resources in organizations and social institutions.

Organizing and planning are complementary activities. Most planning requires some organizing. Both sets of activities require that the practitioner perform *analytic* and *interactional* tasks; that is, he must engage in interpersonal processes with people, and he must think about what he is doing at every stage in strategy formation. His focus is on problem solving.

Organizers and planners may be engaged in a number of phases or stages in the problem solving process. These may be categorized as (1) uncovering or defining a problem, (2) building the structural and communication links for action on the problem, (3) laying out the alternative options and adopting a policy, (4) developing a plan and implementing a program, and (5) receiving feedback, monitoring progress, and redefining the problem. As must be evident, this is a cyclical or spiral process. The planner or organizer may enter or leave the scene at any point.

In our observations, the practitioner is rarely a free agent. Regardless of value and ideological commitments, or of skill and expertise, much of his work is determined by the *contexts* within which he practices. Contextual components include (1) the auspice under which he operates— the legitimating and sponsoring body, (2) the source of financial and other support, (3) the purpose of the organization for whom or on whose behalf he acts, (4) the target of his intervention, whether a population group, organization, or service network, (5) the internal structure of the organization within which he works, and finally, (6) the locus at which his intervention is pitched—the neighborhood, the local community, the state, and the like. Together, these components constrain and limit the *scope* of his activities, and give him the *mandate* for his actions.

Organizers and planners are found in a variety of practice settings or arenas. A growing number work directly with *voluntary associations* of people banded together as self-help groups or social movements, or to provide a service. They may be organized around neighborhood, content, or ethnic concerns. Other practitioners are employed by *agencies* whose primary function is the delivery of direct services. They may, themselves, be direct-service practitioners or administrators. Increasingly, however, many direct-service agencies are employing community-organization and planning specialists. Finally, they may be found in a multitude of *funding, allocating, coordinating, and planning settings*. These may be under governmental or voluntary auspices. They may be at the local or extracommunity level.

We do not suggest, of course, that organizers or planners are captives of their employers or sponsors. The effective practitioner, as our cases illustrate, may focus much of his energies on creating changes within his own agency, voluntary association, or social movement. The way in which a practitioner performs his responsibilities is an individual matter. It is determined greatly by his ideological commitments, his characteristic way of looking at problems, his technical, analytic, and interactional skills, his energy, his personal style, and the like. We think this book attests to the great variety of practitioner types, agency settings, and problems of concern found in community-organization and social planning. This variety, we feel, is not only healthy but also essential at this stage in occupational development. Premature closure on theory, style, scope, or locale would only stifle what is quite apparently a vibrant and energetic occupation.

THE PEOPLE OF THIS BOOK

The people who speak from these pages are organizers and planners at the grass-roots level, in service agencies, in political positions and in Federal agencies. Their positions on social change range from radical to moderate. Obviously a book of this scope could not do them justice. Many organizers and planners are not represented. This was not by choice. Current materials on welfare rights, environment, and women's liberation, for example, could not be prepared in time for this volume. Their voices are being heard elsewhere in this land.

The book was finished over two years before publication. Changes have occurred in that time. These will be readily apparent to the reader. For example, almost no white people are organizing in black communities today and the word Negro used by organizers several years ago, as we quoted them then, would now be unthinkable. However, the issues raised by the organizers and planners have a timeless quality and will always be relevant to people seriously interested in effectuating social change.

We have acquired a profound appreciation for organizers and planners. On the line in a very public way, their successes are difficult to measure. They must often be satisfied with tentative accomplishments. The competent practitioner may be plagued with the feeling that he has not done the best possible job, that alternative choices of action might have led to a closer approximation of his original goal, or that greater skill would have reduced wastage of resources and opportunities.

Few of the practitioners whose work is recorded in this volume are fully successful. There are no easy solutions to complex problems. Yet these men and women know that *their day is short. Their work is great. And they do not desist.*

PART I

Community Organizers

2

Community Organizers and Voluntary Associations

INTRODUCTION TO PART I

Don't mourn for me—organize! JOE HILL

I have a dream. MARTIN LUTHER KING

It is how we use our lives that determines what kind of men we are. CESAR CHAVEZ

ORGANIZING FOR SOCIAL REFORM IN THE UNITED STATES

American history is studded by the growth and decay, accomplishments and failures of voluntary associations. Despite the ethos of rugged individualism and of Horatio Alger shoestring-to-riches mythology, much of America's social progress has been based on the emergence of social movements, trade unions, and self-help associations. Collective rather than individual action has frequently resulted in pressures on the social system leading to reform and resource reallocation. The way out of the slums for teaming millions of newcomers, whether from foreign lands or from rural America, has been through the mutual action of those similarly or vicariously affected by repressive social conditions.

Despite periodic spurts of effort, however, the history of organizing for social reform in the United States has been fragmentary. Organizers and planners of one generation are frequently unaware of the contributions of their predecessors. Traditions, techniques, and strategies have not been passed down or built upon.

Reform efforts of the late nineteenth century and the union and radical movements of the 1920s and 1930s were separated by a period of relative tranquility. The Second World War with its unity of national perspective, and the subsequent homogenization of the Cold War and McCarthy eras,

9

further separated us from the traditions of the union movement. Unions have themselves become separated from their social and reform objectives as the processes of institutionalization and accommodation have taken precedence.

We have frequently been dismayed at the ahistoricism of the many young organizers we have met. The fault is not entirely theirs. The traditions of organizing have not been transmitted intact.

Today's organizers are a mixed lot. The settings within which they practice, the ideological and analytic perceptions that inform their activities, the people with whom or on whose behalf they work—all these affect the roles they play, what they do, and how they do it.

From an advocation or cause, organizing has evolved into a new occupation to help people accomplish what they could not without organization. The practitioners of this occupation may be referred to as grass-roots organizers, community organizers, community developers, and not incidentally, meddlers, outside agitators, and do-gooders. They are meddlers, for in most cases they do come from some "outside" organizations and their expressed purpose for being on the scene is to do some good. While organizing is not a new activity, its professionalization within social work and other professions and its location in university curriculum are a new phenomenon.

Community-organization (CO) practice as an occupation and as a specialization within social work is still in its infancy. There is too little experience on which to build practice principles or consistent practice approaches. Successful practice is still very much an art and an accident, with improvisation a frequent maneuver. Our understanding of social change is still quite rudimentary. We do not know which strategies under which circumstances may be the more effective ones. Further, the goals of organizing are frequently mixed, just as our definitions of social problems tend to be complex. Organizers, whatever their stated objectives, may contribute to a blocking rather than an enhancing progress. Progress is itself subject to varying interpretations across generations and within generations themselves.

THE PURPOSE OF ORGANIZING

The organizer's efforts are aimed at modifying the attitudes and behaviors of people, not as individuals but as members of groups, as employees, as citizens, as clients, and as residents of a neighborhood. While it is true that organizers may represent right-wing reactionary and repressive social forces, the community organizers represented in this volume are generally concerned with the accomplishment of one or both of these ends: (1) the improvement of social provisions for some disadvantaged or disenfranchised population, and (2) the enhancement of social relationships to bring about a greater capacity on the part of some target population to deal with common problems.

Organizing may be viewed as a means of achieving and guiding local control over problems that originate elsewhere in society. Programs and services are aimed at specific populations of the disenfranchised or disadvantaged. Unfortunately, such efforts are rarely adequate or sufficiently comprehensive. If palliative, they may do more to perpetuate the problem they set out to overcome than to solve it. Many action programs aimed at problem amelioration soon become institutionalized into service programs. These same service programs develop needs of their own, and may perpetuate themselves long after the problems at which they were aimed have been redefined or relocated.

Organizers are faced with a welter of social institutions, social problems, and rapidly accelerating social change affecting both of these. They may have to choose between aiming their efforts either at improvements in social services and amenities, at changes in the social structure, at redistribution of power and influence, or at building the patterns of interaction leading to a "sense of community."

The organizer may choose *a strategy that leads to the confrontation of social problems,* or he may choose *a strategy leading to confrontations with the social structure.* If his concerns are primarily with social problems, his organizing efforts tend to become particularized and situation-limited. His efforts will generally be aimed at a particular service system or network. Organizing victories may be manifested in such concessions by the service system as a new street light, greater community control of the schools, greater freedom for students, enforcement of housing codes, maximum welfare payments, and an open employment policy. Groups organized to achieve such limited objectives may have difficulties in joining together in wider associations. Frequently they disintegrate following a major victory. Others may successfully transform themselves into service organizations, or if they are to remain action-oriented, they select new but immediate goals.

If the organizer's efforts are directed at confrontations with the social structure, social actions may take place at the local level, but may have implications for a much wider geographic scope. His concerns may be to expose "the system" as repressive and corrupt and to make the appropriate changes, or to enhance participatory democracy.

Participation is of critical concern to the organizer. It may be seen as an end in itself, or it may be viewed as a means for training leadership and building a power base. Local participation may be aimed at over-coming the increasing centralization of decision-making power at levels removed from the people whose lives are directly affected by those decisions. For some, participation is an antidote to the massive institutions that threaten to destroy "community."

Participation may also be seen as a regenerative force, as an alternative to alienation, and as means of enhancing human dignity and expressing man's humanity. Many organizers express an explicit faith in man's ability to deal with the personal implications of social problems through interaction on a face-to-face level.

COMMUNITY DEVELOPMENT AND SOCIAL ACTION

Two terms have been used to designate organizing approaches: *community development* and *social action*. In community development, the organizer's main target is always the consumer of his services: the resident, the member, the recipient. His goal is to overcome the individual's or the group's ignorance of the possibilities open to them. People are organized to facilitate education and communication, to nurture hope. An immediate goal, if selected, is always considered by the organizer as a means toward another goal: the establishment of "community" and the ability of people through cooperative and collaborative ventures to face their common problems. The process itself and the learning that results from it are more important than the achievement of any particular objective. The process is not time-limited.

The social-action approach differs in that the organizer's goal is to redress a power imbalance, or to open up a service network. The organizer is concerned with specific social injustices. The target, rather than being the consumer of service or member himself, may be a political structure or service system. A particular reform may be important for its own sake, or for the change it effectuates in the way in which the social system functions. Issues tend to become polarized. Successes are frequently measured in immediate, time-limited victories.

Social-action strategies may emerge out of real or perceived conflicts, or from opposing perceptions of social problems. In contrast, community-development approaches generally emerge out of agreement on common goals and a mutuality of perceptions about the cause and consequences of social problems.

There has been a tendency on the part of some writers to stress one approach over the other. We do not perceive them as mutually exclusive, nor do we feel that one approach is necessarily better than another. Both approaches attempt to influence the course of social change or cope with its effects at the local level. In our observations of practice, and as our cases illustrate, organizers are generally involved in both social action and community development at the same time or at different times within an action process. Frequently, a community-development approach may be seen as a stage in a process leading towards action and the achievement of specific goals. Similarly, a current focus on the achievement of a specific victory may be a means to a more long-range development approach. Action becomes a phase of development and development leads to action. We do not suggest that there are no real differences between organizers of the social-action persuasion and their colleagues in community development. We do feel, however, that in practice, these distinctions become muted.

DILEMMAS, CONTRADICTIONS, AND TENSIONS UNDERLYING PRACTICE

The community organizers we interviewed were concerned with advancing the interests of disadvantaged groups, with improving social conditions, with the delivery of needed services or the provision of social amenities, with redistribution of power and influence, with enhancement of the coping mechanisms of target populations, and with strengthening community participation and integration. These objectives, however, are frequently in conflict with each other. The establishment of a multiservice center, for example, may be achieved much more effectively without resorting to broad community involvement. Organizers may represent different constituencies, each struggling for the same objectives in opposition to each other. A focus on delivery of a service may, in reality, do little about the redistribution of power. It may even consolidate it unevenly.

There is an underlying tension between the advocacy of the service-oriented approach and a political or action orientation. Services focus on individual needs, whereas organizing focuses on the location of common problems and joint efforts at their solution. In a sense, each may be considered a corrective of the other. Social action may ignore the needs of individuals, while a service orientation may ignore the impact of social conditions on the etiology of the problem of concern. Some action-oriented organizations—the Black Panthers, for example—have added a multitude of services as supports to their action platforms. Other organizations have built their action platforms on the foundation of an earlier focus on services—Cesar Chavez's community union is an example. Still other action organizations—as is evident in many of the Alinsky organized projects—refuse to deal with service needs during certain phases of the organizing process for fear that these might dilute the organization's purposes. Other agencies—such as Mobilization for Youth in New York and many local community-action agencies—have attempted service and action simultaneously, only to find that the pursuit of one was detrimental to the other. Programs of the National Welfare Rights Organization are marked by this tension.

The question of goals and goal displacement enters here. Every organizing decision, and every action taken, is complemented by a set of alternative decisions not made and actions not taken. Actions and decisions represent commitments in directions that may not easily be reversed. An early focus on service, for example, makes it exceedingly difficult to reorient an organization towards action at a later date. A focus on ethnic or neighborhood solidarity at one stage may make it impossible to progress to a community orientation at another. Goals may be continually displaced as day-to-day activities set precedents for future directions. The relationship between service and action is a case in point. At times, an action program is initiated in order to effectuate changes in a service system, only to become an arm of that system or to perpetuate it once a particular concession is won.

The very existence of a service organization may be the basis for the voluntary association's purpose. Symbiotic relationships frequently exist between service organizations and voluntary associations or action groups organized to effect policy changes in that organization or service system. Tenants' organizations, welfare-rights groups, and unions are examples. An organizer hoping to move a group of people organized for a specific purpose (as in putting pressure on a housing authority) may be sorely disillusioned in his attempt to interest his constituents in broader social issues or political involvements.

Reform-oriented associations frequently disintegrate or disappear once their reform efforts are satisfied, if only partially. As reforms become institutionalized, or as an action organization assumes responsibility for the delivery of services or the monitoring of service delivery, the focus of membership concern frequently shifts to maintaining the service and its efficient delivery. Thus, reform efforts become bureaucratized and institutionalized, the new institutions developing lives of their own. These, in turn, may become unresponsive to further change.

Organizers are frequently caught in a bind between their professional and ideological commitments to long-range goals and the need to achieve immediate objectives, between their espousal of utopian objectives and the need to achieve feasible goals. Most organizing efforts are aimed at the secondary manifestations of social problems. Most organizing, what-ever the rhetoric behind it, is in practice aimed at piecemeal adjustments of the machinery of society. Many organizers, we know, have been accused of applying Band-Aid therapy. We feel this is an unfortunate analogy and offers little understanding of a complex set of phenomena. The magnitude and direction of many social changes may be determined by forces out of the reach of most organizers and their constituencies. Never-theless, the impact is felt by everyone. Organizers know that imbalances and inequities can be righted as powerless populations develop needed skills and perspectives. There are no shortcuts in achievement of long-range goals. They are built out of day-to-day efforts of those who stand to gain the most from being organized.

A further tension exists in the fact that organizers must concern them-selves simultaneously with the achievement of specific changes and the accomplishment of visible victories, while building a network of rela-tionships that make and maintain the voluntary association. How is success to be measured? By achievement of specific reforms, or by lon-gevity of organization? By the establishment of a new network of rela-tionships and a sense of community or by a visual accomplishment? Warren Haggstrom has suggested the term "organizational mileage" as a measure of progress, accomplishment, and development. An organiza-tion may suffer a defeat but become stronger by it, therefore netting additional organizational mileage, or it may win a concession and then fall into apathy, thereby losing mileage. But organizational mileage, useful as a heuristic concept, provides no adequate criterion for the measurement of success. Nor can it, so long as organizing goals are multiple, complementary, and sometimes contradictory.

At once the major strength and major weakness of the organizing effort is that it attempts to deal with the manifestations of social problems at the local level or within particular social strata. It is at the local level or within a certain stratum of society, after all, that problems are manifested and that people are hurt. On the other hand, problems do not originate at the local level. Change efforts located in the neighborhood, for ex-ample, are frequently negated by actions at the state, regional, or na-tional levels.

On the other hand, a viable democracy needs the constant creation of new channels for the aggregation, articulation, and communication of the unrepresented interests of submerged segments of the population. Many observers argue that organizations and institutions do not trans-form themselves, that the pressure for change must come from those ele-ments that stand to benefit most from the application of pressure at those points of decision that materially affect their welfare. Only pressure from the bottom up, the argument continues, can enable a disenfranchised group to have a voice in these decisions. The aggregate effect of many local actions produces social change. It may be true that a single action resulting in the reversal of an urban-renewal policy in Baltimore may be no more effective than a failure at a similar attempt in San Francisco, it is argued, but hundreds of attempts by an organized citizenry will have the desired cumulative effect. Those who maintain this position point to the significant shifts in public policy regarding American military spending and military interventions during the late 1960s as an example of public policy being shaped by the intervention of many local citizens' organizations despite very little national guidance or coordination.

Not accounted for in this somewhat simplistic overstatement, however, are the multiple pressures from other sources, the potential or actual backlash that may overshadow most gains from the organizing activity, and the changes in other sectors of the society, all of which impinge on the problem of concern, and all of which affect it. Organizers are frequently unprepared to deal with repressive measures. They may not be aware that the severity of repression may be in direct proportion to their actual effectiveness in producing structural change.

Whatever one's views on the location of decision-making power in society, it is clear that the power to initiate actions and to precipitate changes is located at every level in society. The ability to effectuate policy changes depends on a number of variables. These include the energy, the resources, the expertise, and the numbers of people dedicated to achieving a certain change. Conversely, the same factors can be brought to bear in favor of the status quo by those who would block reform. Much of the organizer's time will be spent in overcoming resistence to change in addition to promoting support for it. The choices open to him may include engaging in conflict or cooperative ventures. Frequently he engages in both.

Beyond the documentation of impressions, it is almost impossible to verify effectiveness. We have as yet neither the indicators to measure change nor the theory to explain it. We have, therefore, little of what we need to measure the true impact of the organizer's interventions. This is not to suggest that he ought not to intervene in situations where a social need is clearly identified or a social problem is defined to exist. On the contrary, the vitality of our society is dependent on such interventions. It is suggested, however, that he must be modest in his claims and expectations. To act otherwise, we believe, is to act irresponsibly towards one's clients, towards one's constituencies, and towards one's profession.

THE NATURE OF VOLUNTARY ASSOCIATIONS

Voluntary associations of people interested in social change may be cause-oriented, service-oriented, or development-oriented. They are found within every stratum of society. In Part I of this volume we illustrate, in some depth, the nature of practice with disadvantaged populations. We do not describe organizing efforts among the very wealthy, because much of it, conducted by social workers, tends to fall closer to our definition of planning. It is expressed in such activities as charity-raising, the expansion of a service agency, and political pressure for advanced social legislation. Practice at this level will be illustrated in later sections of the volume dealing with interorganizational planning and coordinating of settings.

Some attention is given to organizing a middle-class clientele. Here we stress the relationship between middle-class associations and those made up of groups lower down in the societal strata. Recently, organizers have begun to work in middle-class, white communities for the reduction of both attitudinal and institutional racism. The range of settings is too broad to cover well in a volume of this sort. We have chosen to illustrate only those efforts of middle-class groups that are devoted to either general social welfare or to the benefit of some disadvantaged group.

We have turned most of our attention to associations of the poor, the disadvantaged, and the disenfranchised because this is where social workers and others have increasingly directed their intervention efforts. In the turmoil of the late 1960s and early 1970s, this is where much of the "action is," and where much of it is likely to remain. It is also here that the greatest amount of professional help is needed.

Unfortunately, few of our cases illustrate work with the near-poor, those populations (generally among the lower middle class) whose status and financial positions are on shaky grounds and who perceive themselves to be threatened by upward movements from below. Little community organization is being practiced at this level.

This is numerically the largest stratum of society. It may also be the most conservative. Some organizers feel that it is this population that must be energized towards progressive social change. There are neither enough numbers nor enough other resources, they argue, among the poor. In the absence of documentation and experience of organizing for social change within this stratum, much of the volume is addressed to organizing among the poor.

Among the many disadvantages of the poor and of some ethnic minorities, are deficits in organizational skill, in influence, in technical expertise, and in money. Much of the organizer's time may be devoted to rectifying this imbalance through educational and other means. The absence of money is often made up through the concerted use of large numbers of people who, not having money to spend, can withhold it—as in store boycotts, rent strikes, and the like.

This absence of money, and the limitations on lower-class mobility frequently places geographic limitations on organizing efforts. For this reason, much of the organizing herein recorded is at the neighborhood level. This presents some difficulty for the organizer. How is the neighborhood to be defined? The geographic boundaries of the neighborhood may not be contiguous with its symbolic boundaries, its functional boundaries (schools, shops, and police districts), or with the boundaries of social interaction.

Organizers at the neighborhood level, therefore, may choose to work with people on the basis of a number of criteria: physical proximity (for example, block clubs and house councils); common cultural patterns; specific issues or concerns (for instance, school autonomy, welfare rights, and voter registration); or the objectives of a social movement.

Social movements are increasingly of interest because of their growth in variety and memberships, because their concerns transcend the boundaries of the neighborhood, because they tend to last over a period of time, and because the nature of their protests and the solidarity they engender bring them increasingly into the public eye. They, too, face the dilemma common to most organizing efforts—the need to produce immediate tangible results while promising some deferred state of social betterment. Local actions must be seen against an extended time span. Social movements tend to combine cause orientation with service orientation. For these reasons, they must constantly guard against goal displacement.

Other forms of neighborhood self-help associations arise on a temporally limited basis in response to an individual or community crisis, to a particular situation defined as a common problem. Few such associations emerge spontaneously. They frequently require the intervention of an outsider who can help local residents redefine their problems in such ways that they can be acted on. With the exceptions of new social movements, formal, lasting organizations and associations have not been characteristic of lower-class communities and neighborhoods. It took a massive dose of governmental and voluntary funds and large numbers of organized practitioners to stimulate many of the self-help associations found in American communities today. To a certain extent, even social movements have been indirectly affected by these other organizing efforts originating in the middle classes. Conversely, other organizing and planning efforts have been influenced by social movements. Many observers have pointed to the influence of the civil-rights movement, for example, on the early programs of the War on Poverty.

Many government and voluntary organizing projects are looked at with suspicion by those in social movements. It is a characteristic of social movements that they must question old values and institutions, strengthen their own positions by denigrating the work of others, develop new belief systems, articulate new values, and behave according to new norms. They evaluate their positions in contrast to those of a society whose belief systems, values, and norms have deprived their membership of equal standing.

For this reason, successful collaborative efforts between social movements and other self-help organizations in the same locality that are working on similar problems have been rare. Radical movements among students, in the black community, and among other ethnic minorities engage in action born of a redefinition of the social matrix in which they find themselves. The values they strive for, in our opinion, are not in antithesis to, but in concert with, earlier and fundamental American values. Frequently, it is not the specific reform they aim for, but the rhetoric and the tactics they use, that put them at odds with the rest of society. There are those among them who believe that social conflict and the use of confrontation tactics are an essential ingredient in pressing for meaningful social change. There are others who feel that these tactics are limited in effectiveness and may become even more so, if overused, or if used without some overall strategy. There are others who believe that change, to be lasting, must be based on mutuality of interest and effort.

Alliances between people's organizations and associations increase in importance as the numbers of self-help groups and social movements increase. In order for an alliance to be lasting, the parties to it must be in agreement on both means and ends. That this is rarely the case is evidenced by the continual splintering characteristic of the Left. Alliances are rarely effective beyond time-limited or action-limited periods. The establishment of alliances is of increasing concern to professional organizers working with the poor.

Alliances between lower-class and middle-class associations are also receiving increased attention. Foundations may fund an action program on a demonstration basis. Social agencies may actually organize their own groups of lower-class or neighborhood constituents. These new associations then develop lives of their own. As in the case of the Poverty Program and, to a certain extent, the Model Cities Administration, associations of indigenous people may become continual sources of embarrassment for sponsoring or funding organizations. This is especially so when they engage in controversial social-action issues, or engage in divisive or confrontation tactics. Community Action Agencies, in particular, have suffered from being caught in the middle between the neighborhood councils that they organized for political support and the "establishment" that they organized support against. Rather than have the support of those groups that they consider their constituencies, CAP agencies frequently have to balance the opposition from above (City Hall), and from below (neighborhood councils).

In such circumstances, the organizer is frequently suspect. Generally middle class in orientation and in background, certainly middle class in support, he is only infrequently accepted as really "belonging to the people." Even when indigenous workers are recruited at the neighborhood level, their training, their employment, and their assignments and interactions within the employing organization tend to rob them of the perspective of their constituency or neighborhood.

THE ORGANIZER'S ROLES

Under these conditions, the organizer may be expected to play a great variety of practice roles. These may be dependent on the goals of the institution by which he is employed and the particular position he holds within its formal organization; on the needs and characteristics of the target population; on the particular stage in the organizing process of the voluntary association's development; on the ideological perspective he holds; or on the strategies used to effectuate changes. A worker maintaining a community-development perspective may be expected to stress some roles over others, whereas an organizer maintaining a social-action perspective will stress still others. A representative of the city planning commission, for example, may be expected to function quite differently from an organizer within a social movement, though both may be dealing with the problem of housing for low-income people in a particular neighborhood.

Without attempting to be exhaustive, and at a risk of omission or distortion, we list the roles that are readily identifiable in the case materials that follow. These include:

Communicator
Interpreter
Expeditor
Broker
Negotiator

Mediator
Expert
Advocate
Enabler
Social therapist
Supervisor
Activist
Charismatic leader

These terms are all well defined in the literature. We do not feel that any one or any combination of these roles is most effective or most appropriate under all circumstances. None of these roles is ideologically neutral. Their selection will be based on the training, skill, and ideological perspective of the organizer and on the context within which he is organizing.

Much of the confusion in the roles that workers are called on to play stems from the issue of accountability. To whom is he accountable— his employer, his employer's constituency, the target of his intervention, his profession or occupational group, or his ideological commitments? There was a time not long ago when these issues were relatively clear. When professional behavior tended to emphasize cooperation, normative judgments could easily be made on the basis of consensus regarding "professional ethics." Today, however, the legitimacy of social institutions and service agencies is being challenged by clients and other organized groups. The issues of loyalty and responsibility are no longer clear.

At one time, loyalty to the agency was interpreted as concern for the client. This is certainly no longer the case. Organizations, in fact, may employ individuals with special characteristics to represent a constituency or subgroup that is expected to be in conflict with the dominant factions within an organization. An employee may be expected to represent that subgroup. The employment of black university administrators and communicators in predominantly white institutions is an example in point. Under such circumstances, the organizer may be called on to represent a subgroup in a process of negotiations. He may be called on to mediate disputes. With neither a body of laws nor a body of traditions to govern the mediation of community disputes, these are especially difficult roles.

While setting, auspice, and circumstance may determine the roles an organizer plays, how he plays them is very much a matter of skill, style, and experience. The timidity or the brashness of the individual organizer —his personal style—may be due to a variety of factors. Organizers must be wary of many pitfalls, and be aware of what Alen McSurley calls individual "hangups." An organizer may be overtly manipulative, or he may be afraid to manipulate and exploit people. He may perceive himself as a meddler or intruder in the lives of others, while simultaneously being unable to commit himself to prolonged involvements with those whom he organizes. He may, conversely, work so hard and become so committed as to lose his perspective and burn himself out in a year or two. The organizer may be so personally unable to make decisions or so ideologically committed to "letting the people decide" that he throws responsibility for complex decisions into the laps of those unprepared. He may become depressed by frequent defeats or elated by small victories. He may put too much or too little faith in those with whom he works.

Organizers sometimes play inappropriate roles or play their roles inappropriately. Their efforts may result in failure. We have included illustrations of failure in this volume for several reasons. We think it is possible to learn from failure. Empirically speaking, it is difficult to identify an action or series of actions as a success or a failure. Organizers have differed with us and among themselves in evaluating their activities. Finally, no field of practice is entirely successful. A book cataloging success, even were this possible, would be untrue to reality. We have attempted, instead, to allow practitioners to describe what they actually do, when, and how.

ORGANIZING TASKS AND STAGES IN PROBLEM SOLVING

Organizers are frequently evaluated on the basis of their interactional skills. To be successful, after all, an organizer must be able to talk with people, to influence them, to motivate them, to encourage them, to assess their readiness, and to help them deal with failures and aspire to victories. The stress on interactional skills, however, may relegate to the back door, a complementary set of skills—the ability to use rational processes for the formulation of objectives, the development of strategic efforts, and the evaluation of those efforts. Many organizers, we have observed, are overly involved in the specifics of a particular action, in their commitments to a particular population, or in their commitments to a particular social or ideological perspective. We have no quarrels with commitment. We do feel, however, that blind, unself-conscious commitment yields haphazard practice results. Many of the cases recorded in this volume give evidence of organizing practices in which limited alternative goals and means were explored. Analysis and evaluation are frequently ignored under the press of action. Such practice, we feel, is nonprofessional. The mark of true professionalism is the practitioner's ability to use interactional skills self-consciously, utilizing both empirical and conceptual knowledge in a self-disciplined manner.

Stages in problem solving were outlined in the introductory chapter. They include problem definition, goal selection, structure building, action, and evaluation. Social interaction and analysis are essential at each of these. An organizer moving into a new neighborhood is simultaneously involved in exchanging information, establishing relationships, and defining a problem. The assessment of the opportunities and limitations set by his employing organization, by the social situation, and by the target of his intervention is both an interactional and an analytic task, for it is frequently made on the basis of multiple interactions with relevant actors.

The processes of problem definition and "moving in" are frequently concomitant with the process of goal selection. On an interactional level, the organizer promotes the expression and exchange of preferences. On an analytic level, he weighs these against probable support and probable success. His knowledge of past efforts to deal with similar problems is selectively shared with those who must make the decisions to engage in a particular action. The selection of both goals and means is thus greatly affected by both interactional and analytic processes.

A third stage in problem solving is the actual building of an organization or network of interactions capable of dealing with the defined problem, and acting to achieve the agreed-on objectives. In many instances, the building of an organization is itself a major goal. The establishment of informal and formal communication links, the recruitment of individuals to fulfill certain organizational roles, and the processes by which members and other actors are taught to become more skillful at their roles or more aware of their social circumstances are dependent on the organizer's successful interactions. The decisions regarding with whom it may be most appropriate to interact, and how under what circumstances interaction may be most effective, require analytic skill.

Implementation of an action design requires the detailed specification of the tasks to be performed to achieve an agreed-on goal. It also requires the ability to relate people to resources, to help them in the processes of collaboration, to sustain them under attack, and to draw out and support indigenous leadership. Personal contact may be the essential catalyst to effectuating action. At times, the most carefully planned strategy, well rehearsed and fully agreed on, falls through because the organizer took the fears and anxieties of his constituency or clients for granted. It may be necessary for him to actually assist and accompany them to the site of action and to "walk them through" each step.

Unfortunately, many organizers, in our observation, are frequently too involved in an action process, or too exhausted from the continual and frequently unrelenting demands of their immediate situations, to "step outside" long enough to evaluate their interventions. Even at the end of a particular piece of action, they may become involved in some other activity before having properly evaluated the impact and effectiveness of what they have just completed. A process of monitoring action and getting feedback on effectiveness is, we feel, an integral part of the organizing process. The consequences of various actions and strategies must be analyzed and communicated or exchanged with constituent groups. Evaluation is an essential step in both organization building and problem or goal redefinition. Without such evaluative efforts, organizers may be accused of myopic, situation-bound perspectives, frequently leading to inappropriate and unsuccessful endeavors.

HOW TO READ PART I OF THIS VOLUME

With these cautions in mind, we invite the reader to examine the assumptions and the practices of the community organizers whose work is described in the following pages. To what extent have these organizers actually accomplished what they set out to do? Were their objectives clear from the start? Were their objectives appropriate to the situations in which they found themselves? Were they sufficiently cognizant of alternative tactics? Were their tactics informed by strategy or conscious design? What might be some of the unintended consequences of their actions? The cases, vignettes, and illustrative materials that follow should not be used indiscriminately as guides for action. Their value is more for the questions they raise than in the answers they provide.

In Chapter 3, we examine and contrast the work of organizers of the social-action, community-development, and social-movement persuasions. The organizer is frequently the man in the middle, caught in the cross fire of competing interests and personal commitments. We explore his dilemmas in Chapter 4.

In the next chapter, we explore the types of relationships established by organizers in the communities in which they work. In Chapters 6 and 7 we focus on organizing at the neighborhood level, and give special attention to public housing and rent strikes.

The content of each chapter was selected and organized from among those materials available to or gathered by the staff of the Community Organization Curriculum Project. When possible, it corroborates or illustrates what we have discussed in this chapter. The reader may wish to return to Chapter 2 after examination of the cases that follow.

Suggestions for Further Reading

Although many of these sources complement and give conceptual clarity to the case materials that follow, others go beyond this volume to discuss aspects of community organization for which case materials are not currently available.

A. BOOKS

Alinsky, Saul D., *Reveille for Radicals,* The University of Chicago Press, Chicago, 1946.

Altshuler, Alan A., *Community Control: The Black Demand for Participation in Large American Cities,* Pegasus, New York, 1970 (paper).

Beck, Bertram, *The Neighborhood Service Center: A Study and Recommendations,* Scientific Resources, Inc., New York, 1967.

Clark, Kenneth, and Hopkins, Jeannette, *A Relevant War Against Poverty: A Study of Community Action Programs and Observable Social Change,* Harper and Row, New York and Evanston, 1968 (paper).

Community Action: The Neighborhood Center, Community Action Program, Office of Economic Opportunity, Washington, D.C., 1966.

Coser, Lewis, *The Functions of Social Conflict,* The Free Press of Glencoe, New York, 1956 (paper).

Gurin, Arnold, and Robert Perlman, *Community Organization and Social Planning,* Council on Social Work Education and John Wiley and Sons, Inc., New York, 1970.

Lippett, Ronald, et al., *The Dynamics of Planned Change,* Harcourt, Brace, and World, New York, 1958, Chapters 4–10.

Marris, Peter, and Martin Rein, *Dilemmas of Social Reform: Poverty and Community Action in the United States,* Atherton Press, New York, 1967.

25

Oppenheimer, Martin, *The Urban Guerilla,* Quadrangle Books, Chicago, 1969 (paper).

Perlman, Robert, and David Jones, *Neighborhood Service Centers,* U.S. Department of Health, Education, and Welfare, Washington, D.C. (J.D. Publication 1005), 1967 (paper).

Schaller, Lyle E., *Community Organization: Conflict and Reconciliation,* Abington Press, Nashville, 1966 (paper), Chapters 4–6 on Alinsky.

B. READERS, CASEBOOKS, AND INSTRUCTIONAL MATERIALS

Cox, Fred M., John L. Erlich, Jack Rothman, and John E. Tropman, *Strategies of Community Organization,* S.P. Peacock Publishers, Inc., Itasca, Illinois, 1970.

Dahrendorf, Ralf, *Essays in the Theory of Society,* Stanford University Press, Palo Alto, California, 1968, section on "Attributes and Functions of Conflict."

Herman, Melvin, and Michael Munk, *Decision Making in Poverty Programs: Case Studies for Youth Work Agencies,* Columbia University Press, New York, 1968.

Kramer, Ralph M., *Participation of the Poor: Comparative Community Case Studies in the War on Poverty,* Prentice Hall, Inc., Englewood Cliffs, New Jersey, 1969 (paper).

Kramer, Ralph, and Harry Specht. *Readings in Community Organization Practice,* Prentice-Hall, Englewood Cliffs, New Jersey, 1969.

Oppenheimer, Martin, and Lakey, George, *A Manual for Direct Action: Strategy and Tactics for Civil Rights and All other Nonviolent Protest Movements,* Quadrangle Books, Chicago, 1964 (paper).

The Organizers Library Series, Southern Conference Educational Fund, 3210 W. Broadway, Louisiana, Kentucky 40211.

The Organizers Manual, Bantam Books, 1971.

Shostak, Arthur B. (Ed.), *Sociology in Action: Case Studies in Social Problems and Directed Social Change,* Dorsey Press, Homewood, Illinois, 1966 (paper).

Turner, John B. (Ed.), *Neighborhood Organization for Community Action,* National Association of Social Workers, New York, 1968, especially articles by Project Staff, David Austin, Nathan Cohen, and Lee Rainwater.

Zald, Meyer N. (Ed.), *Organizing for Community Welfare,* Quadrangle Books, Chicago, 1967.

C. ARTICLES AND PAPERS

Alinsky, Saul, "Citizenship Participation and Community Organization in Planning and Urban Renewal," Industrial Areas Foundation, 1962 (mimeo).

Aronowitz, Stanly, "Poverty, Politics and Community Organization," *Studies on the Left,* Summer, 1964, 4, No. 3.

Bennett, John C., "The Church and Power Conflicts," *Christianity and Crisis,* March 22, 1965, **25**.

Bernward, Joerges, "Communication and Change at the Local Level," *Ekistics,* January 1969.

Boesel, David, Richard Berk, Eugene W. Groves, Bettye Eidson, and Peter H. Rossi, "White Institutions and Black Rage," *Transaction,* March, 1969.

Booth, David, and Charles Adrian, "Election and Community Power," *Journal of Politics,* February 1963.

Braden, Ann, "The Southern Freedom Movement in Perspective," *Monthly Review,* July–August 1965, **17**, No. 3.

Brager, George, "Organizing the Unaffiliated in a Low Income Area," *Social Work,* October 1969.

Brager, George, and Valerie Jorrin, "Strategies for Change in Community Organizing: Some Uses of Bargaining." *Social Work,* 1969.

Brager, George, and Harry Specht, "Mobilizing the Poor for Social Action," *Social Welfare Forum,* Columbia University Press, New York, 1965.

Bullock, Paul, "On Organizing the Poor: Problems of Morality and Tactics," *Dissent,* January/February 1968.

Burke, Edmund M., "Citizen Participation Strategies," *Journal of the American Institute of Planners,* January 1968.

Chalmers, Thelma, "Summary of Conference on Negotiations of Public Organizations with Black Dissidents," Institute of Labor and Industrial Relations, University of Michigan, Ann Arbor, (mimeo), March 1969.

Cleage, Albert, "Transfer of Power," *The Center Magazine,* March 1968.

Cloward, Richard A., and Richard M. Elman, "Advocacy in the Ghetto," *Transaction,* December 1966.

Cloward, Richard A., and Frances F. Piven, "A Strategy to End Poverty," *The Nation,* May 2, 1966.

Coles, Robert, "Like It Is in the Alley," *Daedalus,* Fall 1968.

"Community Development Corporations: A New Approach to the Poverty Problem," *Harvard Law Review,* January 1969, **83**, No. 3.

"Consumers Legislation and the Poor," *The Yale Law Journal,* March 1967, **76**, No. 4.

Dellinger, Dave, "The Future of Non-Violence," *Studies on the Left,* 1965, **5**, No. 1.

Deutch, Morton, "Conflicts: Productive and Destructive," *Journal of Social Issues,* January 1969, **25**.

Fink, Clinton F., "Conceptual Difficulties in the Theory of Social Conflict," *Journal of Conflict Resolution,* December 1968, **12**.

Fry, John R., "So Grow Up," *Christianity and Crisis,* July 1968, **28**.

Gans, Herbert J., "The New Radicalism: Sect or Action Movement," *Studies on the Left,* 1965, **5**, No. 3.

Gittlin, Todd, "Local Pluralism as Theory and Ideology," *Studies on the Left,* 1965, 5, No. 3.

Grosser, Charles F., "Community Development Programs Serving the Urban Poor," *Social Work,* July 1965, 10, No. 3.

——————, "Community Organization and the Grass Roots," *Social Work,* October 1967.

Grosser, Charles F. "Organizing in the White Community" *Social Work,* July 1971, 16, No. 3.

Gurin, Arnold, "Community Organization Methods and Skills in the Program of National Agencies," *Community Organization Methods in Social Work Education,* Council on Social Work Education, New York, 1960.

Gurin, Arnold, and Ecklein, Joan Levin, "Community Organization: For Political Power or Service Delivery?" *Social Welfare Forum,* 1968, Columbia University Press, New York and London, 1968.

Haggestrom, Warren C., "The Power of the Poor," in Frank Riessman, Jerome Cohen, and Arthur Pearl (Eds.), *Mental Health of the Poor,* The Free Press, New York, 1964.

Hamberg, Jill, Paul Booth, Mimi Feingold, and Carl Wittman, *Where It's At: A Research Guide for Community Organizing,* New England Free Press, Boston, Massachusetts, 1967.

Handlin, Nathan, "The Organization of a Client's Advisory Committee," *Public Welfare,* October 1967.

Hauser, Philip M., "Environmental Forces Shaping Our Cities," *The Social Welfare Forum,* 1967.

Himes, Joseph, "The Functions of Racial Conflict," *Journal of Social Forces,* September 1966, 45, No. 1.

Howe, Harold, "Organization for Innovation," *Journal of Social Issues,* January 1965, 21.

Hayden, Tom, "The Politics of the Movement," *Dissent,* January/February 1966.

Johnson, Mrs. Charles W., "The Black Community Looks at the Welfare System," *Public Welfare,* July 1968.

Judge, Joseph B., "Brownsville: A Neighborhood in Trouble," *Dissent,* September/October 1966.

Laue, James H., "A Contemporary Revitalization Movement in American Race Relations: The Black Muslims," *Journal of Social Forces,* March 1964, 42, No. 3.

Lipsky, Michael, "Rent Strikes: Poor Man's Weapon," *Transaction,* February 1969, 6, No. 4.

Litwak, Eugene, and Henry Meyer, "A Balance Theory of Coordination Between Community Organization and Community Primary Groups," *Administrative Science Quarterly,* June 1966.

Mack, Raymond W., "The Components of Social Conflict," *Social Problems,* Spring 1965.

McWorter, Gerald A., and Robert L. Crain, "Subcommunity Gladiatorial Competition—Civil Rights Leadership as a Competitive Process," *Journal of Social Forces*, September 1967, 46, No. 1.

Miller, Melvin G., "Increasing Low-Income Consumer Buying and Borrowing Power by Cooperative Action," *Ohio State Law Journal*, Summer 1968, 29, No. 3.

Miller, S. M., "Training and Confrontation as Modes of Change," in Robert Schasre and Jo Wallack (Eds.), *Training Series for Social Agencies*, Vol. III, University of Southern California, Los Angeles, 1965.

Mogelof, Melvin B., "Involving Low-Income Neighborhoods in Anti-Delinquency Programs," *Social Work*, October 1965.

Morris, Dan, and Harold Rothwan, "Partnership Between Social Work and Law: An Essential for Effective Community Organization," *The Social Welfare Forum*, 1968.

Moynehan, Daniel P., "What Is Community Action?" *The Public Interest*, Fall 1966.

Nieburg, H. L., "Uses of Violence," *Journal of Conflict Resolution*, March 1963, VII.

O'Conner, James, "Towards a Theory of Community Unions," *Studies on the Left*, Spring 1964, 4, No. 2.

Peatte, Lisa R., "Reflections on Advocacy Planning," *Journal of the American Institute of Planners*, March 1968.

Piven, Frances F., "Participation of Residents in Neighborhood Community Action Programs," *Social Work*, January 1966.

Purcell, Francis, and Harry Specht, "The House on Sixth Street," *Social Work*, October 1965.

Rainwater, Lee, "Open Letter on White Justice and the Riots," *Transaction*, 4, No. 9.

Rein, Martin, and S. M. Miller, "Poverty Programs and Policy Priorities," *Transaction*, 4, No. 9.

————, "Social Action on the Installment Plan," *Transaction*, January/February 1966.

Reissman, Frank, "A Comparison of Two Social Action Approaches: Saul Alinsky and the New Left," September 1965 (mimeo).

Rose, Stephen C., "Rochester's Racial Rubicon," *Christianity and Crisis*, March 1965.

Rose, Stephen C., "Saul Alinsky and his Critics," *Christianity and Crisis*, March 1965, 25.

Rossi, Peter H., "What Makes Communities Tick?" *Administrative Science Quarterly*, March 1957.

Rothman, Jack, "An Analysis of Goals and Roles in CO Practice," *Social Work*, April 1964.

————, "Three Models of Community Organization Practice," National Social Welfare Forum, 1968, Columbia University Press, New York, 1968.

Rustin, Baynard, "Civil Disobedience," *Occasional Papers,* Center for the Study of Democratic Institutions, 1966.

Schecter, Danny, "Reveille for Reformers: Report from Syracuse," *Studies on the Left,* 1965, **5**, No. 4.

Sherwood, Clarence E., "Issues in Measuring Results of Action Programs," *Welfare in Review,* August/September 1967.

Shostak, Arthur B., "Promoting Participation of the Poor: Philadelphia's Anti-Poverty Program," *Social Work,* January 1966.

Solomon, Fredric, and Jacob R. Fishman, "Youth and Social Action: An Introduction," *Journal of Social Issues,* October 1964, **20**.

Specht, Harry, "Community Development in Low-Income Negro Areas," *Social Work,* October 1966.

"Tenant Unions: Collective Bargaining and the Low-Income Tenant," *The Yale Law Journal,* June 1968, **77**, No. 7.

Thursz, Daniel, "Social Action as a Professional Responsibility." *Social Work,* July 1966.

Trimberger, Ellen Kay, "Why a Rebellion at Columbia Was Inevitable," *Transaction,* September 1968.

Von Hoffman, Nicholas, "Hard Talk on Organizing the Ghetto," *Renewal,* February 1966.

————, "Reorganization in the Casbah," *Social Progress,* April 1962.

Wade, Alan D., "Social Work and Political Action," *Social Work,* October 1963.

Warren, Roland L., "Concerted Decision-Making in the Community: Some Theoretical Considerations," *Social Welfare Forum 1965,* Columbia University Press, New York, 1965.

Warren, Roland, "Types of Purposive Change at the Community Level," in Roland Warren, *Truth, Love and Social Change,* Rand McNally, Chicago 1971 (paper).

Wildavsky, Aaron, "The Political Economy of Efficiency: Cost-Benefit Analysis and Program Budgeting," *Public Administration Review,* December 1966, **26**.

Zald, Meyer N., and Roberta Ash, "Social Movement Organizations: Growth, Decay and Change," *Social Forces,* December 1967.

Zeitlin, Maurice, "Alienation and Revolution," *Social Forces,* December 1966.

CHAPTER 3

Community Development, Social Action, and Social Movements

CASES AND ILLUSTRATIVE MATERIALS

CO-1 LA CAUSA AND LA HUELGA
CO-2 BLACK POWER AT THE COUNTY LEVEL
CO-3 GROW AND THE STRIKE AT MASONITE
CO-4 SCEF RESPONDS TO A CRISIS
CO-5 ALINSKY STARTS A FIGHT

These cases illustrate both the differences and the similarities in the community-development and social-action approaches. In "La Causa and La Huelga," Cesar Chavez reflects on the events leading to the development of a "community union" of farm workers in Delano, California. In "Black Power at the County Level," a young SNCC organizer speaks of the strategy that led to the development of political sophistication among the Black sharecroppers and farmers in Lowndes County, Alabama. Project GROW was composed of some of the same staff members active in Lowndes County. As whites, they left the black civil rights movement to work among Southern whites. The SCEF organizers who responded to a crisis situation in Louisville show how a small, well-organized, and flexible group can move quickly and constructively to combat pressure and exploitation of the black community. The final case describes the events leading to the establishment of FIGHT, a militant social-action coalition in Rochester, and gives detailed attention to both the tactics and the strategies utilized in Alinsky-style organizing.

What comes through so forcefully in the Chavez material is his enormous stress on human dignity and self-respect. Chavez epitomizes a personal style. Quiet, unassuming, and modest, he nevertheless builds on personal charisma. He puts great stress on the role of leadership, in particular the need to lead by example, to have great patience, and to

31

give wholly of one's time and energy to the "cause." Unlike other organizers who may build pride and organization on the basis of denigration of others—whether the "enemy" or another ethnic or socioeconomic group—Chavez sees such temptations as destructive of the very values he tries to achieve.

Chavez takes the reader all the way through the organizing process, from a decision on objectives to the selection of a target, through the development of a strategy and the pitfalls along the way. He shows that organizing can be a rational and self-conscious activity. He also shows that it can be a difficult, slow-moving one.

Chavez built his movement around the development of mutual obligations—to himself, to the organization, and to other workers. He made certain that members would have a deep stake in the organization before he even began to speak about becoming a union or going on strike. He was not willing to risk failure until he felt that the organization's membership was ready. He refused outside help during his early organizing efforts for fear that reliance on the outside would sap him and the membership of the self-reliance needed to take control over their own actions. But he also shows great understanding of human failure and weakness, and the constant need for both organizers and organizational memberships to reevaluate their actions and to rededicate themselves to their tasks.

In "Black Power at the County Level," the organizer puts greater stress on ethnic solidarity and class interest as a motivation for organizing. The issue here is political control or, at the very least, some representation. This case is particularly schematic in its description of the use of educational techniques to prepare a community for action and eventual self-government. It might be compared or contrasted with current emphases in the Black Panther Party in other parts of the country.

Project GROW, an attempt at grass-roots organizing among Southern whites, has many parallels to the work of SNCC volunteers in Alabama. It is no wonder. Many of the white organizers for SNCC joined SCEF, the Southern Conference Educational Fund, when they made a conscious decision to organize whites, leaving black organizers to organize black people. Quite apparently, however, their successes were not the same. The strike at Masonite was destroyed not only by the massive repressions instigated by both the International Union and the company, but also by the divisions between the black and the white union local members. The SCEF organizers could have chosen to work with black people. They consciously chose not to. Later SCEF hired a black organizer to work with the black workers. Many of the same organizers were also at work in the following case.

Conscious community-development and social-action strategies are employed by the SCEF organizers who simultaneously attempt to deal with an immediate *crisis* situation, while building understanding and communication links within the white community and between whites and blacks. Not satisfied to deal only with the manifestations of community hysteria, they sought to expose the underlying hypocrisy of racist institutions. A variety of tactics typical of radical organizing efforts—leaflet distribution, mass meetings, and picketing—are demonstrated.

We note, however, that a number of other strategies including the use of political pressures from "within the system," were not employed. Was this because the organizers did not have access to establishment influentials? Are Southern cities closed to such intervention? Why did the church groups not intervene at this level? Self-conscious and critical as the organizers were, did they limit their strategies because of an ideological perspective? The answers are not clear.

What is clear, however, is the commitment of these organizers to mass participation, their willingness to put long hours and their lives on the line, their concern with basic structural changes, and their awareness of the importance of maintaining communication with organizers in other communities.

The two cases of efforts by the SCEF staff are included to illustrate the commitment by social-movement organizers to long-range, basic, and structural change. In some ways, they complement the material by Cesar Chavez. Their work may be contrasted with that of Alinsky. Who is the more concerned with the creation of a social movement? Who puts major focus on the development of new leadership? Who builds on existing organizational structures? Who utilizes external resources and who does not? At which point in the organizing process?

The Alinsky case is issue-specific and gives attention to the way in which Alinsky and other organizers from the Industrial Areas Foundation prepare a community for engaging in social action. Unlike the SCEF cases, in which the building of an organization evolved out of a series of prior actions, the case of FIGHT in Rochester documents a conscious, well-thought-through strategy for building a people's organization. Alinsky is exceptionally cognizant of the need to select a cadre of qualified local people for leadership, of the need to deal with symbolic issues in a creative and innovative manner, and of the possibility of using humor to throw the stupidity or intransigence of the "Establishment" back into its own face.

The case documents Alinsky's conviction that organizers must win specific victories of symbolic importance and that they must be prepared to exploit situations so as to help the organization perceive itself and be perceived as being more powerful. That perception alone may result in actual power redistribution.

The reader may be struck by the contrast of these cases with those in subsequent chapters. The grass-roots organizers in Chapter 3 are atypical. They live in the constant presence of actual physical danger. While they do not all represent social movements, they are all radical in the sense that they challenge the basic structure of institutional relationships. We have some question about the efficacy of their strategies, varied as they are. But we have no questions about their raw courage. They face beatings, repressive arrests, cesspool prison conditions and, in some cases, the possibility of murder. While the Cesar Chavez material suggests the possibility of gratification, successes are, for the most part, all too rare, the pay is all too low, and the pressures are all too great.

*   *   *   *

CO-1   LA CAUSA AND LA HUELGA[1]

A Community Union is Organized

The strike and the boycott, they have cost us much. What they have not paid us in wages, better working conditions, and new contracts, they have paid us in self respect and human dignity.

Violence

If we had used violence we would have won contracts a long time ago but they wouldn't have been lasting because we wouldn't have won respect. Wages are not the main issue in the strike. If wages were the issue our organization would disappear after recognition and an increase in pay. No, what is at stake is human dignity. If a man is not accorded respect, he cannot respect himself and if he does not respect himself, he cannot demand it.

When workers fall back on violence, they are lost. Oh they might win some of their demands and might end a strike a little earlier, but they give up their imagination, their creativity, their will to work hard enough and to suffer for what they believe is right.

Behaving violently is giving up the will to win. Some people just want to get knocked on the head, to be self-pitying. Violence just hurts those

---

[1] This is a compilation of statements and observations on his own work by Cesar Chavez, director of the United Farm Workers Organizing Committee. They come from a variety of sources: personal interviews, newspaper and magazine articles, statements reported on T.V., and an earlier compilation from tapes made by Mr. Chavez in May 1967, while in Detroit. The tapes were edited by David Leonard Cohen in January 1969, when associated with the Institute of Labor and Industrial Relations.

who are already hurt. Violence in the civil rights movement just makes black people suffer. Black homes are burned and black sons are killed. Instead of exposing the brutality of the oppressors, it justifies it.

There are many reasons for why a man does what he does. To be himself he must be able to give all. If a leader cannot give all he cannot expect his people to give anything. The violence upsets me. When I went on my fast, I told no one. I worked everyday as usual. But I could not keep it a secret long. Finally I knew I had to tell some that I would be going to our headquarters at Forty Acres. But I told only a few friends. It was a test, a dedication. It was not a hunger strike. I did not want publicity. I did not want the press to pick it up and to distort it. It was a personal thing. But the word did get out, and it was the best organizing I ever did. People came to me in lines for days. It was for all of us a religious experience. The fast gave lie to the grower's claim that we had no following. Some people came every night to attend Mass, eighty-five miles. We estimated ten thousand came during my fast. Everyone came, Mexicans, Filipinos, blacks—Robert Kennedy sent me a telegram. Then he came. Others came. They understood.

Friends swore to me they would never be violent again. Filipino women came and decorated the building at the Forty Acres, where I maintained my fast. It was beautiful art by people who are not artists. The fast brought the creativity out of people.

Mexican Catholics can be very discriminatory towards Mexican Protestants. But something beautiful happened during the fast. On the fifth day a Protestant preacher from Earlimart came. I asked him to preach to our Mass. At first he didn't believe it could be done. But I told him it was about time to repair some of the damage that had been done among our people. So he preached and there was a great spirit. A few days later I invited another Protestant to preach and then a Negro minister, and then the minister from Earlimart again. This time he brought his congregation to sing Protestant Mexican hymns. It was a beautiful thing. It has done much for our people.

When I finished my fast at the Mass of Thanksgiving, I was too weak to speak, but a friend explained for me what the purpose of the fast was. I have the paper in which some of my words were written and read.

"When we are really honest with ourselves, we must admit that our lives are all that really belong to us. So it is how we use our lives that determines what kind of men we are. It is my deepest belief that only by giving our lives do we find life. I am convinced that the truest act of courage, the strongest act of manliness, is to sacrifice ourself for others in a totally nonviolent struggle for justice. To be a man is to suffer for others. God help us be men."

On Being Able to Carry Your Own Weight

I started out working under Fred Ross, the organizer for the Community Service Organization, set up by Alinsky's Industrial Areas Foundation. I was his constant companion. I used to get home about 5:30 from work and Fred would pick me up and we would go from meeting to meeting. I observed how he did things and I learned from him. I had a need to learn. After a while I became a chairman of our local CSO group, then I became an organizer and staff person. Soon I was organizing in the whole state.

When I left CSO in April of 1962 I almost cried like a baby. CSO was the first organization to try to help Mexican Americans. I wanted CSO to organize farm workers. I thought the only way to really help Mexican Americans was on the farm fields. I offered to work for them for a year without pay. The organization did not agree, so I resigned. A week later I came to Delano. I turned down a union offer to organize for them. I didn't want outside support. If we were to have an organization, the members would have to support it. Outside offers of support were turned down, for we knew that if we became dependent early, we might not have the courage we needed later. Having studied the mistakes of CSO and other organizations, I did not want to repeat them. We wanted the workers to prove to us, and we wanted to prove to ourselves, that they really wanted what we were doing. The assurance came from monthly contributions of $3.50 in dues. It is true that some members came to meetings because they had an investment. If they had been active in the union for a year, they had $42 invested. They were there to see how their money was being spent and for no other reason. But as they came to meetings, we were trying to educate them, building the brotherhood and solidarity so necessary for the understanding needed to bring about a strong organization.

During the first winter of the organizing I would go out to their homes and call on them to pay their dues if they were one or two months behind. I recall one particular incident that will remain with me for many, many years to come. I went to a home in McFarland, California, seven miles south of Delano. It was the evening of a very cold and rainy day. Because of the weather, there had been no work that day in the fields. I went to this home and knocked on the door. The union member was just getting ready to leave.

I told him that he was two months behind in his dues and that we would have to cancel his membership. He had $5.00 in his hand and he gave it to me. As I gave him back $1.50 in change, he told me that he was just on his way out to the store to buy food. I held the money in my hand for a few seconds trying to decide whether to take the money. If I refunded it, I would have to forget the idea of workers paying their own way while they were building a union. It was difficult. The man hadn't been working and had very little money. I took the money, and for the next week I felt very bad about it.

But something happened about three years later. The same man continued to pay his dues and became one of our best strikers. He also became one of the first workers to benefit from the Schenley contract when it was signed. Of course, there were still a lot of people who remained in between. Whenever a member would come to us for assistance, the first thing that we asked about and the thing we insisted upon was that his dues be paid up. They paid the dues and the services were theirs. Now in our Association the worker pays his union dues and in that way pays for his services. We tell them, "We want you to come and demand service, but first of all you have to pay your dues."

This is where we differ from other organizations, and from the poverty program. Helping people by providing services is not enough. Often people get some service and they ask you: "How much do I owe?" In the hand-out programs they say: "Nothing, it is your right, this is paid by the government."

We say: "Sure you owe something. You owe your participation and your responsibility to help other poor people." But that is not enough. Then you have to be completely ready to tell them exactly what they can do to help. You have to have an activity, a task, a job. And while they are doing it, you give them encouragement and you build them into real members. If a person asks what he can do to help it is because he does not know. You must tell him in clear language he can understand.

People do not know what to do. Do not romanticize the poor. The Mexican and the Negro are not some sort of noble innocent. We are all people, human beings subject to the same temptations and faults as all others. Our poverty *damages* our dignity.

Being disadvantaged is not romantic. It is tragic. We want to see ourselves and to be seen as human beings. We know the truth, even if some of the college people who come to help think we are the innocent and the growers are the devils. This is a very hard-nosed operation. Members who pay their dues get service; those who don't pay don't get any service.

Why Delano?

When I left CSO I knew it was to organize farm workers. I chose Delano as my target area for two reasons. First, my wife's family and my brother lived there. I knew there would be hard times ahead, and at least my eight children would not starve.

The second reason has to do with the composition of the work force in Delano. There are over 70 grape vineyards. Table grapes require tender handling. Laborers have to have some skill in leafing, spraying, binding, pruning. Workers here were the best paid in the industry and the most stable. The season lasts nine months. If you are going to organize and ask for commitment, you cannot go to the most desperately poor. They are not likely to take action. If you stand on a man's head and push it into the dirt, he may not even see the heel of your boot. But if his whole face is already above ground, he can see your heel and he can see freedom ahead.

Getting Started

People ask why we were so successful when other attempts to organize a union failed and when all other strike attempts killed union organizing. The reason is that we did not begin to organize a union. I never talked about a union and I never used the word strike. Instead of staying in one community and trying to organize workers against a background of repeated failures over the past forty years, I decided to visit as many communities as I could in the San Joaquin Valley.

I was counting on my past experience that no matter where you go, you will always find a few people who are ready to take up any cause you may have. This is not always so good. People join the wrong causes and some people join your cause for reasons that are not healthy. But what in poverty is healthy?

My family and I visited something like seventy-eight communities including small rural villages and large labor camps. I didn't go to people and say, "Look you're poor and I'm poor. Let's get together and take on the power structure." They would have looked at me as if I were crazy.

We distributed cards throughout the entire valley. Eight thousand of them were signed and returned. We walked through the fields, and door to door. We didn't ask all kinds of fancy questions. Just one. "How much do you think you deserve to earn for an hour's work?" At that time the average pay was 90¢ per hour. Almost everybody responded that they thought they should be getting a $1.00 or $1.10. Only a handful said

$1.25, $1.50 or $2.00. I was dejected by their low aspirations and feelings of worth.

But some of the people wrote us notes of encouragement. We went and talked to each of these. We said, "If you and I get together, we can solve our problems. We have to help each other." And we tried to demonstrate what we meant. If a man was hurt, I would stay with him until I was sure we could get him medical services. If a man needed legal help, I might stay with him or travel to find it for four and five days. When I went out to visit those who had written the comments, with me I took things that I thought would be important for them to know—Social Security stuff and other useful material. On each piece was stamped the name and address of the Association in Delano. When they saw the name, they wondered about it and what was happening.

At first there weren't too many people to respond, but soon the word got around. Day and night people started coming to our house. We were building up a basic trust. We never talked about building a union, just an association of concerned people. But there were some, about twenty people, who went out and really did a job. They went out and took the time to sign people up. Thus our organization was created out of activity. When you go to talk you go to talk to everybody. The only place that I don't talk to people is at bars. I will talk to them at grocery stores, on the street, or anywhere I can. Your best means of contact in the community where you are organizing is simply to stop people on the street. The first reaction that you are likely to get when you stop someone to talk about organizing is that the person may think you are crazy. But because there is in most cases a natural reaction to pay attention to what you have to say, he listens.

The most important thing about signing up a member was that you made a friend. You visited a place, and they would later write to you. Then we would write back to them. If I would be in their neighborhood, I would try to stop in to visit. I visited them in their homes and ate with them. This I had to do because I didn't have any money. If you really want to make a friend, go to someone's home and eat with him. When you get to know people, their home's open to you. They gave me food and a place to sleep. Some gave me money for gas. They had begun to feel sorry for me because I was poorer than they were. Once we had become friends, they would tell me what they wanted. The people who give you their food give you their heart.

We were able to get about four hundred workers who became the nucleus of our association. The secret was that these people were already organized and that it was just a matter of getting them all together. You can't organize people unless there is a need. Poor people have a need.

If organizers are unsuccessful, it is because they have not learned the lessons of organizing well. Organizers must blame only themselves if people don't respond. I have often heard organizers saying things like, "Well, they don't really appreciate the things that we are trying to do." "Their level of intelligence is so low that they can't comprehend what we're doing for them." Or, "They just haven't any interest in themselves." What they fail to say is "We're just not getting the message across to them." People have a very nice subtle way of telling us that they don't like our program.

There is no substitute for hard work, 23 or 24 hours a day. And there is no substitute for patience and acceptance.

We called our first convention together in Fresno, in September 1962. About 350 people were there. At that time the union was called the National Farm Workers Association. There we adopted a very ambitious program. We wanted to gradually move from a community setting in which brotherhood was created through individual help and attention to personal problems to the solidarity needed for a union that would be ready to strike successfully.

Membership Services

We also developed what is now called the Farm Workers Service Center. This Center is not like a welfare agency.

At first we pooled our resources to get legal help in individual cases. Say for instance that a man was rooked by a salesman with a high interest contract. We put all our pennies together and hired a lawyer. If the contract was for, let's say, $100, the company back in Chicago or Detroit would say, "Gee, you know attorneys would cost at least $100 anyway." So they would drop the case. If one of the workers got a traffic ticket and came to us and said, "Look, I really didn't deserve this ticket," and if we were convinced that he was right, we would spend perhaps $100 on a $5.00 ticket—in some cases even more.

Any time that we felt that an injustice was involved in a problem, we would work on that problem in two ways: First, we would let everyone know about it, especially the membership. Second, we would make sure the person involved had a commitment to follow through.

Soon we set up a credit union and co-op programs to help get such things as insurance and automobile parts. I learned bookkeeping from a government pamphlet. The most important possession for the farm worker is an automobile. A lot of money was being poured into repairing their old cars. So we developed what we call the car service center.

Our car co-op is a little different from the standard accepted co-op program operating in this country today. Instead of making the savings refund at the end of the year, we give a refund right across the counter when the worker purchases the item. In the car co-op we have always concentrated on little items, parts that are needed for a car—not luxury items such as fancy hub caps, but items such as generators, starters and the like.

Now we also have a gasoline co-op, and we are able to sell gasoline three or four cents a gallon cheaper than any station in town. We also organized a newspaper so that we could keep people informed about the things that were going on within the Association.

A Community Union

As word spread, more people heard about what we were trying to do and joined us, thus increasing our resources.

When the other unions were organizing workers, they seemed to approach the problem by using only the issues workers had with their employers. They were not doing anything on the community part of the problem. We wanted to do both things. We wanted to have a community union. We didn't have the name for it at that time, but we knew that we wanted to deal with community problems by getting the people together and showing them that there is some power in numbers.

After winning some victories we began to pull things together, started some programs, and gradually moved into a union setting where we would be really ready to strike and confront employers.

In the four and a half years before the strike we had a lot of time to do this. Only once did the press find out what we were doing. Only once did it get through. Otherwise, for four and a half years no one knew what we were doing except for our most immediate friends.

We had many tests and some early victories. Even before I left CSO we demonstrated. Braceros were getting jobs before resident workers even though the law stated clearly that residents should get first preference. I would take groups of unemployed workers and have them fill out an employer's work card. We did this day after day, keeping records of the results. We then had a protest march and a card burning ceremony to symbolize our protest and to show the worker's contempt for such hiring practices.

Later, when we discovered that Kern and Tulare counties were actually making money on the filthy, slummy migrant camps, we were able to encourage the migrants who lived there to demand that they be closed down and new ones erected. I felt we were getting close to being ready to strike. Our situation was different from that where the other strikers failed.

In many of the early strikes, the organizers who actually were conducting the strikes blamed the people for their failures. In almost all cases, the people blamed the unions and the organizers for the failure. The unions came in with a paid staff and quite a bit of money, but after having spent a considerable amount of money, they all gave up the idea of organizing. There was in all the attempts one most noticeable parallel. The unions were attempting to do two jobs in one: They were attempting to organize the workers and simultaneously to strike.

Most of the unions were going into the fields to organize workers after the workers had revolted. The workers were out on strike (on one of those suicide strikes) and the unions couldn't put things together to hold with any permanence.

In the end the people felt that the unions had sold them out, and the union leaders felt that the people really didn't want a union. With this past history we had a number of failures to contend with and we wanted to change that.

When we came in, we decided that the job was too big to do all at one time. If we were going to organize a union, it would have to be done quietly, incorporating the idea that is now known as a community union.

First, of all, we wanted to convince ourselves that the workers really wanted a union this time. They had to show us that they wanted a union. They did this by their paying for the initial organizing drive.

By building a strong base we felt that someday we would be ready to strike, conduct a boycott, and exert other legal, economic means needed to get our union recognized.

The Strike Begins

In September of 1965, a few days after the Agricultural Workers Organizing Committee (an AFL-CIO union led by two Filipino organizers) struck two of the largest growers in the area, we voted to strike the rest of the industry where we had membership. We called our meeting on September 16, Mexico's Independence Day. We brought in 2700 workers for the night of the vote. This represented 60 to 65 percent of the total work force in the area. There wasn't one "NO" vote. Our members said they too wanted independence—from poverty, brutal working conditions, discrimination. I asked our members not to strike until four days later which would give us enough time to make contact with all the growers, asking them to meet with us to negotiate the issues without a strike. Our demands were identical to those of the AWOC. We sent "return receipt requested" letters to all the growers. We called all the growers. We sent them wires and asked the State Conciliation Service to call them to see if we could get together. They did not answer our letters. They even refused to accept our wires.

We knew that in the many attempts to organize workers, violence had played a large part in the suppression of the unions and we knew that from the moment we struck justice would be about 20 percent for us and 80 percent for the opposition. I asked the workers to vote that this strike be a nonviolent one. Many of them didn't really know what this meant. But many did know that there was another group in the country that had been making progress for human rights with a commitment to nonviolence, the civil rights movement. It was decided that night that we would be nonviolent and we have kept to this pledge throughout our struggle, but not without difficulty.

On September 20, 1965, at 5:30 a.m., our strike started. During the first ten days almost all the workers left the fields. Nothing was done in the fields. Most of the outside strikebreakers stayed away—not because they believed in the strike, but because they feared violence.

The moment they found out that we weren't going to do anything to them, they went to work. Many of those who went into the fields, when asked about it said, "we're with you 100 percent, but we just want to work to get enough money to leave the area. But we are with you." In the first three days wages went up from $1.15 to $1.25 because of the shortage.

We began to send strikers to stand by the fields with picket signs. "Heulga," we shouted. We tried to convince the strikebreakers that they were wrong, that they should be with us. If one man walks off the field during a work day, then an official strike is certified. It is important to get someone to walk off.

The picket line is the best place to train organizers. One day on the picket line and a man is never again the same. The picket line is where a man makes his commitment. The longer on the picket line the stronger the commitment. A lot of workers think they make their commitment by walking off the job when nobody sees them. But you get a guy to walk off the field when his boss is watching and, in front of the other guys, throw down his tools and march right to the picket line, that is the guy who makes our strike. The picket line is a beautiful thing because it makes a man more human.

Some of my best organizers and more faithful members hated the union before they joined. But when they see the light, they never desert us because they have been on both sides. The converted ones are our best members. Nonviolence has made it possible to survive, although there have been injustices and injuries. Union members always get arrested. Growers never do.

The strike brought us many surprises. We thought we were striking the growers. We thought the church groups, the city council, and the school people would at least remain neutral, if they would not come to help us. Within 24 hours the Delano City council had held a special meeting and passed a resolution condemning our "communist ties." Both the high school and the elementary school boards passed similar resolutions. The Chamber of Commerce passed a resolution that was similar except that it was more wordy. The Ministerial Association for the very first time in the history of Delano consented to meet with the three local priests, and they too passed a resolution condemning the strike. This really shook us up. We were looking to them as the arbitrators and conciliators. There was, then, only ourselves on the west side of town, trying to meet all forces.

"Huelga"

For the first nine days of the strike the sheriff's office and the police department in Delano played it cool. The very first day of the strike the Kern County Sheriff assigned a squad of deputies to Delano. The sergeant in charge, whose name was Dodd, told us he was here to look after and protect the farm workers on strike. I thought it was a welcome sign and I thanked him.

Nine days later, I was called to an emergency meeting with Sergeant Dodd at the Special Sheriff's Station in Delano. I was told that there was a lot of feeling in the community about the strike. Those poor workers who had crossed the picket lines had become so incensed and disturbed by our attempts to recruit them that there was bound to be violence. He asked us to refrain from speaking to them or even shouting "Huelga." He told me that if we complied, this would further our relationship, thus helping both groups. We had an emergency meeting of the strikers that evening, and I put the problem to them. They put up quite a lot of argument, but I asked them to please do it for this time to prove that we were fair and wanted to keep our friends.

We voted to refrain from shouting "Huelga" at the strikebreakers.

Three days later I was called to another emergency meeting with the sheriff. This time he was complaining because we were still using the word "Huelga." We were not shouting it; we were just saying it in a normal tone of voice so that the strikebreakers would hear us. When I asked why was there such opposition to the word, he replied, "Well, because all the people know that there is a strike. There's no need to tell them. After all, you are in the United States and you should be speaking English."

He also said that there were a lot of complaints from the powerful people in the county that the only reason we were using the word "Huelga" was that we were trying to attract the attention of the Communist Party in Latin America. When I protested he said, "Well, the word sounds downright nasty."

I brought the membership back to another meeting and I told them what had happened. I said, "We cannot use the word 'Huelga.' Could we use a different word?" They all got up and told me where to go.

The next morning 44 of the strikers and nonstrikers picketed one of the larger growers in the area. Included in this group were my wife, 9 ministers, 11 other wives, and 23 strikers. They lined up about 50 feet from one another and started shouting "Huelga" at the workers at the top of their voice.

Sure enough, as the sheriff had promised, all of them were arrested. I went down to Berkeley to the University to beg money from the students to bail the pickets out of jail. I got there just before lunchtime, and I spoke from the steps of Sproul Hall. I asked the students to give me their lunch money; and they gave me $6600, which was enough to bail the pickets out and cover the cost of legal aid to fight the case.

About a year later all 44 cases were dismissed.

Peregrination: Pilgrimage, Penitence, Revolution

We gave Delano a new word. While the word was very dirty in the beginning, now it has become a very accepted word. "Huelga" is used by the high school kids as a means of saying, "Hello. How are you?" It is our symbol.

A symbol is an important thing. That is why we chose an Aztec eagle. It gives pride. My brother squared off the wings so that it is easier for members to draw. When people see it they know it means "boycott" and we know it means dignity.

A year after the march from Selma, we decided to have our own penitential march ending on the Capitol steps in Sacramento. The American press can make little things into big things and big things into little things. A lot depends on how well they understand them. We tried desperately to put it into the right perspective so that they would understand. Father Keith Kenney from Sacramento wrote a beautiful explanation about the march, but it was not understood.

The first reason for the march was that we felt that personally we had to do penance for those things that we had done wrong during the six or seven months of striking prior to the march. We wanted to discipline ourselves to keep our commitment of nonviolence. When soldiers are drafted into the army the first thing they do is march. They march back and forth all day long. This is discipline training. They don't say that only 99 percent of the people march. They say everybody marches.

We wanted to come back after marching for 26 days and part of the nights with new dedication. On the march we went through much suffering. This helped us find ourselves, understand ourselves, and discipline ourselves for a strike that we knew was going to take a long, long time. The theme of the march was "pilgrimage, penitence, and revolution." People understood a little about pilgrimage, very little about penitence, and hardly anything about revolution. We were talking about changing things to make a better life. We came back with new dedication and more commitment. We had religious services two or three times a day during the march; and, while we were marching side by side along the road, we were reexamining ourselves. Some of our members, some of our organizers, and some of our friends did not like the religious nature of our march. They felt La Causa should not be a religious affair. But self dedication is a spiritual experience.

I am not a doctrinaire religiously. I want to break down the barriers. In my fast, I encouraged much different religious activity. I wore a mezuzah around my neck. Jesus must have worn one. Certainly he did not wear a cross.

The march was very successful. Many of the farm workers to whom we went understood the strike a lot better. After we left them they were really a part of the movement. By the time we arrived in Sacramento on Easter Sunday, one grower was ready to sign. Others were ready to give us support.

It takes a lot of punishment to be able to do anything to change the social order. It is such a difficult thing to do, especially when the matter of money is involved as it is in our case. It was only after we went on strike that we began to accept money from others. Walter Reuther pledged $5000 a month for the duration of the strike as support from the UAW. The AFL-CIO offered $10,000 per month. Other money began to come later.

The Boycott

We have won our major contracts mainly through economic pressure on the growers. As farm workers, we are specifically excluded from the protection of the National Labor Relations Act. Under the present situation we can't go to the employer and say, "We have 30 percent, or 50 percent or 100 percent of the workers signed up and we want you to recognize our union." We can't even go to the Board and ask for an election. Even if we had a thousand percent signed up we would have no rights. So our only hope has been the pressure of a consumer boycott.

When we started our first boycott, we were told by some experienced and very friendly unions that it wouldn't work. But it has, because we have received the support of thousands and thousands of rank-and-file labor, students, civil rights people and church groups. We have developed a nationwide network of support by sending out strikers to cities throughout the United States and Canada. We had pickets in 237 communities at one time during the Schenley boycott. This is what got us our first contract at the time that we got it. If we had not launched the boycott, our strike could never have been successful.

There are lots of people who are ready to say that this generation of farm laborers has to be written off, and that legislation, education, and so forth have to be aimed at the children. Well, I for one am not ready to be written off. This generation of children will get the food and the education it needs when the parents have enough money to take care of them.

UFWOC—A New Union

In September of 1966 our Association merged with AWOC to form the United Farm Workers Organizing Committee. At that point the AFL-CIO chartered our union and gave us the jurisdiction of organizing farm workers. This merger brought together both unions.

I'd say that it took about six months before we really brought the two unions together. For although we were together on paper, there were problems to be dealt with. First of all, AWOC was almost 100 percent Filipino: our union was 90 percent Mexican-American and about 10 percent Negro. Growers had traditionally played ethnic groups off against each other. That way they could keep wages low.

At the beginning of the strike everyone was giving us from two to three weeks, saying that we would lose like the other strikes had been lost. If you had asked me about it then, I would probably have said that failure was very possible.

But in our case something different happened—something that the other unions had never had happen in their attempts to organize workers. We received public support in our attempts to organize like no other union had experienced.

The church people, organized labor, students from SNCC and CORE, and other persons who were interested, came to our rescue, and they were able to see us through to our first victories. From then on the possibility of success was assured.

On Organizing and Being an Organizer

I am an organizer, not a union leader. A good organizer has to work hard and long. There are no shortcuts. You just keep talking to people, working with them, sharing, exchanging, and they come along. People can be organized for anything, even the worst of causes.

The reactionaries are always the better organizers. The "right" has a lot of discipline that the "left" lacks. The "left" always dilutes itself. Instead of fighting a common enemy, the "left" splinters, and the splinters go after one another. Meanwhile the "right" goes after its objective, pounding away, pounding away.

From my experience I would say that bringing about community organization is a lot harder than labor organizing. In a labor union, at a certain point you can say, "Well, it's organized." But in community organization I could never see an end, a time I could say it was organized.

When I say community organization I mean the grass-roots type. It's not the type in which you take existing organizations and put them together in a coordinating agency. When I went into an area as a community organizer, I tried to stay away from the leaders of all existing agencies. I found my best leaders by going deep into the grass roots. Unfortunately, it has been my experience that some grass-roots leaders don't remain grass-roots very long. The more successful they get, the less effective they seem to become.

Another reason it is more difficult to organize community groups is that they often tend to be erratic. The organization of these groups doesn't go along smoothly; instead, there are peaks and valleys. Say you have been working in a community, and after a whole year of hard work it is organized. You go away for a few weeks and when you come back, your organization has crumbled away. You cannot organize unless there is a need for it. And until you have well developed and recognized leaders, there is no secure structure.

A movement with some lasting organization is a lot less dramatic than a movement with a lot of demonstrations and a lot of marching and so forth. The more dramatic organization does catch attention quicker. Over the long haul, however, it's a lot more difficult to keep together because you're not building solid. One of the disappointments of community organization is that it takes an awful lot of time to build. It takes a lot of time because people are not developed overnight. A lasting organization is one in which people will continue to build, develop and move when you are not there.

Everything in life is contagious. If you work hard enough, the other guy is going to work. Not so much because you convinced him, but because he's downright ashamed of his not working. At first he usually doesn't know how to work in an organization. So if you work 16 hours a day, he's going to work 5 hours a day. If you work 24 hours a day, he's going to work 8 hours a day. As an organizer you are going to have to work more hours than anybody else and like it. If you can't work without complaining, then you'd better get out. What it takes you a week to build, you can destroy in one outburst.

If you're not frightened that you might fail, you'll never do the job. If you're frightened, you'll work like crazy.

Being of service is not enough. You must become a servant to the people. When you do, you can demand their commitment in return.

*   *   *   *

CO-2   BLACK POWER AT THE COUNTY LEVEL[1]

The only way black folks in the South are going to get their rights is by taking them. And the best way to take them is to win political control over their lives. Charles Evers proved it can be done. The people did it, and that is a lesson no one will ever forget. The next step is to develop political organizations capable of electing enough officials to take over county governments. It can be done, with organization and education.

When we first began organizing in Lowndes County, we quickly discovered that politicians wouldn't listen to the people if they were working through a civil rights organization. In October and November of 1965, several of us SNCC volunteers began researching the Alabama Code of Laws for every bit of information relevant to setting up county governments. Beginning in December, we scheduled workshops to share what we had learned with the people.

The first three were held in Atlanta. Twenty-five Lowndes County people were there. Fifty came to the third meeting and we were ready to shift to biweekly workshops in the county. Hundreds of people attended. We started by talking about how a person could be nominated for office, then how elections actually take place.

Then we examined each of the offices to be filled: the tax assessor, the tax collector, the coroner, the sheriff, and the school board. If we could assess taxes, then the rich would stop getting away with fraud while the poor people paid. If we could control the schools, then black kids could get their fair share. If we could control the sheriff's office, then we could keep impartial peace in the county and make sure the law is applied equally to all.

Since not everyone could attend the workshops, and not everyone would remember all that went on, we mimeographed complete job descriptions for each of the county offices, and then made up illustrated cartoon

---

[1] Adapted from "Lowndes County Freedom Organization," written in 1967 by Jack Minnis of the Southern Conference Educational Fund.

booklets for those who could not read. The booklets showed what each official was supposed to do and what the people could do, if they controlled these offices. We were preparing to nominate candidates.

The nominating convention took place in May. One nominee was picked for each office. We then ran a series of summer workshops aimed at preparing the candidates to do their jobs well if elected. Other people came too. We focused on "how-to-do-it" kinds of things, but we also stressed the ways in which the powerful people tried to buy off political officials, trading favors and building them up so that they might begin to feel "better" than the folks who elected them.

Both the candidates and the people were beginning to see the dangers, what to watch for in themselves and in their elected officials. We taught them about impeachments, special elections, and so forth, in case some officials did not represent the people well. Our candidates ran under the banner of the Black Panther Party, a symbol of freedom and power. It was the first time the symbol had been used.

On election day, the Party organized car pools and assigned poll watchers. But we were not fully prepared for the opposition. Black Panther party workers were fired on by shotguns, and in one place were beaten by a mob. White poll "officials" gave misleading help to some blacks who could neither read nor write. Half of the registered black voters had to travel across the county to polling places far from home. We captured 43 percent of the vote, but we didn't capture any office.

What we did win was an understanding that poor people can nominate their own candidates, that if they organized, they could capture offices and run the County fairly, and that in the future it would be necessary to stick together even more closely if they wanted to win.

*   *   *   *

CO-3 GROW AND THE STRIKE AT MASONITE[1]

My first experience in the movement was in McComb, Mississippi, in 1961. I was attacked by a group of white men who beat me into unconsciousness. I left only when it became obvious that black men had to lead black men. Now I am back in the deep South, working with the same kind of people who beat me then.

I know Southern whites well. I grew up in Alabama. My uncle was a sharecropper. I have relatives who used to be in the Ku Klux Klan and some who still are. I left the South the first time because I knew I could

---

1 Abstracted from *GROW*, a pamphlet published by the Southern Conference Educational Fund in 1967.

not live in a world filled with racism and hate. I came back the first time because I had hopes that black people were going to change that world.

Four months ago I came back once again—this time to work in white communities. It was like coming back to a different world. I have talked with poor white farmers who must send their children to Headstart centers run by black people. I have talked with white union members who know that in a strike black workers will not support a union that has betrayed them over and over. Yet without the support of the black workers, their union will be broken and they will go back to starvation wages.

I have walked into union halls and talked with men who belonged to the Klan. I make no secret of who I am. I tell them frankly that if they do not want me to stay, I will leave immediately, but they do not ask me to. Instead they say: "To hell with that. What can you do to help on a strike?" GROW is my answer.

Our concept for the Grass Roots Organizing Work project (GROW) is that poor and working whites can make common cause with their counterparts in the black community against the economic and political system that strangles them both. Racism in the white community is our common enemy—the kind of racism that has been deliberately cultivated to prevent such coalitions from taking place. Our strategy is to find situations in which we could show whites that they needed black people to change the conditions of their lives, whether in the midst of a strike, in a struggle for child day care, or in a program of adult literacy.

How to begin to locate the poor and working whites in the South was the first question. The GROW staff has worked in the black communities of the Mississippi Delta, and had some credibility there. From our old friends we got the names of whites to contact.

We don't quite know why, perhaps because of Movement propaganda, but we were afraid of approaching these people. After all, in the innocence of the 1964 Summer Project, we were told that these people were the enemy. They were the ones who shot into the COFO Freedom Houses, beat you when you were walking the picket lines, poured the ketchup over your head when you were integrating those greasy spoons fighting for the right of black people to eat terrible hamburgers they could not afford.

But these were not the people to fear. We met many of them.

Some spoke of the wretchedness of their lives with dreams and illusions, like the woman who was writing songs and sending them to a radio station (along with $2) in the hopes that someone would set her words to music and she would make a bundle, just like the announcer said she would.

We met a woman who was obese—the kind of obesity that comes from eating all the greasy, fatty stuff the poor use to fill their bellies. Her child was what the medical profession calls mongoloid. It was 20 degrees outside and there were puddles of ice in the yard when he walked outside wearing nothing but a torn T-shirt.

And there was the man in the Delta who earned $10 a week, plus the right to live in a three-room shack with his eight children, one a small infant. There was a 28-year-old man who lost all the toes on both feet while chopping wood—who is going to marry his 12-year-old first cousin, and who didn't even have a job prospect. This is what the sociologists must mean when they talk about the cycle of poverty.

We invited about 30 of these people, including small children and teenagers, to New Orleans for a weekend of workshops. It was impossible to meet in their own communities, because they were as frightened of the authorities as black people were until the 1960s. A sharecropper I met wanted to attend a literacy class, but was sure his bossman would disapprove of it. The New Orleans workshop didn't work. Subsequent visits to other poor whites in the Delta led us to conclude that they were thoroughly and tragically beaten. Unlike poor blacks, who had the strength of an organized movement to look to, they lacked the spirit and the vision to alter their lives.

What they desperately need are social services—welfare, housing, food, medicine. We do not have the resources to provide these things. These are people who must be part of any movement we build, but they do not have the strength to be the spearhead of it.

In the summer of 1967 we began making visits to lower Mississippi, where there was a labor struggle between Local 5-443 of the International Woodworkers of America (IWA) and Masonite, the largest producer of hardboard in the world. The plant had been organized since 1939.

In 1967, the local had a membership of close to 3000 and about 75 percent of it white. That year the company tried to push through a reorganization plan (partial automation) that would have eliminated jobs and increased individual work loads. The union struck. The strike lasted seven and a half months and it was bitter; the repercussions have yet to be fully felt.

The company effectively "Klan-baited" the local. It was not hard to do in Jones County. Yet to charge the local with being Klan-controlled is absurd. Management posed as the friend of black people by integrating showers, drinking fountains, and the like. Of course, the company was simply complying with the Federal order. But it must be pointed out that the local had supported certain segregationist practices inside the plant. This simple tactic lured at least half the black strikers back to work.

Injunctions were then obtained against the local to end picketing. Gun towers still dot the plant area. During the strike, five men were alleged to have been killed.

When Masonite production declined both in quantity and quality, the company brought a $3 million suit against the International Union. The International then negotiated a new contract with the company without consulting with the local; imposed a trusteeship on the local, seizing the local union hall and its finances; and then removed the local officers. Masonite then dropped its suit. Five hundred men, many of whom had worked at Masonite for 20 and 30 years, were thrown out of work after the new contract. Many felt that their own International had sold them out. They couldn't even get a local attorney to help them—indeed, the attorney who had represented them received $25,000 on condition that he would not represent the local in any future litigation. At the end of 1968, more than 800 of the strikers had not been taken back, because they are considered strong unionists. About 1600 now do the work that once required 2800 men.

Anyone who is serious about building a movement in the South would do well to recognize what formidable opponents we have. Laurel is a company town. Masonite has economic, political, and propagandistic control. The largest employer in a two- or three-county area, in 1966 it effectively shut out the St. Regis Paper Company by the simple expedient of upping its labor force by 1000. It did not want a competitor in the local labor market. Masonite is a heavy advertiser. The one TV, several radio stations, and the only newspaper all reflect the probusiness, conservative stance. Outside of these institutions are the banks, the businesses, and the Chamber of Commerce, all of which depend heavily on the weekly Masonite payroll. Jones County is a colony.

While the strike was going on, we at the GROW staff met many times with the strikers. At the time of the strike, what the local needed most was to get the black men out of the plant and back on the strike. But the black unionists were bitter over the second-class role they have in the local; on the other hand, they have profited from a strong union and their wages were higher than other black Mississippi workers.

But, we were convinced, whites should not work in organizing black communities at this point in history. Our hope was to form a joint project with some black organizers around common interests to defeat the company in its efforts to divide. We would work with the whites and the black organizers would work in the black community. If we could show that a black-white coalition could be built in Mississippi, its impact on the movement would be tremendous and would spur others. Concessions would have to be made by the white unionists—that is, participation by black men in union affairs—and a strong black caucus would probably have to be built. But the black groups we contacted in Mississippi and on the national level were unresponsive. GROW decided to go it alone. The situation was drastic. The International had deserted the local, morale was low, and people began drifting away.

Jack Minnis, our research director, had a talent for finding flaws in the system. When he was in charge of research for SNCC, he found an obscure Alabama law that eventually led to the formation of the Lowndes County Freedom Party. Minnis pored over all the strike data he could find, and learned that the International Union had violated its own constitution in imposing the trusteeship and signing the contract with Masonite. We went to court for the local. The suit is still in the courts because of charges and countercharges brought by the International and Masonite. The intensity of the court battle may best be appreciated if it is mentioned that Hulse Hayes of the law firm that wrote the Taft-Hartley Act in 1946 heads a five-lawyer team for Masonite, while the International is using a Little Rock law firm that includes one exgovernor, plus the former commissioner of the Arkansas Public Service Commission.

On the organizational level, we have been holding rallies and workshops, building trust and a feeling of unity. Good rapport exists between GROW and the white working-class community in Laurel. We have been able to do this while keeping our relations with black, antiwar, and student movements. It has been honest from the beginning; in our first meeting with the strikers we told them about our backgrounds with SCEF and SNCC.

A five-man strike committee has been formed in the local union to coordinate their struggle. Three are white, two are black. Morale is still a problem, but these are hard men.

Rallies are held every Saturday in a cow pasture. The crowds vary in size from 55 (one cold, rainy day) to over 800 on a nice sunny one. Cars stand in dual lines, many bumpers distinguished by faded Wallace stickers. There are some black people in the crowd, but most are white. A flatbed truck is situated in the middle of the pasture and the speakers are talking about the struggle of working people and their need for black-white unity. Jack Minnis used one rally to explain the law suit in terms of the whole nature of the state and Federal judicial systems. "If there's justice in the courts, we will win," he said, "because the law's supposed to be on your side. If we can't win in the courts, we will have to try something else." His theory is that if you are going to change the system, you must first understand it. A lot of people in Jones County are beginning to.

We have finally made contact with working whites. Our relationship with them is good. We have been accepted into their homes and have eaten and slept there, and they have visited us in New Orleans at the GROW educational center. We have fraternal relations with rank-and-file members of the Klan. We've sipped moonshine, discussed Wallace, and drunk beer into the wee small hours in a bar that we were told was the headquarters of the Klan. There is hope in these people, while there is little hope among the poor whites we originally tried to organize.

If there is any possibility of changing this country for the better, these white people *must* be organized. George Wallace has exploited their plight, and they voted for him because they did not have anyone else to vote for. We want to give them an alternative.

*   *   *   *

CO-4   SCEF RESPONDS TO A CRISIS[1]

The White Community Responds to the Black Rebellion

The rebellion in Louisville erupted on a Monday night, May 27. It followed a street-corner meeting in the heart of the ghetto to protest a flagrant case of police brutality. There would have been no violence if police cars had not roared into the crowd of black people who were peacefully leaving the meeting.

Our city and state governments responded to that night's uprising by an immediate and tremendous crackdown. All available police converged on the area and the Governor sent in the National Guard—2,000 of them by the next day. An immediate curfew was imposed. Before dawn more than 100 black people were arrested, mostly for curfew violation. Four were shot.

Our first thought was to get white observers at the jail to try to discourage the mistreatment of black people being arrested. At the jail, we found that the Louisville Council of Churches also had observers on

---

[1] Based on a report prepared by Ann Braden and distributed by the Southern Conference Educational Fund (SCEF) in June 1968 in Louisville, Kentucky. Suggestions for further reading on projects by the Southern Conference Educational Fund, 3210 W. Broadway, Louisville, Kentucky 40211 include Robert Analavage, *GROW: A New Movement in the South,* SCEF, 1968; "Appalachia: Case Study in Repression" (pamphlet), SCEF, 1969; Jack Minnis, "The Care and Feeding of Power Structures" (pamphlet), SCEF, 1967; Alan McSurley, "Hangups—Common Problems of People Who Organize Other People into Communities" (pamphlet), SCEF, 1967; and *The Southern Patriot* (monthly newspaper), SCEF, Volumes 23–28, 1965–1971.

hand—ministers, mostly. The Council had set up its own skeleton organization back in the winter to respond to a possible rebellion and to set up a "rumor center." They had a telephone number where people could call to see what was happening. Because things like this were being taken care of by the church group, we were able to turn our attention to other kinds of action.

Early Tuesday morning, we decided that our job was to attempt to get some kind of public expression from the white community protesting the imposition of a police state to deal with the black rebellion. It is our opinion that this is the task of the white activist at this moment in American history. We saw it as our job to help the white community to see that as long as there is oppression there will be rebellion and that if the white community attempts to crush this rebellion instead of facing the conditions that cause it, this can only be done by the imposition of a police state that will enslave everyone. In other words, aside from all the moral questions involved, it is in the self-interest of the great majority of people to stave off a police state—because the kind of society it would bring is one they would not want to live in. This was the political and philosophic base of all our actions in Louisville—and it still is.

That first morning, a few of us got on the telephone, called all the white people we could think of who might respond, and asked them to meet at City Hall at 3 p.m. to attempt to see the mayor. The demands of the delegation were to be (1) removal of the National Guard, (2) lifting of the curfew, (3) release of prisoners on their own bond (bonds had been set at $2000 for curfew violation and $20,000 for looting), (4) firing of the police officer whose misconduct had caused the protest in the black community, and (5) establishment of a program to deal with the real problems in the West End of Louisville where the rebellion was in progress. Militant black leaders were making similar demands on the city. We also distributed a leaflet in downtown Louisville calling on white people to support these demands and to meet at City Hall.

The downtown leafleting recruited only a few people for our City Hall demonstration. However, it served the purpose of letting great numbers of whites know that other whites were opposing the policies of the city government. Most of those who actually came to City Hall did so in response to the telephone campaign. There were more than 50 of them—a good turnout for Louisville on something like this and one that included some people we'd never seen at a demonstration before. White Southerners don't often demonstrate on the behalf of blacks.

Terrified city officials locked the doors of City Hall when we got there. We waited on the steps. Finally, the executive director of the Human Relations Commission came out to talk with us. We insisted on seeing the mayor, and when he insisted that the mayor was seeing no one, we insisted that he immediately take our demands to the mayor. He did— with no results, of course. But our delegation stayed an hour or more talking on the steps with the Human Relations man. Police were crawling all over the place; we asked why, and he finally asked them to leave. We had two official spokesmen—a Catholic priest and a Baptist minister—but everyone whom the spirit moved was able to talk, and we did. We made two main points: (1) the practical short-range one that the use of force, the presence of the Guard, and the like were actually making matters worse and prolonging the disorders in the West End, and that (2) if the city continued its policy of meeting rebellion by force it could only succeed by increasingly repressive measures, a garrison city, and an unthinkable and unlivable situation. We fear that the officials were moved more by the former short-range argument than by the latter, more basic one—especially since our argument was at that moment being documented (we learned later) by new West End outbreaks in the very areas where the Guard was heaviest.

Finally there was nothing more to say to the Human Relations man— so one of our delegation hastily went into town and bought cardboard and we made picket signs and set up a picket at police headquarters. When it came time for the 8 p.m. curfew, everyone left except seven people who decided to stay and be arrested—which they were. We later had some doubts about the effectiveness of this kind of protest against the curfew. There were hundreds of black people in jail by then and no one really had time to fight about these people's right to picket. However, those who went to jail had important and significant experiences in communicating with the Black prisoners—many of them understood why the white people were there too, and important lines of communication were set up.

The City Hall delegation did have an impact in the community far beyond those who saw us there—as it was written up in the paper the next morning and others knew about it by word of mouth.

That night there were more disorders throughout the West End, more blacks arrested, and four more shot.

The next morning we decided that instead of spending our time getting out a new leaflet and organizing a continuing picket line, we needed to take time to get more white people together to broaden our base of planning and decision-making. We didn't want the white protest to be just a SCEF thing. The value of a group like SCEF in a situation like this, we felt, was that it was mobile, could move fast, had a printing press handy, and had a few full-time people who could drop other things and act. But the turnout at City Hall had shown us that many white people in the city were concerned, and we felt we should not be making the basic decisions alone.

So that day we spent on the telephone inviting people to a meeting the next day—which happened to be Memorial Day and thus a holiday when no one would be working but certainly not in the mood for a picnic.

Meantime, that day (Wednesday), in response to the pressure from both the black and white communities, the city deescalated. They partially withdrew the Guard, lifted the curfew, let may of the prisoners out of jail, and granted the request of black militants that they be allowed to set up a marshal system to patrol their own streets. Things quieted down considerably in the West End—although that night tragedy struck as two black people were killed. One was a 14-year-old boy shot by a policeman; the other was a 19-year-old youth shot by a merchant. The youth was eating a fish sandwich in front of the store when he was slain.

Our meeting of whites was held the next afternoon in a church, and 70 people showed up—with a number of others expressing support who could not be there. The temporary chairman, a young Presbyterian minister, opened the meeting by saying we were meeting because a number of white people felt the need for a "radical response" to what was happening, that we were having "liberal" responses but we needed a "radical" one. The group got off on that foot—and continued in that direction.

The upshot of the meeting was an ad hoc organization that named itself the White Emergency Support Team (WEST), the stated purpose of which was to support the black community at this time. It was made clear that it was not to be a negotiating committee or a go-between, that its purpose was not to "quiet things down" but to try to bring influence to bear to see that Louisville faced its basic problems.

We set up three committees immediately: (1) a policy committee to meet right away and draw a policy statement to be mailed that night to those present and others seeking signatures that could be publicized; (2) an action committee that was given freedom to proceed with direct action, leafleting, picketing, and the like; (3) an information committee that would seek the facts on how the rebellion started and its real causes to the community by all possible means—the press, radio and TV, and our own publications.

Part of our policy statement was borrowed almost verbatim from a statement issued by white people in Washington during the April uprisings there. If radical organizers and organizations keep in touch with each other, we would learn a good deal by sharing our experiences and become more effective by sharing our materials.

The policy committee also drew up and publicized a list of "immediate demands"—including the original ones made at City Hall, plus a demand that the policeman and mechant who had killed the black youths be charged with murder.

By Friday morning, the West End was quiet—and we thought WEST could settle down to a long-range task of educating the white community. But we had underestimated the will of the city administration to counterattack, its blindness in facing the real issues, and its determination to crush activists instead of solving problems.

On Friday afternoon, the City-County Crime Commission met and issued a blast. It ignored the basic social problems and recommended that "proper authorities" investigate an out-of-town black speaker at the original Monday night rally, the "role of antipoverty workers" in the disorders (some VISTAs had been active in WEST), and the role, "if any," of SCEF leaders in starting the riots. Meantime, the grand jury had met and brought charges of assault and battery against the black man who had been struck by a policeman—the incident that had produced the original protest against police brutality.

In other words, powerful people in the city had apparently decided to "blame the victims" for what had happened and to try to solve its problems by scapegoating. This is the traditional way of handling thorny problems in Louisville.

That night (Friday), police moved to implement this line. They arrested the out-of-town speaker mentioned by the Crime Commission and held him incommunicado until late Saturday morning. Then they picked up two other speakers at the Monday night rally, two young leaders of the militant Black Unity League of Kentucky (called BULK). A "court of inquiry" was hastily convened in police court for Saturday afternoon. Police charged that these three black people were plotting to dynamite oil refineries in the West End. They produced no evidence whatsoever to support these charges, but all three were jailed under a total of $175,000 bond.

WEST had got into operation Saturday morning as soon as we got word from the black community that a court of inquiry was to be held. Our action committee did a telephone campaign to get people to the courtroom. After the court hearing, we immediately set up a picket line at City Hall and issued a statement to the news media about scapegoating.

On Sunday, movement lawyers got a habeas corpus hearing in Circuit Court, attempting to free the three men. This failed. The hearing went on until 10 p.m. Immediately afterward, people from WEST, BULK, and other groups met at a West End church until after midnight to plan a counterattack. We decided that the main thing that must be done at that moment was to raise a voice in the community challenging the hysteria that was being built up by the scapegoating process—and to get the facts on what was happening to as many people as possible. We knew we could not depend on the commercial press to do this for us— even though the Louisville papers are better than most. So some of us stayed up all night and prepared a leaflet. The leaflet was headed "City Shifts Blame for Civil Disorders; Frames Black Leaders." The leaflet briefly stated the real causes of black rebellion, reviewed the facts of what had happened in Louisville, stated the circumstances of the arrest of the three black leaders, pointed out that this followed a national pattern of framing and jailing black militant leaders, and then said:

"On June 1, in Louisville all of the court machinery and official apparatus sprang into action. Why? Because police said they had heard a rumor that black people planned to dynamite oil refineries.

"Just four days before, police had shot into the homes of black people. Just three days before, two black people had been shot dead. This was no rumor; it was real. But no court of inquiry was convened, no official machinery sprang into action.

"White Louisville must face the fact that this set of circumstances says one thing very clearly—that when white property appears to be threatened we do something about it, but when black lives are taken we do not." There followed the obvious specific demands.

In the next few days, WEST—mobilized by the action committee— distributed tens of thousands of copies of this leaflet—in downtown Louisville, in the courtrooms where hearings were being held, on campuses, at meetings throughout the city, by mailing to various lists. We also set up picket lines at City Hall and at the jail. The following weekend WEST, along with other groups in the black community and in the white one, set up a mass protest rally. A movement attorney from New York came and spoke about the national pattern of repression. Other speakers included local leaders—militant blacks, young and old; Muslims; and white activists. After the rally, many of the participants went to the home of the police-court judge to picket and attempt to see him. The meeting had been billed in the leaflet announcing it as a "rally against a police state," and it produced the greatest show of unity Louisville has seen in some time. The Steering Committee Against Repression, a coalition of Southern human rights groups, joined the local groups in sponsoring it and brought people a feeling of support from outside the community.

Meantime, other people in WEST were working on different levels.

Some of them formed a more "respectable" delegation to City Hall—"respectable" not in the sense of who took part, as it was open to all, but in the sense of being made up of people who preferred not to picket or take part in direct action but who wanted to make a determined attempt to actually talk with the mayor. They did have a conference with the mayor and presented the WEST viewpoint. Other WEST people were contacting press representatives and giving them information on the real situation in the ghetto and a viewpoint they might not have otherwise had.

There is no doubt that within a week's time these efforts had had an impact on public opinion in this community. Newspaper articles and editorials were making note of the charge that the city was seeking scapegoats to avoid facing the real problems in the West End. The word "scapegoating" was getting into the popular vocabulary in Louisville—and at meetings throughout the city there were discussions as to whether this was what was happening. We believe this is testimony that if you speak the truth insistently, even in these times of hysteria, it *can* be heard.

After a week, bonds of the three "scapegoats" were reduced, and as this is written two have been released. The battle for truth is far from over, because the city is continuing its efforts to becloud the issues and to crush all who have challenged them. Also, the new Kentucky Un-American Activities Committee has been set up (KUAC—pronounced QUACK—we call it), and the governor has told them to look into the Louisville disorders. That's about all we need at this moment—those people dabbling in the serious social problems in this city.

However, for the time being we have at least slowed the steamroller of hysteria that was launched by the city in the wake of the uprising, and we have found that a voice of sanity can be heard. Temporarily at least we have built a little beachhead of resistance against the encroachment of a police state, a sort of liberated area. We will continue to build on this experience.

Meantime, WEST has started some long-range efforts. A legal committee has been set up; we raised money for an answering service, recruited seven lawyers each to be responsible for responding to calls one day a week, and made a mass distribution of a brochure "Know Your Rights" with a telephone number for people to call when they feel they are mistreated by police.

Also, we are preparing a brochure with pictures and information from interviews with shooting victims, documenting some of the things that happened during the rebellion.

In addition, a special committee is planning an information campaign in the poor-white areas of Louisville.

Meantime, too, other groups in the community have been doing other things. The local Religion and Race Council has been holding "truth sessions" each night at various churches in the white community where black speakers "tell it like it is" and things like the Kerner report are discussed. At the height of the rebellion, we found that while the Council of Churches telephone service functioned well as a "rumor center," it was not really able to be a service center for people in the West End—for example, people whose relatives were injured and needed to get through the curfew to care for them. Therefore, a start was made on a service center to be operated by a community organization within the West End. Since the disorders quieted so soon, this never really got into operation but would be able to, should the necessity arise again.

From our experience here, we are able to make these general suggestions to those who may be faced with similar crisis elsewhere:

1. Find out as much as you can about the experience of other communities. A report sent out by the Center for Emergency Support in Washington in April was invaluable to us. We didn't follow that model exactly, because circumstances here were different, but the ideas from Washington helped us. We have copies of the Washington report if you'd like to see it. We also have extra copies of this Louisville report. If other communities wish to share their experiences, we will help distribute them.

2. Don't underestimate what a few people who are ready to move can do. Only two or three people did the telephone campaign that gathered our first demonstration of white people. It could have been done by one person. The main thing is the will to act—rather than to spend time talking.

3. But don't forget either that many people who have not responded before will do so in a crisis. One of the most important things we did, even though it delayed action for a day, was to take the time necessary to gather together a larger group of people to share planning and decision-making. At a time like this, any sort of desire to dominate or creditmonger is fatal—we are in a life-and-death crisis and the point is to get the job done.

4. Assess the resources in your community, what groups already exist, and what they are doing. That way you won't waste time in a duplication of effort—but you may also find you'll have to do things we didn't have to do here in Louisville. For example, in a community where no white groups are actively concerned with the ghetto crisis, an ad hoc group would need to do a number of things that other groups were doing

in Louisville. If the Religion and Race Council had not already been planning discussion groups throughout the white community, our ad hoc group should have tried to stimulate such meetings. It may seem more moderate than direct action—but it is essential to reach the unreached. If the Council of Churches had not been organized to provide some of the service functions needed during a rebellion (ministers at the jail, and the like) an ad hoc group would need to do this. In our own situation, because we did have other resources in the community, we were able to concentrate on public political positions and direct action—also very necessary and not likely to be done by more moderate groups.

5. Obviously you don't need to wait for a crisis to act in the white community. People usually do—unfortunately—but the educational work should be going on all the time. And efforts should be made to stimulate action against repression of black people *without* a crisis.

6. Once you are in the midst of a crisis, it is important to set up a mobile machinery—democratic and with as broad participation as possible in general policy-making, but able to act quickly when action is needed, without interminable board meetings and discussions. One way to do this is by seeking general agreement on basic approach and philosophy as West has done and is doing with its policy statement—and then giving a small action committee the freedom to act within the bounds of that policy. For example, it was important here that people were willing to meet at midnight on a Sunday instead of waiting until morning and that some were willing to stay up all night to issue a crucial leaflet.

7. And finally, remember that we're in for a long struggle. You can build a beachhead in a week, as we did, but you can't win in that period of time—and the repressive forces hover on all sides. Saving America from a police state at this point in history will require the sustained and tireless efforts of all of us—and there will be times when we feel defeated—but we must keep on, on every front where we have maneuverability. The frightened people who are trying to settle our social problems by repression are many and powerful. They are playing for keeps and the stakes are high—involving no less than democracy itself and the future of all of us and of our children.

Postscript

Two years later, Louisville's "Black Six" (three more black community leaders were indicted after the above case was written) who were charged with conspiring to destroy private property during disorders in May 1968 won a directed verdict of acquittal. On July 7, 1970, Circuit Judge S. Rush Nicholson said that the prosecution had failed to prove the charge of conspiracy against them. He instructed the jury to return a "not guilty" verdict after the prosecution closed its case.

The prosecution had asked for repeated delays in the trial—and at one point got it moved to rural Munfordville, Ky., after material charging the city with "scapegoating" was circulated widely in Louisville. It was moved back to Louisville after two white staff members of the Southern Conference Educational Fund (SCEF), Martha Allen and Mike Honey, sent a letter to everyone in the Munfordville phone book asking them to protest the trial. Honey and Allen were charged with jury tampering because of the letter, but have since been acquitted.

According to a SCEF communique, ". . . The Black Six case was won in the court of public opinion in Louisville at least a year ago—long before it came to trial in a court of law. The most important part of this, of course, was the support in the black community from the time of the first arrests and indictments. . . ."

Over the two years the White Emergency Support Team (WEST) did a great deal of work to reach sizeable sections of the white community. The SCEF staff plan to write up a report on how some of this work was carried on, and it may be obtained from them.

* * * *

CO-5 ALINSKY STARTS A FIGHT[1]

The Scene Before FIGHT Was Launched

Rochester, New York State's third largest city, has a population of approximately 350,000. It is principally a manufacturing center, with 45 percent of its labor force employed in some 800 plants, Eastman Kodak being the dominant firm and Xerox a rising newcomer. The city had a Democratic administration, Republicans regaining control in 1970. It was estimated that there were 35,000 blacks in the city in 1964; there are close to 50,000 today. This represents a tremendous growth since the early 1950s.

Unemployment[2] of both blacks and whites was exceptionally low in Rochester, about one percent at the time Alinsky arrived at the scene, and the industrial leaders are "enlightened," far more so than, for example, in Syracuse. Rochester has a highly skilled labor market. The public schools had been doing some things to meet the need of blacks: In 1965, 1000 black children were placed in schools outside the ghetto.

---

[1] Edited version of a case written by Robert Perlman of Brandeis University.
[2] Unemployment of black men may currently be up 5 percent and that of black females 10 to 12 percent.

It may be of interest that the late 1960s witnessed a rise in lower-middle-class racism, putting a stop to integration. The housing occupied by blacks, however, was and still is generally substandard. The city's blacks, regardless of social and economic status, are concentrated in two ghettos. The Third Ward contains most of the better-off blacks. The Seventh Ward, which had been the receiving area for blacks displaced elsewhere by urban renewal, contains the bulk of low-income people who live in an area with prostitution, numbers, rackets, and the like. Transportation in Rochester is a mess, but this is not peculiar to the black community.

In the face of strong civic pride about what the city has done for its people, there were what some whites and blacks considered "serious riots" in the black community in the summer of 1964. Others considered these as the beginning of "black rebellion." One opinion held that the riots were a revolt against the Rochester police, following a history of incidents of police brutality. Protest committees had accomplished nothing. Then three whites and three blacks staged a sit-in at City Hall and received support from some of the University faculty. The clergy wanted action through a Police Advisory Board that had been set up by the Democratic administration. Black leaders wanted two or three men on the police force fired.

The NAACP and the city's Human Relations Board were considered to be ineffective in the situation. The press, radio, and TV—controlled by the ultraconservative Gannet chain—opposed the interests of the black community. Shortly before what the press subsequently defined as "riots," Malcolm X had a meeting attended by 800 blacks. Some observers feel that his presentation may have sparked the "riot." Other observers disagree. During the disturbances that followed, four men from Martin Luther King's organization (Southern Christian Leadership Conference, or SCLC) were invited to organize in Rochester. They came. After surveying the scene, however, they indicated that SCLC was currently committed to its endeavors in the South. Because of the press of these involvements they did not feel equipped for organizing efforts in a Northern city.

The Urban Ministry of the Rochester Council of Churches then turned to Saul Alinsky's Industrial Areas Foundation (IAF). The Council is a corporation of denominational churches, supported by local contributions collected through its member churches and affiliated with the National Council of Churches. The Urban Ministry is a somewhat autonomous group within the Council; its function is to develop strategies for inner-city church programs and to administer such programs. The Urban Ministry has its own board of directors and its own executive. It gets its funds from national and local judicatory bodies of the various denominations and is therefore, to some degree, free of control by the local churches. The Urban Ministry's executive director—with full support from the Executive Director of the Council of Churches and from the lay chairman of the Urban Ministry board—sparked the first move toward Alinsky by bringing together a small, informal group of white and black laymen and clergymen and arranging for them to go to Chicago for an initial contact with Alinsky. The group invited him to come to Rochester to discuss an organizing program.

Preparing the Way for Alinsky

In January of 1965 a meeting was arranged in a black church in Rochester, but Alinsky's plane was grounded in Chicago and he did not appear. In his absence there was a brief discussion revolving around such questions as whether the black community needed a "white Moses" or a black leader. Some felt that the black community was divided and needed a miracle. Perhaps Alinsky could provide it. Others argued that the black community should not depend on a white man but should organize from within. Later in January, Alinsky came to a similar meeting and answered questions, described the organizing work of the IAF in other cities, explained the role the IAF would play if it came to Rochester, and clarified the possibilities and requirements of an organizing drive. He was very clear on the financial arrangements. These would have to be secure, not subject to political promises, and capable of supporting the first two years of organizing efforts.

Meanwhile, public knowledge that Alinsky might come to Rochester had begun to agitate and polarize the whole community. The Protestant ministers were busy explaining and defending Alinsky and neutralizing the growing opposition. Petitions asking Alinsky to come were circulated in the black community. Individual civic leaders (a member of the board of the Council of Social Agencies, a Jewish businessman, a prominent Republican, and others) let it be known, mostly in private conversations, that they favored Alinsky's coming to Rochester. Ranged against them was the press, the business community's top leadership, the President of the University of Rochester, the executive of the Council of Social Agencies, and some members of the Divinity School faculty. During this period, the Urban Ministry obtained commitments, from its national and local sources, of funds in the amount of $100,000 for a two-year organizing drive, half of it in cash for the first year and pledges for the second year. This fact was widely publicized in Rochester.

In mid-February, a Citizens' Committee for Alinsky created by the Urban Ministry held an open meeting in the ghetto. Black and white ministers fielded questions from the floor. Again there was discussion of goals and tactics, of the need for unity among blacks, of their responsibility for organizing, and the like. In this meeting the Ministerial Alliance, an organization of black clergymen, took the stance that they were inviting Alinsky to Rochester.

A few days later, there was a second meeting attended by an all-white audience in another section of town. Members of the Urban Ministry saw to it that the proposed arrangement with Alinsky was explored from all angles. Would there be violence again? How does IAF proceed? What would be the effect on social welfare agencies? Shortly after this a meeting was held in a black church to bolster the campaign for signatures on petitions to bring Alinsky to Rochester and to give evidence of growing support for him in the black community. The Ministerial Alliance took responsibility for this one.

Throughout these weeks Saul Alinsky had not given a direct answer to the black and white leaders who were urging him to come.

Alinsky Agrees to Come

The next significant event was a meeting in Syracuse between Saul Alinsky and 18 people from Rochester, with more blacks represented in the delegation than had been the case in previous meetings. Alinsky again explained his approach, what could be expected of him, and what he expected of those who wanted to organize. He stressed the fact that there must be no rioting in the summer of 1965. If riots occurred, he said, it would be the end of the organization. Alinsky told the group he was willing to come to Rochester, but that some steps had to be taken to define issues and rally more support before a public announcement could be made.

A Militant Core and a Larger Organization

In March, a crucial meeting of blacks who had been involved from the beginning was held by a small group in which they tested among themselves what they were prepared to do and risk if Alinsky came. They decided to assume leadership and planned a public meeting to consolidate the decision to have Alinsky get started. Two hundred people took part in this meeting. At the end of March, Alinsky held a second meeting in Syracuse with the Rochester leaders. He introduced Ed Chambers as the organizer he was assigning to Rochester. A press and TV interview was arranged to follow this meeting. This constituted the public announcement that Alinsky was going to organize in Rochester's black community.

Chambers assumed the organizational responsibility at this point and recommended some structure—an organizing committee, a steering committee, and preparations for a "convention of delegates" of local organizations to be held within six weeks. On April 20, 400 people, half of them blacks, met as "the body" of FIGHT and heard representatives of organizations give evidence of their support. Four committees were set up:

1. Constitution
2. Policy and Issues
3. Convention Arrangements
4. Urban Renewal

The Steering Committee was legitimized by "the body" and was authorized to take action against slum landlords. This issue was selected by the Steering Committee and Chambers because it would draw universal support and was a symbolically meaningful target.

The IAF organizer at this juncture made a decision to concentrate organizational effort in the Third Ward, where the church-oriented people who looked at themselves as "respectable" lived because it was stable, and he felt that the important thing at that time was to get the organization started. Alinsky and Alinsky organizers have subsequently been criticized for this approach and for their frequent reliance on already organized black middle-class groups. The IAF organizer did not, however, give up his determination to maintain and in the long run increase the participation of the antichurch, more militant group from the Seventh Ward. Chambers then hired some organizers, all blacks, from the neighborhoods in which the organization was beginning. Soon thereafter, FIGHT staged a picketing demonstration against a landlord.

During this period the Steering Committee was meeting every week or two. In mid-May a public meeting took place at which new organizations affiliated with FIGHT. A Nominating Committee was established to prepare for the "convention" that was to be held on June 11. About 700 people participated as delegates in that convention. Some 130 organizations were represented. While about 70 percent of these organizations existed before the convention, the others were paper organizations. Hundreds of white people attended the convention as observers. The constitution was presented and some sections were discussed and amended from the floor before it was adopted. A slate of officers was elected. All the preparatory work had been handled by a convention committee under the general direction of the Steering Committee. FIGHT was established!

Reexamination of Alinsky's Strategy

Alinsky's operation resembles the process of organizing a local labor union. As the union moves into a plant or a community that is unorganized, the organizers make contact with some people who have indicated their interest if not their commitment to organizing. The union then tests whether there are sufficiently good prospects for expanding this nucleus to warrant an investment of a union's resources in an organizing drive. The union may also be concerned about exposing a small group of militant people to defeat. During this feeling-out process, the union explains that the goal is to set up a permanent organization. The union also makes clear that the basic responsibility for organizing rests with the workers and particularly with the nucleus of emerging leaders. The union brings to bear its previous experience and offers, in effect, a kind of technical assistance to the organizing drive.

Ths analogy breaks down in one important respect. The union must ultimately be able to produce a majority of workers as card-carrying members of the union. In the Alinsky type of operation it is not at all necessary to enroll a majority of the target group. In fact, in Alinsky's *Reveille for Radicals,* he points out that building an organization with 5 percent of a target population will constitute success. In this respect it may be more appropriate to compare Alinsky's operation with the organization of a local chapter of an environmental action group. These considerations lead directly to the first of a series of propositions about his organizing methods that will be advanced and illustrated here.

Step 1. There needs to be a nucleus of support and the availability of financial resources outside the disadvantaged community in order to initiate an organizing process.

The process begins when an actor or group of actors makes the decision to undertake organization of a target population. In the early and mid 1960s this target population was usually a black community or a low-income neighborhood without regard to race. While individual members or leaders of such groups often initiated the goal of organization, they rarely if ever possessed the financial resources needed to carry it out. The growth of social movements in the mid-1960s and the experience of population groups with the anti-poverty programs considerably changed this picture.

The leadership of the Urban Ministry in the Rochester Council of Churches first took the initiative in bringing together a group to seek out Alinsky. It was also this group that raised $100,000 for the organizing drive. It was necessary, however, to help the community shift the responsibility from the white Protestant leadership to the leadership of the black community. Alinsky made it clear at his first meeting with the Rochester group that he must have an invitation "from the people" as well as financial support from the churches. He explained that if a church group wants to make money available and is able to get the support of the people, then the Industrial Areas Foundation must have the money in advance in order to protect its organizers' income when the going got rough and pressure was applied to call off the organizing. Once the sponsors advanced the money, however, they would have nothing to say about what happened after that; the people would make decisions.

While the initiating group was not without some anxiety over this, some of the people who favored Alinsky clearly saw him as an alternative to more nationalistic and "dangerous" leadership emerging within the black community. From the outset, Alinsky faced the test of avoiding "the riots" that the white community feared in the summer of 1965. This made it necessary for him to move more rapidly than usual.

Step 2. Alinsky sets certain tests as conditions for his coming and in responding to these conditions, the local leadership begins the process of organization before Alinsky commits himself to enter the situation.

Over a period of months Alinsky structured the situation so that while he did not give a definite answer about his coming to Rochester, more and more people were asking him to come. He held two meetings in nearby Syracuse, where he had been a consultant to Syracuse University, rather than in Rochester itself. At the first meeting he held in Rochester, Alinsky was asked whether he would come, since he had whetted the people's appetite. He replied that he was not sure, that he had many other bids for his services in other cities. At the next public meeting, which was held without Alinsky, the question was asked, if the black community is unorganized and divided, how can it respond to Alinsky? When Alinsky next met with the group in Syracuse his first question was, "What is the mood of the churches, is it militant?" He was told that the churches were not leading and that some of them feared reprisals. At the end of this meeting Alinsky made the statement, "We will come when you are organized."

This process of testing reached its climax at the meeting in March, when a small leadership group consisting only of blacks met to discuss their position. They were still uncertain at this time and were asking themselves whether they were willing and able to act. At this meeting the leaders finally committed themselves to bringing Alinsky in and then asked how they could prepare for this and how they could mobilize support to convince Alinsky that there was a sufficiently strong base to warrant his coming in.

Step 3. Alinsky helps the local leadership meet his set of conditions.

He used a variety of devices to educate his leadership: he recounted past successes in order to convince the local leaders that it could be done; he sought to increase militancy by polarizing the situation, by identifying the enemy, and by developing a situation in terms of "good guys" and "bad guys"; he helped the leadership to anticipate some of their problems, such as the role of informers and sell-outs; he provided leadership in setting goals and helped them to anticipate the kind of tactics they would need to employ; and he schooled them over and over again in the mutual rights, responsibilities, and expectations of his role as the professional organizer and their role as the local leadership.

This approach may be illustrated in some detail by quoting from Alinsky's early meetings with the Rochester group. At the first meeting in January, Alinsky began in his characteristic way, not by making his own presentation but by asking for questions. One of the first questions was, "Is integrated housing a goal?" Alinsky answered, "The whites don't want to live with Negroes." He went on to say that he would not be telling the blacks what to do; that after they had put together their organization they would have only black organizers, he would not be present much and would sit in the back and only speak up if asked to. Alinsky said, "I am not after anything for myself, but white skin can be useful in getting an audience downtown."

Alinsky was asked how leaders are recruited. He answered that you start by looking for angry people who are willing to learn and if they are intelligent, you take them. He added that the IAF does not reject existing leadership and went on to recite the history of the Back-of-the-Yards movement. This presented a problem that Alinsky had to deal with again—he explained the growing tendency of workers in that part of Chicago to become part of the establishment and said that he might have to go in and start a new organization there. A question was raised about his attitude toward social workers and Alinsky warned that settlement houses would try to buy people off by giving them certain services. He emphasized that he tried to organize people so that they could acquire dignity and a sense of identity that can only be achieved by fighting the enemy. "Power is organization," Alinsky said, "and the sources of power are either money or numbers." Since blacks lack money, they must organize power through the use of numbers. "Power is neutral," he continued. "Whether or not it is desirable depends on the values involved and the immediate situation."

When asked about sit-ins, pickets, and similar demonstrations, he answered, "We do nothing so unimaginative." He cited the instance in Chicago of mobilizing three thousand blacks who went to one of the department stores as a means of getting jobs there for other blacks. They carefully looked over all the merchandise and made small purchases to be delivered C.O.D. (in order to tie up the department store's trucks). Purchases were all for $5 worth of merchandise, the minimum that could be purchased C.O.D. All orders were refused on delivery. The presence of so many blacks turned away many white customers. Alinsky then used "Uncle Toms" to get the message to the department store that they were willing to negotiate. Within a matter of hours and at the insistence of the department store, 113 jobs were made available for blacks. Alinsky was asked whether he could bring a factory to Rochester as a source of employment for blacks, and he answered that the IAF had done this in several places in Chicago. He was asked about salaries for his organizers and said that they usually started at about $4700 and if the individual did a good job he could work his way up to about $6500. In a press conference following this meeting, Alinsky was asked about violence and replied that violence occurs when people are discontented and have no understanding of their potential power. He said that organization overcomes that sense of desperation and removes the need for violence.

It is important to note that this process of interpretation was carried on by other individuals in Alinsky's absence. At one such meeting it was explained that Alinsky would organize politically and that he would use the techniques and tactics of the union movement. In the course of this discussion more and more stress was placed on the development of pride, self-help, self-responsibility, and the like. One speaker said that blacks need to organize in order to unify themselves in the way that Italians and Jews have done in Rochester. Some interest was expressed during this meeting in generating public opposition in the white community as a means of lending legitimacy in the black community to Alinsky's presence as an organizer.

The process of preparing people for the struggle ahead continued when Alinsky met with a leadership group in Syracuse. He warned the group that the antipoverty program would try to control black churches by moving in as tenants, paying rent and providing funds for their programs and then insisting on certain controls. He also warned against "professional Negroes," by which he meant the gradualists. He expressed his concern about people being bought off and kept out of the organization. Alinsky told the group that his staff would guide and offer their experience, but "the job of liberation is yours." He said he would pick the local director who in turn would recruit and train black organizers.

Immediately after Alinsky told this meeting that he was willing to come to Rochester but that this was not the time for a public announcement, he added, "Let the whites worry, let's first find the issues and get people to declare themselves." He urged them to put together a list of people for the organizing drive. All of this had its impact on the small leadership meeting that was described above. At that meeting there was a discussion of the major issues, which were defined by various individuals as jobs and education, urban renewal, and the need for real and lasting representation downtown. The strategy that was suggested was to line up black leadership and organizations, and the man in the street would follow.

Alinsky used the events of the moment to define for the leadership his role and his tactics. At his March meeting in Syracuse he said that he had received an invitation to meet with the City Manager of Rochester. He first assured the group that they would decide by vote whether or not he would accept this invitation. He then made three points: "(1) They want to know me as a person. If I say 'No' to their invitation, they will think they are dealing with a madman; (2) I assure you they will be more nervous after my meeting with them. I'll show strength and toughness; (3) We should realize that we will have to negotiate sooner or later, we can't be suicidal. I also want them to know I keep my word but that we are strong. I will stress treating Negroes with equality." In the discussion that followed, someone wondered whether Alinsky's meeting with the City official would jeopardize trust on the part of blacks. The group made a decision to approve the meeting because they felt that Alinsky was going as their representative and not as someone picked by "downtown."

While Alinsky was concentrating on preparing the black leadership for what lay ahead, the white Protestant ministers were equally hard at work in the white community preparing both friends and enemies. At the meeting in February attended only by white people, the white leadership recounted the history and experience of the Industrial Areas Foundation, pointed out that violence was not a part of this plan, and emphasized that Alinsky had worked with churches in various parts of the country. It was emphasized that Alinsky had no program for Rochester but that he would make the black community work together and gain power through such devices as a rent strike, efforts to improve code enforcements, and the like. No answer was given at this meeting to the question as to whether Alinsky would be working with white people to educate them. There was a discussion of the reasons for the riots in Rochester, and these were given as the flooding of southern blacks into the city and the antagonism of blacks to merchants and to the police.

One of the ministers reviewed the TWO experience in Chicago and said that social workers do some organizing but prove to be helpless when their demands are rejected. The Alinsky-type organizer was compared to St. Paul as a passionate man and at the same time a strategist. With regard to relationships to existing organizations, it was pointed out that in Chicago settlement houses, the American Legion and others have cooperated with Alinsky organizations. As to whether there would be conflict with social agencies, the answer was that this choice would be up to the social agencies.

Throughout this meeting it was reiterated that Alinsky's operation is not a program but a process. In dealing with the question as to whether Hitler-type leadership could arise in this process, one of the speakers made it clear that the white community could not control the process and was not in a position to organize the black community.

The stage in the organizing process that this material illustrates might be restated as follows. *Alinsky helped the local leadership to meet the conditions he had set and thereby accelerated the process of organization. Simultaneously he offered them technical assistance, such as instruction in how to set up a press conference, and confronted them with the choice of whether in fact they wanted to play the role that he defined for them.*

Step 4. As soon as Alinsky commits himself to organizing, the development of a militant and disciplined core of people becomes the overriding objective. Issues and programs are converted into tactics to achieve that objective.

Alinsky suggested using a "program ballot" in which people were asked to state their goals at the beginning of an organizing campaign. However, this is essentially a tactical device that Alinsky used to build and protect the developing organization. Alinsky's rationale for this device is that it makes people in the community aware of the organization's existence, it gives some of them a feeling of participation, it helps to identify potential recruits for the organization, and it is a defense against the charges of lack of democracy in the organization. In other words, Alinsky used this program ballot not to formulate goals but to build the organization.

The data on the first few months of organization, which bears on this point, will be summarized here. When Alinsky moved into action, one of his first statements to the group was, "Don't be specific on issues." This can be interpreted as a recommendation to keep the stance of the organization flexible in order to seize opportunities as they present themselves. He also stressed the use of humor, ridicule, and surprise to throw "the enemy" off balance, while unifying "your side."

At the same meeting Chambers reacted when, in the discussion, it was made known that the local Community Chest was giving $40,000 to start an Urban League in Rochester. He said, "If the Urban League is getting $40,000 to educate Negroes, let's ask for $40,000 to educate poor whites about Negroes." This brought an immediate and favorable response from the group. Chambers then got down to the real business quickly. He asked if there was a need for the nucleus of an organizing committee and which community groups should be signed up as part of the selling job that would take place during the next six weeks before the nominating convention. Chambers always threw out ideas as questions.

When the steering committee met, there was some discussion and listing of issues. These included the needs of migrants, youth problems, enforcement of housing codes, school segregation, police activities, vocational conseling, and urban renewal. The committee then discussed the coming convention and agreed that every organization would be invited to send five delegates. It was in this discussion that the rules for group discipline began to be made explicit. Chambers urged that none of the officers or committee chairmen leak information prematurely and that they not take their disagreements outside the executive group. Throughout these meetings in the spring there was considerable concern with questions of solidarity, not breaking ranks, being seduced by the establishment, backbiting among blacks, and identifying and removing Uncle Toms from their midst. The sense of black solidarity was further reinforced at these meetings by making it clear when welcoming whites that this was a black organization.

It is evident from the record that as an organizer, Chambers made a clear-cut decision in his own mind concerning strategies. He would present his strategies and argue them before the leadership group. Subsequently, over a period of time, he would seek out those people who supported his strategies, and in turn support their rise in the organization if they corresponded to his image of leadership.

Chambers also recognized that there was strong factional feeling between the Third Ward where the "respectable" people lived, and the Seventh Ward. He made a conscious decision to begin working through the more stable, church-affiliated neghborhood where the ministers told him they could count on mobilizing 2000 of the 10,000 to 14,000 black adults.

Wanting to see some balance maintained between the two groups, Chambers saw himself as a catalyst. He encouraged them to bring their conflict out into the open and battle it through. Apparently Chambers hoped to build the organization with support from both wards. Consequently, he embarked on a strategy of involving the ministers of black churches and encouraging them to assume roles as militant, visible, and committed leaders. In one tactic, for example, he set quotas for black ministers to bring a certain number of people to the picket line that was demonstrating against a slum landlord. He cautiously walked a middle ground between the factions and hired two organizers from the anti-church area and one from the church-oriented neighborhood. Alinsky and Chambers chose as the president of the organization, Reverend Franklin D.R. Florence, a minister known as a militant and a black nationalist. Chambers was careful not to move without the support and approval of his new president and, in fact, held off from action for many weeks while Florence had to be out of town.

Chambers defined his role as one of constantly trying to push people into doing things they wouldn't otherwise do. He moved through the community and kept widening his contacts. He set goals and tests, such as by telling the leadership that if they could not produce 60 pickets for a demonstration, it should be called off. He suggested program ideas such as negotiating with landlords who were holding back on maintenance and also complaining about their tenants, and suggested arranging to reduce the rent for "a house mother" who would then keep order in the house. He saw this as a prelude to starting tenants' clubs later on. It seems clear that Chambers screened and selected the issues for action. He resisted efforts to involve the organization in service programs. When it was suggested at one meeting that FIGHT participate in the literacy program by providing teachers, he pointed out that this was not a central concern of the organization.

Alinsky is concerned with "people's organizations" and strengthening their influence on service organizations. Working at the level of the local community, he seeks to change the attitudes and behavior, with respect to power, of both kinds of organization. The essence of the Alinsky process is to exploit action situations so that a "people's organization" will perceive itself as more powerful. Forming a disciplined organization, it may test its power, inevitably finding itself increasingly effective in asserting its interests against those in authority who have hitherto disregarded the group because they perceived it as powerless. The salient point here is that the Alinsky-style operation is designed to redistribute power in the decision-making arena and to place more of it in the hands of the previously powerless. This quite different from efforts that are directed toward some specific policy change, such as improving the quality of education for disadvantaged children or enhancing the job skills of school dropouts. Concrete program objectives are the means for Alinsky, not the ends.

Two Years Later

There are, of course, a series of epilogues to FIGHT's early history. No organization stays the same for long, and a militant organization based on a shaky alliance cannot expect to maintain allegiance of all its supporters forever. Some of the organizations founded by Alinsky foundered after some time. Some, like Back of the Yards, became conservative and reactionary. Most changed their character considerably. Alinsky counters his critics by explaining that this is the nature of the dynamics of all organizations and all collaborative efforts. His job is to help a community organize, not to tell it what it should do with itself after it is organized. If helping the "have-nots take it away from the haves" results in giving more than its rightful share to the group he is helping, then maybe "I'll have to help another group of have-nots take it away from them," he says.

Two years after Alinsky and Chambers began organizing, where was FIGHT? In keeping with the times, the "I" in the organization's acronymic name was being largely ignored (the letters stand for Freedom, Integration, God, Honor, Today). Whites had been firmly pushed out of the organization, but were now all organized into the Friends of FIGHT. FIGHT as an organization was now a conglomerate of more than 100 organizations, including settlement houses (those social workers Alinsky had argued against), pool halls, gangs, and Black Panther clubs. According to its chairman, it was led by "dissident young blacks ready for a change."

The Council of Churches was trying to raise $35,000 for a third year. Several denominations were refusing to contribute. Others pledged money, but only after bitter internal struggles, and with victories of small minorities. Still, most gave, and the money was eventually raised.

Friends of FIGHT were in disagreement. Some deplored attacks made by some of FIGHT's leaders on several Jewish community leaders. Stokely Carmichael, then chairman of SNCC, came to town to address a FIGHT rally, promising that in a forthcoming battle with Eastman Kodak over 600 jobs for hard-to-employ, unskilled blacks, he would organize a national boycott against Kodak. When it came, the boycott was a dismal flop, proving that FIGHT could not rely on help outside Rochester, and that there was a certain aloneness in a local organization that is not part of an organized national movement (another criticism leveled at Alinsky). "When we are through," Carmichael had claimed, "FIGHT will say 'Jump,' and Kodak will ask 'How high?'"

The Kodak issue provided good press for some time. A vice president of the company whose wife was a member of Friends of FIGHT had signed a rather confusing agreement with Florence to allow FIGHT to recruit the 600 blacks to be employed. "Kodak's killing FIGHT with kindness," wrote a local news columnist. A few days later, higher-ups within Kodak repudiated the agreement. "If I were Alinsky, I would have bribed Eilers (president of Kodak) to repudiate the agreement," said Ben Phelosof, acting president of Friends of FIGHT.

FIGHT at the time was engaged in a number of fights, perhaps too many. The Gannett chain picked up on its attacks. Prominent white supporters were repudiating the organization, or at least wavering. The Urban League, organized by middle-class blacks to counter the Alinsky organization, was picking up some support and somehow weathering the accusations of "Tomism." New, more militant organizations were expanding within the Seventh Ward, where Chambers had not organized early enough. But FIGHT continued to maintain its rather characteristic Alinsky style for some time. It should be noted that while this case illustrates Alinsky-style organizing, vintage 1960's, he has recently moved progressively out of the black community and into organizing lower- and middle-income whites around other sets of issues.

4

The Organizer as Man-in-the-Middle

CASES AND ILLUSTRATIVE MATERIALS

Organizers are frequently caught in the middle: between their boards or sources of support and their constituencies; between their professional or ideological commitments and commitments to clients; and between political factions in the community. These vignettes illustrate dilemmas frequently faced by community organizers as they strive to make difficult decisions or sort out the ambiguities in the roles they are called on to play.

In "Black Students Take Over," a black employee of a university administration agonizes over the issues of responsibility and loyalty. Does he represent the students with whom he has been thrust in a situation not of his making, or the administration that has employed him to serve the "needs" (kept under control) of black students?

Documenting the episodes in which a confrontation occurs, this case illustrates difficulties in negotiating settlements in community disputes. Neither side has agreed to a set of negotiating rules, or even that negotiations are to take place.

The administrator, speaking of his predicament in "Unleash Your People and You Stand to Lose Your Job," found himself caught between his professionally trained staff members, his indigenous nonprofessional staff, his board, the press, and neighborhood councils that his agency had organized to give voice to the poor. He was also caught between the

79

competing objectives of providing better agency services through the use of indigenous workers, serving the personal needs of those workers, and serving the needs of community groups through the leadership that these workers could provide.

The VISTA organizer who became the scapegoat provides a moving example of what happens when the interests of powerful community groups are threatened by the actual or perceived intent of an organizer's activities. The organizer, who in this case did not go through regularized channels because he felt them to be too slow, was trapped in a cross fire of his own making. The easiest way for various community groups to relieve tension and to remove immediate pressures was to find fault with the worker and to have him removed. The regional representative for OEO was also caught in the middle. He was forced to choose between doing what he thought was in the best interest of saving a program (that had already weathered a year's activity) and protecting a worker who represented the essence of the antipoverty program's avowed philosophy.

"Social Brokerage and Social Action" analyzes the experiences of the staff at Mobilization for Youth in New York. The tensions in using social brokerage to increase services to individuals on the one hand, and to encourage or stimulate social action on the part of citizen's organizations on the other, are fully detailed.

Andrea Cousins, the director of "A Tutorial Project in Harlem," gives vivid portrayal to the distance between good intentions and community-organization skills; and between staff assessments of neighborhood needs and the reactions of community residents not involved in creating or monitoring the resultant project. Although the workers were not bound by the usual constraints of a formal social welfare organization with its hierarchy and authority, their very lack of a legitimating body made them suspect in the community. Despite their freedom to experiment with techniques and programs, they were bound by their own middle-class orientations and ideological prejudgments of community need. Here were a group of young organizers caught between their ideological commitments to fundamental change in society through action at the grass-roots level, and their debilitating naiveté, paucity of experience, and lack of organizing skills.

This chapter ends appropriately with a statement by Nicholas Von Hoffman. "The Good Organizer" is very much the man-in-the-middle, aware of the precariousness of his position, of his personal hang ups, and of the need to stay in the background, playing up to the community leadership that he helps to recruit and to develop.

In a recent letter (August 1970), Mr. Von Hoffman told us that he no longer feels that this material is of "practical value." To the extent that he speaks of white organizers finding and building leadership in a black ghetto, he may be quite right. Although we still know a number of white community organizers working effectively in black communities, the times have changed politically and socially since Von Hoffman shared his insights with SDS organizers in the mid-1960s.

Nevertheless, we feel that this piece is not dated and that it abstracts a number of important practice principles for organizers in the ghetto, in rural hamlets of West Virginia, in the farm fields of northern California, and in the prosperous suburbs of Chicago. We invite the reader's reaction.

* * * *

CO-6 BLACK STUDENTS TAKE OVER

Role Ambiguity

Being black in white America can be difficult enough. But being a black employee in a white institution is particularly difficult. The job becomes almost impossible when one has to represent the institution's administration to its black constituency while helping the blacks organize themselves effectively to deal with the same administration. That's the position many black university employees find themselves in as representatives of the dean of students' office, coordinators of black studies programs, and the like. When the inevitable conflicts arise, it is easier if one can identify entirely with one side against the other. That is rarely possible; too many questions always come up.

As an employee of an institution, to what extent can one ethically organize from within or gather support from without in order to change the organization's basic policies? At what point are one's actions ethical and at what point unethical? Who defines ethics—one's constituency or one's employer? Is the term "constituency" appropriate or should one think of "clients"? At what point does one say "I've had enough?" And who is hurt by one's leaving—the institution or the students? Can one play a truly professional role in a conflict situation or is one a captive of one side or another in such situations?

I'm not certain. I sense that bureaucracies are becoming less rigid, allowing for greater role freedom and more flexible relationships between functionaries. But it makes selecting one's roles all the more difficult. I was able to stay on after our crisis at the university—but not without some difficulty. When it was all over, many of the "hawks" ("get-tough" faculty and administrators) saw me as the troublemaker. I don't perceive my role as having been one.

When I was hired last February as a student-activities specialist, there had been a number of threats of disruption, but no major crisis to date. Having graduated from the University and having worked in the city's poverty program, I was well known to both students and administrators of the University. I had to be acceptable to both or I would not have been hired. My two years in the Urban League taught me a good deal about working with people in and out of establishment institutions. I was used to working with both whites and blacks.

Which Side Are You On?

Even before I officially began, a small group of black students had tried to get me to commit myself by telling them where I stood. They were angry, resentful at not having a black studies program. They condemned the institution for its racist admission policies and its curriculum, which they felt, with some justification, was irrelevant to the cultural needs of black students. "Things can be done," I told them. "Let's see what's holding things up from being as they should."

It didn't take long to find out. Black students were hurting in their minority status, and felt they were insufficiently represented on both student committees and faculty and administrative bodies. In both of these feelings they were supported by most of the white radicals and a majority of the liberal and moderate students. While there seemed little question in the minds of most of the black students that they had legitimate grievances (nor in mine), I soon found that (as they had found before), their concerns were not treated seriously by the administration. Earlier requests for a black dorm, for soul food, and for more scholarship money had been put off until a "black student-activities specialist" would be hired. The administration, from the dean of the students to the president, had met on request with the black students, but these meetings, I found, had been agreed to only in the hope of cooling off the students, of letting them express their feelings in the hope that this would satisfy them.

But the students were neither satisfied nor pacified. By the time I came on the scene, many of the blacks saw themselves in an adversary position. What they were at first asking for or suggesting, they were now ready to demand. I tried to convey these feelings to the deans and administrators. Although many were well aware of them, they tended to dismiss what I thought were legitimate grievances as the unrealistic demands of "a group of extremists," "black nationalists," "radicals," or "unbalanced kids." I was frankly disturbed by these labels. If you define someone in narrow terms, you are limited in your behavioral responses. When I worked with street gangs years earlier, for example, I found that behavior towards an outsider was standardized in accordance with whether he was defined as a "punk," a "stoolie," a "square," and the like. If a guy was a "punk," you could "stomp" on him. In fact you were not only justified, but almost duty-bound, to do so.

The labeling process was no less pronounced on the student side. Just as I was beginning to feel pressure from the students ("Which side are you on"?), I began to sense a good deal of support for their position among the faculty and administration. Several professors issued statements of support through the student press. At a small but significant faculty meeting, a resolution was passed directing the administration to deal more rapidly with the demands of black students. The dean of students himself was saying that the administration had procrastinated long enough. We all felt that progress was being made. There was a marked reduction of tenseness among the blacks. When it came to action, however, every meeting led to further meetings and further delays. The president was away in Washington. The trustees had to be consulted on this. Other channels were needed for that. The student government must make a request for something else. Everything seemed to end up with promises, but no progress.

Throughout all of this, some of the other radical groups on campus— SDS, the DuBois Club, Progressive Labor, and others—were encouraging the black students to take "positive" action. They indicated a willingness to follow the black students' lead in any confrontation—a march, sit-in, class boycott, takeover of a building, and the like. The black students, however, felt that this was their issue. "We got to think this through and do our own thing," was the general response.

Nonnegotiable Demands

On April 24th, four days before a national track meet was to be held at the University's athletic field, 17 black students, most of them athletes, barricaded themselves in the locker rooms of the stadium. In an imaginative statement, they proclaimed that locker rooms would be occupied until a set of attached demands were met. The stadium was selected for appropriation because it "truly belonged to the black people —the athletes whose bodies attracted the crowds" and who earned the money that was used to finance its construction. It would be returned when equal funds would be pledged to "the nurturing of black souls and minds." The attached demands were "nonnegotiable."

The administration was shocked. Until only a few days before, even I had been under the impression that there was still some real possibility of rapprochement. Now everyone's hand was forced. The 17 students issued a call to all black brothers—faculty, students, and administrators —to join them. Now I had to choose sides. I felt that my ministrations to the administration had not borne fruit. The students in the locker rooms must be scared, confused, and unsure of how long to hold out. I thought it made the most sense for me to join them. I called the president and informed him of my decision. I also informed him that I intended to help them accomplish their goals with whatever means at my disposal.

Sixty-three other black students, accounting in total for 60 percent of the University's black undergraduates, joined the original group. Most had until that moment been "moderates," content to give verbal support, but concerned primarily with getting through and completing their degrees.

The students *were* scared. The administration could have chosen a number of courses—to capitulate to all the students' demands was a solution that seemed highly unlikely. It could have chosen to do nothing, to wait us out. The students did not know how long they could hold out, but this solution was unlikely. Community pressure would be too great. The administration could agree to negotiate the demands but punish the "ringleaders" for the takeover. Should this be the reaction, the students were prepared to go to jail or be expelled en masse and to refuse any negotiations. (The kind of togetherness that civil disobedience can engender is unbelievable).

Then again the administration could choose to agree to negotiate on the demands but to ignore the takeover of University property. This was the most disquieting possibility. Just how nonnegotiable were the demands?

Finally, the administration could use force. If it did, it might wind up with a Harvard or a Columbia on its hands. If it did not, it might end up like Cornell, looking stupid and losing face (and several key administrators) or like Brandeis, coming up smelling like roses. I don't know how the students would have reacted to force.

One or two apostles of violence were argued down in what may have been one of the most important dialogues these students will ever participate in. Positions on the nature of self-defense shifted from day to day, hour to hour. On the third day, the students had developed some exercise periods. These included training in the use of the body in nonviolent resistance (going limp, protecting your head) for those who were interested. Some shared what they knew of karate and other defense-offense tactics. Much of the time was spent in discussing ideological issues, in sending messages back and forth to sympathizers on campus, and in examining the implications of the latest word from an administrator, a faculty member, or a student group.

Polarization and Integration

You could sense from the inside that there was a polarization going on outside: there were some who wanted to punish the students for their illegal take-over (the track meet had to be shifted to another university); there were some who felt that the tactic was wrong but the grievances legitimate, even if some of the demands were excessive; there were others who felt that this tactic was the only correct one—that without it, the administration would never have acted, nor the University experienced the necessary trauma of self-examination.

There were round-the-clock discussions inside the locker room, and round-the-clock discussions outside—on the rest of the campus. The campus was increasingly polarizing between those who supported us and those who opposed us. The students inside were increasingly unsure. Few seriously wanted to jeopardize the institution, only to change it and make it more responsive to black needs. Most of the students were suspicious and a bit resentful to the white radicals who were in an almost constant vigil outside. The rhetoric of both groups was similar, but the objectives were quite different.

On the evening of April 28, the administration put the students on "temporary suspension," to be revoked when they left the building.

On April 29, we had our first serious understanding. The next day we left the locker rooms. There had been constant meetings with the administration. Usually one or two students went, representing the rest. I refused to go to these meetings. I was with them to help them think through the issues, not as their representative. At first my role was some-what unclear to them and to me. It emerged progressively during the course of the "occupation." I don't perceive of it in the fashionable term of "liberation."

I had three objectives: (1) to deal with the psychological and emotional issues that the students were grappling with; (2) to help them establish coalitions with supporting groups on the outside that could help them not only to accomplish their objectives but also to see that they were not completely alone in society; and (3) to develop a leadership group and some consensus on the next steps so that they could negotiate a solution that would not be destructive of either the University or the individuals involved, or to their aspirations.

Keeping open a communication channel to the outside was vital. Without it, the imagination plays all kinds of tricks. On the 28th, the Student Council voted to change its structure so as to ensure more minority-group representation. This was successfully negotiated by three of our students. Developing a leadership cadre that could negotiate with the administration was my most difficult task. There were too many feelings and ideological shades of "blackness." At first, those students who might have wanted to negotiate a compromise were shouted down. The more militant you were, the more accepted you were by your brothers in bondage.

For many of these students this was their only real taste of power, of having some command over a white institution. After a few days, it became evident, and I tried to point this out, that the control would slip out of our hands if we did not agree to negotiate. But negotiations were dangerous. Our previous experience with the administration suggested that they might try to use the negotiations to reshape the students' demands. Further, agreeing on negotiations assumed that following some sort of settlement, the black students would actually be better off than they were initially. Cooptation and the "white man's tricks" were the greatest danger. The paranoia with which students reacted, an understandable and justifiable paranoia, made it impossible to deal with any of the administration overtures during the first few days. By the 29th, however, a breakthrough was imminent. The Student Council action had given the students some hope and some faith.

On the 29th the faculty had voted, although not unanimously, to recommend amnesty for the students, and to support their major demands. The president, if nothing else, had shown some good faith by refusing to be pressured into calling the police. He had not panicked during any of the preceding five days. His handling of the students had been firm and somewhat sympathetic. The students were still suspicious, but some who had been in negotiations with him tended to blame the system and the bureaucratic machinery rather than the man.

My major contributions to the students, I think, was in helping them "psych out" the opposition—especially the president. I had known him from the poverty program where he had been on the board. I also know that he had been a successful labor mediator prior to accepting the presidency of the University. I spent a good deal of my time teaching the students how to negotiate, pointing out to them that labor unions, too, used nonnegotiable demands at the beginning of a session.

Negotiations are a tricky thing. I constantly stressed that this wasn't a game in which someone had to win all and someone had to lose. If anyone lost, we all lost. The issue was to have both sides wind up winning. The students would benefit from achieving the major part of their demands, from the winning of respect for the way they handled themselves. The president and the administration could come out ahead by the very same victories the students won, and by "handling the issue" without recourse to violence.

The difficulty in these kinds of negotiations is that it isn't clear who you are representing, or with whom you are negotiating. The president, for example, had to satisfy other administrators, the trustees, the faculty, the rest of the student body, alumni, and various other community influentials. There certainly was no unanimity within his constituencies. The faculty and student votes had strengthened his hand to act, but not without some risk.

The black students had trouble deciding among themselves who would be their delegates. Every time a student came back from a discussion or prenegotiation session with someone from the administration, he tended to take a more moderate line, trying to convince his brothers of the need to give in a little. Invariably he was shouted down and replaced by others who took a more militant line. It wasn't until about 20 of the students had actually had a negotiating experience that the group seemed willing to allow two of the students to represent them and to accept their agreements with the administration as binding.

What I tried to do with the students was to show them how to help the administration understand their position. At the same time I tried to help the students understand the constraints that the president was under. It was not easy, and there were many, many times that I lost my self-control and found myself reacting with black skin instead of with professional objectivity. It was because of my very personal struggle, I think, that I was successful at all.

The Agony of the Aftermath

Still, I don't think I can ever convey the agony and the anguish—the pressures I was under—of being in that situation. I wish it were over. It's not. The aftermath of the affair is the most painful part.

Somehow, even though their suspension was temporary and lasted barely a day and a half, the names of the students in the takeover were fed to their local draft boards. All were reclassified 1-A. I'm sure the University administration was not responsible for this, but the black students and their white radical supporters are blaming the president. The paranoia of the black kids, I can deal with. I live with it myself. The cynicism of the white radicals, I do not comprehend. I am at a loss as how to deal with it or if I should even try.

One of the black students was from Trinidad. The U.S. Immigration Service contacted a white faculty member surreptitiously to ask if the University wanted that student deported. It is to the University's credit that they refused to consider it. This helped me deal with the paranoia.

At the same time, however, several students received bad end-of-the-semester grades. I could deal with their feelings of having been discriminated against. In one case I thought it was true and I spoke to the instructor. In several cases, they were poor students—a condition of being black and of going through ghetto schools. There was nothing I could do except to help them understand their limitations. In some cases, the poor grades resulted from time lost and assignments missed during the take-over. Well, that's the price you pay for activism, for a belief. You can't have it both ways. It is something they must come to understand.

What was toughest for me was dealing with the students who undeservedly got high grades and with the instructors who gave them those grades. Call it guilt or call it sympathy, but in a number of cases, white instructors gave students A's for courses in which they did no work. One sociology professor asked me if I didn't think his student should have gotten an A for the sociology he learned during the rebellion. I just don't know how to deal with that kind of patronizing, mawkish sort of thing.

What I could deal with was the fact that several students lost their stipends for bad grades. The machinery of the bureacracy is something I'm well aware of from my OEO[1] days. It is tedious and often frustrating, but it can be negotiated with.

Perhaps the biggest problem is one I'm still dealing with now—relations with the black community. Many of the students in the take-over lived in the ghetto not far from the University. While in the locker rooms, they were frequently visited by parents and friends with food and encouragement, and by representatives of militant organizations with further encouragement and with strategic advice. If the University had used a hard line, I think there would have been a major demonstration in the ghetto. Perhaps that is why the president kept his cool, and the city authorities did not pressure the University directly.

But the communication lines established between the black students on campus and community organizations are now well established. My biggest fear is that the community groups will try to extend their hold on the students and use them for their own purposes. Understand, I'm a black man, myself, but my allegiance, on the job, is to these students. It is their concern that must be my own.

*　　*　　*　　*

CO-7 UNLEASH YOUR PEOPLE AND YOU STAND TO LOSE YOUR JOB

When the board meets next week, they'll be deciding on whether to keep me or "can" me. I'm caught in a cross fire. I'm damned if I do and

---

[1] Office of Economic Opportunity.

damned if I don't. When you start a process in motion, you can't always control it. One of my professors in grad school told us that if you're going to be a successful organizer, you have to take risks. The best community organizers, he said, rarely stay on the job more than three years. And it's not because they get promotions or solve all the community's problems. Well I've been here less than one year.

The issue that caught me by the heel was the one about the staff. When I came to Bradford (a fictitious name for this West Coast community of about 130,000), the poverty program had been in operation for about three years. Stanley Kimoto, the director who preceded me, had been well liked. He was a gradualist, well established in the social welfare community. He spent his first six months assuring the "establishment" that the community-action program was there to enhance the social welfare community in its efforts to deal with poverty. His theme was cooperation and collaboration towards the achievement of community goals. So when the "flack" started getting militant about a year ago, Stan was in the clear. He played the role of conciliator to the poor and interpreter to the people downtown. Nobody could fault him for not doing his best in what was developing into an explosive situation, except maybe the poor, the militants, and the activist students who were doing tutorial work. Kimoto left to take a position with a sectarian foundation.

When I took over, the situation had deteriorated tremendously. I doubt that many people on the board fully understood the situation. Some of the neighborhood-council people on the board might have, but they had either been intimidated, brainwashed, or co-opted by their participation in the program. Some of the more militant were boycotting the board.

That's how it is with much of the poverty program. You can't come in to a community, promise them a war on poverty, real participation, control over the forces that shape their lives, and then accept cuts in federal funds, knuckle under to established political pressure, and accomplish little more than helping already inadequate agencies simply provide reenforcing apathy, making people feel they'be been betrayed, and opening yourself up to charges of irrelevance.

On the other hand, there is no question in my mind that the programs have done some good—people who were never organized before, are organized (though how they will remain so, without staff help or being under the aegis of a social-political movement of some sort, is the big issue), and a lot of people have begun to develop and express leadership that no one knew was there. The staff issue really brought this home to me.

I hadn't been at the agency for more than a week before a group of paraprofessionals, representing all eight neighborhood centers, came to my office with a list of grievances and set of demands. Their concerns really pointed up the problems in our program. On the one hand they wanted more recognition and better pay. On the other, they were complaining about how their work kept them out of touch with what was "really happening" in the community. "Sure, people come to us for help," one explained, "but they don't trust us." "We're not doin' anything about jobs, about the racist cops and the racist schools," another exploded. "We set out to change the system and now we are captured by it. My buddies say I've sold out. Damned if I ain't."

Lets face it. The poverty program put these people in an impossible position. Like a lot of other well-intentioned poverty directors, Kimoto and his staff went out to recruit neighborhood people as paraprofessionals. It seemed to make a lot of sense. By using neighborhood residents you could dispel some of the distrust they were bound to have. You could get people on the front line to communicate in the language people spoke, not bureaucratese like a lot of social workers use. It was a way of reaching the community, using poor people as common carriers, carrying our message to the community and serving as a barometer of community attitudes to the rest of the staff. And it was a way up, out of poverty for many of those we recruited.

That's the way it worked out theoretically. In practice, the agency paid them about half of what a "professional" staff member earned. The salary may have seemed good at first. It was degrading after a while. At first they had helped locate community leadership and recruit people to the neighborhood council, and even organized block clubs, but shortly after the agency organized the neighborhood councils, and as the helping stations were being converted into multiservice neighborhood centers with center boards, the subprofessional staff was for all intents and purposes removed from the community.

When I arrived at the scene they had all been assigned to buildings, some in multiservice centers that weren't even in the neighborhoods from where the staff came. They had been given desks and phones that not only served as props, but also resulted in their wanting to imitate the professional staff, and discouraged them from making home visits. They were taught to fill out forms and to make written reports. We called them case aides, intake workers, job-referral trainees, and the like. Like the rest of the staff, they began talking about clients and hard core cases, instead of about neighbors and friends. In essence, they were identifying with traditional structures and agency practices rather than with the community. Instead of being messengers or links between the agency and the community, they found themselves accepted as equals by neither the community nor the rest of the agency staff.

My own reaction was that we had to unchain these people. I saw two roles for the paraprofessional: the case aide (which is the only role they were currently playing) and the community worker, group organizer, and community agent. In each, they need a good deal of support.

My first action with the board was to push for a pay increase for all subprofessionals. My first action with the staff was to reassign workers to teams made up of professionals and indigenous workers. Case aides were reassigned for desk jobs to spend more time with clients, working them through the job-application process, taking them to medical services outside the neighborhood, functioning as advocates at the welfare department, and helping them fill out complaints against the police.

A core group in each neighborhood center was attached to the CO unit to work with neighborhood boards and to establish links with other community groups. It is here where I got myself into the most trouble. I would follow much the same procedure if I had to do it over again, but I think I would spend more time bringing my board along.

The neighborhoods are different than they were when the poverty program started four years ago. True, most people are not too vocal about change, and there are more moderates than militants. But the militants are plenty vocal. And the mood is such that it doesn't take much to provoke intense feelings, and even less to give some of the militants an excuse to disrupt and attempt to polarize the community. We're in for some tough times.

I specifically instructed the paraprofessional community workers to make contact with as many community groups as possible. If we are going to create some real changes in the community, it wasn't going to be through the neighborhood councils and center boards alone. I wasn't sure of what the end results might be, but I knew that increasingly the militants and even former block-club and council members were looking at the neighborhood councils as irrelevant. The Panthers, Muslims, welfare-rights groups, other black nationalist organizations, church groups, gangs, and fraternal organizations each had their own programs. I felt it was as much our job to encourage them and to give them staff help as it was to develop our own constituencies.

As I said earlier, once you start a process, it's hard to control it. The trouble for me converged in a short time-period last fall. Too many things were happening at once. Five of my staff, four paraprofessionals and one student in field placement, were arrested during a welfare mothers' sit-in. One of them and three other staff members were involved in a dispute with the Board of Education over the hiring of a new vice

principal for P. S. 13. One of my workers on Cooley Street, a neighborhood half black and half Irish, provoked an arrest in a bar that ordinarily did not make blacks welcome. He gave the arresting officer some
"lip" and was beaten in front of witnesses. We're now pressing for a
review and dismissal of the officer.

A number of members of the Ivan Street club (one of our councils)
had participated in helping the Panthers operate their soup kitchen, and
two nurses who had once worked for us in the Page Center are now running the Panther "free clinic." They were still on our payroll when they
started working with the Panthers. You can guess what the newspapers
did with that!

The neighborhood council presidents are pushing for more representation on the board. They want 50 percent plus one representation from
the neighborhoods. If they get it, they'll vote as a block and the program
will be theirs. I think that's how it should be. On the other hand, if they
do get the program, a lot of our leading citizens, black and white—especially those with influence downtown, in Washington, or with the business community—may resign.

The mayor, you can imagine, is not too happy. The city administrator
is hardly pleased, what with the "flack" he has been getting from the
mayor, the cops, the public-works supervisor, and so on.

Even I am under pressure from the neighborhood people. Two of my
neighborhood councils are pressing me for more say in running the
neighborhood centers. Our center boards are generally made up of professionals and lay people from outside the neighborhoods. Now the
neighborhood councils want control over these too. The issues have to do
with gripes about some of the professional staff. I don't mind telling you
that some of these staff members are uncomfortable with all of this. A
number may be leaving, but most like the action the way it is.

An interesting thing about neighborhood groups—you organize them
as your constituency, hoping that they will give you the backing and
support you need to conduct your program or push for reforms. But if
you are successful, if you give them their head and help them become
really independent, they take a life of their own. And they begin to put
the pressure on you just like on everyone else—even more so, because
you are the most visible and easily accessible.

Things are popping and that's the way it should be. Neighborhood
people are increasingly independent and vocal. They don't depend on
us as much any more. Why should they? Neighborhood organizations
aren't going to be staffed by federally supported employees forever. I only
hope I survive long enough to see it through. Ironic, isn't it? Unleash
your people, and you stand to lose your job.

*   *   *   *

CO-8   ON BECOMING A SCAPEGOAT

The mayor was running the CAP[1] program. You can understand how it was. The CAA[2] board was made up of nine people, mostly Chamber of Commerce or welfare-council and social-agency types—clean, conscientious citizens, spokesmen for progress. In a city like this of 100,000, they all knew each other pretty well. The mayor avoided choosing politically dangerous types.

It was 1965, a few months before the new OEO guidelines were issued that said the poor had to be represented on CAA boards. So the neighborhood councils had no real voice in policy making. In fact, about all they could do was act in advisory capacities to the neighborhood centers and out-reach stations being set up by a professional staff. The staff kept administrative and fiscal policy decisions fairly well centralized, so there wasn't much the neighborhood people could do anyhow, even if they had been aware that there was something to do.

Well, that's how it was when I got to town. I was in one of the first VISTA training programs, and there weren't more than maybe 200 of us around the country, so the local CAA people didn't know exactly what to do with me. I told them I wanted to be in the most deprived neighborhood in town, so I was assigned to Buena Vista. At the out-reach station, the program director welcomed my Spanish, and suggested that I just wander around and find out what people wanted.

They wanted jobs, a playground for the kids, paved streets and street lights, a branch library, and a real community center. They needed a place for the kids during the day and help with the old folks at home. "Most of these programs are beyond our present scope," the program director told me. "About all we can do now is refer them to the proper agencies, and help the people to get to these agencies. Maybe in a few months we can get some of the agencies to try to put some of their staff here in the neighborhood."

Well, the people knew about the agencies. They aren't too well educated, but they know pretty much about what was available and what was closed off to them. Six months went by and most of the programs people wanted were still beyond our scope; neighborhood-council people lost interest. There was nothing for them to do, and they probably wouldn't have known how to do it anyway. Nobody knew what was going on in the other neighborhoods.

---

1 Community-action program.
2 Community-action agency.

I checked around and found out that none of the neighborhood councils were going strong. Leadership was underdeveloped, and none had been able to settle on a single action program. But the issues in each neighborhood were the same as in mine. People wanted better city services, jobs and job training, and the like. It just seemed as though the OEO structure wasn't going to open up and listen. I took three of the council presidents to the mayor's office to talk about better lighting. He promised to do something about it. But the next day my supervisor called me in and told me the mayor had called him, and didn't I think I should have cleared through the center first (we were now a "center"— in name only—instead of an out-reach station).

"So let's do something," I argued. "Let's get the people together, pick one project, and get it going—street lights, a park, better transportation, anything." "Play it cool," my supervisor advised. The OEO was about to issue some new guidelines about participation by the target populations, and the mayor's office was pretty powerful. "Let the more experienced staff handle these matters."

Well six months of my one-year hitch were over. I just wasn't about to play it cool. I called the three council presidents who had gone down to City Hall with me, and asked them to call all the other neighborhood council presidents together. We met one time, and decided to meet again, not for any specific purpose, but just to share ideas, frustrations, and the like. We figured that with some moral support and just finding out that the other guy felt like you did, it would be easier to be a council president. Most of these people had never been active in formal organizations before and few had been officers. They knew each other from a series of training sessions and seemed anxious to keep meeting with each other. I was glad because I knew that unless they did things for themselves, nothing would happen. This was the only way to prod the mayor, the board, and the staff.

I decided to invite a reporter I knew to the next meeting. I reasoned that the right publicity would be as good a way to start prodding as any. He came. We shared some more frustrations and decided to meet regularly on Tuesday evenings, with or without staff support.

The next day, the morning papers carried the headline: NEIGHBOR-HOOD COUNCILS QUIT OEO. I called my friend on the paper and asked "Why?" Didn't he know that we weren't quitting, just trying to strengthen the organization? He explained that he had written up the meeting just as it had taken place, but that the city editor, a political enemy of the mayor's, had decided on the twist to the story as a way of embarrassing the mayor. Two days later, the new OEO guidelines came through and the regional office was pressing him to appoint neighborhood council people to the board. He agreed, but there was a deal. I had to go. The mayor denounced me as a troublemaker in the press, and publicly welcomed participation from the councils. The VISTA director in the OEO regional office pulled me out and reassigned me to a school on an Indian reservation.

I explained the whole thing to him, that the councils were not quitting, that they wanted "in," and that in reality we had just anticipated the OEO directive by a couple of days. "Try to understand," he said. "We were in a tough position. We wanted the neighborhood people on the board. The mayor didn't and he didn't want you around either. What should we have done—stuck up for you and let the whole program go down the drain?"

*   *   *   *

CO-9 SOCIAL BROKERAGE AND SOCIAL ACTION[1]

We are more than ever convinced that the worker as "broker" served a much needed function. Bureaucratic systems are, at best, difficult to manage, and low-income persons, who need them most, are least able to manage them. By intervening in the client's behalf, the worker insures at least minimal redress in the balance.

Unfortunately, vast numbers of the poor and undereducated cannot acquire the ability to "negotiate the system" as does Mrs. I. in the following case summary. The summary suggests the range of services provided by social "brokers" on the Mobilization staff.

"Mrs. I. was referred to me because of acting-out problems on the part of the two older children. At this point, she was hospitalized for a tubercular condition, and the four children were living with the paternal grandmother. . . .

"My first encounter with Mrs. I. was when she was released from the hospital. She was extremely hostile and suspicious . . . viewing me as a white power person who was trying to keep her children from her. I set about helping Mrs. I. set up a household for herself and the children. . . . We ultimately located $3\frac{1}{2}$ rooms. . . . I spoke with the Administrative Assistant of the Department of Welfare concerning the upper price limit for such an apartment. This was done in her presence, and was significant in that DW had quoted a lower price for her. That DW was actually able to go higher and that I was able to get this information for her seemed to be significant. Next we worked

---

[1] Excerpted from *Action On The Lower East Side: A Progress Report and Proposal*, Mobilization for Youth, Inc., New York, 1964.

on additional clothing and blankets from Welfare, which came through. . . . Mrs. I. learned from these experiences how to negotiate with Welfare, particularly in relation to her rights as a client. She has subsequently been able to deal effectively with a series of DW workers through persistence, directness, and confidence in her position.

"The civil-rights issue is central to this case. I took this up with Mrs. I. specifically in relation to the March on Washington. Mrs. I. seemed stunned that I, as a white person, would be concerned with this, and surprised that Mobilization was to some degree involved. Her attitude toward me gradually began to change. . . .

"In another instance, one of her children was involved in a physical altercation with a woman who subsequently filed a minor delinquency charge against the child. Mrs. I. came to me for help, and we consulted the Mobilization Legal Unit together. We helped her to go to the courthouse and file a countersuit. The matter was ultimately settled without going to court.

"Mrs. I. became much less guarded with me. She let me know, for instance, that she had a phone, of which DW was unaware. . . .

"We discussed the Voter Registration campaign at great length, and for the first time Mrs. I. came to believe there was a possibility of attaining a change in her life conditions through the ballot. She voted for the first time in a number of years, and brought several friends with her.

"Throughout, my approach has been respectful, supportive, non-probing, with the emphasis on concrete assistance and education in relation to negotiating social systems. This has already had some carryover, not only in relation to DW, as previously mentioned, but also in terms of school. She has begun to form a nonhostile, rather open, relationship with two of her children's teachers, both of whom are white. I have had contact with both teachers as well, interpreting this family's needs to them. Mrs. I. now feels free to go to both schools and has welcomed both teachers into her home."

The broker must be as free as possible from institutional pressures. Since he represents the client, the role cannot be performed without constraint from within the service system with which the client is engaged.

Long-term intervention is often required. Extensive negotiations may be necessary, and they may not be so successfully concluded as in Mrs. I.'s case. To aid in this effort, a Housing Clinic and, recently, a Welfare Clinic have been incorporated into the Neighborhood Service Center program. The Welfare Clinic, which the Centers operate jointly with the

Community Development program, provides direct service for clients with specific welfare problems. This not only cuts down on the caseloads within the Centers, but also exerts greater pressure to encourage Department of Welfare service to the client. The Clinic structure provides for the handling of some problems on a group basis, and offers greater possibility for documenting the nature of welfare problems.

In assisting persons to deal with community resources, the broker may be implicitly encouraging other ways of affecting one's environment, such as through collective activity. The converse may also be true: collective action may encourage individual understanding and assertion.

Social Brokerage to Increase Participation

The participation of low-income persons in community activities presupposes that these activities are meaningful to them. The willingness to participate is prompted by the conviction that something can be done to solve the problems of daily life; the capacity to participate develops out of successful experience in solving these problems.

The Community Development Program has attempted to increase participation by recruiting isolated individuals for group membership. These individuals are attracted by the offer of services to fulfill their immediate needs; the groups that are shaped by such social brokerage tend to be primarily groups that serve as liaison between their members and public or private agencies. Although this is the most personalized form of social action, it affords greater access to agency resources and a more efficient utilization of available services than any one client could achieve. It is assumed that action of this sort will foster participation in action of less individualized and immediate consequence.

Groups have been organized by Mobilization for Youth to deal with such problems as lack of heat or hot water in tenements, overcharging of rent, language barriers between parents and teachers that impede discussion of children's work, fraudulent installment plans and shoddy merchandise, and inadequate welfare allowances. The worker first does whatever is necessary to solve the problem before the desirability of other group activities becomes evident. Examples of such direct action are:

No Heat: Contact tenants who can speak English well enough to call the landlord and the city agencies until heating is resumed. Buy electric heaters if necessary, and tell tenants to deduct cost from the following month's rent.

Rent
Overcharge: Help tenants fill out forms requesting information on legal controls on rent. If there is an overcharge,

	follow it up. Meanwhile, begin taking action on other violations that may exist in the building.
Parental Fear of Going to School:	Start a class with a part-time teacher in one of the parents' homes. Go with the parents to visit school personnel.
Consumer Fraud:	After checking with the State Attorney General's office, go to the store with the consumer and discuss the matter with the manager. If fraud persists and the manager refuses to correct it, threaten to picket with other consumers unless charges are reduced.
Welfare Allowance:	Call (or help client to call) the investigator and insist on immediate action. In emergency situations, lend the client the money to purchase items immediately.

Thus, the organizer's function in his initial contact is to serve as a broker between the clients and the appropriate person or institution. A shared problem leads to the formation of an informal group, and in the cooperative attempt to solve the problem, the members learn how to meet some of their needs through group processes. Although considerable time may elapse before the initial problem is solved, the group may use this time to become involved in programs ranging from social action to recreation.

During the first two years of the Community Development Program, the following groups were formed as a result of social brokerage.

Tenants' Associations were formed in approximately 100 tenements. Each of these groups was related to one of two housing clinics located in the Neighborhood Service Centers and staffed by professional community organizers and local people, mostly from the organized tenements.

Urban-Renewal Site Committees are composed of tenants living in buildings that are slated for urban-renewal projects. Frequently landlords discontinue services because the city is going to buy their buildings. In addition, the tenants are not involved in the planning for the project, and their interests, particularly in regard to relocation, are not taken into account.

The *Consumer Aid Clinic* was a group, no longer in existence, that formed around the special problems of merchant fraud, overcharging, loan sharking, and the like. About 50 families have been served by the clinic (which was jointly staffed by the Legal Services Unit and a community organizer). Members testified at the Senate hearings on the Truth in Lending bill and later participated in the formation of a citywide group to fight for legislation to protect consumers.

School Parents' Groups have been formed by community workers who visit families new to the community. They try to help newcomers to utilize available services and encourage the parents of schoolchildren to meet in small groups and attend PTA meetings. Parents learning to discuss their children's school experiences and ways of dealing with these experiences. Ten such groups have been formed. Their activities include attendance at larger meetings with speakers on school problems and recreation such as bus trips and dances.

The *Welfare Clinic,* newly formed, is run with staff from Community Development and the Neighborhood Service Centers. Residents who are having difficulties with the Department of Welfare receive advice, guidance, and direct assistance. When appropriate, it is expected that some participants will be able to take concerted action on some of the problems.

Groups with less specific functions have also been formed. The United Puerto Ricans, for example, emerged out of a worker's efforts to help one family. The Puerto Rican Mothers' Association was begun by a worker who was visiting mothers who did not participate in any activity; this group now wants to learn English. The Committee Against Discrimination in Housing was formed by three families who were arbitrarily refused housing.

The organizing experiences of Mobilization for Youth have had varying outcomes. A few of the groups failed to survive the first year. Among these were an association of small merchants, an organization to handle cases of police brutality, a group of unemployed men, and an attempted organization of patients needing the services of the local hospital clinic. Some groups dissolved after solving the problems that brought them into existence. Others continue to meet, some on their own and some with a Community Development worker. Still other groups have joined such local organizations as PTA's and settlement houses. In some instances, the members of several groups have merged to form a larger organization.

The difficulties of organizing informal groups increase with greater social differentiation and geographic dispersion. Although social brokerage attracts a wide variety of unaffiliated individuals in need of service, it serves as a source of social organization only for those who share similar social characteristics and live in a geographically circumscribed area—for example, Puerto Rican mothers of children in the same school, the tenants of one apartment building, and the black tenants of a housing project. Informal groups grow out of primary relationships, and primary relationships presuppose peers. The more differences that exist among individuals, the less able they are to see themselves as equals, eligible for membership in the same groups. The attempt to encompass a broadly defined membership thus fails to attract unaffiliated individuals interested in primary relations with peers. Rather, it attracts more organizationally sophisticated persons who already participate in other activities. The structure of the groups formed by social brokerage bears more resemblance to an extended family than to the goal-directed organizations of the middle class. Interpersonal relationships, rather than abstract issues, are the source of social cohesion.

The justification of the use of social brokerage in a program oriented toward social action is the expectation that the informal groups that emerge out of individual needs will develop an interest in community problems. The assumption implicit in this expectation is that community organization involves processes of social maturation—that is, that successful experience in informal groups results in a willingness to experiment with other forms of group life. Presumably, then, satisfactory primary relationships will ultimately support and sustain social action.

Some of the groups formed by social brokerage did in fact undertake social action beyond that required to resolve their immediate problem. One group of mothers who were meeting to learn English became involved in a campaign for increased police protection for their neighborhood. Another group of parents who set out to "find a place for their children to play after school" not only did so but also became embroiled in a controversy with the Board of Education that eventually led to several changes in policy for the school district. This was achieved in spite of the fact that the chairman was a mother of seven who lived on the sixth floor of a tenement with neither elevator nor telephone. She not only lacked resources critical for maintaining communication and organization but was also often without the assistance of baby-sitters to enable her to attend the meetings that precipitated social action. Still, some goals of the group were achieved.

Perhaps the failure of social brokerage to stimulate social action is less a function of the problems inherent in the group than of the assumptions implicit in the strategy. It may be unreasonable to expect a group that has found a meaningful *modus vivendi* to change its form and purpose. Since modern life is mediated through formal organizations rather than informal groups, the satisfactions of the members' primary relationships may in fact be dysfunctional for bringing about social change. The informal groups that mitigate the suffering of slum life deflect energy from organized social action. When immediate needs are met, there is little motivation for social action; when such needs remain unsatisfied, there is little capacity for sustained action. Social brokerage has not yet succeeded in resolving the dilemmas of organization that its use creates.

* * * *

CO-10   A TUTORIAL PROJECT IN HARLEM[1]

ANDREA COUSINS

Early last fall an integrated group of students began a community-organization project in the heart of central Harlem. Our group, the Harlem Educational Project (HEP), was at that time attached to the Northern Student Movement, which had similar programs in seven other Northern cities.

Our staff consisted of three college graduates and four college dropouts; two of the black males had grown up in Northern ghettos, while the remaining five people (two white females, one white male, and two black males) were of middle-class backgrounds. None of us, whatever our roots, had ever had direct experience in community organization.

The area where we set up our office is primarily residential, with the exception of some small business establishments on one avenue. On the east side of the avenue—at the border of our community—there are a number of large businesses (a chain restaurant, a supermarket, a drug store), usually owned and operated by white people. An elementary school one block away was built in the late 1800s; it has a student population of more than 2000 and a predominately white administrative staff.

In the neighborhood there are no social or political organizations such as the Elks or the Democratic Party. The only municipal establishment is a recreation center, once used as an armory, located on the site of a city park. There is no place in the neighborhood that belongs to the people who live there, no place—with the possible exception of a large empty lot—where people can independently direct their energies and create something of their own—the "Commons."

When we began to work on 147th street, our staff shared two objectives, though we did not often discuss them formally. We wanted to bring the people of the local community into greater control of their own lives, and consequently of the institutions that exerted power over them. At the same time, we hoped to enlarge the community to include persons of varying interests, skills, and economic and racial backgrounds. But even at the start there was some confusion over whether these two

---

[1] This case was adapted from a presentation entitled "Harlem: The Neighborhood and Social Change," made by Andrea Cousins at a national conference of the Students for a Democratic Society in April of 1964, at Ann Arbor, Michigan. Miss Cousins, then a recent graduate of Sarah Lawrence College, had been director of the Harlem Education Project for nearly a year. Portions of her presentation were reproduced and printed in the Chicago Maroon on May 8, 1964 (page 7).

aims were complementary or mutually exclusive, and whether they could be achieved simultaneously.

In the early days of the project, however, these theoretical problems seemed somewhat irrelevant to the work that was already in progress. A member of the staff had already involved men and boys in the neighborhood in the planning and construction of a community park. This effort to build a Commons had brought about the creation of a Neighborhood Council, which was to determine, in a democratic fashion, the nature of block redevelopment beginning with the Commons itself.

A second staff member had involved a score of older boys in a science workshop where they attempted to relate problems of logic to the actual working of particular mechanical tools.

There was also a tutorial program designed to bring tutorial relationships into close contact with community concerns. In conjunction with the tutorial program, one of our staff members hoped to work with the curriculum-research division of the Harlem Parents' Committee. He wanted to use the tutors' experiences to formulate teaching methods that would be relevant to Harlem schools.

Although these projects were well underway, our group failed to face up to the problem of reconciling two apparent needs—to define long-range programs and to respond to the immediate problems and desires of the local community.

The question of timing was at the heart of the issue. To be specific, while the tutorial program provided our organization with a definite framework for sustained work, we failed to present the parents with an explicit description of our plans before beginning to recruit our tutees. Unlike other such projects, which had enlisted their students through guidance counselors or teachers in the schools, the new tutorial was expected to grow through immediate neighborhood contacts. We felt that this would be a more democratic process.

But what we failed to take into account was our own lack of knowledge about the community. For example, we failed to realize that there would be substantial conflicts of interest within the area. While the interest groups were not defined in precise economic terms (as they might have been in a more developed area containing local business interests and outside investments) it quickly became apparent that sex, age, and particular places of residence made for their own particular and conflicting concerns.

Mothers of younger children, for instance, expressed a need for a child-care center; among the older boys and men the problem was to get jobs; the younger students felt trapped by the local school system; some tenants wanted to do something about their dilapidated homes; some persons wanted more space for recreational purpose; some tutees wanted their own hangout; some parents wanted more ways to get together with each other; and others only wanted peace and privacy.

A general conflict was evident between the older and younger generations of the block. The young people wanted more freedom of movement, and the power to strike back at the policemen, the truant officers, the probation officers, the teachers, and the building inspectors—at the whole code that says no drinking, no gambling, no singing in the hallways, no loitering on the stoops, no playing in the streets, no sex in the alleys, and no pigeon coops on the roof. The parents generally wanted to enforce "respectability."

With our lack of knowledge about the neighborhood, our relative youth, and our concern for democratic government, we found ourselves in the position of choosing sides among the varying interest groups, rather than acting as an effective mediator between them. This was the result not only of our failure to involve the parents in the planning of a program like the tutorial, but also of the fact that we had our own investment in the neighborhood (development of the lot, use of the basements and the office-apartments, and participation of people in the tutorial), which made us an interest group like any other.

In midautumn we relocated our office to the middle of an apartment building, and this created a conflict of interest between the teen-agers who hung around us and the tenants who lived in the house. Despite the fact that we had moved there with the express purpose of cutting down on the social activity that had taken place in the Eighth Avenue storefront where we previously worked, the persistent curiosity of the teenagers on the block and the need to have contact with all people mitigated against the need for a "business office."

It was the white women on the staff whose work required organized office activity, but they were the workers least equipped to enforce order. The men, whose work took place outside the office, were reluctant to spend long hours in supervisory roles away from the street. There was never any clear restriction on the sort of activity that could legitimately take place in the office, and naturally the confusion increased as the younger people realized that we were unable to back up our own immediate demands.

The presence of a 16-year-old black girl who had volunteered to serve as a secretary aggravated the problem. She found herself unable to distinguish between her role as a teen-ager and her role as a staff worker. This difficulty was increased by her ambivalent feeling about working for an integrationist organization, whose demands she was supposed to communicate to a group of black boys her own age. In time, this group managed to persuade her to let them use the office at night as a place to play bongo drums, sing, and drink. The tenants in the building could not understand why the disorder persisted.

Other people who volunteered injected similar problems into our relationship with neighborhood adults. For example, one man turned out to be a junkie, which of course was no secret to anyone who looked out his window. The fact that we had never reached any formal agreement with him, and the fact that we ended all dealings with him as soon as we discovered his avocation, never changed the community's initial impression that he had been a regular, full-time worker. Both to the tenants in the building where we worked and to other parents in the neighborhood, it appeared that we were instigating immoral activity among the younger generation.

But it was not only in our individual relationships that we aroused the suspicion of the adults in the community. We also incurred a kind of political anger. One of the staff workers, a white student, stated publicly that he would uphold the right of the teen-agers to representation in all decisions that affected them. In response to this, one of the dominant citizens of the community called a meeting to find out what the boys wanted to do. Two police commissioners and a board of adults were present to advise them on ways that could solve their problems.

Individually, the boys were summoned to the front of the room and asked to state their personal concerns in front of this imposing board. None of them showed much desire to speak. Soon, the man who had organized the meeting began to reprimand them, and then he called a recess to permit them to think over their behavior, and reform it.

When the meeting resumed, the white HEP organizer stood up to assert that the procedure was entirely wrong, and that the boys were not being treated with any respect. The fact that other HEP workers were sitting in the audience next to the teen-agers added to the adult community's sense of antagonism.

The meeting organizer became increasingly hostile, and he used most of the rest of the session to denounce HEP. He argued that the boys should talk with their parents about their problems, and not to a group of outsiders. The hostility incurred at this meeting was one of the causes of a campaign in which about ten parents were persuaded to withdraw their children from the tutorial program.

Our problem, then, was twofold: it involved both the young people, whose behavior in our presence remained disorderly, and the adults, who accused us of instigating disrespectfulness among their children. It was not only that our hopes were too high and our objectives too broad: they were expressed with the kind of conviction that tends to alienate people who are not of a similar mind.

A kind of religiosity developed among members of our staff, and this is certainly a danger that faces most current civil rights organizations where individuals have become deeply and personally identified with a particular set of ideas. It is a source of personal frustration and organizational confusion. In place of dogma, no matter how deeply it is felt, there should be a clear and functional description of particular programs. This not only sharpens a staff's awareness of what can actually be accomplished, it also reduces the inevitable disappointment that mounts as ideology departs further and further from the facts at hand.

In our case there was an additional difficulty rooted in the fact that most citizens of the neighborhood, despite our ideological pronouncements, wondered why we had come there in the first place. This distrust increased as our promises, which emerged more out of our ideology than out of what was materially possible, persistently outran our accomplishments. Of course, many people in the neighborhood broke a promise or two during the course of several months, but for us such failures were different.

When working with a formal organization, one is viewed not only as an individual but also as a part of some strange impersonal entity. This entity might be the very thing that increases hostility. As an organization we were expected to have money, to know exactly what we were doing and how we were going to do it, and to possess a power that was considerably greater than the sum of our actual parts: a handful of staff members, a secretary, a telephone, and an apartment with our name (for awhile) on the door.

It would be a much simpler matter if individuals without substantial organizational means, such as money or administrative machinery, could go and live in an area, come to know the people personally, get a close sense of their concerns, their way of talking, and their way of thinking— and then begin to think up organizational possibilities.

HEP failed, then, to become an organic part of the community in which we worked, and a large part of this failure can be attributed to our actual style of life. In September, when we began our program, several of the staff members hoped to find apartments on the block, and thus fasten their private as well as their organizational lives to the community. But there was a shortage of available space, and high rents for whatever was open, so all but one of us found apartments outside the immediate area.

For this reason, the people on the block could never feel that our interest was an abiding one. The effect of seeing us leave each night for unknown places was to sever the sense of solidarity between the staff and the people of the neighborhood. With this arrangement, it was difficult to say "Why don't we do such and such?" when the personal circumstances of our lives made for *us* and *them*. The price of understanding a community, of becoming accepted there, is steep. But unless one invests one's life in the life of a neighborhood, there is a serious question as to whether one's involvement can be more than superficial. And it may be destructive.

In our case, the fact that we set up an office in the community long before we had established a program geared to the people's needs proved more of a liability than an asset.

Although our meetings with the boys seemed to progress in good spirits, the raids on the office continued. It soon became a contest to see who could claim the most territory, with HEP succeeding during the day and the boys triumphing at night. The attacks grew more hostile; chairs and books were stolen, pictures slashed, and drawers and shelves overturned. The remaining paint was splashed less discriminately over the floors and desks. HEP couldn't afford to spend more money on locks.

By this time, tenants would visit the office during the day, shaking their heads and advising us to turn the boys over to the police. There was no solution that appeared to be feasible or to promise effectiveness in the long run.

The strangest part of the struggle was that no individuals, either from the staff or the group of boys, could personally confront each other with the problem—the contest did not seem to exist between any single persons. Although boys would come in singly to ask in amused puzzlement what we were going to do, even going so far as to say "I did that painting on the wall near the desk," each would add remarks like "But I wouldn't have messed up that typewriter" or "I wouldn't have put that shit on the walls."

In a peculiar way, the hostility was not directed at any of the three staff members who remained; in similar fashion, it was hard for the staff to feel that any of the boys was really accountable. Apparently the boys considered the attacks to be on a collective entity called HEP and on an impersonal office, rather than on X, Y, or Z; the staff felt that "the boys" had done it and found the raids impossible to connect with individual people, most of whom laughed and joked with the staff members by day.

Part of this can be explained by the fact that the boys were usually high when the raids took place, and perhaps it is also true that the staff was "conned" by a semblance of friendship. But the matter was far more complicated. A definite group psychology was at work, obscuring all individual relationships. In fact, the leader of the boys' group would take much time to explain to us how the raids happened, and would warn us about the individual boys who took part in them. Not only was it difficult to reconcile the need for a business office with the idea of a place for people to gather and talk (and excluding people did not seem to resolve the problem; it created another), but the fact of having to protect our own property put staff members on the defensive.

The most dramatic instance of this problem was the recent wrecking of the office. The group of older teen-aged boys had been coming into the office nearly every day looking for a way to spend their time; this was obviously frustrating to everyone concerned. At the time there were only two men left on the staff, neither of whom had the energy or force to direct the energies of these boys into a sustained and imaginative program.

Even if this had not been the case, the steady presence of a white woman in the office caused some sexual frustration that probably needed more than a program to alleviate. In addition to the daily visits to the office, the boys asked to use the office at night as a place to sing and drink. When they were denied this by one of the male staff members, the boys took it as a challenge and proved that no lock—even a $60 steel bar—could hold them back.

The first raid was highly strategic, rather than destructive. That is, rather than breaking windowpanes or furniture, the boys carefully put the typewriter and phones out of commission by pouring white paint over both. (The office had just been repainted, and cans of white and black paint were stored in the back room.) Large drawings of naked men and women were painted in black in the central room: on file cards and on several walls the boys had painted "Fuck H.E.P." (sic) and a globe of the world was completely covered with black. A photograph of a small boy building something in the back lot was carefully retouched; black paint filled in the boy's face and arms. The slogan was repeated underneath the picture. The windowpanes were filled in with black, but the red curtains had been removed and replaced after the operation.

One of the tutors felt that instead of taking it personally, we should be able to "read" it as a message. The paint job said to him that the boys had felt blocked out of the organization, and wanted to make their power recognized by the staff. In talking with them afterwards, a male staff member explained that he didn't have the energy to paint the whole thing over and at this point some of the boys said they'd help to fix it up.

Some of them did help, sporadically, in getting the paint off the walls, but the job was pretty much taken over by a bunch of the younger children who clamored to do it after school. At this time most of the older boys were setting up plans to build a basketball court on the Commons. This appeared to be one of the main sore points with them, since the Commons was supposed to have been completed with their help the previous summer.

Under different circumstances it might still have been possible for us to move the actual administrative apparatus out of the neighborhood and keep the apartment open as a field office, attempting, among other things, to redirect the energies of the gang who had raided us into creative channels. But by this time the male staff member who lived in the neighborhood was demoralized and weary, and the other black student in our group was not suited to supervise such an obviously tough operation. We would have to find another "strong black male" to make a field office effective, and this was impossible since we didn't even have enough money to pay our present staff regular salaries.

We finally decided to close down the office altogether and move to an empty room in the VISTA building ten blocks south of the neighborhood. It seemed to us just as absurd to run a neighborhood office designed as the center for a grass-roots organization on a strictly business-like basis as it did to keep open a room that would become more and more a hangout for teenagers.

To an extent this plan has proved effective. Without so much need to socialize with the community, we can carry out our daily business with considerably greater efficiency, and after hours we can fraternize with neighborhood people in apartments or on the street. Since we no longer need to defend a piece of property, these relationships proceed with greater ease. But there is still a problem. The boys in the neighborhood, especially those who carried out nightly raids on our office, feel that we have run away and ducked a challenge. Whenever we meet with them now we are reminded that, in some way or another, we have failed.

A neighborhood like 147th street now appears to us to be one of the most difficult, as well as one of the most important, places to begin, if one wants to understand and bring about change in this country. To work in such places one must have a far more concrete sense of method than we started with last fall. If some of us had been living more ordinary lives in the neighborhood since last September, instead of initially approaching it as the object of our organizational efforts, we would most likely have gained by now a far clearer sense of its problems and possibilities.

On this basis, programs could have been developed from the start with the cooperation of local citizens. The problems that a stranger, particularly a white one, would have in moving into such a block might be impossible to overcome. But it is just as impossible to think of moving back out at night, on weekends, or during the summer. In the equation for social change there is at least one factor that stays constant—the need for people to clearly understand themselves, each other, and the ways in which their freedoms are related.

*　*　*　*

CO-11 THE GOOD ORGANIZER[1]

Building an Organization

My first objective in any ghetto is building an organization that wields power. I don't go for the flash-flood demonstration kind of thing that Northern big shots quickly get blasé about. An organization that wields power, as opposed to the kind that throws an intermittent stinkbomb, must be big, broad, and quasi-institutionalized.

The kinds of leadership it must have to operate successfully are the kinds that are not simply "found" in communities where no one has had the chance to gain any experience with big organizations. Most of the people we organize will not even have been in the army or will have served in low echelons. They have not acquired a feel for the big organization, how it is put together, how it stays together, and what you have to do to run it.

We are speaking of people whose organizations are mostly small, and whose leaders are schooled in techniques that work for small groups. Large enduring organizations would have had the leaders to run them, and community organizers would be superfluous.

It is also true, however, that every community has a few naturals, that is, a few people who by accident of life experience, an exceptional intelligence, and some other qualities, can begin to move to the forefront almost as soon as the first organizational beginnings are under way. Who are they? How do you find them? It would be much easier if we could spot these people in advance. Unfortunately that is impossible. At the beginning of the organizing process, you are the leader—natural or otherwise—because at least theoretically you know more about what you are doing than anyone else around. If any of these three conditions doesn't hold, get out and give the job to somebody else.

---

[1] Abstracted from an article by Nicholas Von Hoffman entitled "Finding and Making Leaders" and distributed in mimeographed form by Students for a Democratic Society.

Being Scared

Recognize the fact that the organizer who comes into the community for the first time is internally in a precarious position. He is afraid—or at least he should be if he has any brains that he doesn't want beaten out.

He is afraid because he doesn't know the people, and we are all vaguely afraid of people we don't know. If he is white and he is going to work in a black community, he is doubly afraid. If he is a middle-class black, he is afraid too, for similar but not quite identical reasons.

He is afraid because he is the bearer of a new idea. Mankind does not cotton to new ideas in general, but especially not to the new ideas that organizers bring. This is so because they may mean trouble and because the organizer's mere presence in the community is a tacit insult. The organizer's presence says, in effect, "You are so dumb that you need me to think your way out of this mess you are in." Don't kid yourself about this. Nothing absolves the organizer of this sin.

The organizer is also afraid because a failure is a crushing blow to his ego or his self-respect. Even a bad organizer puts a tremendous part of himself on the line when he goes into a community. In his own eyes, he is being tried as a person, as a huge test of his own worth. To fail is to be adjudged a capon, a sexless, impotent thing by one's self, or so I always found it.

These fears work on most organizers to make them very susceptible to thinking the people they meet in the community who are sympathetic are the people to listen to and work with. I can't count the number of times I have wandered into communities to find the people who were supposed to be building a mass organization mucking around with pious, middle-class clergymen or teenagers.

Or, of course, there is the organizer who sees the weakness in himself, and overcompensates by finding a bunch of social outcasts, usually winos, addicts or semicriminal types, the kind that talk a good fight but lack the self-discipline to make hard-core organizational material. This kind of organizer may also be playing to a gallery of middle-class friends (often white) who will be mightily impressed by his acquaintance in the demimonde. It's nice to have one's outside friends think you are "in," but the question is, in what?

Picking Leadership

For the organizer who gets beyond acting as a reaction to himself—in my experience, few do—plucking out "natural leaders" by dint of casual observation and conversation is very chancy. I recall having picked a number of these on-first-sight gems and I also recall spending months kicking myself for having done so.

The guy who is indeed the natural small-group leader may turn out to be the guy who gets hopelessly and permanently confused by committees or simply by having to keep in mind that now instead of dealing with ten old faithfuls in the block club he's got to worry about what 400 people think. The guy you met at the barber shop, who seemed so articulate and understanding, may turn out at second meeting to be a dogmatist of the first water or a flannel-mouthed idiot. The guy with the big line about how "it's about time the black man showed those m-f's" can turn out to be one great big chicken, or what can be worse yet, a lazy bum who only comes to meetings to make long theatrical monologues.

The leaders in the third month or an organization's life are seldom the leaders in the third year; a few leaders, ourselves included, are really all-purpose; and the best organizations create a "collective leadership."

The first leadership is usually the closest leadership at hand. It is usually selected in the enthusiasm of the first campaign, because it is available. You don't have a choice and you have to go with what you've got.

It may be a rent strike, a school demonstration, or what-have-you. Reverend So-and-So says he'll be the spokesman, and you want him because he's a clergyman and you figure he'll cut more ice because he's respectable. Maybe it's Mrs. Jones, because she's the only one of the tenants who shows signs of being able to speak out in front of a judge. Or perhaps it's so-and-so because he has a reputation (with you anyhow) as a regular freedom fighter.

Note all these people were picked on the basis of what they could do in a one-shot affair. And the beginning of every viable organization smacks of being a one-shot affair, for the simple reason that theorists who fiddle around waiting and delaying until they've got a full-blown across-the-board organizational program set are never ready to commence swinging into action.

But you will notice too that the reasons for your picking the first leaders (and you know it's you who picks them) say nothing about how they will wear over a period of time. That respectable clergyman can turn out to be a timid jerk; the lady who was so good at sounding off in front of the judge may be good for nothing else; and that big freedom fighter can look like a vain egomaniac living off the reputation of a deed done many years ago.

The lesson I draw from this is that at the beginning keep the organization very loose, and spread the responsibilities and the conspicuous places around. This permits you, and the new membership that you are supposed to be recruiting, to judge the talent, and it keeps things sufficiently porous so that new talent isn't blocked off. Nothing is more absurd than an organization that's six months old, without a dime in the treasury and with a membership that can fit in a Volkswagen, having a cemented-in, piggy leadership. Vested interests are only tolerable when they are protecting something of value, not fancy organizational charts, letterheads, and research programs.

Don't laugh. This kind of thing is a clear and present danger. Vain men frequently prefer to be members of obscure executive committees where they can spend years expounding doctrine. It is safer and easier than the realities of making and using power. Men with the most to lose or men with the most to give in talent, money, and experience are often not the first to join an organization. They will never join if they see that there is no room for them in the top leadership. Why should some of the most talented people hang back? One reason, of course, is that they want to check you and the incipient organization out. If they are worth having, they won't be the kind who must bet on a guaranteed winner, but also, by the same token, they don't want any part of a born loser.

On Being an Organizer

Many organizations are killed off by their organizers even before they get close to a second leadership generation. It is pure charity of course, to speak of such preliminary groupings as organizations at all. Most of these endeavors never grow to look like much more than an aborted six-month fetus. They have been murdered by their own parents, the organizers who were supposed to give them life.

In the case of young organizers, their youth is enough to do it. People may admire youth, they may praise, they may believe that youth is showing the way in which age should follow, but they are very, very reluctant to trust youth with anything of immediate value. Youth is not an insuperable handicap, I rush to add. I have known top-notch organizers in their twenties.

Impressions do count. I'll mention clothes. It is one thing to wear overalls in Mississippi where many of the people actually do wear them—it is another to wear them as an occasional stunt in a big Northern city. To indulge in peculiarities of dress and speech simply makes you look like faddists. I apologize for saying this to those of you who know better, but those will also know it has to be said. Fadism makes you look like a horse's ass. White middle-class girls from Des Moines, to be extreme about it, did not grow up referring to males as "cats," and when they do it on the South Side of Chicago they sound either patronizing or idiotic —take your pick.

Nothing is so reassuring as a person who acts like himself. If you don't know who you are, stay out of organizing until you do and are willing to accept yourself as yourself. When you do, you will find that other people will.

Drop as much of your excess ideological baggage as you can outside the place where you are organizing. You are building a power group, a mass organization to serve a particular constituency, one that has certain paramount demands to be met. The demands are remote from "peace" or from any number of other perhaps laudable but irrelevant interests.

In other words, don't act like cultists. If you are a vegetarian, keep it to yourself, hide it, because there are a certain number of butchers in the community and you want them in the organization too.

This work demands self-discipline in every way. It means that you either get your rest or hide the fact that you haven't because people who arrive at sixes and sevens and announce they haven't slept for 26 consecutive hours give the impression of being unstable. It also means that you recognize that you have no private life, or put differently, you do not offend against the public morals of the community. Why? Not because the morals are necessarily correct, but because organizers who do not seem to be observing them alienate potential members for no good reason.

Some people may read what I have just said and think "Aha! White man's conventional middle-class values—ethnocentrism, etc., etc.," to which I reply, these are the public values held by substantial portions of the people you hope to organize.

Whether they practice them is as beside the point as whether middle-class whites do. The cultist will say that there can be no surrender and that freedom of the individual is involved. Perhaps it is, but he who wastes time debating such abstractions, or, worse, insists on making it clear by his behavior that he believes otherwise, is enjoying a luxury that is organizationally ruinous.

As organizers, apostolic vegetarians can only organize and inspire confidence among other vegetarians.

The best organizers have single-track minds. They care only for building the organization. When they alienate a potential member, they do so out of organizational need, not out of the egotism of irrelevant personal values. The best organizers stifle their tastes, their opinions, and their private obsessions.

Organizing Comes First

The organizer's first job is to organize, not to right wrongs, not to avenge injustice, and not to win the battle for freedom. That is the task of the people who will accomplish it through the organization if it ever gets built. When things are looked at through the glass of organizational calculation they assume new shapes.

A couple of examples may help to explain my meaning:

1. When the cops pick up a whore, shake her down and beat up her pimp, they have done wrong. Both the whore and pimp have rights that have been grossly violated, but the thinking organizer may wonder how good an idea it is to commit his new group to their defense. What will the public at large say? More important, what will the different segments of the community say?

The caballeros hustling on the street will love you, but what about the solid family types? Should these solid family types be taught the relativity of all human values, and will they consent to learn? Six months from now will the caballeros think enough of the organization to support it by coming to one meeting, by contributing one dollar?

2. Rent strikes are very popular now, but as with leadership, they are seen as something that is good to do merely if you can do them. However as anybody who has ever run one can tell you, they gobble up an organization's time, which should be a valued asset—and may produce very few organizational dividends.

How might an organizer look at a rent-strike proposition? (I am spinning this example out to illustrate the mentality that one might call organizational calculation.)

Of course he looks at the building. He does this for two reasons— the first is defensive; he wants to make sure the tenants aren't lying to him. Who doesn't think his landlord's a louse? Nothing is worse than getting into a fight in which the enemy can publicly prove your facts are wrong—note I said *publicly* prove.

The second reason he looks is to see how the building will photograph and will strike the eye of the often not very sympathetic press. I recall once having an argument with a photographer from the *Saturday Evening Post* as to whether a dead rodent in a slum building we were striking was a rat or a mouse. In short, the rats should look like rats.

If it still appears that a strike is feasible, he must ask what it will do for the organization. I will list a few possible things it might do, again by way of illustrating the organizational mentality.

1. If the political climate is right and you know that local government is with you it may provide a quickie victory—something every organization needs on occasion.

2. It can be a device to show people via face-to-face confrontation

that a big, important white man like a slum landlord can be humiliated and beaten.

3. It may be a way to force a municipal government to begin rigorous enforcement of minimal housing standards.

4. It may be useful in building up general organizational cohesion. I recall one rent strike during which the landlord retaliated by such tactics as failing to buy coal for the building. The organization responded in its turn by taking a portion of the sequestered rents to buy coal. The coal truck was decorated with appropriate signs; the gentleman from the Teamsters Union who customarily drove the truck was replaced by several local leaders in the cab, while other people from the organization surrounded it as it paraded around the neighborhood before finally coming to its destination. Humor, color, the relish of a small triumph, and greater organizational solidarity came out of the little episode.

5. The strike may also be a useful method for organizing the people in the immediate locals around the building in question. Unless you have all of officialdom on your side, a rent strike is liable to be a protracted contest of nasty little surprises that each side springs on the other. The landlord's surprises are usually legal ones—bailiffs, court orders, and the like. If the whole area is mobilized and organized into a big warning system, the landlord can't pull off much.

But if the fight is really you and a few tenants versus the landlord in the midst of an indifferent populace, you are likely to invest hundreds of hours keeping the tenants' morale up, with little to show for it but some publicity.

The Purpose of Organizing

There are other reasons, good organizational reasons, for having rent strikes, but the point to bear in mind is having some reason other than the pure injustice of it all. It is, of course, very hard for an organizer to know when he has a valid reason for doing something, and when he is conning himself.

By nature most organizers are optimists—they have to be or they wouldn't be doing what they do. Optimists tend to be credulous. They get so fascinated by the putative advantages of a proposed line of action that they never seriously examine either its drawbacks, or—and this is just as important—how they might be better spending their time.

I found in my own experience that my ego was incessantly trying to sabotage my judgment. For instance, I would argue in favor of striking a slum on the basis of organizational advantage without ever realizing that actually I was in a rage over the conditions the people in the building were living in. A good organizer cannot afford to vent his anger, any more than he can use his position to push miscellaneously irrelevant pet social beliefs.

The ego works in other ways to deform the organizer's powers of judgment. Promising young organizers are prone to come up with clever ideas—and in their pride of invention, or in the egotism of mischief-making, to attempt to carry them out in circumstances that are neither propitious nor even apropos.

The calculating organizer is forever suspicious of himself, forever mistrusting his analysis of the situation and his plan of action. He is always asking himself questions like, What am I doing? Why am I doing it? What if I succeed in doing what I am trying to do—will we really have gained anything worth gaining? However, the organizer with a calculating mentality will assuredly fail if he is trying to do the undoable.

The purpose of organization is power. As a practical matter, the organizing of two percent of the population is more than sufficient for the purpose of power. This you know from the history of modern revolutions—or if you look around, from the composition of the most effective present-day political machines. Indeed, even two percent of a population actively participating in an organization is an immensely formidable number. With two percent of a district's population closely organized, the organization should have an unbreakable control over things.

When the problem is viewed this way, it becomes more manageable intellectually and actually. It now becomes possible to see the plausible places to start organizing and to sort out what elements in the community demand organizational attention and which are purely optional, to be courted providing the occasion arises and you have the time.

An organization needs three things: (1) a network of people spread out and in position to reach and mobilize the inert majority, (2) continuity, and (3) money.

The majority of small groups in the ghetto districts I am familiar with turn out to be potentially strongest in one of these three qualities. Thus a block club adds a good deal to the mobilization network and has some money potential, but is usually quite low in supplying continuity. The same can be said of the sorority or the poolroom gang, while a business group scores higher on the money and may bolster an organization's continuity.

Obviously what is needed is the right mix of groupings to make up the sinews of organization. Sometimes this is accomplished by finding what the textbooks call the most common denominator. But the catch is, the most common denominator evokes the least general interest. Everybody is against juvenile delinquency but who cares enough about it to do anything? An issue that lines a whole community up on one side is most often so innocuous as to be organizationally useless.

There is an exception to this, and that is the outrage, the atrocity—the bad slum fire, the rat-bites-child incident, the bombing of the Sunday school. However, such crises are of limited organizational value. The shock and anger they cause are soon dissipated. Furthermore they are of much greater value to an existing organization than they are to the building of an organization.

Where an organization exists, the emotion the momentary crisis causes to be released can be harnessed to well-thought-out political maneuvers and demonstrations; it can also be exploited for money raising and recruiting in sections of the district where you are organizationally weak. But where there is no organization, there is no way to capitalize on the opportunity. There may be a few indignant meetings, or even a riot, and then all collapses back to its previous shape.

The foregoing should suggest that the right balance of network, continuity, and money is engendered by an organizational program containing a balance or mix of goals or would-be payoffs (which organizationally is all that a goal is) for the various groupings you need to recruit. For homeowners the program may be a defense against venal building inspectors; for welfare mothers it may be a defense against snooping welfare inspectors; for the unemployed it may be pressure on some well-known local firm that discriminates; and for the church group or local civil rights sentiment it may be some sort of an assault on the local educational system. Hence it has been said that organizing of this nature is, at least in part, building up a communitywide set of interlocking log-rolling agreements: "You scratch my back and I'll scratch yours, but if we don't combine, nobody's back'll get scratched."

Purists may find such a procedure intolerable. For example, you don't put pressure on the white small-store owner past a certain point—even if he can hire an extra black clerk. The reason is, you need his money, which you will get if he fears you, but not if he hates you. You will also get his money, I hasten to add, if the organization's program includes objectives that are worth something to him. Purists will find picayune many, many of the things the individuals and groups that you are courting want. Yet these "picayune" wants are the stuff of which organizations are built. They are the things that must of necessity most occupy people and that move people to action as great abstractions seldom do. Moreover, it is by meeting through organizational conquest the picayune demands that the great issues are made immediate and divested of their abstract distance. The mother learns about segregated education by fighting for school books for her child. The homeowner struggling with urban renewal learns about the society's huge engine of residential segregation by battling to save his property. The people learn these lessons, and the most important lesson is about how the world that bears down on them actually functions. If the organizer is there to present the lesson and to make the experience valuable, he must lead the people on to the next and larger round in this match, which will be won by those adaptable enough to use victorious methods.

The organizer who merely sees the people's day-to-day problems as the proof that oppression demeans men and not as the chance to be exploited, lacks the patience, ingenuity, and opportunism that makes success. The I-can't-be-bothered-with-that attitude is self-important, and the organizer who is mostly concerned with "big issues" will never meet success outside the debate room.

Again, I am speaking of the ability to see with calculation and act with calculation. It is not easy, particularly once you have sensitized yourself to the importance of little favors, little worries, and little preoccupations to know which are the organizationally useful ones and which are heart-rending but profitless. I remember a newly founded organization that was offered several thousand dollars worth of Christmas baskets by a group of terrified local businessmen hoping thereby to placate the popular wrath. First we battled with the local sufferers-for-humanity about putting whisky in the baskets. They wanted the money spent on extras for the children. After that we argued over who should get the baskets. They wanted to give them to the needy! The organizers wanted to give them to the strategic ones, the flat janitors and other key people whom it is good to have obligated to the organization.

A big organization demands a variety of leadership talents—money-raising leadership, oratorical leadership, tactical leadership, leadership for routine, leadership that can measure community sentiment, and leadership that knows when to move and when to stay put. The different kinds of groups that come into your organization train their natural leaders with greater skills in one area than in another. You need them all, and for that reason, I spoke earlier about collective leadership. It is just unrealistic to expect a big organization to produce more than a few all-purpose leaders who can perform most of the various leadership tasks exceptionally well.

Like it or not, white men have their uses. Organizationally, an astute pretty white boy with an ivy league manner can run circles around anybody else in certain kinds of highly proper middle-class situations. White organizers can be useful in dampening the often destructive battle for prominence that has wrecked many a promising black endeavor.

Remember, your white organizer has no political future in the ghetto; therefore, he can be used as neutral absorbent material for out-of-control ambitions that are emitting dangerous rays. The white organizer sometimes can be a reassurance when making deals with outside white groups —and I hope there is no one here in such retarded political babyhood as to think such deals are not necessary.

On the other hand it grates in this time of rising independence to see the old dependence on whites—to see the old razzmatazz of whites leading blacks. But for the good organizer this should be no problem because the good organizer should never—or virtually never—make a public speech, never get his name in the paper, and never enjoy any formal authority in the organization. The big-deal organizer who becomes a figure in his own right was never serious about developing leadership. He is the man who always meant to be the leader himself; when this type asks how do we find an indigenous leadership you can translate his words to mean, "How do I get myself a personal following?"

The good organizer is the self-effacing mentor who judges his work a success when he can leave the organization without even being missed. He is rare, rarer than first-rate leadership, but he exists and he comes in a variety of colors and he can work in almost any situation.

CHAPTER 5

Building Relationships

CASES AND ILLUSTRATIVE MATERIALS

This chapter includes some rather complete case materials and a number of short, illustrative vignettes. They represent practice in a number of settings, under a variety of auspices, for a multitude of purposes, and with diversity of constituencies or target populations. While all these contextual components affect the nature of the organizer's practice and may influence each of his actions, the setting in which he finds himself and the people with whom he works emerge as the critical variables in the cases that follow.

In "Hollow Hope: Community Development in Appalachia," a young organizer and his wife find that they must overcome community suspicion and build personal relationships before they can even begin to help an Appalachian community to help itself. Just as important, they find that they, too, have come with a number of misconceptions, that their neighbors have a number of strengths and skills they did not expect. The reader may wish to reflect on the organizers' initial decision not to combat the exploitation of the mining companies they knew to be the basic cause of the misery and poverty of the county.

"Getting to Know You—Talking At or 'Rapping With,'" documents the differences with which a director and his associate approach a community meeting. The former has thoroughly researched the community and its problems and is prepared to fully disclose the benefits of an antipoverty program to the residents of an urban neighborhood. The failure of the director in communicating with his audience, and the concomitant success of the associate director, illustrates the importance of establishing a personal rather than an organizational identity in working with lower-income consumer groups.

The organizer in the following case discusses the use of "The Survey as an Organizing Technique" to identify neighborhood problems, to spot potential community leaders, and to build the relationships necessary for further organizing efforts. He has developed a rather standardized survey procedure and is convinced of its universal value as an entry point into a community. He does, however, discuss some of the shortcomings of this technique. The reader will recall variants of his approach utilized in the cases describing the work of Alinsky and Chavez.

The curbstone caseworker utilized her experiences in delivering services in the neighborhood to identify the need for legal aid to the poor. She does not, however, build an organization of the poor to bring those services into the community. Instead, she prefers to work directly with those groups and individuals that have the resources necessary to sponsor legal aid services. She uses her relationship to the poor only to convince others of the need. Later, she concludes, she might not even have needed their help for that. She is evidently cognizant of the sources of opposition and support in her community.

There seems to be little doubt that the organizer in "You Stand Up and They Ain't Gonna Knock Me Down" knows his community. And the community knows him. The organizer speaking is a national figure. We've been asked not to divulge his name. It may be obvious.

"Cool the Cops" is more than a single case. It contrasts the working styles of two organizers, each working with a different clientele, but each concerned with a similar issue—police brutality. The case is not complete because the actions described therein were still in process at the time we gathered our materials. We include it as it stands because of its richness. The case deals not only with police-community relations, but with the relationships between two organizing efforts, each having different long-range purposes, and each concerned with changes in populations that differed according to racial, ethnic, and socioeconomic characteristics. We suggest that the reader might like to contemplate the alternative strategies flowing from the data and analysis presented.

* * * *

CO-12 HOLLOW HOPE: COMMUNITY DEVELOPMENT IN APPALACHIA

Coal miners were the first to fuel the technological and manufacturing explosion that made America the world's foremost industrial and military power. Since extraction began in Appalachia more than 100 years ago, an estimated $500 billion worth of raw resources has been hauled out of the region on rafts and barges and by trucks, railcars, and pipelines.

The region, still incredibly rich in natural resources, could not survive without social security and welfare payments. In many former mining communities, public assistance supports 60 percent or more of all local sales or exchanges.

America has been unwilling to reclaim the land and the lives that deteriorate in Appalachia. In 1963, John F. Kennedy set up the President's Appalachian Regional Commission. Its major accomplishment, the Appalachian Regional Development Act of 1965, earmarked 80 percent of its funds for highway construction. Those who have entered the region through these new roads know they are far from modern. Rather than bringing people, services, and products into the region, they serve as an escape route for the young, the disheartened, and the disabled, and as further tax supports for the already well-endowed mining companies.

Of those who are employed or who have worked, more than 125,000 Appalachian men have been permanently injured, their lungs impaired by inhaling coal and rock dust. There are only 150,000 miners in this country. U.S. Public Health research on black lung and related diseases is 25 years behind the British, who spend nearly 10 times as much on mine safety and research as do Americans. Even tiny Belgium spends more than we do.

Until recently, neither the industry, the union (UMW[1]), nor the legislatures of the states involved recognized black lung as a disease worthy of prevention, cure, or compensation. It took the aftermath of the Farmington disaster in November 1968 (strangely reminiscent in cause and description of the infamous Black Heath disaster that claimed 54 lives near Richmond, Virginia in March 1939), and a wildcat strike in February 1969 to move the West Virginia legislature to pass a law compensating workers whose lungs are permanently damaged by coal dust. The union did not support the strike, which lasted three weeks, included 40,000 miners, and closed the industry.

If the gainfully employed are poorly protected, what of the unemployed—those left behind in blind hollows, far from modern roads, jobs, and schools?

Straw Hollow was a good place to find out. We selected it as a target area precisely because it was so typical of the region and we wanted to demonstrate what could be done with community-development techniques. We were a staff of five from the State University's Institute for Regional Development: a professional community developer who taught

---

1 United Mine Workers.

at the University, two graduate students from the school of social work who spent their three days a week of field placement in the hollow, and my wife and myself. I have my MSW from a school in Boston where I grew up. My wife and I both wanted a rural experience of this sort. We met as volunteers in the Appalachian Summer Program two years earlier, and decided then to come back here some time to work.

Straw Hollow, along with Silver Creek, Loon's Lake, Unforeseen, Slattertown, and the whole Black Ridge area, had once flourished with mining activity. Under the leadership of John L. Lewis in the 1930s and 1940s, miners secured good wages after bitter labor wars. The region was prosperous enough during World War II. It was good times even for those mountain folk who had scratched out bare livings along the steep hillsides and stony bottoms for generations.

In the late 1960s, however, times were no longer good. The best seams had given out. Mechanization of strip mining had thrown many out of work. The union's efforts in securing high wages had never extended to securing adequate health and accident benefits. Many who had once been employed by the mines were now in ill health, disabled by accidents or with lungs impaired years earlier from inhaling coal and rock dust. Of the 93 families in Straw Hollow, only 8 men were gainfully employed. Eighty-seven families drew some form of relief. Those on the county welfare roles knew their meager checks were dependent on their good behavior, political and otherwise. The sheriff, the judge, and the welfare administration were all related, as were the principal storekeepers in Slattertown, where all local shopping was done. Hollow dwellers accepted these facts. They reacted to them as they reacted to most outsiders —with mistrust bordering on apathy.

Before going to Straw Hollow, we talked to organizers—a young couple like ourselves—who had helped people from another county fight the strip miners. They were convinced that the only way to help the region was to confront the exploitation of the coal industry head on. They used tactics from the civil rights movement—demonstrations, sit-ins in front of the bulldozers, walk-outs, and voter registration. What happened to them scared us. They were arrested on sedition charges, thrown into jail, and investigated by the McClellan Committee. Their library was stolen, and their house was bombed. We didn't want that to happen to us. Above all, we did not want to be singled out as outside troublemakers. The University could not have withstood the political repercussions, and we felt that in the long run, we would have misused ourselves.

Bad feelings existed between hollow dwellers and school officials and teachers, each of whom represented very different cultures, and both of whom presented convincing arguments about the worthlessness of the other. Children dropped out of school before they were legally allowed. Many did not attend during the winter months, when a two-mile walk on muddy or icy roads with inadequate shoes (or no shoes at all) made the trip an excruciating hardship.

About the only social institution that attracted some following was the church, a fundamentalist, other-worldly, doctrinaire institution. There being so few involved in mining, the union had no interest in the hollow. No focal point existed for solving community problems. Bereft of the skills, the imagination, and the will to solve common problems, forgotten or defined as worthless by outsiders, the residents of Straw Hollow withdrew among kin and select neighbors.

The project director and the two social work students were the first to visit the community. They came regularly on Thursdays and Fridays, beginning in late September, trying to establish contacts and become acquainted. Although they introduced themselves as staff members and students from the University, they offered no specific program. "Whut you all goin' ta do out hyer?" was the usual question. "What can we help people do?" was the usual reply.

I suppose their wandering around, their refusal to make decisions about what to do for people's welfare, and their nondirectiveness must have been very disquieting for the residents. A preacher who had warned that they might be dangerous outside agitators could not find anything to accuse them of agitating about. Some residents must have decided that the visitors were freeloaders (they did accept invitations to meals at people's homes on two occasions), or goof-offs or goldbricks. The one thing they were not seen as were representatives of the outside community's exploitive and degrading institutions.

A month later, my wife and I came to town. We had decided that, unlike the other staff members who had part-time commitments to the project, we would live in Straw Hollow. The only available building was the school, a one-large-room affair that had been closed by the county authorities about four years earlier and that was in a state of disrepair almost beyond belief. We had secured permission from the county school board to use it. In this case our university credentials were useful. Had we been VISTA volunteers or poverty workers, we would have been turned down as outsiders, government intruders, and meddlers or troublemakers.

The old school was in worse repair than we had imagined. It took my wife and me two days of hauling timbers from discarded machinery crates at one of the mines in Silver Creek on top of our old Saab, and three more days of sawing and hammering, just to fix the floors. We ran out of lumber when it came to patching holes in the north wall, and fell to using tar paper, old canvas, and oiled newspaper (we saw this done in an old movie once). As we worked, some of the teenagers and younger children came by to see what we were doing. Two of the boys offered to help. One girl who lived nearby said her mother wanted us to use their well until we could get our own going.

By the third week in November we were finished and feeling pretty good about things. My wife was outside splitting off cords of wood for the fireplace and I was inside fixing up some makeshift furniture out of branches and twine, when a number of our new friends came by. As we were thanking them for their help, it suddenly occurred to me that it was getting awfully close to Thanksgiving and that we might show our appreciation by organizing a Thankgiving feast.

Well it was really quite a blowout: turkey, squirrel, and pheasant. Of course not everyone came. The fact is, we hardly knew anyone in the hollow. We had decided not to go out aggressively to meet people, but to let it happen naturally as we met them on the road, at the Post Office, as they came by to check on who we were and what we were doing, and the like. Four families and some children from as many more came to the dinner. Some were having other dinners with kinfolk as well.

The next day about fifty people more, many of whom we had never seen, came by to look or to introduce themselves. We had them in for coffee. It was like an open house. And then we realized something that hadn't really occurred to us before. Our home was a familiar building to them. Many of the parents and the grandparents and some of the older children had gone to school there. It had been a community building. It still was the largest single room in the hollow, and it seemed natural for it to become a community building again. Had we kept it strictly to ourselves we would have been like squatters taking over something of theirs.

Our success in patching up our own living quarters suggested to us that we might be able to get a "clean-up" or "face-lift" campaign going before the winter set in and it got really cold. We failed to get any support at all. But some of the men who visited did like what I had done with the furniture. Some copied my ideas, and others offered their own. One old-timer taught me to whittle a funny little propeller stick, a children's toy. He and another old-timer and some teenagers began coming over two afternoons a week. We carved all sorts of things.

My wife had a loom of her own, different from anything that anyone in the area had seen. Between her weaving, the sewing and darning that had to be done, and the needlework that some women had almost forgotten how to do, we had a women's folk craft program going. On Saturdays, my wife started a sewing club for the school girls. To make a long story short, by spring we had a folk craft co-op going, sent some things to an exhibit at the University, and arranged for the sale of some items at Cape Code and in Cambridge, Mass., where we had a number of friends with small shops.

Not once had we suggested to anyone that we wanted to help him seek a job, but after a while young men and older boys began coming in regularly asking for help. We found ourselves dividing up responsibilities. My wife and I were dealing with things internal to Straw Hollow. The students in field placements began to assume responsibility for negotiating in the external environment. One of them took on the employment task.

Periodically almost every male in the hollow tried to look for employment. Few were content to stay on relief. But each spurt of enthusiasm had resulted in failure and renewed lethargy.

One young man, a recent father, told us that he wouldn't go on ADC[1]: "I haven't sunk that low yit!" He had been to the Employment Office in Charleston on many occasions and filed applications. He was told once that he was due to enter a welding training program soon, but the next time he went, he was told that there was no application in the files for him. This happened twice and he was furious and desperate. We went to work on his case and, after some fifteen phone calls, managed to locate and expedite his application. The problem had been one of communication. He had no phone and his neighbors had not been home when the crucial call came through. This would have happened again except that we made our phone available as a backup and made sure he got the word. He is now in the training program and we are considered wizards at dealing with these matters.

As a result, we are in constant demand as aides in tracking down lost applications, advising on employment matters, making appointments for kids at the Department of Employment Security, and so forth. The employment people have been cooperative and spared some of our charges the psychological hazards of the bureaucratic machinery of their office by personalizing the service for them as much as possible. Three have been lined up so far for training programs and several others have received temporary employment. Many others were unable to be placed due to a sheer lack of salable skills. Contacts we established with a Job Corps camp about 30 miles away, and with a job training center for adult males in an urban community in this part of the state, made it possible to serve 11 of the unskilled.

We also started a tutorial project, encouraging some children to stay in school, helping many do better, and encouraging two dropouts to return. Based on our work with children, we were establishing some cred-

---

[1] Aid to Dependent Children.

ibility with the teachers and the principal, which we were to cash in on later.

The teens were a special problem. Except for those we were able to get jobs or job training for, most were in dire straits. Relationships at home deteriorated if the teen-ager had any gumption of his own. Other teens were trapped in a cycle of interdependence. Some had delinquency and arrest records. A Saturday social we planned for New Year's Eve was the first they had had in four years.

With some of the contacts we made right after our Thanksgiving feast, we organized a turkey shoot with around 40 people participating, and netted $78.00 to go towards a Christmas program. We used the money to decorate a Christmas tree one of the men cut down for us. By this time we had a small "social" committee and were able to arrange a party at which 150 children attended. We played games, had treats, and were able to send candy home with everyone. Some of the teen-agers who were planning the New Year's party with us joined in caroling around the community.

By this time, we thought we were ready to call a general meeting. Some of our friends in the community had discouraged us. "Ain't none of them hill folks give a damn." "All y'll git is fightin' and arguin'." But we decided to try anyway. We asked people to spread the word, and put up a sign at the Center (what our house was now being called) and one at the Post Office.

I must tell you we were more than pleased at the outcome. The crowd began to arrive early. We had called the meeting for 7:30. By 6:45, twenty people were here, and by 7:30 we had nearly 80 people, about twice as many as our building could hold. We were afraid our crate-board floor might cave in.

The project director had come in from the University to give a talk. We reviewed the kinds of things that were beginning to develop in Straw Hollow. The co-op hadn't been organized yet, nor had we placed many in jobs, but all these projects had been begun. When the project director spoke about our concerns, he made it very clear that what was happening was a natural thing, and that we hoped we could be helpful in a number of ways. We needed to know what people in the community wanted, and then maybe with some of our know-how and outside connections we might be able to help them get it to happen.

The condition of the road was mentioned. Some wanted a school bus. Others encouraged us to continue with the tutorial work. One father felt that the most pressing need was some sort of teen-age center, but, in the only fight of the evening, was bitterly opposed by some church people who felt that a teen-age center would only "encourage sin."

Crowded as the meeting room was, somehow people seemed to be forming committees. Somewhat to our surprise (I suppose we had been full of preconceptions about Appalachians), people seemed to be rather sophisticated about committees and were well aware that little could be done in so large a group. One committee took on responsibility for contacting the school authorities about meeting in the public school two miles down the road and also agreed to work on the busing problem. Two men volunteered to contact the county commissioners about improving the road. The crafts committee, later to become the co-op officers, was a natural group by then. Three mothers volunteered to be a parents committee. They had children either in our tutorial program, in the crafts group, or in both.

The school officials at first were lukewarm to our request to use the school auditorium (fearing the place would be left in shambles) for our next meeting, but were convinced by a combination of our University credentials and the relationships we had made with some of the teachers who attested to the progress made by our students. The place was not left in a shambles after our first meeting, and we met there regularly once a month thereafter. It took a while, but eventually we got the school bus.

These were real victories for the hollow. The neighborhood was beginning to develop a certain sense of self. We felt it and were constantly reminded of it. "Never did think I'd live to see Clara Bolton give one hoot about anybody else." "Imagin Ned Holsger's boy helpin' fix that well." "Them school folk ain't so bad as I had them figured."

By spring we felt ready to suggest a "clean-up day" again. We had it. We hauled away five two-ton truck loads of trash. By the end of the summer we had gotten a crew of men to repair a bridge, getting so much newspaper publicity that we were able to pressure the county road commissioner to fix the rest of the road (school officials were with us on this one, if only to protect the bus from too much wear and tear).

The co-op was fully incorporated. Some of the teens had organized a newsletter that included not only news about our own hollow, but also news of happenings in other neighborhoods as well. It was run off on the mimeo donated by one of the mining companies and kept at the Center. We repaired several wells and built a small dam and an irrigation ditch and elected three permanent "water commissioners."

None of these are really tremendous accomplishments. There is still much to be done in linking the hollow to the rest of the world. We hope to bring the Boy Scouts and 4-H in. But unless the vast majority of the men get jobs, many of our accomplishments are meaningless. And we understand full well that the future of the region is controlled by political and economic forces outside it. Still, we leave our assignment this fall with some hope for the hollow, and it is not a hollow hope.

*   *   *   *

CO-13 GETTING TO KNOW YOU—TALKING AT OR "RAPPING WITH"

The Director Meets the People and Tells About It

I really prepared myself for the first meeting on the West End. I had read several studies on the neighborhood and talked over the problems with people from the social agencies. I met with the City Planning Commission, with a councilman from the district, and with the people from the parks and recreation department, the schools, and the traffic department. I talked with some of the police officers assigned to community relations. I was new to the CAP, but I knew what OEO could deliver if Congress didn't throw us any curves. But prepared as I thought I was, I just wasn't prepared for the reception I got.

For the first half hour or so after the councilman introduced me (there were a priest, a Baptist minister, and the chairman of the Community Action Council sitting on the stage with me), I sensed almost no reaction from the audience at all. I wondered if it was my approach or the people who were up there with me. Then all hell broke loose.

A young black in the back of the hall asked, "What you white folks aim to do, tear our houses down and build some nice apartments nobody can afford?" I barely had time to answer that one before someone else asked me what I was going to do about jobs. Then it got more personal. Why did I take the job in the first place? Why did I move to this town? Why did I want to run the Community Action Program? And then impersonal again. When was the City going to do something about the potholes in the street?

When people asked their questions, they always accentuated the *Mister,* in addressing me, or ended with *Sir.* I felt I was being put on. I certainly was feeling harassed. I knew I was bombing it. But I just didn't know how to stop the slaughter. Finally I said that I appreciated their interest, that I thought it showed we could really get something going in this community, and that I was sorry I didn't have all the answers now, but would try to get them by our next meeting.

The Associate Director Meets the People and Tells About It

When Lou told me how he had bombed out at the first meeting on the West End, I laughed. I told him he had done just right and that he had softened them up for me. It was a good thing it happened. Lou is a very open guy, and this incident helped us divide up our responsibilities. It's obvious he does better with the people downtown. I do better with the people in the neighborhoods.

I started out as a shop steward for the UAW and then became an organizer, so I know how to talk to people. Before the next meeting I made sure to get the names of those people who stirred up most of the trouble from the councilman and others I knew had been present. Then I went and talked to them.

Now it's like this. When you're dealing with people downtown or in some big organization, it's important to tell them who you are—your title, what you expect to accomplish, and the like. You play it like an organizational "rep." But when you're in the neighborhood, people don't want to know your title. They want to know *you*. Can they trust you? Are you afraid of getting your hands dirty? Are you going to play square or just promise the world?

I talk plain, straight from the shoulder over a cup of coffee or a beer. I never make promises. I always stress that "we" (them and us) have a problem. If I told them all the resources I was going to bring in or used a bunch of bureaucratic words, they would throw me out on my ear. If a guy uses big fancy words and I don't know what he's talking about, I'd walk out, or toss him out.

Once they get to know you, then you talk about your organization—but only about how it might help them deal with the problems and the gripes they've already shared with you. By the time I had my meeting with them, they were softened up. We could really "rap."

*   *   *   *

CO-14   THE SURVEY AS AN ORGANIZING TECHNIQUE

Over the years I've developed a standard procedure for opening up new neighborhoods to organizing efforts. It works almost all the time. I'll tell you about the potential problems in a minute. The indirect, more than the direct, results of a survey are what you use for organizing. I don't care if you're trying to organize the residents in a housing project, a neighborhood, or a whole town. The survey is a quick, easy way to get information and to build a support network.

Let me give you an example. Last year our agency was awarded a contract with the Housing Authority to organize residents in each of the low-income housing projects in town, to bring services to the projects, and to bring people out of the projects and to services. We set up offices in the Barton Street Project in an apartment set aside for us. Now, our agency is well known in this part of town. We have a reputation for delivering whatever we set out to do.

It didn't take more than a couple of days, what with residents looking around as we moved office furniture in, and as some of our staff hung around the parking lots and entrance ways in the early mornings and late afternoons, to find out what the real problems were. The old folks needed protection—too many muggings and petty robberies occurred right in the buildings themselves. Mothers needed day-care help. Teen-agers needed recreation facilities, tutorial help, and jobs. The men needed jobs and job training. Everyone needed help with transportation. The management of the project was often arbitrary in establishing rules. Residents weren't involved, and earlier attempts at developing a tenants' council resulted in a takeover by a very vocal lady and a small group of henchmen.The place was demoralized. People just wanted out. If there was no hope of escape, there was no hope of improvement either.

Now, we didn't need a survey to find all this out. We were told quickly enough. We knew pretty much on the basis of informal discussions what the results of a survey might bring out. From the organizer's point of view, what we already knew was more important than statistical indices of broken washing machines, nonfunctioning toilets, and muggings.

Unless your project is of long duration, or unless you can gather your data long before you begin organizing, or unless you think the information will influence some group to action, the results of your survey will not be ready in time to be of any use. By the time you've completed the analysis, circumstances will have moved you in certain directions. The information you gathered may be less than useful. More important, if you try to get everything into your survey, the people you interview will begin to think you really don't care about what is important to them. You may gain in information and lose in relationship.

Let me get back to Barton Street. Residents were segregated pretty much by demographic variables. Old folks lived in one section, mothers with kids in another, and married college students in still another. In our informal contacts, we were quickly able to line up some volunteers. Together, staff members and volunteers from each building or building complex interviewed someone in each apartment in that building. We asked similar questions everywhere, but we put the stress on certain issues in each place. For example, with the old folks we focused more on questions dealing with transportation and with muggings. With mothers of young kids we focused on child-care needs and on the broken washing machines.

The canvassers who went from door to door did not just ask questions and leave. They stayed and talked—about anything people had on their minds, and about why we were there in the project. A 20-minute interview could easily stretch into an hour. It was never time wasted. We identified potential leaders, located the disinterested, and got insights into the politics of the housing authority. Most important, we began establishing communication links—not just between ourselves and the people—but among them too. Bringing residents along and having them do some of the canvassing was very helpful. They were able to dispel some of the mistrust people showed strangers. On the other hand, sometimes people in the apartments were not about to open up and tell one neighbor about a problem they were having with another neighbor. So there are some disadvantages too.

Sometimes you get information that could never come out in a formal survey, and we shared this information rather purposefully. Like, we would tell Mrs. Cooley on the sixth floor that Mrs. Robinson on the third had had the same trouble with her sink and how she managed to maneuver through the bureaucracy to get it fixed. We gave her Mrs. Robinson's phone number so she could get the whole story.

So much for one example. The survey does something for your staff too. It forces them to learn. They learn how to talk with people, how to elicit information. And they have to think about it and decide sometimes on the spot what is relevant and what to pursue. This takes a certain sophistication, and not all your staff members are going to be so sophisticated.

In the early stages of organizing, during this survey period, I have staff meetings every day, sometimes even twice, just so my staff can talk over and share the information and the impressions they have been getting. The analysis is important. It shapes how they will function when they leave the meeting, and in a sense it is the building block upon which all the rest of our strategies may be founded.

So now you have it in a nutshell. A survey can give you accurate information. It can furnish you with knowledge about conditions that don't get reflected in any formal document. It is a way of getting known and of establishing relationships. It helps you begin to focus on an organizing issue. And it educates your staff and whomever else you want to use in canvassing. Like I say, I've used residents. But I've also used officials and board members when I wanted to influence them.

One tip! People in low-income neighborhoods may not be accustomed to generalizing about their feelings. You can't make a question too open ended. Like you can't ask how they feel about schools, or living in the project. They'll just shrug their shoulders. On the other hand, if you are too specific—like asking about the plumbing—you may get too specific an answer and never get to the more interesting and important issues.

You don't have to reach 100 percent of the population. Sometimes your time and your staff will be limited. There are some who say it doesn't make much difference whom you talk to and when. But I think it does. After all, whom you ultimately involve and who your leadership will be does make a difference. I like to pick certain times of the day for strategic reasons—because I know certain people will be in. If I want to talk to the man of the house, I don't pop in at two in the afternoon. If I want to talk to the teen-agers, I don't come in at 11 in the morning. On the other hand, if I want to talk to the mothers alone, I might pick just these times—before or after she gets hung up on mealtime.

I did mention that there are some drawbacks to the survey. You can get awfully hung up on tabulation of the results if you don't have the staff or the equipment to work on it. You do have some obligation to the people who answered your questions to tabulate and use the results.

More important, though, the whole thing may backfire on you. One time a funding agency put the screws on us because we were working on voter registration in a neighborhood, whereas our survey indicated that most people were concerned about having a "minipark" or some other recreational facility for the kids and the old folks. We tried to explain why a voting citizenry was necessary to get those things, but we got slapped down for playing politics.

Another time our canvassers came on too strong. We had contracted to start a project in another town. We had planned to start with a survey, locate some indigenous leadership, and then train them to organize and eventually hire someone as their own organizer. But we frightened people. Suddenly, there we were, an army of us asking questions at every door. We talked about organizing and an organizer. The words turned people off. They got scared and looked at us as outside agitators. I think someone must have started up a whisper campaign. Anyway, we really goofed it up. Never did get anything going in that town.

*   *   *   *

CO-15   A CURBSTONE CASEWORKER BRINGS LEGAL-AID SERVICES TO A COMMUNITY

I'm a maverick in this town, and my board knows it. I think they like me for it. I run a small family agency with two other full-time caseworkers and three or four part-time staff members. I try to keep the agency tuned in to developments in other agencies around town.

Things were getting a little too comfortable around the office—middle-class clients, fifty-minute hours, that sort of thing. At one point I felt my board members out on completely changing our focus and targeting in on only the poor in town. I made the pitch incorrectly and horrified some of the stalwarts. But I did get them to buy my idea of "curbstone casework." We opened a little storefront on the Puerto Rican side of town. I started spending my afternoons and one or two evenings a week there. The rest of the agency was pretty much running itself. I didn't have to be around all the time.

I was well known by the Puerto Rican community. I'm Puerto Rican myself, and I've been involved in a lot of causes. I don't live in town, but the Spanish community thinks of me as one of them. It's a lot of bunk that social workers are no longer regarded with respect among the Spanish Americans.

Many people walked into the store or stopped me on the curb for assistance with their problems. I would take five minutes on the curb for an interview. This curbstone casework is always a major part of C.O. work. Uptown I'm a caseworker. When I'm down here, though, I think of myself as a community organizer. Many people brought problems that obviously required legal assistance beyond my ability. I am not a lawyer. I thought that I should have some assistance in answering the questions —someone to lean on. This became evident to me after about six months in the neighborhood. I guess the idea for the actual project was mine, but it ultimately came from the people's expression of their needs.

I got a guy to give his time as a lawyer in the evening, once a week. This was a trial balloon. I knew it wouldn't be permanent because no volunteer service can be counted on to continue on a permanent basis. I wanted only to get an idea of the scope of the problems involved. Because I'm a layman there are many legal problems that the people of the community will not normally tell me. For example, a young lad with whom I had worked for weeks told the lawyer that he had gone AWOL from the Army and yet I never knew of this. The flocks of people that went to the lawyer also provided *evidence* that legal assistance was badly needed.

I talked with the president of my board of directors about the need for legal aid. He asked for my suggestions. I recommended a trip by board members to a legal-aid society in a nearby city. I picked it because I knew that the town had a legal-aid agency that was separate from other agencies. I also knew the founders. Mobilization for Youth of New York City has the best legal plan in my opinion, but I did not suggest a visit there because our people favor this state over New York. I also avoided suggesting any agency in New York City because many people in the community already look at me somewhat askance because I presently live there. My choice of a nearby agency in this state for illustrative purposes thus avoided a needless difficulty.

Following the board members' trip to the agency I sent for material on the topic of legal aid from OEO. I made a packet of this material and mailed it to all board members who had expressed an interest (through a show of hands) at a previous meeting. However, the board president killed the idea for a legal-aid project by simply failing to talk with the key people we had agreed on. He also told me that our agency should leave the legal-aid project alone because the resistance put up by the local Bar would be too great. None of the board members knew of the president's hesitance to act in the face of the Bar. It never came up in a board meeting, but I must admit that I shot off my big mouth a bit about just what had happened.

When the president of the board killed the project by his inaction, I stopped activities on the issue also. But only until it looked as if I might get the support I needed.

In June of this year, several local people went to a civil rights meeting in Washington. On their return, the participants concluded that the city needed some kind of legal-aid agency. On learning this, I decided to completely circumvent the president of my board by gathering a large following from the community. In doing so, I intended to use neither the sponsorship nor the physical facilities of the Family Service Agency. I planned to use only my skills and connections (I have done this many times on other projects. In such instances I don't condemn the president of my board—I just ignore him).

A second factor played an important role in my decision to move the project. A minister from a wealthy town nearby asked me how his congregation could help the poor people of my city. I suggested the legal-aid agency. In the weeks that followed I met with the board of his church. I took a grass-roots leader with me and permitted him to do most of the talking because I thought that the liberal drive with the minister's board members would be better satisfied if they heard about the poor of the city through the *broken* English of a grass-roots member of the community. The presentation was intended only to be a general orientation to the problems of the poor of the city.

In the initial contacts with the minister I pumped him gently for information about his congregation's membership, personal influence, and willingness to contribute money. The likelihood of forthcoming seed money for beginning the incorporation was a strong asset. I also viewed the personal influence of several congregation members as an important asset to the project. This was just an exploratory meeting. The minister and I kept in touch.

I thought that the new agency should be set up on a regional basis because I thought that OEO would be more willing to give money to the whole county and because the idea was unusual (OEO will grab anything that has the slightest hint of being original). And the minister, more or less, went along with my suggestions. After we had finished the discussions on the proposals, I said to him, "Okay, you get me five people from your community and I will get some from mine." As time went on we consulted more and more. Incidentally, I frequently had to deal with his fears of difficult fights and of making enemies.

As we agreed, the minister brought four or five people to the meeting and I brought eight or nine. I brought the three chairmen of the only three grass-roots organizations in the community; one board member because he had done much and because he was knowledgeable about the community; a lawyer from my board because he had showed interest; and several others. For the meeting I also asked a legal-aid assistant of the nearby town to come to familiarize us with his experience. I intended only for him to give us an overall orientation and to answer questions. After this, we would, I figured, kiss him goodbye and go on our own.

I introduced the speaker and others present introduced themselves. I tried to make it free and easy. I then turned over the meeting to the legal-aid assistant. I went to get Cokes for everyone and in general stayed far in the background during the meeting. After the legal-aid assistant had spoken briefly, the meeting participants asked questions. They asked about the cost of the undertaking (mostly), the kind of cases such an agency could handle, involvement with local poverty programs, how the board was set up, difficulties they had experienced with the bar, what the men thought our next step should be, and how they had made use of voluntary personnel.

At about this time I also appealed to the lawyer for his assistance. The man is a rather inactive member of my board, but the proud possessor of a high reputation and considerable wealth as well as being a participant in community government and an extremely influential member of the Bar. Who can go against such a man? It is simply not to his advantage to do so. I approached him in the vein of "Of course this is something you are interested in." I asked him to arrange a meeting between the Bar and the interested community people from the meeting. In view of the general reaction at the meeting, he could hardly refuse.

That's pretty much how I work. I try to involve people. I listen to what they tell me at the grass-roots level. I try to get their support. But I don't go for demonstrations. No sense in stirring up hostilities if it doesn't get you the program you want.

Tomorrow, we have a second meeting of the group representing both cities. The lawyer from my board didn't get too much resistance from the Bar. In fact, several attorneys from the Bar Association have agreed to submit plans at tomorrow's meeting. I'll take all the suggestions that come up, take into account the objections and feelings about each, and redefine a plan of action. I'll help the minister sell it to his board. They will have to provide us with the local share of matching funds. For someone who doesn't like to go through channels, I certainly am taking a long time to get this thing set up.

If I had it to do over again, I would have bulldozed my way through. I would have written the grant myself, gotten a few to buy it, and sent it off to OEO. More specifically, I would have gone through the Mayor instead of through the lawyer on the board. The Mayor wants to run for governor and can't stand bad publicity. He knows that I will give it to him if he does not cooperate. Cooperation of the Mayor would have prevented a power play on the part of the bar. If the legal-aid agency we created had flaws in it, we would simply have taken the bugs out in the second year. Ramming it through would have taken less time and would have been successful because the opposition had not yet hardened.

* * * *

CO-16   YOU STAND UP AND THEY AIN'T GONNA KNOCK ME DOWN

You cats listen close, and I'll tell it to you like it is. You ask me to come down here and get you organized, but you show up with nine scared people in a room. I been in this town twice before, and been arrested twice. I'll be in jail before I get out of town again. Ain't never been one of you raised a ruckus about it. The police could stomp me and lay my brains on the dirt in niggerville and ain't none of you would do a thing.

But when the pigs messed with me in _____, niggers got themselves up and tore up the town. They let me go, cause the people told 'em to. They wasn't gonna mess with all them niggers.

Now this is the last time I'm gonna come here to get thrown in jail or to get messed up. Next time you invite me, you forget about your nine people. You get three, four hundred to meet me at the bus depot. You tell the pigs I'm comin' and that you invited me. *You* stand up, and they ain't gonna knock *me* down. *You* stand up and they ain't gonna knock *you* down neither.

Lots easier to push a man over if he's shufflin' or bowin' low, than if he's standin' tall.

* * * *

CO-17   COOL THE COPS

Police Overreact

Our big break came when the police attacked the Free Clinic on Howell Street. Like most incidents between the police and the community, it was an irrational one. According to reports, at about 11 a.m.

officers in a patrol car had flashed a driver they suspected of being drunk to pull up to the curb. The driver did so, was ordered out of the car, and was given a "highway test" for inebriation.

Howell Street is in the ghetto. The driver was black and the two officers in the patrol car were white. Howell Street is where 15 boys were arrested last spring for playing softball and ostensibly blocking traffic. The neighborhood was alert to an incident involving the police. A crowd quickly gathered. The drunk, finding himself with an audience and with some people in the crowd egging him on, became abusive. An officer pinned his arms back, handcuffed him, and began pulling him towards the patrol car. Onlookers called the officers names and yelled to let the "brother" go.

Someone in the back of the crowd, probably a teen-ager, threw a pop bottle at the officers. One of the policemen called for help, and within minutes the street was cordoned off by six other patrol cars. The show of force enraged the crowd. It was an awful lot like the incident that triggered the riots in Watts back in 1965, and a lot like countless other incidents since then. Shouts of "pigs" and four-letter obscenities were hurled at the policemen. Perhaps fearing the outbreak of a riot, or in order to retaliate or simply to force the crowd to disperse, the police threw tear-gas canisters into the crowd. There had been no warning, no use of a bull horn. Several of the gas victims were brought into the free clinic just up the block.

The clinic is an experiment in self-help. It was organized by a black doctor with community residents, but is staffed by volunteer physicians, medical students, and nurses of all races. The majority happen to be white. By about 11:30 there was a great deal of confusion. More police cars arrived at the scene. The gas fumes, the choking, the stumbling crowd, people yelling and crying—it must have been quite a scene. Two physicians and a nurse, all of them white, stepped out of the clinic onto the street to help other victims of the gassing. One of the physicians asked the police to stop using gas, at least near the clinic. "You nigger-loving sonofabitch," the officer replied, shoving him down and throwing a tear-gas canister directly at the doctor on the ground.

Two other officers then picked him up, threw him through the open doors of the clinic, lobbed in two more canisters, and then closed and barricaded the doors behind them. No one could get out.

The policemen had miscalculated. Eleven witnesses signed dispositions describing the incident. The physician who had been attacked is an extremely prominent surgeon in this town, active in the AMA and a number of medical societies and prominent in civic affairs. Three other prominent physicians were at the clinic that morning as well. All suffered temporary debilitating effects from the gas. One of the patients, blinded by the gas, had fallen down the stairs and had to be hospitalized with skull fractures. A white news photographer, trying to record the incident, had his camera smashed and was clubbed by three policemen.

The press picked it up, and the Police Commissioner's "love-in" was over. We moved in with our demands at that moment. Luckily, we were ready, although the turn of events moved us faster than we had anticipated. But I'm ahead of myself. Let me tell you how the whole operation began.

White Racism: The Basic Issue

I was hired by the Polish archdiocese last year to coordinate an effort aimed at "white racism" in our community. The Kerner Commission had made white racism the target. The black community was not letting us forget it. James Foreman's demands in the "Black Manifesto" had set the issue square in the laps of the churches. It was issued, after all, at a meeting funded by the Interreligious Conference for Community Organization.

Here in the Polish community you get a lot of denial. Poles aren't exactly noted for their liberal voting records. They are subject to a good bit of discrimination themselves, and tend to look down on others when they can. I know this is a broad sweeping generalization, but it is important to know with whom you are dealing. Anyway, you see the manifestation of racism everywhere—not just in attitudes, but also in the entire institutional fabric of our society. It is the society that generates the attitudes and society's institutions that perpetuate them.

That is why, in our early discussions with lay leaders and clergymen in the archdiocese, we decided to focus on institutional racism rather than on the attitudes of individuals. Any institution was a fair target— schools, the police, business and industry, welfare—you name it. My first task was to develop a board and to seek out appropriate issues. The board was made up of leaders of various Polish organizations and a number of prominent citizens concerned about the racism issue. At the second meeting, we named the organization the Catholic Anti-Racism Committee. It didn't take long for us to find a focus.

The First Incident on Howell Street

The police issue came alive for us within a few weeks. Conservative elements in the Polish community had been calling for more law and order. They were criticizing the police for not cracking down on "crime in the streets." The black community interpreted this as less protection for themselves and an encouragement of more police brutality. The white press played up the muggings, rapes, and holdups in the ghetto. The blame always seemed to be placed on the blacks rather than on inadequate police protection. The black press conversely played up inadequate protection and frequent issues of police brutality.

The mayor supported the police, and the City Council, which opposed the mayor on most issues, found it easy to fault the police for almost everything. To a certain extent the police were vulnerable. It would seem that positive community relations would be the policeman's greatest ally against crime. But community relations were bad all around. In the ghetto, at least, the police were suffering. In the white community they were not doing so well either. I've seen cops under pressure before, and I've seen them retreat into a defensive and dangerous military posture.

Last April, several boys, twelve blacks and three whites, were playing softball on Howell Street. A patrol car cruising in the area stopped and an officer made the boys line up along the curb. One of the boys said something wise. A crowd was gathering. The other policeman called for a wagon, and all fifteen were handcuffed and taken to the station where they were severely beaten while still cuffed. For a while, it looked as if the white boys would be spared, but when one of them spoke up on behalf of the blacks, they were hit too.

If the white boys, all of them Polish, had not been involved, it is doubtful that much would have happened. As it was, members of their parish, several of whom were on the CAR Committee, were incensed. They wanted an investigation. We pursued the incident with the State Civil Rights Commission, with the Mayor's Citizens Complaint Bureau, and with the Police Commissioner's public-relations man. We also set about getting some press, concentrating especially on the black press. We wanted blacks to get the message that our organization was concerned and acting. I have personal contacts with reporters in the black press. They interviewed and then published statements by both the white and the black boys and their parents. My name and the CAR Committee's was mentioned in many of the articles. This gave me an "in" to call a meeting of our board and to get clearance to call a meeting of the parents involved and other interested citizens. I did so, and then arranged a meeting with the Commissioner. A settlement house in the area where the incident took place assigned a worker to attend the meeting. He brought many of the black parents with him.

Three weeks after the incident and on a scheduled appointment, we met with the Police Commissioner and demanded a progress report on the investigation of the "incident." The Commissioner took out a pad and paper and asked the people to describe their complaint. These people had gone through hours of interrogation and knew that the Commissioner had the information. The 30 or 40 indignant parents and people of the neighborhood who were there let the Commissioner know how they felt. They really let loose. It was a good thing that there was a big desk between the Commissioner and the people.

Prior to the meeting with the Commissioner, I had met with my executive committee. We talked about two things: how to utilize this as an opportunity to get support for our organization in the Polish community (while engendering some support within the black community) and what we wanted from the police department. We decided to push for a police review board, more blacks on the force, redress, and redetailing of the officers involved. The first two items were priority for us. The third item was probably the most important for the parents and boys involved.

We really hadn't expected that the Commissioner would help us by acting like such an ass. Two members of my executive committee were with me. One was an important lay leader in the Archdiocese, but unknown to the Commissioner. He immediately contacted a black state senator with whom he had had previous dealings, and two members of the City Council. It's funny how things were shaping up. We were getting some informal alliances between low-income parents in the black and the Polish communities, and between some of the lay and political leadership in both (rare other than in times of national election).

Joe Garbo, the settlement-house worker, built on the excitement felt by some of the blacks there. They had created a press, they had "told the man," and they had seen him act the fool. He formed a neighborhood group, "The Howell Street Cop Watchers," to patrol the neighborhood. As summer approached, reports of alleged incidents of police brutality increased.

The Cop Watchers Make Demands

About five weeks after the beating incident, a boy was shot in a housing project. The Cop Watchers knew that they were in a reasonable position of strength. They marched downtown and met with the Police Commissioner and a representative of the mayor's office. I was there with several members of my board. We had been in communication with the neighborhood group and had agreed on some specific demands. They looked on us as supporters. We looked on them as a carrier group for our program and a link between us and the black community.

There were three demands: put more blacks on the police force so that black cops could patrol black neighborhoods, thereby reducing incidents of racially motivated police brutality; give Cop Watchers some muscle—

get a police review board; and put more cops on the street to give protection instead of riding around in their cars or giving out traffic citations.

The neighborhood people gave the Commissioner a nightstick with a sheath around it, and told him that they didn't want more cops around and that those around now should not unsheath their nightsticks until there were more blacks on the force. Then they gave him a little bag of black and white jelly beans and told him that was what the force should look like. Every once in a while in the session with the Commissioner, they threatened to open up the little bag and give him another look at what they meant. They really used ridicule to their advantage.

My board members were a little less given to frivolity than the neighborhood people, but went on record as holding the Commissioner personally responsible for any further incidents. The Commissioner promised to look into each of the demands. This time he kept his cool. This threw us off. We heard nothing from him for two weeks.

In the meantime, a black policeman who had been present at the April beatings decided to make a statement about the incident. He gave details to the black senator who in turn reported the event to us. Since nothing had happened in terms of either our three demands or our original demand (that the beating incident be investigated and the officers responsible punished), we sent another letter to the Commissioner and one to the Civil Rights Commission threatening to publish our evidence if action on our demands were not taken soon. We were certain the Commissioner would have to act soon. He did, but not the way we had expected.

The Commissioner Calls for a "Love-in"

On July 1st he took to the air and made a special plea to the people of the city. The City Council, he explained, had not seen fit to increase the Department's budget, because as everyone knew, the city was in financial difficulties. But in order for them to do their job, to protect citizens, and to enhance public safety, several new pieces of electronic equipment were absolutely essential. The equipment would make it possible to reassign more officers to street duty. He declared a one-month "love-in" between the police and the community, during which time he hoped citizens would, on their own volition, send contributions of a dime, a dollar, or more. It was a stroke of genius!

In one act he was reaching for public sympathy, rebuking the Council, and avoiding the issues for which the police were under criticism. On the other hand, if he miscalculated, there would not be too many other chances for public appeals of this sort. It looked as if he was not the ass we thought him to be. I felt I had to call a meeting of my executive committee together again. We had been reacting to events, and now the Commissioner threw something else at us. Would we do better in keeping up our attack and denouncing his "love-in" as a sham? Or would we get further by offering the carrot of citizen support as a swap for concessions from the Department?

Just before our meeting, two events took place that were to shape our deliberations and our strategy. On July 4th, in the afternoon, the police came around to the neighborhood where the incident with the boys had taken place. They were in station wagons and had big blocks of ice. Chipping some ice off at every stop, they gave it to the people. My wife and I chuckled over the fact that there just wasn't enough ice, just as there wasn't enough police service of the right kind to go around. It *was* funny. The Commissioner was trying to have a "love-in" with the people in a potential riot area to "play it cool" with some chips of ice.

Putting The Ice on The Cops

Joe Garbo called me that evening and asked me if I would come to a meeting. The people in the neighborhood had somehow gotten around to thinking of "putting the ice on the cops" on the Howell Street issue with the theme of "why ice the handcuffs?" A lot of neighborhood people were there: Cop Watchers, parents, boys who had been arrested. Someone suggested they get 1500 pounds of ice, 100 pounds for each boy arrested, and bring it down to the Commissioner's office. It was agreed. Mrs. Johnson had a little toilet that was cut in half with the sign, "For our half-assed friends." She wanted to imbed it into the ice. Other people suggested a softball or handcuffs.

By the next day, the message had changed to "Cool the Cops." It was a hot day, and the ice melted considerably. On the way downtown, the piano skid that they were using broke and the group decided to leave the ice on the steps of the closest police precinct. My newspaper friends were there, and the TV cameras were on hand. It was good copy. Mrs. Johnson, who had earlier received some notoriety at a welfare rights sit-in, was the spokesman for the Cop Watchers. She said she wanted to love the cops, but it was hard to feel much love for someone who beat up your kids. She demanded to know why there had been no investigation of the incident, or, for that matter, of the shooting.

I had to hand it to Joe. Through the whole bit with the nightstick, and now with the 1500 pounds of ice, he was using ridicule, almost in taking the police position, but against them. He was mobilizing greater anger, really keeping the neighborhood cool like the cops never could, and building an organization.

The CAR Committee Investigates

The second event that took place was in the Polish community. A young Polish policeman, a nephew of one of my board members, told his uncle about how distressed he was over the racial tensions, the bad name the police were getting, and so on. He said he had become a police officer because he liked people and wanted to help them. His uncle brought him to the executive committee meeting. "I've always wanted to be a policeman," he told us. "Somebody's got to do something. You can't live without laws. I like kids, I'm interested in PAL—helps keep kids off the streets and out of trouble. Being a cop is like being a social worker, lawyer, arbitrator, marriage counselor, and psychologist."

I sensed considerable sympathy for him at the meeting. A lot of people in the community had kids or relatives on the force. The Polish community is certainly not antipolice. They want more, not less, police authority. If given the vote, most would allocate more power to the police. In this group, however, we were concerned with institutional racism. "What about racial tensions?" my chairman asked. "What about police brutality?"

"Look, cops are scared," the officer replied. "You step out of your car to question someone or to make an arrest, and a crowd gathers around. They call you 'pigs,' might start throwing rocks. You can get knifed in an alley."

His testimony provoked a lively discussion. We decided on two things: to set up a subcommittee to investigate police attitudes and overt expressions of racism, and while investigating, to continue support for the black group in the neighborhood. We would not push for any new programs or reforms until we got a report from our committee. Father Zaminsky was appointed chairman. The group was given two weeks. We wanted to take some action before the end of the "love-in."

I thought the committee did a remarkable job. In the two weeks, members interviewed about 20 to 25 local area policemen, a member of the police-community relations staff, people from the mayor's office, a well-known criminologist at the University, and a great number of people in the black and Polish neighborhoods. The criminologist, a resident in this part of the city, volunteered to write the subcommittee's report. Committee members decided to leave out items that might be inflammatory.

For example, no specific incidents of police brutality were reported on, although dozens of really hairy situations were uncovered. Last year, for example, there were 11,372 reported cases of physical altercations between policemen and citizens. One out of every four policemen on the force was involved (consider that half the force is rarely on the street). Of the 1039 citizens injured by policemen, 511 were Negro, 211 were Spanish Americans, 208 were Caucasian, 6 were Oriental, and 3 were Indians. Six hundred and twenty-eight suffered face, scalp, head, nose, eye, and jaw injuries. Of the 489 policemen injured by citizens, 323 suffered hand, knuckle, and finger injuries. Arrested citizens rarely bring charges. They may be highly vulnerable to blackmail, and often agree to keep quiet in return for a lesser charge on the books. It is the citizen's word, with few if any witnesses, against the arresting officer's. In this state, the law makes it very difficult to sue (and collect) from a public official.

The subcommittee's report included some very useful information. It put things into a perspective so that our board could begin to devise action strategies. The breather was helpful to me too. The trouble with community organizing is that you often have to shoot from the hip. You don't have enough time to think through what you are doing, to pick your target, or to take careful aim. Here is a copy of the report. It will help to explain why we moved the way we did.

CATHOLIC ANTI-RACISM COMMITTEE
Report of The Special Subcommittee
On Police—Community Relations

There are a number of reasons why policemen abuse their authority, behave impulsively in certain situations, or engage in purposefully hostile activity against certain populations.

These reasons may be described as follows:

1. *Hostile Attitudes Towards the Community.* Policemen may be hostile towards residents of the ghetto or other groups in the society for a variety of individual or collective reasons. There is no question that such hostility exists. The issue is how much; how much may be expected under which circumstances to erupt into violent or brutal behavior.

   Race and class prejudice contribute to this hostility. The vast majority of the city's policemen are white. They come from lower middle class and working class backgrounds. They and their families have struggled hard to achieve a certain class status. They are fiercely middle class in their orientations, are protectful of the accompanying values. They may feel strongly about individuals denigrating those values.

   A rigorous screening process during recruitment and training of new officers should presumably bar undesirable candidates from becoming policemen. This process does bar the psychotic and for the most part the functionally prejudiced policeman. . . . the man who believes that Negroes are inferior beings and that it is the policeman's job to "keep them in their place."

Indeed, many policemen, on entering or applying to the force, express the desire to be of service to the community. Conventional prejudice, however, is not barred. The city's policemen, after all, are products of the city's high schools, community colleges, and universities. In situations in which the police may not be certain of themselves, of their social status, or even of their public support, they may shore up their own images by speaking in derogatory terms of others. Abusive speech may culminate in abusive behavior.

A white policeman who wants to get along with his colleagues may not risk objecting to injections of race in "shop talk." Policemen may have certain attitudes they bring with them to the force. While on it, they develop a common perspective. Perspective arises out of facing common problems. When such problems include threats of violence to themselves, threats to their authority as representatives of middle-class values, they may react with fear and hostility.

2. *Lack of External Controls.* Public opinion, when combined with political clout, can both sanction and control police activity. The ghetto lacks sufficient political power to threaten party politicians. It has few friends at court. Black residents of the ghetto have little of what it takes in money, business and professional leadership, or even numerical strength to influence the city power structure.

The city's opinion makers—the white press, radio, and T.V.—show only enough of the ghetto to let the outside world know how bad it is inside. The Negro is stereotyped as shiftless, criminal, prone-to-violence. While the Negro press gives continued reportage of police brutality, there is no reason for the police to fear that harsh treatment of Negroes will bring opprobrium from the white press.

Fragmentation within the black community makes it ineffective in defending itself against attack by the police, the power structure, or the press. Frequently, the threat of counter violence against the police and against what may be perceived as "white racist" institutions, is the only tool readily available to the ghetto. Its actual or threatened use increases the public image of the black community as a dangerous "jungle." Police may consciously or unconsciously react to such threat.

There is in this community no impartial police review or police advisory board which might serve to balance the power between the police and the community. The Police Patrolmen's Association and other police fraternal groups have successfully campaigned against the establishment of any such citizen's group.

3. *Inappropriate Conceptions.* Policemen may have false notions of the effect of their behavior, of the reasons for social problems, of the real motivations, attitudes and aspirations of the populations they are charged to protect and to control.

Unaware of the factors which have shaped the lives of American Negroes and the patterns of the black community, white policemen may act only on the basis of the information they have—the crime rate, rate of illegitimacy, overt behavior of Negroes in the street, press statements of black militants, etc. It is surprisingly easy to see only surface behavior, to see only what one is prepared to see.

4. *Intergroup Tensions.* Police are a distinct minority within the ghetto itself. They are highly visible not only for what they are but for what they represent—an exploitative and unresponsive white society. The patrolman never strolls through the ghetto. He always rides in a closed automobile and with a partner. He is not known by name, and certainly not by personality.

Policemen and members of the community are remote from one another. The police officer can be expected to suffer strain under such circumstances. Fear and hostility exist on both sides: the one representing what it perceives to be legitimate authority; the other frequently perceiving this authority to be misused at the very least, or illegitimate, erratic, and oppressive, at the worst.

5. *Inappropriate Functions.* The public image of the police is further compromised by the variety of functions assigned them. Rather than their spending the majority of their time fighting crime and delinquency, their actual work week is given to extraneous and un-rewarding assignments.

Paperwork could more easily be automated or delegated to non-police personnel. Court appearances on their own time make officers reluctant to arrest and charge most offenders. It is frequently more "efficient" to mete out punishment on the street or in the confines of the patrol car. Overemphasis on prostitution and nar-cotics use, neither of which ought properly be called a crime, puts the average officer in a position where he is called upon to be judge and jury. There are obviously more situations in which he could make an arrest than he would ever have the time to. On what basis does he make his decision?

Public praise for public service is rarely heard. The news media do not print stories about quick rescues on the expressways, about the sensitive handling of a confused senior citizen, about the expert first aid given a school boy, or the effective counselling of a poten-tial suicide. Perhaps the most frequent contact with the citizenry is in the act of giving out traffic or parking citations, neither of which are truly police functions, and both of which are bound to engender public resentment.

THERE CAN BE NO EFFECTIVE REDUCTION OF INCIDENTS OF POLICE AND COMMUNITY CLASHES UNLESS THESE IS-SUES ARE ADDRESSED OPENLY AND HONESTLY. THERE IS LITTLE ENOUGH TIME LEFT TO ACT.

At about the same time as the subcommittee was writing its report, the second incident on Howell Street occurred. This time the white press played up the gassing incident big. The "love-in" was for all intents and purposes off. The Commissioner took to the air and promised a full investigation of the affair, although he made the point that officers are frequently subject to such abuse and hostility by crowds, and that under pressure they may make bad judgments. That wasn't the issue, however. Provoked as they may have been initially, in this case the police had violated every one of their own procedures for crowd control. How were the police to be controlled? We sat down to map out strategy.

6

Organizing at the Neighborhood Level

The eight vignettes that comprise this chapter represent a variety of action pieces. In "Green Light, Red Light, Black and White," an organizer tries to build an organization of organizations (block clubs) in an urban area slated for Model Cities intervention. She moves from optimism to dismay. The difficulty of finding issues that will hold people together to accomplish even limited objectives are nothing as compared to planning long-range community objectives. Finally, she executes a very effective, if limited, program.

In "Organizing Block Clubs," the worker points to the same problem: the difficulty in finding an issue "broad enough to involve everyone but specific enough to get accomplished in a hurry." In the next vignette, the organizer discusses "The Limits of Neighborhood Councils" and wonders whether, beyond a certain point, their maintenance is more costly than their value. The organizer who tries "Importing Leadership" shows a marked misunderstanding of the nature of neighborhood organizations and their meaning for the membership.

"Preparing a Neighborhood for Urban Renewal" illustrates another form of neighborhood council. The community organizer was not interested in building a network of block clubs, nor in the general objectives of community development. His concern was to involve the community in whatever manner feasible to plan for a neighborhood marked for urban renewal. While the case material refers almost exclusively to his major concern—getting together an organization of "representative citizens"—representation remains limited to the end. Still, he concludes, "We accomplished what we set out to do."

The administrator of a new multiservice center still in the planning stages gives an even more graphic picture of the difficulties in developing representative groups and working with neighborhood leadership. One would hope that the process of "Building an Advisory Committee" might be accomplished more smoothly by a more competent or experienced practitioner.

The "Radical Action at the Franklin School" is not properly a case of community organization in a neighborhood. Although the action takes place at the neighborhood level, the locale and the target of intervention were chosen only because the Franklin School seemed to be the most vulnerable part of the "system"—the easiest to attack and to win a victory over. The case illustrates a number of commonly used confrontation tactics. It also illustrates an almost total lack of strategy beyond the initial selection of a target.

"Safaris into the Ghetto" represents the beginning of a conscious strategy to change a community's image of itself and its image to the outside world. Unlike the Franklin School issue, which arose out of the ideological commitments of the organizers, the social action herein described emerged accidentally (albeit with some careful guidance by a skilled settlement-house worker). It grew out of a discussion that might have led to a much more defensive posture, doing little but exacerbating the negative image of the community. Colleagues have suggested to us that this case may be offensive. We are fully aware of that. We include it because of the controversy we hope it will engender.

* * * *

CO-18   GREEN LIGHT, RED LIGHT, BLACK AND WHITE

A Neighborhood Organizes

When we first began organizing the neighborhood, there was plenty of interest. Model Cities was getting a big play in the press. Some of the neighborhood people had gotten their feet wet in the poverty program. The school issue last year really brought them out. People were used to going to meetings. People are being reached. We don't even call the neighborhoods slums anymore, just low-income neighborhoods.

Our notion was to build an organization of organizations that could successfully bid for a significant voice in the Model Cities program. At the first meeting, we had a fairly good cross-representation; some merchants, churchmen, welfare-rights mothers, and other local residents—about 50 percent white and 50 percent black. We laid the issue on the line. If we could mobilize residents around their needs and discontents, we could get our licks in on the Model Cities grant. If they were really organized, they could demand a dominant voice in the program. We were promising big, but there wasn't much time. The mayor wanted the money. He was popular in this part of town. He really did not care about citizen participation. I don't think the feds did either, but they wanted a proposal with a semblance of neighborhood involvement. It was a good meeting. Issues were laid out.

Then we called the second one to develop some organizational structure. If this group went well, we could organize several more, and then our organization of organizations. Well, only 18 people came. There were 82 at the first meeting. And only 2 of this group were white. By the third meeting there were about 30 people. Up again, but they were all black.

It was impossible to focus on organization. We (the staff) didn't want an all-black group. And the people at the third meeting were so full of issues, we couldn't decide where to start first. Staff members were playing a passive role, partly because of our conviction that leadership had to come from the group and partly because we really were not sure how to move. There were lots of issues: high prices and poor-quality food at the local superette, rat- and roach-infested housing, local control of the school, fights between white and black teen-agers, and the need for a traffic light across Bearsley Street. One of the men present said he knew someone on the City Council, and he was sure he could get the traffic light.

It's like this. In organizing you have to have a concrete issue. You can't go to a community and ask them what they want or to write up a plan. The traffic light seemed like a good place to start. I volunteered to work with him on a strategy. We got a few others to volunteer, and we set another night for the traffic-light committee to meet.

At the next meeting, the idea of petitions came up. Someone suggested that seeing the city councilman wouldn't be as useful as going to the traffic commissioner. After some discussion, the group decided to have a trial run with the councilman, and perhaps get some ideas for further strategy from him. I was very firm on two things: I didn't think we should go to see him unless we were clear on what we were going for and how we would talk to him (I suggested role playing the scene), and I felt that we should do all we could to include some white people on the committee. The group agreed to both. Mrs. Barker said she was pretty sure she could get some of the white members of the welfare-rights group to join us at the next meeting.

They did. We role played. The man who knew the councilman made the appointment. The group went downtown. The councilman was very helpful. He suggested petitions, a chart of traffic flow, and the like. He also suggested direct contact with the mayor, who, after all, was interested in the neighborhood and in its development of an organization.

The group followed his advice. They submitted a petition with over 300 names and a document complete with a traffic-flow chart and so forth. The traffic commissioner never replied. We called him several times in the next two weeks. He was always out. The members of the committee were really let down. "What's the sense of talking about Model Cities if we can't even get a traffic light?" one of the members said. She summed up everyone's feelings. A lot was riding on this issue. I suggested a symbolic demonstration.

Everyone was worried about the kids crossing Bearsley Street. Why not act as a green light and red light during peak traffic hours? We could make green and red signs and flash them manually, like traffic monitors. Someone volunteered to get a bunch of cardboard pizza trays, and we were in business. We met a few days later to color them in. We agreed that mothers would become the traffic lights.

On the morning of the demonstration, a co-worker and I arrived at the corner at 7:45. The mothers were supposed to be there at 8:00 a.m. Only Mrs. Barker showed. She had the red and green signs. Reporters were due at 8:45. We rushed from house to house. Some women hadn't found baby sitters. Others were still asleep. One said she just couldn't go outside and make a spectacle of herself. A white woman was clearly uneasy about demonstrating with black women. We asked each one if they still wanted the traffic light. The question worked. Most of the women did appear. Reporters took notes. We promised we would demonstrate again at noon and during the 5 o'clock rush hour. We would have a statement at 5:00 p.m.

At noontime, they were better organized. The morning had been a trial run. The women now knew what to do. A crowd of neighbors milled around, joking and giving encouragement. A reporter from Channel 4 news made sure the demonstration would take place again in the evening. He wanted to do a TV tape interview and to show it on the 6:30 news.

Now things were serious. The mothers selected a spokesman. We rehearsed her all afternoon. By five, the neighborhood was packed with blacks and whites. Other mothers volunteered to join the "traffic lights."

The mothers showed almost military precision. The TV cameramen and the reporter showed up. He had also arranged an interview with the Commissioner in his office that afternoon. A week later they got the traffic light.

It was what we needed. That piece of electronic machinery became the symbol of our organization. It was on view daily as a monument of organizational victory. When we next called a meeting, it was well attended. The first order of business was getting a name for the new organization—The "Red and Green Club." Of five officers, three were from our traffic-light committee: two whites and one black.

*   *   *   *

CO-19   ORGANIZING BLOCK CLUBS

In the neighborhoods I made door-to-door contacts. I let one person lead me to another. I tried to find out who the people were in the neighborhood who were interested in community programs, such as Sunday School programs. As you go along, the more people you interview, the more the same names crop up. My job was very difficult because there are few local leaders, although there were 18,000 people in the two target areas.

I first started out with the idea of organizing the whole area, and then I found out that this was ineffective. To do the job and get participation, you must do it on a small basis. You must organize block groups and then get the block groups to join together.

To organize a block club, you go out on the street and you talk to one individual on the street and you ask him who has been doing what in the neighborhood. Then he might express an interest himself. You also ask people that are standing around on the street what they want. It is important to find out if they want the street cleaned up, if they want a sewing club, and the like. Then you tell people that you talk to on the street that it is possible that other people have the same thoughts that they do about what they want and then ask them if it is possible to have a little group meeting on the block to find out how many people want the same things, and what they want. Then you get somebody working for you to develop that block. You try to get that person to have a little group meeting of her neighbors in her house. You need a person who will act as block leader right away so that she can take information from you to the people in her block. After she has had a block meeting, you try to get the five block leaders together in one group or section. I had actually selected the block leaders but I didn't think this was very good.

I had a great deal of difficulty organizing the block clubs. Some of the people were very vocal and elaborated on many things when I was in their living rooms. When I called them together to work as an advisory board on the beginning stages of a neighborhood council, I was sure that once they got together they would all want the same things and they would all talk to each other. I was shocked to find that at the first meet- when I asked one of the ladies to act as chairman, she declined and none of the other women would take a temporary chairmanship either. I don't know why but I had had every confidence that when they got to- gether they wouldn't be shy because they had talked at such length with me.

The biggest problem is finding some issue broad enough to involve everyone but specific enough to get accomplished in a hurry. But if your issues are too immediate, you defeat your purpose. Once they get re- solved, the group has no reason to keep together. I learned this lesson years earlier when I was a grad student.

I had been assigned to work with a block club. The biggest issue we could find was getting rid of the squirrels that were eating up the flowers. After a few weeks I discovered that the only reason the club had been in operation for the past two years was because several of the residents felt they owed an obligation to the director of the settlement house. They knew the director had to have field placements for students from the University, so they faked having an organization. It took me five months to convince my field instructor that the assignment made no sense.

*　　*　　*　　*

CO-20   THE LIMITS OF NEIGHBORHOOD COUNCILS

Let's face it. Neighborhood Councils have very limited uses. We spend a lot of time developing them. Day and night, it sometimes feels like. You may have to go knocking on someone's door five or six times before she even begins to talk to you. I've worked so hard on this one, I rarely have the time or the energy to sit down and think about what I am doing.

People don't develop lasting commitments to a council. Sure, you can get a street light, better garbage pickup, and a few other things, but the issues have to be immediate. Interest wanes on long-term items. The real advantage of the neighborhood council is that it helps you spot and then develop leadership so that the next time around, when a new issue arises, you can just reactivate the network of relationships and build on the skills and experiences from the last round.

When we first started, for example, our people had no idea of some of their rights, or that they could pressure the city to condemn a landlord's property. After a whole series of other steps, they attended a public meeting of the housing commission. Ten people—we spotted them around the audience—were coached. They asked the right questions and pressed the right points. It was obvious that they were developing a mood of approval in the crowd. The commissioners had no idea these people had been coached. We carried the day.

It is best to work this way, quietly and unobtrusively. If you go after publicity and dramatic victories, they'll break you eventually. You can't protect your people from reprisals. All you can do is help them learn to do what they want to on their own behalf. Beyond a certain point, however, keeping a council going requires more energy than it's worth. You reach a point of diminishing returns. You have to know when to quit.

* * * *

CO-21 IMPORTING LEADERSHIP

We had four block clubs already organized in the neighborhood. They had been going strong for about a year and a half. The problem was, while they could do lots in terms of their own self-help activities, most of the rest of the neighborhood was still a mess. What is more, four block clubs were hardly strong enough to engage in any meaningful social action. We wanted to expand the number to 26.

As you can imagine, getting a good block club off the ground takes a lot of energy and a lot of staff time. We were really short-staffed. So I hit on the idea of importing leadership from the block clubs that were going strong, and having experienced leaders start new clubs on adjacent streets.

I asked Mrs. Erlich of the San Vicente club to help me organize Simpson Avenue. I don't think she was particularly enthusiastic, but I had known Mrs. Erlich for some time and we had a good relationship. She is quite a dynamic woman. She is well respected on San Vicente and is responsible for much of that club's dynamism. Since her name has appeared in the press and since she has been active in local organizations, she is fairly well known in the entire neighborhood. I reasoned that her stature and her experience would be invaluable in starting the Simpson club.

As I said, Mrs. Erlich was a bit reluctant, because she said she had too many things going already, but she agreed to come to an organizing meeting. I got ten other people together from the block on the basis of some contacts I had made earlier. One person led me to another, and so forth. I thought we could start with 10 families and Mrs. Erlich, and then expand further.

I met with the group at its first meeting, and explained what kinds of things block clubs could do. Mrs. Erlich was very enthusiastic in describing the work of her block club. I thought she was making too much of an emphasis on the San Vicente club as being her club, and made a mental note to discuss it with her later.

Things were kind of hectic around the agency during the next two weeks, and I was unable to continue meeting with the Simpson club. However, Mrs. Erlich went to the second meeting and was elected secretary. The club now had officers and I felt sure that with Mrs. Erlich there it would develop as dynamically as had the San Vicente club.

You can imagine how surprised I was when Mrs. Erlich called me after the fourth meeting to tell me the group had decided to disband. The members had decided there was no purpose to organizing a block club. "They just didn't see anything in it," Mrs. Erlich told me. "People have got to want to improve themselves if an organization like this is to be successful."

* * * *

CO-22 PREPARING A NEIGHBORHOOD FOR URBAN RENEWAL

As a community-organization specialist for a city-planning commission, I perform a liaison function between the commission and citizen groups. My job is to organize any section of town that the city intends to designate an urban-renewal area. I usually launch an area community council that can make recommendations to the city. My task is to put the neighborhood in a position where it could deal with the city. The city pays my salary but never interferes.

The last area that I worked in was New Davis, setting up a community council. The project began in April of 1968 with a declaration of intention by the city to consider the New Davis area as an area with sufficient physical and social problems to warrant a study for a possible urban-renewal program.

I had to evaluate the purpose of the city in going into New Davis, what my role would be, and what my purposes would be. The city had by this time recognized the intensive problems in the ghetto area of New Davis and also the need to relate to the local citizens there.

I found that if I wanted to go to New Davis as an entry point for the city, I would have to go through the overall area first. The black community is a maze of power conflicts, various levels of group pressures, and a variety of other conflicts—for example, black-white feelings, working class versus professional, political black versus anti-City Hall black, and the like.

I realized that I had to thread my way step by step so that at each point or layer I would be able to involve key individuals and groups and gain sanction of the people on that particular level.

The first step was a direct move into the central political group consisting of the New Davis YMCA crowd and the New Davis businessmen's luncheon and professional group. These two groups were centered around the New Davis YMCA. This group already had its system in terms of giving everyone a chance to be an officer, to be visible. The white community knew them and this was the sanctioned group that could deal with the white community on the governmental level. I met with both groups and they arranged for a series of meetings at which the city proposal could be discussed. This immediately brought the proposed study into the open, and for a month there were a series of meetings. Several things were gained by this. I became visible. People knew that I was willing to come and explain and interpret what was going on.

Notice, I was Jewish, I was white, and I was middle class; I had all of these strikes against me. But notice what I was doing: I was preparing the way for the next level, to get to the proposed renewal area and talk to the people there directly.

I met with a minister's group, some black professionals, and some homeowners. These were all a series of meetings, and by this time (5 or 6 weeks), people were getting to know me. There was no formal group, but people in the target area were beginning to receive signals about the city's intention to study this area. I did not know who they were, but they began to react to the rumors, and at one of the meetings we were invaded by a group of 30 or 40 of the homeowners who had heard about the proposal. They wanted to know what was going on and why we were not dealing with them.

I welcomed them into the meeting and told them I was a guest and was prepared to talk to anyone without regard to his group affiliations. From this point on the shift began from the YMCA and other power groups to the local people. I asked them to bring in a group of people to talk about what could be done to improve their target area.

There was a great deal of hostility and questioning that evening, and I accepted it and explained that I understood it, and that I was working my way toward them and that their coming tonight helped me. I also pointed out that there were no blueprints from the city. Just before the meeting ended a group of ministers agreed to call a meeting in the target area.

At the same time, I began to go into the area openly and visit white merchants, knowing that the merchants are natural "gossip centers." For instance, I went into a local pharmacist, knowing that he would discuss what I said with every other Jewish merchant in the area. He also spoke to some of the key black families in the area. So by the end of the week I became visible on a local level. If I had gone directly to the area, I would have found closed doors. But by going to the gatekeepers, I had been able to prepare the way. At all times I was telling them, "I would like to talk."

I insisted that the ministers make all the arrangements for the meeting. I also made it very clear that I would talk with any responsible group. In addition, I insisted that there be both afternoon and evening meetings.

For the next two months, there were about a dozen meetings in the churches and in the hospital. At these meetings, I had the opportunity to present the city's proposal and tell them that there was no blueprint. I emphasized that it should be a process of working together. Local leadership now began moving ahead—leadership that had been there, for example, two or three young housewives. In the black community, the women are generally somewhat well organized. One became chairman of the New Davis study committee. Women were also the temporary officers.

I now had triggered the local community to organize themselves. We defined the study, our roles, and the time schedule. They knew that their responsibility would be to interpret to the neighborhood what the project could do and to bring to the planning commission what the neighborhood's ideas were. I had to provide support in terms of procedures, how to use community resources, and agendas. They were in business.

We worked all summer from July to October. There were monthly mass meetings of 75 to 400 people. An executive committee was set up and by the end of November the temporary group wanted a more permanent setup with officers and responsibilities established. The New Davis community council came into existence. I now had a visible group with an identity and sense of purpose—it was trained leadership of a fairly sophisticated nature.

The next step was to have physical planners come in to make traffic and resource studies. But on the other hand, I told the community people that they had a special competency that we did not have and that their own knowledge of the neighborhood was vital. Workshops were organized around community needs: education, recreation, health, welfare, commerce and industry, community services, and institutional services. A chairman was set up for each, and each chairman brought in a different group of people. They were responsible for recruiting, getting a meeting place, chairing the meeting, and taking notes. I was trying to get them to set up a group with leadership that could bargain with the city. All this time they were suspicious of the city, but realized that it was better to be on the inside in dealing with the city. They were also impatient to become better organized so that they could "stand up" to the city (they were telling this to a city official).

A leadership group of about 20 people emerged and all either worked or lived in the area—homeowners, a few tenants, and some white businessmen. They also conducted their own questionnaire with my assistance, and a team of men and women canvassed the area. We also set up a series of walking tours for the city planners, and this gave them a feeling of confidence in the concern of the commission. Committee chairmen met and evaluated workshops and then brought the results back to the community. People felt that this was a down-to-earth project, and many identified with it.

We then brought the results of our study made by physical planners and this showed that the group had matured. The meetings became a dialogue in which mutual information was shared. At the end of one and a half years, we wrote a final report that was reviewed with the leadership and for the most part, was found acceptable. We interpreted to them the fact that the area had such basic problems that, until the city was ready to commit to an all-out redevelopment program, we would not be involved in any further recommendations.

About three months ago the Mayor announced the policy of committing large quantities of money to ghetto areas. New Davis was one of the areas selected.

The leaders came to a meeting and accepted the proposal from the city.

Along the way, there were some problems that we had to surmount. In the early stages, I was approached by some of the black middle-class real-estate people who thought that this was a chance to clean up the area and clear out the welfare families. And by interpreting to them what we wanted to do and by involving them, they were, a year later, the greatest proponents for getting special housing for the "poor families in our midst." The change came as they learned the facts about the problem.

The group that finally emerged as leaders—the black homeowners, a few tenants, and a few white businessmen—rejected completely the middle-class black political group and the white industrial factory owners, and chose to work through one or two representatives of the white businessmen. This is a problem I was never able to solve even though the committee remained an open-ended structure. The leadership kept representation limited. They were no longer suspicious of the city, but rather of certain members of their own community taking over.

In summary, I had to bring a problem to the community and at the same time develop a group. One of the dangers was that I would never get beyond the YMCA group. However, there would be no basic changes in the way I would operate if I were to do it again. We accomplished what we set out to do; to study the community, to involve the community, and to develop leadership.

*   *   *   *

CO-23   BUILDING AN ADVISORY COMMITTEE

I was a supervisor in the City Welfare Department before going on loan to the mayor's Human Resources Commission. My job was to set up a multiservice center in a mixed middle-income, working class area. In trying to organize local people into an advisory council, I found out that local leadership is jealous and self-serving. Grass-roots representation is hard to locate and harder still to get moving.

I had a conference with the Commission's program director in his office. I was to set up a community center that would promote a supermarket of social services. (There had been much beating of the chest by politicians about the program.) I was expected to more thoroughly acquaint the people with the available services. In that conference the program director gave me the impression that the local block club, church groups, and the like were grass roots in nature. He gave me the names of two people whom he thought to be powerful community leaders and springboards to effective action in the community. I was to organize an area advisory committee. He said little else. The conference was in fact very brief.

One other man, several years my junior, was also transferred from the Welfare Department to be my assistant in the area. We sent letters to all the groups in the area stating what we were in the process of planning for a multiservice center. We received many invitations to speak that we accepted as rapidly as we could. I thought that that was the best means available to familiarize the community with the services that would be offered through the center.

We had no physical facilities for the center. The people of the community were theoretically supposed to, and I believe, expected to, have a hand in selection of the building. I soon realized, however, that this process would take too long. My assistant and I personally combed the area by car in search of a building that would be near the center of the target area, easily accessible by public transportation, and large enough to house the proposed services. After weeks of frustration, I finally chose one that is poorly located but of adequate size. We planned several storefront operations to correct the poor location of this building.

Shortly after the acquisition of the physical facility, I sent a letter to the block clubs in the area inviting them to attend a public planning meeting. During these weeks I also talked with the two people suggested by the Commission's program director: Mrs. Clark and Mrs. Coombs. Mrs. Clark assured me numerous times that she did not seek an official leadership position in the area advisory committee. She said she already had enough to do as president of the neighborhood association of block clubs. With this in mind and in an effort to convince the community that I was willing to place the leadership in their hands, I named Mrs. Clark as the temporary chairman for the meeting. As the meeting got underway, rather than talk about substantive issues as I had anticipated, she led the discussion to structure and organization. Mrs. Clark was nominated from the floor for the position of chairman of a "steering committee." She was quickly elected by a fairly large majority. A Mr. Wolfson and several other community people also received nominations. I sat on the stage dumbfounded and not sure of what to do as the events quickly followed one another. Later in that meeting several members of churches complained that the procedures used by Mrs. Clark were poor and unfair. I believe that Mr. Wolfson led in voicing these complaints.

Mrs. Clark's tactics in the meeting produced many ill feelings and represented a step backward for the Commission. Mrs. Coombs confided in me after the meeting that she felt betrayed by her friend Mrs. Clark. She said, however, that she had anticipated something of this sort. She maintained her relationship with Mrs. Clark and with the Commission, and was, in fact, elected vice chairman of the steering committee. At the meeting and after it I think that animosity toward Mrs. Clark oozed from many in the community. I felt that this animosity probably spread to me and the Commission because of my selection of her as meeting chairman. My presence on stage coupled with inactivity in the case of Mrs. Clark's tactics gave the impression to everyone in the meeting that we backed Mrs. Clark.

In the light of both this situation and my proven unfamiliarity with its petty politics and the like, I decided to back off for some time. In the one month before the next planned meeting of the steering committee, my assistant and I did accept speaking engagements from the block clubs, churches, and so on. We spoke at least once a day and sometimes as often as four or five times a day. There was nothing else we could do.

We tried to disseminate accurate information about the program and sought to explore program possibilities with the area's residents.

In the week after that first meeting I also attempted to disassociate myself from Mrs. Clark in the eyes of the community. I wanted to make it clear that she was officially supported only by the organization of block clubs of which she was president. As chairman of a steering committee for the advisory committee for the center, she was to call meetings, nothing more. I did retain some contact with Mrs. Clark. More specifically, I accepted an invitation to speak at a meeting of her block club organization. At one point she also had me over for lunch. It became evident that she was not a very smooth operator and that she rather openly sought patronage. She wanted a staff position in the in-service training program of the new center. Mrs. Coombs and others in the community openly sought jobs.

A few days before the scheduled second meeting of the steering committee I met Mr. Wolfson on the street, totally by chance. I suggested that he might come to the scheduled meeting (simply because I sought as much community participation as possible). Mrs. Clark came late for the meeting. Early in the meeting, Mr. Wolfson asked me, from the floor, whether it was legally possible for the steering committee to transform itself into the advisory committee. I replied from my position in the audience that this was indeed possible. The idea, of course, appealed to all of those on the steering committee and Mr. Wolfson's motion quickly carried. Correct procedure dictated that a new chairman and so on should be elected. Mr. Wolfson was immediately nominated and elected to the position of chairman.

I learned later that Mr. Wolfson and Mrs. Clark were the leaders of rival factions in the block-club association. There was considerable personal rivalry between them as well. From the discussions after the meeting and from observations during the meeting, it also became evident that the community representatives on the steering committee were by and large rather middle class. Mrs. Clark, for example, had a good home, as did many others. I also realized that these people were very skillful in the use of parliamentary procedure.

In the regular monthly meeting of the advisory committee that followed, I attempted not to get too involved. I did not want to take sides. During the meetings of the advisory committee I sat in the audience and participated only to give official views on issues that arose. In a way, I played the role of a technical guest. During these months my administrative tasks multiplied immensely because of the assignment of regular civil-service personnel to the Center.

During these first months of operation, each community contact pressed home more firmly to me the realization that the block clubs were not as potent as my superiors had led me to believe. My feeling that the advisory committee did not reach the man in the street also grew. A month or two after Mr. Wolfson was elected, I explained to him in detail what I thought about lack of representation in the advisory committee. He concurred.

On my own initiative, I talked with school community agents in the area in an attempt to obtain a sampling of ADC and welfare recipients. The school community agents contacted a sampling of welfare recipients and invited them to participate in the advisory-committee meetings. Twenty-one in all were contacted. Of these, only eight showed up at any of the meetings. All of them were very ill at ease. Four agreed to serve on the advisory committee. Only two ever came to later meetings. Only one ever opened his mouth. Inadequate representation on the advisory committee of the people we are supposed to be serving still stands as my major problem.

A few months after his election, it became evident that Mr. Wolfson had personality problems: at a minimum, it was evident that his motivations for assuming the chairmanship were something less than laudable. For example, after several meetings he began boasting of the fact that he was a public servant through his role and also boasting of the fact that his outside work yielded him an income of $12,000 per year. He also began making decisions with the consent of the advisory committee.

Mr. Wolfson came up for reelection in June of this year. I did nothing to influence the course of the election. I felt that he was OK and that his opponent was not too strong. I also felt that although Mr. Wolfson and his opponent, Mrs. Downs, were about equally qualified, Mr. Wolfson was more thoroughly versed in the matters of the community.

As it turned out, Mrs. Downs received a very substantial vote but did not win. Mr. Wolfson grew more militant almost immediately after he was reelected. At the next meeting he took the occasion to demand undefined powers for himself. He threatened to resign if he did not receive them. No one wanted him to resign.

Last week he came to the Center at about lunchtime with two people who needed service. Later he complained that the people had had to wait 45 minutes before they received attention. He failed to mention that one woman got the job she sought and that the other woman was unqualified for the specific job she sought. In private, Mr. Wolfson is still very agreeable. However, in public meetings he is a heller. He is not interested in solutions; he wants only to select issues and beat the desk with them.

A few days ago, Mr. Wolfson proposed to me that the community aides be rotated in order to further personal and professional roles. I pointed out to him that the aim of the Commission was public service and not professional growth of personnel. He persisted with a fury that has become characteristic of him. I finally suggested to him that if he wanted to pursue the matter further he should take it directly to the central office.

To my frustration, I find that as an administrator for the Commission I am dealing primarily with the area advisory committee and with the Commission personnel. I feel that I should be working personally (and through my staff) more directly with the grass roots of the area. However, I do not have enough people. The VISTA volunteers that we are scheduled to get this year may be a shot in the arm. They will be living in the area and are sufficiently idealistic to get a following. If these volunteers are not successful in engaging the grass roots, I have contemplated propagandizing every fifth person in the target area to make them aware that there is an advisory committee of which they can become a part. I have also contemplated trying to get key contact people on each block.

*   *   *   *

CO-24   RADICAL ACTION AT THE FRANKLIN SCHOOL[1]

In November, the executive secretary of the Chester NAACP conferred with several Swarthmore student leaders about what steps could be taken to put life into the Chester civil rights movement. The CFFN[2] existed as a skeleton committee and it was decided to attack a specific school about which Chester residents in the area were very concerned. A letter was sent to the school board demanding that it be replaced by a new school and that in the meantime several conditions that were unsanitary and hampered good education be corrected. A boycott of the schools was called immediately and was about 60 percent effective, and picketing was started.

The area was extensively leafleted and the leafleters talked to as many residents as possible. The boycott and the picketing were called off after three days, since parents did not want to keep their children out of school for long. However, most said they would participate the following

---

[1] Excerpted from *Chester, Pa.: A Case Study in Community Organization* by Danny Pope, Alain Jehlen, and Evan Metcalf, with Cathy Wilkerson (then members of the Swarthmore SDS) and distributed by Students for a Democratic Society, 119 5th Avenue, New York, New York.

[2] Committee for Freedom Now, a loosely-knit organization of civil rights groups.

week when they were told that the plan was to force the issue by blocking the doors of the school. After more leafleting, talking, and a successful mass meeting, about 100 people blocked the doors and many more
picketed or watched. The school was closed for the day and demonstrators marched downtown to City Hall and the School Board headquarters.

In the next two days, some 250 demonstrators were arrested for sitting
in at the City Hall and blocking doors of the school. The School Board
finally agreed to all CFFN demands. Mass meetings had gotten larger
every night, and the last one was especially successful and spirited because it included the first group of arrested demonstrators. All charges
against the demonstrators were dropped. CFFN negotiators could not
get a written agreement, and as a result the School Board later went back
on most, although not all, of its promises. No new school appears to be
in sight.

Several factors appear to have made the demonstrations successful:

1. The school is probably the worst in all of Chester.
2. The area near the school is a housing project, which is a fairly
tight-knit community.
3. The demonstrations all started at the school, which is near where
the demonstrators lived.
4. The very militant nature of the demonstrators, their radical and
very specific demands, and the confident attitude of the leafleters apparently convinced people that things were finally going to change.
5. Initial success was achieved probably because the police and the
School Board were caught by surprise. As a result, the school was closed
the first day with no attempt at arrests. Had the police arrived early
and made arrests when those blocking doors were mostly Swarthmore
students and CFFN leaders, it is possible that the additional Chester
residents would not have taken their places, although this factor may
not have been decisive.

While the demonstrators were in jail, there was a great deal of discussion. A provisional executive committee for CFFN was formed.
Several Chester residents began to take leadership roles, and many contacts were made between students and residents that were later very
valuable in organizing the first three block organizations. (The block
organizations are dealt with below.)

During Swarthmore's intersession in January, when some 20 to 30
students worked full time in Chester, a CFFN storefront office was set
up, a voter-registration campaign was conducted, and publicity for a
citywide school boycott began while a list of demands for the boycott

was discussed. The school boycott was part of the nationwide series of boycotts in February and, according to the School Board, was 40 percent effective. A great deal of the leafleting and publicity for the boycott and the preliminary mass meetings was done by block organization members; support for CFFN still came principally from high school students and residents in the vicinity of the Franklin School. The boycott was most successful at the high school and least successful at the elementary schools.

It was also at this time that the city began to harden its attitude towards CFFN, apparently finally convinced that it was not a one-shot affair. An ordinance forbidding leafleting without a permit, or leafleting anywhere except door-to-door even with a permit, which to our knowledge had never before been enforced, was used to arrest ten people distributing leaflets before the boycott. (The cases are now on appeal.) By the preparations made (chartered buses, for example) the police appeared to be ready to arrest an entire demonstration of 400 people unless it got off the street and onto the sidewalk, although previous marches in the street had been permitted. This attitude reached its peak (thus far, at any rate) during a series of demonstrations late in March. The demonstrations, organized while almost all Swarthmore students were away for spring vacation, included blocking intersections by sitting down in the street. The first night this was done, police generally ignored the demonstrators; only about six arrests were made. The next afternoon, however, the police marched up the street swinging their riot sticks; as a result of the ensuing brutalities, six demonstrators were hospitalized and several others hurt. The demonstrators were convicted on two counts without counsel and were not even aware that they were being tried. As a result, the convictions were thrown out and the demonstrators were released on bail for a third charge. For the peaceful demonstrations that followed, the city deputized not only the fire department, but also the city trash collectors. Four days after the first arrests, the CFFN leadership, including in addition to Branche, Philip Savage, Tri-State Secretary of the NAACP, and Gloria Richardson, chairman of the Cambridge Nonviolent Action Committee, decided to hold another sit-down; 113 were arrested, this time without passive resistance and without police brutality. The city again raised as many barriers to bailing the prisoners out as possible. Property equity would not be accepted after 3 p.m. on Friday, for instance. In view of this attitude on the part of the city, the tactical problem of when to use a demonstration that involves breaking the law becomes more complex. Particularly with so entrenched and unresponsive an establishment, it is important to be able to apply pressure to the power structure, and disruption is a tactically effective and relatively easy means; but on the other hand, large and fairly long jailings are financially highly burdensome, and discouraging both to the people stuck in jail for a week and for the rest of the people who don't want to go in for longer than a day or two. The problem is partly to find a safer but equally effective tactic, and partly to use the situation "educationally," to evolve a deeper commitment so that a week in jail becomes accepted as the necessary sacrifice, just as a day in jail was after Franklin School, and also to have the demonstrations point out further the nature of the power structure they are aimed against.

*   *   *   *

CO-25 SAFARIS INTO THE GHETTO

Two years ago, white safaris into the black ghetto would have been unthinkable. In fact, the whole program began because of neighborhood resentment of white intrusions into the lives of local residents. Ever since the August rebellion two years ago, white sociologists and political scientists have been coming in asking all sorts of questions. The University organized a special program for government officials and community influentials to tour through the ghetto, interviewing welfare recipients and talking to jobless men on the street corners. Faculty members sent their seminar students in to observe. I'm sure they learned a lot, biased as their insights might be, but it doesn't make someone who lives here feel much better about conditions.

White people knew only the seamy side of the area. Newspapers carried stories of muggings, prostitution, narcotics, kill-crazy militants. After what the white community called the "riot," suburbanites began arming themselves, afraid that angry, murderous blacks would make terrorist excursions into their communities. Really, the image of this community in the white world has got to be absurd. People don't know us, and they're scared. Our people are scared too.

We have a social-action committee in the settlement house. It is made up of a number of citizens active in community affairs or in business. It has never been a very militant group, and acts almost more like a local chamber of commerce. A number of members were concerned about the intrusion of white investigators. All white people seemed to see was what they wanted to see—the poverty, the squalor, the crime. At a recent meeting, Marcus Lomumbo, owner of an Afro-American crafts shop on Central Avenue, wanted to find some way of barring whites from snooping, even if it meant barring them from the neighborhood altogether. Mrs. Parsons agreed that the snoopers weren't wanted, but was concerned that if whites were afraid to come into the neighborhood, the image of the blacks would never be changed. "That's all right," replied Mr. Lomumbo, "It's about time we stop worrying about what white folks think about black folks. Let them think what they want." There was considerable sentiment to that effect in the group.

I rarely interject opinions into committee deliberations. As assistant director of the settlement, I long ago learned that what would be, would be, only on the basis of what community people wanted. I felt, though, that isolationism was not the answer to either this community's problems or to the deterioration of black and white relationships.

"I know just how everyone here feels," I interjected at one point, "but barring whites is bad for Mr. Lomumbo's business, and what's bad for neighborhood business is bad for the neighborhood." The conversation ceased. I explained. I gave the example of Chinatown in San Francisco and Greektown in our own city. People came to these places because they were exotic. They offered a taste of a different culture, new foods, new visual sensations, new products to buy. "The trouble is," I went on, "that white people have been coming into our community only to look at our troubles, not at what we have that's good, that's really us, or that we have to offer."

I must have hit a sensitive nerve, because the discussion changed markedly after that. We began listing the things in the community that people could look upon with pride: the new shops with local art in the African style like Mr. Lomumbo's; the Freedom and Liberation mural painted on brick walls on Moody Street; the Black Theater productions right here at the settlement house; the new coffee shops and soul food restaurants. The list wasn't very long. But it did make the point.

Lomumbo could see the advantages to his business of bringing tourists to the area. Jackson, who was also active in the theater group and very much interested in getting wider acceptance for black poets and playwrights, suggested tours or theater tickets. "Well, all right," agreed Lomumbo. "If white folks think we're living in a jungle, let's sell them places on safari tours."

It was said in jest, but that's how *Safari Tours, Ltd.* was born. It is now in process of becoming incorporated as a profit-making enterprise. It set out to encourage tourism to the neighborhood as a way of fostering community pride among residents, and to bring new income to the community. It currently includes guided tours to shops, historical landmarks, cultural events, theater productions, and several restaurants with specialized food. Open discussions with the actors are a highlight following each theater production. The morning and evening dailies now list restaurants and special events for the neighborhood just as they do for other parts of the city.

At first it was a little difficult to attract whites to the tours. We began with the kids in summer day camps run by settlements and private agencies in other parts of town, and then invited parents of the white children who visited to sign up for evening tours. We also approached church groups and all kinds of fraternal and civic groups in the white community. Newspaper publicity and word of mouth has been so positive that it looks as if we've not only started one viable business enterprise but stimulated a good many more. Some people are thinking of developing our own local newsletter or magazine. Who knows what they may develop into?

Organizers, Rent Strikes, and Public Housing

Since the mid-1960s, organizers have increasingly directed their attention to problems related to housing. The concern is easy to understand. Most organizing with low-income groups has been neighborhood based. Housing and neighborhood conditions are intimately interrelated. Two of the three cases included in this chapter describe organizing efforts located in public housing. In each, tenants' organizations were perceived as a means whereby specific injustices or indignities could be rectified, and whereby the power imbalance between tenant and manager could be redressed.

On our request, Lawrence Grossman prepared the materials on "Organizing Tenants in Low-Income Public Housing." This case is distinctive in its description of the analytic and conceptual steps the organizers undertook in formulating their objectives, their strategies, and their tactics. Their selection of a "core committee" of residents was based in part on a prior categorization of tenants according to a typology of adaptation to mitigating environmental circumstances. Their decisions to intervene manipulatively in the tenant decision-making processes was also based on careful analysis. One may quarrel with their analysis of the situation and with their handling of some of the issues, but one cannot find fault with their efforts to be critical at every stage in the organizing process.

In sharp contrast, the material by Nanci Gitlin entitled "Intimidation,

Red-Baiting, and Paternalism in Public Housing" gives little evidence of sophistication regarding the predictable responses of residents or of management and other public officials regarding an emerging tenants' association. Good will and hard work were no compensation for inexperience and inadequate conceptual tools. The case is also interesting in its documentation of intimidation and Red-baiting, and in pointing to the need of officialdom to deal with outsiders in formal ways. ("Who are your superiors?").

"The Rent Strike on Girard Street" is a much different setting. Circumstances dictated a rather different set of responses. The tenants did not face the administrators of a service agency (public housing), but had to maneuver through a morass of legal and municipal authorities. There was no way in which they could, as an organized group, successfully negotiate with the landlord. The case presents considerable evidence to the effect that the legal system often works to the detriment of the poor. It also suggests that organizing efforts at the grass-roots level may not always be in the best interests of those directly involved.

This case raises a number of important questions. Should the Girard Street Association have moved into the housing issue in response to someone else's initiative? Were the tenants properly prepared by the organizers for the risks they were to take? What did they learn from their experience? What did the Association gain from its participation in these actions? What were the things that the organizer left undone? How better might she have used her sophistication about getting around downtown—on behalf of the tenants involved, and on behalf of Girard Street and the Association in general?

* * * *

CO-26 ORGANIZING TENANTS IN LOW-INCOME PUBLIC HOUSING

LAWRENCE GROSSMAN[1]

On Organizing Perspective

As an organizer approaching a much violated or disenfranchised population, you can either "play-it-by-ear," doing whatever seems to work at any given time, or begin by consciously facing the implications of your intervention. As students and faculty at a graduate school of social work, all with some organizing experience, we chose the latter route.

---

[1] Prepared especially for inclusion in this volume.

Our intervention strategy flowed directly out of the analysis of society that brought us to organizing in the first place. More specifically, our action design emerged from an analysis and understanding of the problems being faced by the people we chose to organize. Self-determination of the target population was of major concern to us. But self-determination without leadership by a cadre of organizers, we knew, had resulted in the deteriorated social conditions that we faced at the start of our program. We were not going to be passive.

In order to test out our assumptions, we decided to organize a large, sprawling low-income housing project in Brooklyn. We selected this particular housing project because of its far-ranging reputation as one of the worst places to live in the entire city. Persistent thefts and muggings, urine in the hallways, and a recent rape in an elevator resulted in the tenants not answering knocks on their doors after 3:00 p.m. More than half the apartments were occupied by single-parent families. There was a pervasive sense of hoplessness. The locked doors not only kept people out, but also added to the feelings of those inside that there was no exit.

This case history is the result of our early decision to think through each of our actions and each of our decisions before and after the fact.

We began by just hanging around benches talking to mothers with their youngsters, picking up ideas as to what they thought was wrong with the project and what they wanted to change, but it was obvious that we were compromising our original intent. We had to know the population better to be able to work out our design, but each such effort caused us to be perceived a certain way by the people, in advance of our reasoned presentation of ourselves. Our initial contacts also partially committed us to some relationship with the contacts.

In our first meeting with the housing project's manager, in which we discussed our self-help concepts, he suggested the names of twelve tenants. These, he said, would be good material for a tenants group. After brief interviews with seven of them, it was clear to us that any organization built through these individuals would not be action-oriented.

At this point, we ceased our organizing contacts, and took two days for stock-taking and a work-up of the population.

Analysis of the Social Scene

We believed that:

1. As a consequence of their residence in this particular project, the tenants shared exposure to a particular set of social conditions.
2. The nature of these conditions had relevance for the life choices and life styles of every tenant.

3. Every tenant had to find some way of adapting to these conditions.

4. The social milieu of this housing project created pressures inimical to the maintenance of self-respect on the part of an individual tenant, inhibiting any achievement of community or general well-being among the tenants as a collectivity.

With regard to this last point, we felt that the following environmental features mitigated against self-esteem and self-respect.

1. *Managerial Monopolization of Power.* There was an elaborate set of rules and regulations governing such tenant behavior as walking on the grass in front of one's own home, hanging towels out of windows, sink overflow, making noise at night, and riding bicycles in the project. There were multiple criteria for eviction and income levels. The manager acted as a "legal guardian" towards the tenants. He could enter apartments at will. He had wide discretionary powers in interpreting, changing, and enforcing rules. He had a set of "discretionary" fines at his command that he used when he wished. Tenants had no legal recourse.

2. *Managerial Monopolization of Knowledge.* Not only were there myriad rules, but the exact nature of these rules was kept a secret from the tenant. Many of the infractions that brought fines were not listed anywhere, but fell within the manager's "judgmentary" powers. A tenant could not challenge "laws" that he did not clearly know. There was wide differentiation in the manner in which different tenants were treated by management, but there was not enough circulation of knowledge among tenants to establish this. There was no orientation process to adequately prepare the new tenant for living within the project. Half-understandings and tenant isolation began the moment residence began. There was a further imbalance in knowledge in the accumulation of personal information on each tenant in the manager's files. Any contacts the tenant had with a city agency, for example, resulted in material being sent to the manager. There was no reciprocal knowledge in the tenants' hands of management's activities. The manager also used knowledge gained from tenant informing on tenant. In such a "Kafkaesque" environment, the bewildered individual came to feel quite helpless before the vast resources of the manager. There was a case of a tenant breaking a neighborhood store window. The owner came to the manager to complain. The manager fined the tenant, and the tenant paid the fine without even knowing it had nothing to do with project life.

3. *Lack of Tenant Access to the Decision-Making Power.* The manager was a distant authority. Behind him he had the shadowy omnipotence of the state legislature and City Housing Commission, both sources entirely beyond the reach of the individual tenant. The manager

stood behind his receptionist, housing assistants, assistant manager, and secretary, all people with power to close off entry to the manager, but no real power to make basic decisions in the manager's place. If a tenant could gain an audience with the manager, he would have nothing to offer him in the way of bargaining material to barter a compromise. The individual tenant was completely vulnerable.

4. *Prisonlike Uniformity and Monotony of Housing Units.* All apartments were painted in one drab color.

5. *Societal Perception of Tenants.* The project has been written up in the newspapers as a bed of crime, filth, and corruption. Tenants felt a stigma from the project's reputation, this being added to the general stigma of being low-income and black in a national culture that respected neither.

6. *Breakdown of Relations with Housing Police.* The management and the housing police were under separate administrative control, and they did not cooperate. The tenant suffered from the lack of reciprocal responsibility. The manager sometimes charged a fee for a tenant's calling the police. Tenants thought the police were doing the charging, and this, combined with the slowness and erratic quality of police response, caused tenants to be afraid to use their own legitimate means of protection.

7. *Tenant Informing as a Control Measure.* The manager put very little responsibility in the hands of his assistants and so relied little on information they gave him. With his lack of trust of the police, he had come to encourage tenant-informing as a control measure. This further separated and degraded tenants.

Uncertainty, even more than exemplary punishment, is a keystone of terror. In order to survive in this environment the tenants developed styles of behavior in response to power and status deprivations. The basic types of adaptation were as follows.

1. *Anonymity and Apathy.* A large group of the tenants came to *accept* the situation as it was. They retreated into passivity under the overwhelming nature of the threats and pressures. Their greatest success was in avoiding being noticed, avoiding fines, avoiding eviction, and avoiding trouble. Their basic way of minimizing the constant pain of unjust deprivation was to "believe" in its "deservedness." They came to incorporate second-class citizenry, pessimism, and fear into their overall self-image. They had little belief in themselves.

2. *Hostility and Anger at the Management.* There were fewer tenants maintaining this adaptation than the first. It was hard to continue anger when there were no outlets for carrying it through. Most of the people

who remained angry carried their hostility as a secondary strain beneath one of their other adaptations. Open, conscious anger could not be maintained because it kept the deprivation wounds open and reinforced the individual's awareness of his inability to do anything about it. Anger thus became diffuse and undirected towards what was hurting the tenants most—a momentary response that could not seriously contest the circumstances of their lives.

3. *Manipulative, Operating, Cynical "Roll with the Punch" and "Get Yours" Adaptation.* Other people developed a "cool self" and a "worldly self." They cynically participated in a whole number of procedures to which they gave no emotional significance. They gave authority what it wanted, kept out of trouble, and manipulated all they could for small, petty gains. They gloried in victories like cheating the manager out of a few dollars or having an auto while on relief. By minimizing the uniqueness of pain they minimized their deprivations. Implying that this was the usual way people lived, they denied any emotional significance in the struggle between manager and tenant. In fact, they came to deny the emotional significance of most of their activities.

4. *Upward Striving—Identification with Authority.* Those tenants who informed on fellow tenants were a striking example of this type. Informing for petty personal advantage, they also succeeded in separating themselves from the masses of people in the project. Cherishing any exceptions that were made for them, they eagerly sought contacts with authority as entry point to an upper-class world. In effect, they acknowledged the severe nature of the limitations on dignity in the project, but tried to deny that they suffered such limitations. They were harder on the other tenants than the manager himself.

People who adapted by retreating (type 1), by becoming cynical (type 3), or by identifying with the repressive authority (type 4) were themselves enemies of the community. The apathetic feared the exposure and commitment of "community." The cynical rejected commitment and reciprocal responsibility. The last refused to identify with the community for fear that such identification would symbolize all they despised in their life circumstances.

Four other conditions interfered with the development of community. These were *rootlessness,* which came from the fact that added income could bring eviction, and thus inhibited motivation to build and strive; *isolation* from the surrounding communities, on a physical as well as a cultural basis; *managerial perception of tenants* as control problem, which resulted in minimal efforts to keep the grounds in top shape and repair appliances rapidly; and the *initial strangeness* of all the people, who had been uprooted from somewhere else and moved into this strange new world.

Laying Out Programmatic Objectives

Based on this analysis, we defined our general or broad objectives as follows.

1. The development of a powerful tenants' self-interest organization.
2. A systematic restructuring of the destructive features in the milieu (through the tenant associations' choice of targets for action, for example, forcing the manager to negotiate and to publish the rules, and the bridging of isolation).
3. Through a style of fighting such issues that emphasized the uses of power, the development of political and democratic skills to facilitate the emergence of dignity and the kind of communal interaction that would support self-esteem.

Starting the Tenants Organization

Our selection of members for the "tenants association" we decided to create was based on our understanding of that combination of tenant types most likely to result in an action-oriented group. Our concern was that it survive over time, and that it have potential for relatively democratic interaction.

We decided to get a group of 10 to 12 together at the start, of which we hoped that 2 would be of the anger-adaptation type, 2 of the "identified with aggressor" type but less deeply "identified," and the rest from the "apathetic" group. We expected that many of the apparent apathetics" would soon turn out to be angry people or level-headed people ready, given a viable means, to do something about conditions. We wanted some of the success and energy of the least obnoxious "identifiers" at the start.

We met with 11 women—2 "identifiers" from the manager's original list and 9 from among those we had met on the benches around the project. Of these, six were "apathetics," one was "angry," and two did not fit neatly into our classification scheme. Only one organizer was present. We wanted it to be clear that this was to be a tenants' organization.

Recruiting a Leadership Core for an Action Organization

We brought these women together by telling them that "they had come up with so many good ideas, that we thought it was a good idea to bring them together so as to figure out which things might come first."

It was an interesting meeting. The tenants, perhaps because of experience, showed very little confidence in their ability to effectuate change. The organizer, by contrast, effused a good bit of confidence.

During the course of the meeting, the organizer made appointments to see each participant in her own apartment, asking each to invite other residents from their own and adjacent floors. We used this tactic because we knew that the easiest way to have members drop out is by not having anything for them to do.

We also felt that these meetings were essential if we hoped to spread the word about an open meeting we planned for a short time later. Heavy attendance at the opening meeting was essential if we were to impress the manager with our strength. We hoped, also, to recruit more angry and committed people to our core. Meetings took place around stairwells.

Tenants and organizers rang doorbells. There were approximately 12 apartments on each floor. Counting the floors above and below the one the tenant lived on, this meant that 36 families were contacted. If no one answered, a slip was left under the door indicating that there was to be a meeting in the hall in 20 minutes. At the end of 20 minutes doorbells were rung again to remind people to come.

Approximately 20 to 25 people congregated around each stairwell. They were in housecoats, carrying children. The tenant who had been to the first meeting would introduce the organizer as someone who would talk about "our association."

These were very successful meetings. Word of the association spread effectively. Our first open meeting had over 300 in attendance. We also found five new active recruits for the "core"—one of whom was an "angry," two of whom were partly "identified" and partly other things, but very competent at organizational tasks, and two of whom were really "untypeable," somewhat apathetic but also quite ready to work to change things if a strong organization was presented to them. Two of these five were males, the first men in the core group. The act of standing up in front of their neighbors and introducing the worker also bound the original women more closely to the organization, as it caused them to be identified as a key part of it by their neighbors.

Organizing Activities

We had approached the manager before attempting any organizing because we had assumed that our presence would soon be noted anyway. Our approach had been aimed at developing communication channels, reassuring some of his fears, and establishing our clear independence. We understood his position towards a possible association as ambivalent

—it certainly might make for a better housing project community (nothing could really make it worse, even from his point of view; he was a young hotshot manager, fairly new to the project, sent there to improve it). On the other hand, a "runaway" tenants' association over which he had no control was the one thing a manager feared most. We certainly meant the association to ultimately be "runaway"—beyond his control—but not runaway in the sense that it would be beyond the possibility of rational negotiation. We emphasized the rational-negotiation part in discussions with him and left his vanity to complete the task of reassurance that the association would not get "out of hand."

We traded tactical strokes with him, gaining a slight advantage. Prior to the first open meeting, we discussed his possible roles with him. We relayed to him three issues that concerned the core committee, one of which involved a request for a bicycle path, and asked him to prepare answers on them. He agreed to. We also agreed that there would not be a wide-open question-and-answer period at this meeting, to avoid its deteriorating into the kind of gripe session that would make the members feel either frightened or frustrated.

We arranged that this first large meeting would take place in a room a little smaller than the ideal size for the number we hoped for. Over 300 tenants came to a room that ordinarily held around 200. The manager was somewhat intimidated upon his arrival, and at that moment accepted the fact that he would have to negotiate with this organization, at least for a short while.

The manager reacted at the meeting itself, however, by going back on some of the agreements that had been determined with the organizers during their earlier discussion, and presented some of the issues in a manner that implied that he had always been working for their solution; in fact, he would have done nothing had not the tenants pressed the issues. He also barged into a question-and-answer session that broke the meeting up with diffused frustration.

These changes in his presentation had either been planned, or were a consequence of our having intimidated him. They had some immediate small success in taking some of the steam away from the tenants, but the lasting impact of the meeting in the minds of the tenants was the picture of the manager sweating to keep up with them, in front of a room where their members overwhelmed him.

The manager and the organizers retained a successful, guarded relationship with each other throughout the entire organizing period. The manager felt more dependent on the organizers than we did on him. He saw us as something of a safety valve or buffer—another level of possible negotiation and possible compromise.

Once a strong tenants' association was a fait accompli, he needed us more than we needed him, and it was easy to maintain complete independence of him while still receiving information and a number of concessions. Both sides paid some attention to preserving communication lines with each other.

Programmatic goals were selected with great care at all points of the organizing process.

There were three basic types of program issues attacked by the group. These aimed at the following.

1. Ameliorative changes.
2. Significant structural changes.
3. Symbolic changes.

At the start all victories have symbolic as well as substantive significance.

It was necessary to aim for small, likely successes at the start. The "apathetics" would have fallen back into pessimism and the "identified" into formalism, if we had not proved that the organization had potency.

A number of early programmatic victories included the following.

1. The manager's accession to weekly negotiative meetings with a committee of four tenants.
2. The waiving of the rule about bike riding and the promise of a bike path for the future (later fulfilled).
3. The publication of the rules and regulations presumably governing tenant-manager relations.
4. The discontinuing of favors given for tenants informing on tenants.
5. An agreement that an explicit rationale would be given for every proposed tenant fine.

The major extended "short term" objective was the winning of a traffic light. Without it, a park and a middle-income neighborhood across the street were inaccessible. After repeated letters to the traffic commissioner, we received contradictory responses (one saying "we cannot respond to your request until we do a traffic survey," and another received just prior to the first saying "we have done a traffic engineering survey and the street does not justify a light"), and were able to exploit the situation through a liberal newspaper that requested an explanation from the traffic commissioner. At this point he conceded the light. We had won a first victory!

There were no early program failures. There were, however, a number of internal struggles over program issues. These struggles generally resolved themselves into struggles between "identifier" types and other tenants. In most cases, the organizers openly threw their weight behind the non-"identified" tenants, as we believed that the organization no longer needed the identified types. They could either adapt to the new philosophy or get out.

The five issues around which there were differences between groups of tenants were the conviction that:

1. Children were the major cause of trouble in the project and something should be done about their hanging around hallways in the afternoon.

2. The fine for extra calls for the exterminator should be dropped because the roaches were not immune to it.

3. We should write the Governor to veto a Welfare Residence Bill.

4. We should pressure the manager to stop giving favors to informants.

5. Since a successful new start was being made, the name of the project should be changed.

The tenants who were still actively identified with authority voted as follows:

1. Yes on doing something about the children.
2. No on dropping fines.
3. No on writing the Governor.
4. No on putting tenant pressure on the manager.
5. Yes on changing the Project name.

The other tenants generally took opposite positions.

All of the decisions except the one on cockroach fines went *against* the "identifiers."

The cockroach fine was continued because the organizer working with the Health Committee had difficulty either confronting its membership or turning to other organizers for help. He let the Committee make a decision that he should have prevented.

Some tenants had brought the request to the Health Committee. This was the only committee that was dominated by "identifiers." The organizers had been slow to notice this. It should have been obvious. What kinds of people are usually attracted to "keeping things clean"? These same tenants had punitive attitudes toward their dirtier brethren. They saw themselves as dispensing rulings for the "good of the people," rather than as representing the people. They saw fines as a just deterrent for dirty apartments.

The issue around changing the name of the project was particularly gratifying to the organizers. The manager had suggested the possibility as a public-relations move by changing the housing project's name. The firmness of some of the original apathetics *against* such a move, their burgeoning dignity and pride in their project, was sharply satisfying experience. Instead of changing the name of the project, they voted to have a big celebration over winning the traffic light, and invited three big-name baseball players (one black, one Cuban, and one white) to join them.

Later in the organization's history, the tenants became involved in the surrounding neighborhoods, and the association becoming a major part of an area council.

Evaluation and Analysis

There were a number of heated and prolonged discussions among the organizers relating to the degree of our interventions appropriate to our objectives. What types of decision-making structures should we strive to develop within the organization?

Our goals for the organization included giving it an action orientation, building tenant skills and confidence, assuring a respect for democracy, and priming effective and democratically-oriented leaders in anticipation of our withdrawal. These objectives had some contradictory implications. The "apathetics" were a problem in terms of general participation and the "authority-oriented" ones a problem in terms of democratic participation. The "apathetics" required quick movement on issues to maintain their confidence, while the "authority-oriented" ones could manipulate fast movement into a strengthening of their nondemocratic style. The fewer people who participated in decisions, the faster they went. The "authority-oriented" ones also used slower processes to entrench formalism. Some insisted on intricate procedures that supported their greater experience, and upon which they built up their power. For these reasons, the organizers decided to keep full control of the association for the first seven months of its operation. We forestalled any elections during that period.

We were afraid that early elections would have resulted in control by the "identifiers." We used every means to build up some of the non-authority-oriented talent that was emerging. We put them on the committee that met with the manager. Thus they controlled information and at least seemed powerful. We mentioned their names whenever possible.

We maintained an action focus rather than a formal or organizational focus in a variety of ways. We only called large open meetings, for example, when there was something large to be done. We made sure that certain larger policy decisions were struggled through by as many members as was possible prior to the open meetings.

The issue of tenant informing was used as a direct teaching tool and as pressure against the "identifiers." We stimulated a number of discussions around the subject. At first the identifiers argued against approaching the manager on this subject on grounds of its "triviality," and then on the basis of its "lack of feasibility." The organizers manipulated such discussions so as to force the informers to publicly denounce the "principle of informing." By the end of these discussions, it was clear to the informers that they had to quit their informing behavior or quit the organization. One did drop out; the rest adapted.

As a counterbalance against our generally aggressive role, we made a strong point of never going with the tenants when they met with the manager. This was a way of signifying our esssential respect for their own accountability. They lived in the Project, not we. We discussed what happened with the manager when they wished to, but after the first two visits, never prompted such discussions ourselves.

The dilemma concerning our intervention and their independence was strikingly exhibited at election time.

Among the serious candidates for the chairmanship, the three most active women seemed to be:

1. A clear "identifier" type with significant organizational experience, who had done much of the letter writing on the traffic-light campaign.
2. A younger, moderate "identifier" type who chaired the Health Committee.
3. A bright young nonidentifier, non-"any type," who usually spoke for the group that met with the manager.

The organizers were rooting for the third. We had primed her by putting her in the position of reporting on the meetings with the manager. She was clearly the most politically intelligent and flexible of the candidates, with a real appreciation for other people. Candidate No. 2 was acceptable to us, but Candidate No. 1 was not. We were sure that her relative rigidity would kill off the organization.

When the time came for nominations, at a "core group" meeting, a surprise occurred. A man was the first nominated. He was as much of an "identifier" as No. 1, but considerably less hard working.

The organizer present took this nomination as in part a tribute to his own maleness, and in part a falling back on old images of authority. He acted against it in whatever ways he could improvise. He suggested that the man in question had "Boy Scout meetings on Tuesday nights, didn't he? Well the chairman could not afford to miss meetings. Maybe someone else should assume the role first."

The group responded positively to the rather blatant manipulating, probably out of a degree of gratitude towards and confidence in the organizer who had performed it. They then went on to bypass woman No. 1 and tentatively suggest No. 2 (whom they rightly sensed was more to the organizers' liking than No. 1). Sensing the tentativeness and having already gone this far, the organizer went one step further and mumbled something about No. 2 already being chairman of the Health Committee (which she would gladly have given up for the chance to chair the entire organization). They chose No. 3.

This behavior was consistent with the approach of the organizing team, even though it had an improvisational character. The organizer faced the dilemma of organizational effectiveness versus self-determination, by choosing effectiveness in such a way that it would engender greater self-determination over the long run. No. 3 was the one candidate whom no outsider (the organizer included) could possibly push around successfully.

At the close of one year of organizing, there remained a fairly powerful tenant organization with 387 family memberships, 4 active committees, and a reliable core of 20 and 23 hard workers.

As organizers, we attempted quite sincerely to rationalize our actions before the fact rather than after, and in the main succeeded more than is usual. The tenants usually knew exactly what the organizers were after, particularly when it affected them directly. They *let* the organizers "manipulate" them at times because they wanted to be "manipulated" into a successful organization. They were also testing our skill, and thus "using" us.

This does not in any way obviate the organizer's need to know what and how he is doing; it merely takes the tenants out of a one-dimensional aspect and validates their subjectivity. A clumsy organizer would still fail out of clumsiness, and an incorrect analysis would probably lead to a stillborn organization.

* * * *

CO-27 INTIMIDATION, RED-BAITING, AND PATERNALISM IN PUBLIC HOUSING[1]

On the day before my group's first big meeting, the group in another area was having a planning meeting. Janette Green went to the recreation director, Robert Malachio, to talk to him about the recreation pro-

---

[1] Excerpted from an unpublished mimeographed paper prepared by Nanci Gitlin while an undergraduate student, and entitled "Public Housing: The Welfare State in Action."

gram and he blew up at her. He said he had lots of programs but people were not interested in them. She invited him to the meeting to talk about them. Later that afternoon, Mrs. Burns, who had been at the leaflet meeting, went to ask Robert if it would be possible to use the gym for babysitting the next night (her idea) so more people could come to the meeting. Robert then showed what was on his mind. He screamed, "You people had no right to print those leaflets; you are using communist tactics. There can be no closed meetings or communism here." Mrs. Burns, by then furious, tried to warn the meeting for that night that Robert would probably be there, but she failed to get there in time. Robert came to the meeting with his superior from the recreation department. When some of the tenants said that he ran the recreation center without ever consulting them, his defense was, "There is the wrong way and the army way."

That evening after talking to Mrs. Burns, who felt we should "stand up to Robert," I called the Joneses to see what they thought; they agreed. Since we knew there would be trouble the next night, it was decided that I should go to the Community Center during the day and try to feel Robert out a little, if he was at all rational. With much trepidation I went, only to find him calm, pleasant—almost saccharine. Everything was in order for the meeting; we did not know what he had planned.

Though I do not often fall back on psychological explanations, this is an excellent example of an authoritarian personality, developed through a role of domination, yet constantly forced to submit to a higher official. Robert's superiors had told him what to do; now he could be calm in the knowledge that he was carrying out orders.

The tenant meeting finally arrived with a huge turnout, about thirty people out of fifty units. None of the management was present. After I had introduced myself and explained about the Lake City Community Project and the planning meetings we had had in Shoreside, a man on my left interrupted and introduced himself (he was the same one from the recreation department who had been called by Robert the night before). He began to ask who my "superiors" were and where my "headquarters" were, and said we should have checked with the recreation department before doing anything in the project. This started a good many other people asking similar questions, and a general interrogation began.

Mr. Jones tried to change the subject, saying we should get on with the meeting. At that point someone asked why the management was not there; she said she had been to see them and they denied knowing anything about us. I explained my conversations with O'Connor, how he had helped me reserve the room. After that we were accused of misrepresentation by Mrs. Koslic, who said that the first time we had talked, I did not mention anything about an organization and only talked about the problems in Shoreside. So it continued until the recreation official finally left, saying that my "superiors" should contact Mr. Smith, the director of the Lake City recreation department.

As soon as he left, the meeting began to pick up. Joe Collins, a young college-age man, saved the day saying he thought there should be another meeting in a week and he would arrange it and notify everyone. The only concrete work to come out of the meeting was the initiation of plans to bring feature-length movies to the Community Center, and Mrs. Burns planned to go to the office demanding that the Center be open on weekends, "even if it gets me evicted!" Mrs. Koslic seemed satisfied with us again and asked me to visit her soon to talk about other things that we should be doing.

This meeting showed the project, the management, and the environment in its true light; it is necessary to discuss several aspects of what we learned from it.

We had been told from the very beginning that the Golden Agers were the most influential group in the project; they usually got their way and were "buddy-buddy" with the management. We had purposely avoided them because the first rule of finding and developing new leaders is to stay away, at least at first, from the older, established ones. The chairman of the Golden Agers Club was at this meeting where she said she was glad the young folks were doing something for a change. She obviously came out of more than just curiosity.

The great dependency on the management was revealed in a number of ways. As soon as they got the leaflets, many ran to the office to see whether it was OK—to ask permission to attend the meeting. At the end of the meeting a few people shouted that the management had better be at the next meeting or they would not come.

But the greatest reaction came from the management itself. As the succeeding will show, Red-baiting and intimidation had a latent function beyond uncovering some kind of evil conspiracy. They wanted to get rid of us, make us ineffective, stop us—anything to end something that might get out of hand and threaten their power. James Cass, the director of the Lake City Metropolitan Housing Authority, is known to be one of the most influential men in the city and a leader in public housing nationally. He is said to fear two things more than anything else. First— publicity. Not one word hit the press when members of CORE picketed several housing projects calling Cass a racist and demanding an end to the discriminatory practices in public housing in Lake City. Second, he fears a tenant council in any of his projects that is not management controlled. Once he decided to step into the situation, we were not sure what would happen.

The day after the meeting I went to several people to get their impressions and reactions. Mr. and Mrs. Jones were glad to see me, and said that they did not understand all of this "outside agitation" concern. Koslic was excited about the progress of the group, though she admitted being scared at the meeting. She had continued to waver back and forth and would probably side with the management in the long run. Mrs. Burns said that a lot of people were afraid that we were sent from CORE to "agitate the place and make way for more Negroes," or that we were communists, or both. She was concerned about this also, but she was more concerned about the success of the group. It is easy to understand their fears; these were new decisions, new situations, and new conflicts.

Two days later there was a meeting to which we were not invited, although it was called to talk about the Lake City Community Project. Present at the meeting called by Miss Cook were two ministers who were sympathetic to us, O'Connor, Robert Malachio, and the recreation official. Although the ministers defended us, after the meeting Miss Cook called the chairman of the South Side Civic Council, asking her to tell us not to use the community center. When the chairman of the Council called us, she said she was calling in the name of the Civic Council; however, the Council had never discussed the matter at all, nor had they any jurisdiction over the community center or us. It was beginning to be quite clear where the real power in the community was centered. Miss Cook had been able to cow the ministers and control the Civic Council.

That afternoon, I called Mrs. Burns to ask if she had been to see O'Connor yet about the center being open on weekends. She was quite cool to me, and said she had talked to Miss Cook, who was in favor of the organization as long as it consisted only of residents (the management never used the word "tenant"), with no outsiders. The intention of Miss Cook's remarks was obvious enough, yet slightly ironic too. Community centers were built in housing projects in the hopes that they would attract community residents from outside the project to help integrate the project tenants into the surrounding community.

There seemed to be only one thing left to do—go to see Miss Cook with some of the tenants, forcing her to make her accusations in front of them. We went to see her to make an appointment for the following day, when a few tenants could come with us. She decided to talk with us right away. The interview was marked by friendly, smiley tones and sugary words; we tried not to be argumentative. First we asked for the appointment, but Miss Cook refused, saying that she did not have time and wanted to see us alone so as not to embarrass us in front of the residents. She then accused us of misrepresentation, indicating that she thought we were coming to do voter registration work only; we had started the groups without her knowledge or permission. I explained my discussions with O'Connor, but she maintained that they thought everything was for voter registration. There was no misunderstanding; she was lying.

Then she started on the leaflet with the following analogy.

"Suppose you wanted something for your very own, what would you do? You might ask your father. Let's say you wanted a car and you asked your father to give you one. He might answer it would not be possible this year, but if you were to earn honor grades, maybe next year."

And her analogy:

"My door is always open if anyone here has any gripes or wishes; now, don't you think this leaflet should have been cleared with me first?"

She continued:

"These people are living in government housing and therefore, do not have the means to get things for themselves and must rely on management to do things for them. Their lives are burdened with hardship. What right have you to come in here and unsettle them, to make them unhappy and dissatisfied? I have tried hard to keep them happy and content; have you noticed that the children here always smile and have good attitudes toward adults? Now people have started coming to me complaining that rents are fixed arbitrarily and the lease outdated, the community center inadequate. It is not true—rents are determined by income and number of dependents, the lease was reevaluated last year, and the recreation department does all it can, since these people can't afford to pay for their services."

But she did not explain why rents are raised when children get summer jobs, then do not get lowered again—why the lease gives the manager the right to enter a home at any time without previous notice—why the tenants cannot decide what programs they would like at the recreation center.

Miss Cook was not yet through. She said she assumed we were withdrawing our request to use the community center with groups of residents. Fortunately, at that point she was momentarily called out of the room. When she returned we again asked for another meeting with her and the tenants and for some reason she agreed. As we got up to leave she pointed out the two WPA pictures in her office, telling us how proud she was of "her" people.

Her paternalism reached extremes I could not believe. This little old white-haired lady sitting with her hands folded at her desk could have been the Grand Inquisitor—freedom from choice keeps the people happy *and* under control.

The next morning Janette Green phoned to say that Miss Cook had called her, asking whether she wanted a meeting with her today. Janette, assuming that we had used her name, said yes and that a few of the Lake City Community Project people would be coming also. Miss Cook answered, "I'll take care of them." We had only mentioned Janette's name to Joe Collins, who was also going and wanted to know who else would be there. We had been suspicious of him for some time and now felt confirmed in the belief that he was talking to the management about everything anyone said.

We gathered outside her office, four of us and four tenants. Miss Cook met us inside saying, "Residents, please go into my office now, but the SDS people stay here." In they went like sheep; she closed the door after them so they could not hear what was to follow. She continued, "We have nothing more to say to you, we are only interested in finding out what the residents want. So you can leave now. Please, I do not want to be rude." A member of our group said we would wait in case there were any questions about us. Miss Cook rebuked that with, "You will not wait. Leave!"

However, two of us did wait for an hour and a half until they emerged. Joe walked out first and as he started talking to us, O'Connor called him into his office. Then Janette said they were going with Robert to reserve a room for a future meeting and told us to wait at her home until she returned.

The tenants' rundown of the meeting confirmed our worst fears. When the subject of the "organizers" was brought up by the tenants, it was quickly changed, but the management was able to get in several points—we misrepresented ourselves, we were subversive, they could not locate our "superiors," etc. When the tenants asked for names or proof, again the subject was quickly changed. If the residents wanted an organization, they were told, they must stop associating with us; if we were involved, they could not use the community center. O'Connor went so far as to suggest that they select a temporary chairman right there, but they protested on the grounds of democracy.

Our relationship with the management had become very tenuous by the time of the first big meeting in my area. We decided on a course of least antagonism because we were not sure of the support we would get from the tenants, especially in the face of intimidation and Red-baiting. Furthermore, we saw no point in focusing all attention on us. It was important that the battle with the management not be seen as our fight, but as the tenants'. They would be the ones affected by any decisions. We talked to them about it and did everything possible to assure them that we were not communists, not from CORE, and not outside agitators. It was more important to retain their confidence at this time than to preach about the evils of Red-baiting or why it was unimportant whether we were associated with CORE.

When I found a person who was sympathetic with the situation or more concerned with the success of the tenant organization than anything else, I was frank with him, trying to show the inevitable conflict that was beginning to come to light. Some began to see beyond the intimidation to the cause of the problem—power. But many remained fearful and left the field of conflict to once again isolate themselves from their community. The most tragic part of the whole thing is that it happened a couple of weeks too soon. If the group had already been engaged in something important to its members, these questions would have annoyed them instead of scaring them away. All we could do now was continue to hold the group together and fight the new foes beginning to emerge.

A few days later we had a meeting with Mr. Smith, the director of the recreation department. Again, a few tenants went with us. Nothing came out of the meeting beyond Smith's defense of the recreation department, but a new character appeared. A man who had remained silent throughout the meeting was introduced as Jack Fisher of the recreation department; he was subsequently identified as Sergeant Harper of the Lake City Police Subversive Squad. Harper is infamous for his Red-baiting; he appears at every gathering and demonstration with his trusty, well-used camera. The very next day, an Officer Doran approached our headquarters with a "complaint" that we were running a hotel and had rats and roaches. He said he was from the Sanitary Department of the police. A call later found that no such department existed and such complaints were always signed, as this one was not. Moreover, these problems are handled through the health department, not the police department.

A member of Sergeant Harper's crew was in Shoreside a few days later visiting tenants and Robert Malachio with pictures of us from "various CORE demonstrations"—we had been on one demonstration sponsored by the Women's International League for Peace and Freedom. They also visited various other members of the community to check on us.

Our strategy did not change after the encounters with Miss Cook and Sergeant Harper, but our activities were considerably limited. I found it very difficult to contact new people, not knowing which rumors they had heard and whether they had been shown pictures or otherwise intimidated. Practically all we could do was keep in contact with the people who remained interested.

Finally the management-called meeting arrived; this was the one planned on the day the tenants talked to Miss Cook and O'Connor. We went to it but were told by Miss Cook that we had no right to be there and certainly could not speak. Joe Collins chaired the meeting, on the decision of himself and O'Connor, the latter saying, "I would recommend . . ." before Joe did anything. The meeting succeeded in little beyond choosing a name and deciding on a constitutional committee. Most people felt that it was entirely unsatisfactory, since O'Connor had manipulated the whole affair.

In October, one woman who had been very active throughout the development of the council was evicted. She received a mimeographed, impersonal notice from the office giving her 15 days to leave (the lease calls for 30 days). No reason was given and when she asked for one, she was told that her son was working on his car in an area where this is not permitted. There is nothing in the lease to cover this offense.

*   *   *   *

CO-28   THE RENT STRIKE ON GIRARD STREET[1]

The Girard Street Project was sponsored by the All Souls Unitarian Church in Washington, D.C. to help residents in its immediate vicinity, a ghetto slum, to overcome some of the myriad problems resulting from poverty. "It was felt that a trained social worker capable of understanding the problems of an underprivileged community must be found to supply what the community lacked most—contact with the resources of the metropolitan area, organizing skill, and a steady push towards the realization that the community was not helpless and must find ways to help itself." The organizer, beginning part time, had started out by getting to know people in the area on an informal basis, forming a mothers' club, a sewing class, and finally the Girard Street Association. The Association worked on such problems as street safety, rat eradication, a playground, and tutoring needs. Of major significance was the Association's attack on the problem of the miserable housing conditions endemic on Girard Street.

---

[1] This is excerpted from the publication entitled "The Girard Street Project," issued in 1961 by the All Souls Church Unitarian, 16th and Harvard Streets, N.W., Washington, D.C.

Housing

The Project Director, Miss Bellamy, had planned from the beginning to attack the appalling housing conditions of the street. In fact, the Association had considered a "clean our street" program to improve the appearance of the block, but, while its efforts were sincere, they did not bring about the expected results. It is hard to improve a street when the houses are in hopeless condition, and housing in the Cardozo Area is very bad. Out of the total of 25,674 dwelling units, 4747 are over-crowded, one out of every five of the units lack private bathroom facilities, and 13 percent of the housing units have been defined as unsound by the Bureau of the Census. Between 5000 and 8000 dwelling units are in substandard condition.

Overcrowding in Washington is caused by the lack of available housing at reasonable prices to large black families. Eighty percent of the new apartment buildings in the city are of the luxury efficiency and one-bedroom type, and progressively the old, large apartments are broken into smaller units suited for single persons and childless couples, barring families with children. The incentive to build small apartments is an economic one; the rentals are proportionately higher. Apartments for families with children are built in the surrounding suburbs where land is cheaper—Arlington, Fairfax County, Bethesda, Rockville Pike area, Prince Georges County, and the like, but this housing is closed to blacks.

The problem was aggravated when thousands of low-income families were displaced by the Southwest urban renewal program. Housing there, formerly occupied by the poor, was replaced by middle-class apartments or deluxe town houses suitable for the single or young married government employees. Other areas formerly occupied by blacks, such as Capitol Hill, have been renovated and refurbished inside and now belong to well-to-do white families. The problem is aggravated yet further by the steady inflow of the black population into Washington from the South. These newcomers are squeezing into the already crowded black areas. As a result, a black family pays a higher rent for its substandard housing than a white family does for an up-to-date new apartment in a pleasant neighborhood.

The Landlord is King

Under these circumstances it is reasonable to expect the municipal authorities to enforce the minimum standards of the Housing Code vigorously and efficiently. The opposite seems to be true of the approach adopted by the Bureau of Licenses and Inspections, the agency in charge of Housing Code enforcement. Inspections of apartment buildings are conducted only once in two years (for license purposes). If a violation is found, the offending landlord knows that by various extensions of deadlines, appeals and excuses, he can postpone repairs for another year and a half. If after all that time he still has not corrected the violation, even then nothing happens to him. His case is referred to the Cooperation Counsel, the public prosecutor for the District of Columbia. He is then granted another hearing and given another three months' extension, and, if his excuses are good enough, he may be given yet another one.

Only if he neglects to begin his repairs by the time this second extension runs out is the landlord brought to trial for the criminal offense of negligence. If he loses in court, the worst that can happen to him is a $300 fine or 10 days in jail, and up to the day of this writing no landlord has ever served a jail sentence for breaking the D.C. Housing Code. Thus, landlords have no fear of violating the Housing Code. Houses "below code" are sold and bought on the real estate market as freely as those "up to code." To buy a house below code presents no problems for the new owner; the record of violations by the previous owner is automatically expunged by the change of ownership. Legally, the new landlord starts with a clean slate. He then can use the same techniques to postpone by another two years any corrections of violations.

To be a slum landlord is a lucrative occupation in the District of Columbia. The financial risks are few, the rewards substantial. There is no rent control, and landlords charge whatever the traffic will bear. Due to the acute shortage of housing for blacks, a one-room apartment rents for $60 to $75, and a one-bedroom apartment cannot be found below $75 to $85 in neighborhoods such as Girard Street. Utilities on top of this are paid by the tenant. The tenants never have the protection of a long-term lease. With or without cause, they can be evicted on thirty days' notice. This power of eviction is frequently used by the landlords. In 1963, there were 92,000 evictions in the District. Retaliatory eviction of the tenant who complains about Code violations is common.

Housing authorities rightly contend that strict enforcement of the provisions against overcrowding would result in eviction of many families, who would then be homeless. But they claim further that unless these provisions are enforced, other provisions of that Code cannot be enforced. They take the position that it is therefore more expedient to try to stimulate the cooperation and good will of the landlords than to incur their hostility by strict law enforcement. The Corporation Counsel's official in charge of enforcement of the Housing Code has often stated that "it makes no sense to antagonize the landlords on whose good will the enforcement of the Housing Code depends." His recommended approach was friendly collaboration and gentle persuasion. He pointed out that landlords frequently defend themselves by stating that the tenants are destructive, that they overcrowd the units without the landlord's consent or knowledge, that repeated repairs are costly and that the tenants have no will to cooperate in the upkeep of the property. But the fact of the matter is that "friendly collaboration" is not a very effective approach to Code enforcement. This was brought to public attention in 1963, when a series of articles in *The Washington Post* described the terrible housing conditions in many parts of the District and brought to light the case of a man who owned 375 rental properties, many of them in slum areas, and against whom enforcement of the Code had been virtually suspended.

At the outset, the members of the Girard Street Association talked about housing conditions with despair bordering on apathy. However, after the group succeeded in some of its other objectives, the Director and the members began to consider ways in which to achieve a stricter enforcement of the Housing Code on the block. It was clear that such an effort would not be easy and that it would be difficult to change the established ways of doing business. But she was not prepared for the discovery that in her efforts she would have to buck not merely "the system" but the law itself. An incident that occurred in the summer of 1963 made this clear.

Encouraged by the Association, Mr. Charles Smith, a young man, living with his wife and child in one of the apartments on the block, complained to the Bureau of Licenses and Inspections about the grave violations of the Housing Code in his apartment. Other people from the apartment building joined him, and they drew up and signed a petition to the Bureau requesting that the violations be corrected.

The building was in terrible condition. A hand-stoking coal furnace supplying heat was in such poor condition that it had been condemned by the Bureau some time previously, but the landlord had never replaced it. It was operated in the most unreliable fashion by a janitor who did not have a proper license to operate a furnace. On many days in the winter the building was not heated. The building was eight stories high and had six units on each floor. The first four floors had no elevator service at all, the floors above were serviced by an elevator that was continually out of order. There was no lighting at all in the halls at night. Women tenants were subjects of assaults by drunks who were hiding in the dark. Plaster was falling off the walls and ceilings in the apartments and plumbing was stopped up. The halls were littered, trash was not collected, and there was an inadequate hot-water supply.

All the tenants had joined in the petition to the Bureau of Licenses and Inspections. The name of Mr. Smith, who drew up the petition, appeared first among the signatures. Shortly after the petition was sent to the Bureau, he received an eviction notice from the landlord. His rent was paid up, there had been no complaints against him by the landlord, and there was obviously no other reason for his eviction than his audacity in complaining. The names of the petitioners were known to the landlord. The Housing authorities had passed the petition and the names of the complaining tenants on to the landlord. At this point, the Director and the representatives of the Association got in touch with the landlord to discuss the matter with him. During the interview, the landlord made it very clear that he would evict whomever he pleased and that he would not deal with any "outside troublemakers" or associations but only with individual tenants. He was well aware that the threat of further evictions or increase in rents would prove sufficient to quell any further unpleasantness with Code enforcement. Help was sought from the Legal Aid Society, which only confirmed that there was no legal remedy against retaliatory eviction, that the 30-day eviction was legal, and that the only thing Mr. Smith could do was to vacate the premises. Although the Director used every resource and every connection at her disposal, she was unable to find suitable housing for the evicted family. After a great deal of travail they were resettled in an efficiency apartment not too far from Girard Street. In spite of this setback, however, Mr. Smith did not leave the Association and continued to be active in it.

The Official Run-Around

The Director seemed to be facing a hopeless housing situation while realizing that improvement of housing was the crux of her work on the block. While other aspects of the Association's program would undoubtedly improve the block somewhat, a real improvement in the lives of the residents could not be made without extricating them from the housing stranglehold in which the landlords' greed and racial discrimination held them. How to do it, how to find a way for them to help themselves when the entire legal and social system was against them, became the center of the following year's activities.

Mr. Charles Vizzini, a young attorney and a member of All Souls Church, became interested in the case at this time. He was drawn as a volunteer into the work of the Association. With his help the following plan was formulated: the Association would conduct a detailed housing survey of the bad apartment buildings on the street and make a catalogue of violations and then he, as an attorney for the Association, would complain about these violations to the Bureau. Thus between the hapless tenant and the irate landlord a third, unevictable party would be interposed. The complaints would not emanate from individuals but from an impersonal association. The Association set to work along these lines. Progress was not easy; after the eviction of the leader of the petition, the morale of the members was very low. Some members drifted away altogether, disheartened by the defeat. But Mr. Smith himself stayed and headed a new housing committee. Painstakingly, a survey of the worst houses on the block was made. After several weeks of work a list of violations in two buildings was compiled, and the attorney presented it to the Bureau of Licenses and Inspections. His experience in doing so was most instructive in demonstrating what a tenant is up against if he requests correction of housing violations.

Although there is a central office of the Bureau of Licenses and Inspections, not all complaints about violations of the Code can be filed there. Thus, the issue of the condemned furnace had to be handled by a complaint separate from that about the faulty elevators. A novice can spend several hours just finding out where and to whom he should complain. Even when he succeeds in filing a complaint, his complaint does not set off a general inspection of the building. The inspector looks at the specified apartment complained about and disregards the rest of the building. After the inspection the landlord is duly notified by the Bureau of the violation and given the customary grace period to make the repairs. Even then, the tenant's troubles are not over. If repairs are not made, a new inspection follows, usually followed by a new grace period for the landlord. Some landlords, in order to maintain "good will" at the Bureau, make partial repairs, usually the less expensive ones, and let the others go.

In the case of the Girard Street Association, it took six months for a trained lawyer, backed by the detailed surveys listed above, to force a landlord to make partial repairs in one apartment building. Even then, the repairs were not satisfactory. For example, cracked plaster was cemented and not repaired with plaster, a cheaper and quicker but not durable method of repair. No painting was done over the patched spots, although it is explicitly required by the Code and is considered to be "interior decorating" and not structural repair. Yet, without the persistent effort of the Association and the lawyer, not even these minor repairs would have been made. The fact that the tenants bear the burden of proof and that a most persistent effort is necessary to require the landlord to make even minimal repairs is well understood by slum landlords. Every time the Association tried to negotiate with a slum landlord on the block it met with the same rebuff: The landlord declared himself unwilling to deal with "outside troublemakers," "do-gooders who have no business on the street," and "self-appointed representatives" and declared over and over again that they have no interest in the Association's aim to protect the houses from deterioration. It was plain that they resented having to deal with an organization that could overcome the handicaps placed in the way of individual tenants—lack of know-how, lack of time, and vulnerability to retaliatory eviction.

The Rent Strike

Late one evening, January 16, 1964, events took place on the 1400 block of Girard Street that gave the Association a chance to test another approach to the issue of housing in the slums. Near the 14th Street end of the block stands an apartment building with nine apartments, each containing five rooms, a kitchen and bath, and a smaller basement apartment. The building is about 50 years old and was, in its day, a pleasant, solidly built structure. Traces of former comfort are still present. The walls of the stairway are lined with solid wood paneling, and the apartments are large and spacious. But in January 1964 the building, No. 1414, was the worst slum on Girard Street. What used to be the front yard was a heap of trash with broken liquor bottles strewn around. The hallways were dark, without a single light bulb. Near the entrance mailboxes without locks and doors were no longer depositories for letters; the Post Office had stopped delivering to 1414 Girard Street more than a year earlier. There seemed not to have been any trash collection in the building for at least that long, and the floors of the halls were so dirty that one could no longer guess their original color and texture.

In one of the top-floor apartments of the building lived Mrs. Katherine Schuler with her five children. She paid $90 a month for her five-room apartment. Her total monthly income was $215. She was on relief. She had lived in the apartment for five years. For the last three years the roof over her apartment had had a bad leak. During a heavy rain in the fall of 1963, water cascaded into three of Mrs. Schuler's five rooms and the hall as well. Several inches of water accumulated on the floor. The plaster fell off in giant chunks from the walls and ceilings, exposing electric wires. There were rat holes in the kitchen. In the living room several windowpanes were broken, patched only with cardboard.

For several years Mrs. Schuler had been complaining to the rental agent about the leaking roof. She had also been trying to locate another place to live, but large apartments are hard to find and small apartments do not take families with many children. Furthermore, most rental agencies require a month's rent in advance before accepting a tenant. For Mrs. Schuler to save up $100 out of her monthly income for such a deposit was simply impossible. Yet, if she requested repairs in her apartment, she was told by the rental agent that she would have to move out while such repairs were being made. Preceding the events of January 1964, there had been an empty apartment in the building, but the rental agent declined to accept Mrs. Schuler as a tenant for it.

The other apartments in the building were not in much better shape. In fact, the owner of the building had been ordered in May 1963 to correct no fewer than 31 Housing Code violations, including holes in walls and broken windows. Although subsequent inspections had been made of his property, he still had not made any repairs, when, in October, he was referred to the Corporation Counsel's office for enforcement. According to the Counsel's policy of good will, he was given until February 3, 1964, to comply. More than 40 people, mostly large families with small children, inhabited the rat- and roach-infested building. One of the tenants complained of "rats as big as kittens." A girl, while taking a bath, was struck by plaster falling from the ceiling. Her parents were paying $110 a month for their apartment. Another apartment had such a bad leak in the ceiling from a broken water pipe that the tenants used an umbrella to avoid getting wet. Another apartment had no front-door lock.

On the night of January 16, Lorenzo, the teen-age son of Mrs. Schuler, came into the office of the Nonviolent Action Group, a local affiliate of the Student Nonviolent Coordinating Committee, popularly known as "Snik" from its initials SNCC. Lorenzo had been helping out with collection of clothing for blacks in Mississippi and was known to the students from Howard University who had formed this group. He reported that his mother had received a court order of eviction for nonpayment of rent and that the federal marshals would evict her the next morning. Mrs. Schuler had fallen behind in her rental payments in December and January. She had not appeared on January 7 at a hearing at the Landlord and Tenants' Court at which the real-estate agent received an eviction order for nonpayment. This is a routine procedure for slum landlords. Some of them use court orders instead of reminders that rent is due. No cost to them is involved. They add a penalty payment of $3 to the rent, although they have to pay only $2 for the eviction order at the court. Evictions are a usual occurrence in the poor sections of the city. A collection of furniture deposited on the sidewalk by the marshals when they forced a tenant to vacate an apartment is a familiar sight.

The SNCC students went to see whether there was anything they could do to help Mrs. Schuler. When they saw the condition of the apartment, they were appalled to think that a District Court was forcing payment of rent for such living conditions. Remembering a case recently handled by the courts in New York, they decided to act. Several tenants of a dilapidated unheated slum in Harlem had refused to pay rent until repairs were made. The judge ordered them to put their rental payments in escrow, out of which the landlord could draw money only for repairs of the building. While this decision had been reached not in the form of a judgment but in the form of an agreement between the parties, it received wide publicity as an indication that the court was willing to come to the aid of slum tenants. As such, it was a departure from the doctrine that as long as a tenant occupies premises owned by the landlord, he is responsible for payments of rent no matter what the condition of the premises might be.

The SNCC students decided to try the same approach in this case. Under their guidance, Mrs. Schuler refused to vacate the premises or to pay rent until the apartment was repaired and fixed for human habitation. When the marshals came to evict Mrs. Schuler the next morning, they found the apartment full of determined looking young people who refused to budge from the furniture. The marshals left without having succeeded in evicting Mrs. Schuler. The SNCC students followed this incident with a meeting to which all the tenants were invited. They proposed a "rent strike" agreement in which the tenants would pledge themselves not to pay rent to the landlord until their apartments had been repaired to comply with the Housing Code. The despair of the tenants with respect to their living conditions can be measured by the fact that they all were willing to take this step. They were familiar with retaliatory evictions and knew the bleak prospects of a family with many children trying to find a place to live in the District of Columbia. Nevertheless, they joined with Mrs. Schuler, and the next day the Washington papers reported the first rent strike in the nation's capital. The owner of the building stated to the newspaper reporters that the tenants were "ungrateful, sloppy, filthy housekeepers," and declared herself "not above emptying the building and boarding it up." The rental agent went on record that he was "persecuted" and that SNCC was "the most arrogant, contemptible group." He said that "the poorer class of people are an awful hard lot to handle."

The Girard Street Association held a special meeting to brief its members about these developments. Their frustration over their lack of success in enforcement of the Housing Code led them to declare their solidarity with the aims of the rent strikers. Although none of the tenants of the 1414 building was an active member of the Association, the strike was a great morale builder for the entire block. A special effort on the part of the members was now made to get the rent strikers to come to the Association's meetings and to support them in their hour of crisis.

The students appealed to a professor at the Howard Law School, Herbert O. Reid, to undertake the defense of Mrs. Schuler. The minister of All Souls Church, Duncan Howlett, together with other prominent citizens, agreed to serve as a trustee of an escrow account into which the tenants would pay their rents instead of paying them to the landlord, until such time as repairs were made to bring their apartment up to the legal required minimum.

Hearings

A hearing of the case in the Landlord and Tenants' Court was set for January 27. The sessions in this Court are usually the most routine and dry affairs. The rights of the landlord are explicit. The landlord owns the premises and has complete control of them. For the privilege of occupying the premises, the tenant has to pay rent, and he enters into a contract to that effect with the landlord. Both the tenant and the landlord have the freedom to dissolve the contract. If the landlord does not like the tenant, he can evict him with or without cause. If the tenant does not like the apartment, he can move away. This presumed equality, however, is fictitious under the circumstances of housing shortage and racial discrimination prevailing in Washington. The tenants, because of their economic status, have virtually no protection on the real-estate market. Leases are virtually unheard of, written rental agreements signed by both parties are rare, and the customary arrangement is one of "30 days' notice." If the tenant falls behind in his rent, if the landlord no longer wants the tenant, or if the tenant wants to leave, a 30-day notice is the extent of legal protection for either side. Since the law is clear, hearings before the Landlord and Tenants' Court are usually limited to simple statements of facts: whether rent was or was not paid, and whether notice was received or given. The clerk reads out the names of the defendants in one case after another. Few tenants who fall behind in their rents ever appear at the hearings, and most of the judgments against them are by default. Occasionally, if a tenant appears and answers his name, a brief sentence or two from the judge disposes of the case: "Be sure and pay the rent by Monday," or "Go up to the renting office and see what arrangements you can make."

The hearing of Mrs. Schuler's case presented a departure from the usual monotony of this process. The tenant was represented by a lawyer, and the courtroom was filled with spectators. The Girard Street Association chartered a bus and brought some 30 residents to follow the court proceedings. SNCC sent a large group of representatives. There were several news reporters present as well as observers from the Washington

Planning and Housing Association, a volunteer organization trying to find ways to deal with the scandalous laxity of enforcement of the Housing Code. It was obvious that this was not a routine case.

Mrs. Schuler's lawyer concentrated on getting into the record all evidence pertaining to the deplorable conditions in the apartment. Witnesses were called to testify about the holes in the ceiling and walls, the exposed wires, the water on the floor. Pictures of the violations of the Code were entered into the Court records as exhibits, and the file of the Bureau of Licenses and Inspections pertaining to the violations and to the orders for repairs were subpoenaed and brought to court. The lawyer representing the owner repeatedly objected to the introduction of this evidence, stating that the condition of the apartment was in no way relevant to the issue before the Court, which was nonpayment of rent; that if the tenant did not like the conditions, she should have moved out; that no law exists to force the landlord to make repairs or to prevent him from renting the premises "as is."

When the owner's lawyer was overruled and the evidence was admitted, he contended that to keep up the interior of the apartment was the obligation of the tenant, not the landlord. He argued that the damage to the roof was not sufficient to cause the condition of the apartment and tried to establish as fact that Mrs. Schuler's children made the holes in the ceiling. Despite the appalling evidence presented by the defense, he protested that the apartment was livable, using as his supporting argument the fact that, after all, Mrs. Schuler did live in it and had not moved out. He argued that the law was unquestionably on the side of the landlord, and that there was no need to go into any of the facts regarding the condition of the apartment beyond the simple finding that she did not pay the rent.

Mr. Reid pointed out that Mrs. Schuler in point of fact had no choice: she could not move due to the shortage of housing. He cited the testimony of Mr. Walter Washington, D.C. Director of Public Housing, before the U.S. Civil Rights Commission pertaining to racial discrimination in housing, and the declaration of Commissioner Tobriner on the shortage of housing in the District, and pointed out that they amounted to a declaration on the housing emergency in this area. His contention was that public policy overrules private agreements, that legal rights must conform to public policy, and that to enforce a contract for an apartment that is openly in violation of the regulations of housing as represented by the D.C. Housing Code, is to enforce an illegal contract. He asked the judge to decide the case on the basis of public policy and not solely on the basis of the private rights of the landlord. Mr. Reid argued that by not complying with the Housing Code the landlord had forfeited his claim to the rent. Because the premises were not in a condition deemed by law as habitable, in effect he had evicted the tenant. The presumption of "constructive eviction" was not voided by the fact that Mrs. Schuler did not vacate the premises.

The case was argued on two consecutive mornings. The judge decided in favor of the landlord. Her decision, while disappointing, was not unexpected and did not mean a final defeat. In fact, her effort to establish a record of all pertinent facts in the case and her willingness to admit evidence about Code violations prevailing in the apartment indicated that she was aware of the importance of the case. At the end of her decision she said to Mr. Reid, ". . . you have made a record, and while it is not my place to overturn the law in this jurisdiction . . . I think you will get a judgment from the Appeals Branch on it." The lawyer indicated his intention of appealing the case.

To enable Mrs. Schuler to remain in her apartment while an appeal of the case was prepared, the execution of the judgment of the Landlord and Tenants' Court had to be suspended. This the Court agreed to, on condition that Mrs. Schuler deposit a bond. The lawyer of the landlord requested a $2000 bond, but upon objection of the defense lawyer the sum was reduced to $1000. The amount was calculated on the assumption that it would take four months to appeal the case. If the judgment went against Mrs. Schuler, the landlord would be assured payment of the rent due him and rent for the period during which Mrs. Schuler would remain in the apartment pending the appeal. Although the Court seemed to be giving Mrs. Schuler a chance to seek justice in a higher court, in reality she was in a hopeless situation. The Court was requesting a $1000 deposit from a woman whose only reason for living under the intolerable conditions that had created the issue was her extreme poverty.

With the help of friends, SNCC posted the $1000 bond for Mrs. Schuler, thus enabling her lawyer to appeal the case. His intention was to appeal directly to the U.S. Supreme Court, in order to shorten the litigation. He was aware of the fact that the type of decision he wanted to obtain would entail a revision of the existing precedents, a step reluctantly taken by lower courts. He also feared that the normal course of appeals through the hierarchy of federal courts would exhaust the financial resources available for Mrs. Schuler's case, long before the case could reach the Supreme Court. There was the further anxiety that if at any point Mrs. Schuler should be evicted from the apartment for lack of money for a bond for further appeal, the whole case would lose substance. Therefore, reasoning that the Supreme Court had direct jurisdiction over all the courts of the District of Columbia, Mr. Reid decided to appeal directly to the Supreme Court.

Eviction

Meanwhile the lawyers for the landlord undertook to evict Mrs. Schuler and the other tenants as the most effective method for defeating the rent strike. Again they brought eviction proceedings in the Landlord and Tenants' Court. Again Mr. Reid argued that no rent was due, on the doctrine of "constructive eviction." But under existing law, a landlord may evict a tenant without giving any reason at all. The law requires only that he give due notice. Having given such notice to Mrs. Schuler and the other tenants, the landlord now demanded that the Court order eviction forthwith, and for no reason but the landlord's wish. The Court, in accordance with law, granted the eviction orders.

These orders led to another hearing in the Court. Herbert Reid again represented the tenants and pleaded the same defense as in Mrs. Schuler's case. The judge who heard the case this time showed little sympathy for the rent strikers. He denounced the rent strike as impractical and declared that "other remedies were available." He did not specify what they might be. How completely ineffective those remedies would be was evident from the fact that although the corrections of violations had been repeatedly requested by the tenants and by the Bureau of Licenses and Inspections, even then, after the first trial of Mrs. Schuler's case, there were more that 140 deficiencies in the building.

The Court again ruled for the landlord, and the condition under which the second case could be appealed to a higher court was once more the deposit of a bond. This time it was set at $8000. The tenants of course were in no position to raise such a large sum. Appeals by SNCC, the Director, and the Association to raise this sum were unsuccessful. This meant that the decision of the Court could not be appealed, and with the exception of Mrs. Schuler, for whom a bond had been secured previously, the tenants faced inevitable eviction.

The tenants held one last meeting and decided not to wait for the marshals but to move prior to the date of eviction. They did not want to go through the ordeal of a forceful eviction, when the marshals pile up the furniture on the sidewalks in front of the building. Often the furnishings stay there until they are stolen, broken, or spoiled by rain and snow, while the tenant searches in vain for a place to go. A passerby wonders what happened to the people who used to own them. Often they are also scattered. The children of such a homeless family often end up in the crowded barracks of Junior Village, the D.C. institution for destitute children. Mothers and fathers live with friends or relatives. Sometimes as a result of such an eviction the family is permanently broken. SNNC volunteers worked with tenants all day and late into the night to help them move and to store their possessions, but they could not provide housing for them. The tenants had to double up with friends and relatives, and some had to divide their families into several households.

The next day a large body of police appeared with the marshals who came to evict the unfortunate tenants. Squad cars blocked off both ends of Girard Street because the police feared trouble. But there was no disturbance, only the singing of "We Shall Overcome" by some SNCC members standing on the sidewalk opposite. As a monument to the landlord's greed, the dilapidated building stood empty except for Mrs. Schuler, who had remained in the rain-soaked apartment on the top floor, the roof of which still had not been repaired. It is interesting to note that the fees paid by the landlord to his lawyers for these hearings had by now amounted to much more than would have been needed for repairs to the leaking roof.

The eviction of the tenants of 1414, who had shown such a fine spirit of solidarity, was a bitter defeat. They were even more disheartened when the Supreme Court declined to review the case and referred it back to the District Court of Appeals. Other legal technicalities now presented themselves. During the time of the appeal to the Supreme Court, the 30-day period for filing an appeal in the District Court had passed. Mr. Reid's appeal was therefore rejected on the technicality of being filed too late. The case could not be pursued further, and Mrs. Schuler was evicted. She disappeared from Girard Street, and her children were scattered into different homes.

Aftermath

This was a hard time for the Association. The members were crushed by the injustice of the rent-strike case. During the successive phases of litigation they had become increasingly aware of the importance that a favorable decision could have for them. It would provide a legal weapon by which tenants could obtain the enforcement of the Housing Code and thus achieve a minimum of decent housing standards. All through the proceedings, they felt the landlord had had an unfair advantage. Although he came into the court as one who had broken the law, both the legal and the financial advantage was on his side. The burden of proof was carried by the tenants, who entered the legal arena with the double handicap of ignorance and poverty. Without the assistance of Mr. Reid, who donated his services, they would have been helpless. Their financial inability to pursue their case prevented them from getting another hearing in a higher court. They saw a landlord, who for years had avoided compliance with the law, upheld by the Court that ruled for him. It left him free to collect future rent for an unhealthy, unsafe building. The members of the Association knew that this was part of a standard legal procedure. The simple human injustice of it hurt them. In their eyes it meant that a rich man can win in the courts, and the poor man does not have a chance. To them it meant that the Court simply refused to see the true facts of the case because the facts did not fit the law.

With bitterness, the members of the Association spoke about the fact that the landlord was never forced to deposit a bond as a guarantee of his intention to fix a roof that had been leaking for several years and for which he was clearly and undeniably responsible. They pointed out that, although he was repeatedly requested to make repairs, he was somehow always able to obtain postponements and was never forced to make them. Basic questions about the work of the Association were asked. Housing was the most bitterly felt need, and the high rents paid for crowded, deteriorated apartments the most serious drain on the inhabitants. The defeat in the rent strike had followed upon their own unsuccessful effort to have the Code enforced. It seemed that no matter how hard a civic group might try to help itself, it was up against such overwhelming odds built into the law and the administration that there was no use trying to do anything about it.

The Second Run-Around

A sense of futility pervaded the meetings of the Association as the morale of the members drifted lower. They saw the strike as additional evidence that no matter what they did they could not beat the system. The Director was as troubled and disturbed as the members of the Association. She realized that the organization had come to a crucial point in its existence, and that some way must be found to attack the housing issue.

The first task, they agreed, was to see to it that the landlord of 1414 did not rent his dilapidated, still unrepaired apartments to new tenants. The Director, therefore, approached the Bureau of Licenses and Inspections with the request that they obtain an injunction against the landlord to prevent him from renting the premises until minimum Code requirements were met. The Bureau does not usually seek such injunctions. It gives as a reason the fact that such injunctions result in further evictions, thus increasing congestion in other buildings. In this case, however, the building was already empty, and there seemed to be no valid reason for not insisting upon enforcement of the Code. It was therefore with utter bewilderment that the Director learned from the Bureau that it was not in position to request an injunction because it had no evidence to support a request. The record of violations had been subpoenaed by the Court, said the Bureau; it was now included in the Court's records. On that basis, the Bureau disclaimed any responsibility for further action on the building.

Knowing that the landlord was ready to rent the apartments again, Miss Bellamy began to pursue the missing records from one court clerk to another, from one court building to another. But the missing records never turned up. Miss Bellamy then appealed to the head of the Bureau of Licenses and Inspections, drawing his attention to the facts about the building. As a result of this intervention, the regional office of the Bureau finally notified the owner that his building would be closed until repairs were made.

The objective was thus reached, but the fact that it took a social worker who "knows her way around City Hall" several days to get this result, which should have been part of automatic law enforcement, gave the members of the Association and the volunteers working on the street a deeper insight into the ways of law enforcement. A tenant in one of these dilapidated apartments is in no position to take several days off his job to go from one office to another to find out how to make a law-enforcing agency enforce the law. Even if he has the time, he does not have the knowledge of the structure of the agencies. In the light of these handicaps most would not have the perseverance to do what the Director accomplished only with the greatest effort. The summary of the rent-strike experiment was a sad one: nine families evicted, the effort to achieve a favorable legal ruling frustrated, a complete lack of cooperation by the Bureau of Licenses and Inspections, and a seemingly inability on their part to understand the desperate plight of the tenants.

Two Buildings Are Purchased

Clearly, if any progress was to be made, a completely new approach had to be tried, one not dependent on the collaboration of the city agencies or of the courts. What was needed was a direct, simple approach that would produce results within a reasonable time. In searching for it the Director learned of the existence of another block organization that had developed a new approach to the problems of slum housing. This block club was organized by two young men, an insurance salesman and a lawyer, who worked in the Second Precinct, the worst slum area in the District of Columbia. Having met with the same frustrations as the Girard Street Association in trying to improve their housing situation, they decided that the only way to improve the houses is to buy them. This they began to do. They repaired the houses themselves and then rented them to tenants who were willing to collaborate with the block club to keep them in decent shape. Thus Better Homes, Inc., was organized in July,

1962, as a nonprofit housing corporation under the Nonprofit Corporation Act of the District of Columbia.

When the Corporation began, it was composed of three persons, a lawyer, a staff member of the Peace Corps, and an insurance salesman. None of them had had any previous experience in the building business. The Corporation bought its first house in November 1963, and within two years it owned eight buildings. The money for these purchases came from two sources. The first mortgages were placed with savings and loan associations. The down payments on the buildings were made with loans by private persons interested in helping the project. The loans were backed by promissory notes of the Corporation at a maximum interest rate of 8 percent. While the Corporation was glad to accept donations, it relied primarily on small loans from people who were not able to make large donations but who wanted to help. The directors of the Corporation believed it possible to provide adequate and healthy housing for fair rent while paying the interest on the money borrowed to finance the purchases and for necessary improvements. They cut costs by having tenants and other persons in the block make as many of the improvements as they could, such as painting, laying tiles, and the like, and by using volunteers to do the accounting and legal work involved. They collected their own rents rather than using agents.

The experience of the Corporation in its first two years of existence was heartening. Although the houses purchased were renovated and brought up to Code requirements, the rents were not raised. The Corporation was able to pay interest on its notes and to meet its financial obligations. It was a bold experiment, and experience demonstrated its basic soundness.

Miss Bellamy approached one of the directors of Better Homes, Inc., with an inquiry as to whether they would be interested in extending their operations outside the Second Precinct area. It seemed that the purchase of 1414 Girard Street by Better Homes would present a chance to improve the housing situation on the block. Better Homes had recently received a grant from the Edgar Stern Family Foundation that enabled them to hire a construction foreman with expert knowledge of real-estate values and reconstruction costs as well as the ability to work alongside the people actually making the improvements. The Corporation was also hopeful that it will qualify under FHA specifications for a 100-percent low-cost mortgage and improvement loan under the FHS program of housing rehabilitation.

It had been learned that the owner of 1414 Girard Street now wanted to get rid of the building. The property could not be rented without repairs having been made on it, and the owner was not willing to invest anything in it. As a matter of fact, it was learned later that he had no cash investment in the building. The total amount of his first and second mortgages exceeded the amount he had paid for the building. Now that his income from the rental had stopped, he was willing to sell. A smaller apartment building on the block was also for sale. At this point Miss Bellamy and the Girard Street Association decided to turn for help to their sponsoring organization, All Souls Church. Would the Church grant a loan to Better Homes, Inc., they asked, to enable Better Homes to purchase one or both of these buildings? After careful consideration by the Social Welfare and Finance Committees of the Church, the Board of Trustees granted the loan. All Souls Church then became the first church in Washington, or perhaps in any city, to take such a step. Other friends also joined in the effort, and as a result two buildings in the 1400 block of Girard Street were purchased in the early summer of 1964. One of these was the rent-strike building, the other a small apartment building with five units. Both were in a below-Code condition and in need of extensive renovation. Applications have been made to the FHA for mortgage and rehabilitation loans. When this financial support has been obtained, the buildings will be renovated by the expert repair crew maintained by Better Homes, Inc. The tenants, who will be selected by a committee of the Girard Street Association on the basis of need, cooperation with the group, and contribution to the aims of the Association, will have to contribute their own labor in finishing the repairs. Sanding, painting, finishing of floors, and other easily accomplished tasks will be left to them. Thus, rent costs will be kept low. The rental will be a division of labor between Better Homes and the Girard Street Association. Better Homes will handle all affairs dealing with financing, accounting, and major renovations. The Association will select the tenants, collect the rents, and supervise the administration of the building.

A Sequel to Girard Street

In July of 1970, William J. Gardiner, Associate Minister of All Souls Church, wrote to the authors, bringing us up to date on the developments in Washington's Cardozo Area. Four years had elapsed since the materials had originally been gathered for publication. Reverend Gardiner writes:

"Better Homes Inc. did renovate 1414 Girard Street. However, the renovation costs were so high that it was impossible to admit low-income tenants without some form of rent supplement. At that time the federal government did not provide rent supplements, so All Souls Church provided $1000 per year to make it possible for three low-income families to move into the building. Many of the people who were originally in the building never returned because the Girard Street Association filled the building with friends and relatives of members of the association.

"In April of 1968 the 14th Street corridor was destroyed in the civil disorders which were touched off by the murder of Martin Luther King. The terrible condition described in the Girard Street Report finally led to the destruction of the 14th Street community.

"However, a new thrust by the residents of the Cardozo Area has brought a new vision to the 14th Street community. The leaders of the various community organizations have come together to control the planning for the urban-renewal process that will be used to rebuild the area. This is the first time in the history of urban renewal in this country that a local group has controlled the planning process for the benefit of the people living in the urban-renewal area. In the first year the Ford Foundation provided funds for the local coalition to do its own planning. In the second year, after the Ford money ran out, the Coalition for the Rebuilding of 14th Street turned to the churches to raise money for planners and site developers. The plans call for new housing, community facilities, and opportunities for economic development. So far, the government has allocated $14 million for land acquisition. Land acquisition and site development is about to begin. All who are involved hope that this new thrust will provide the core for a new community in the Girard Street Area."

Social Planners

CHAPTER 8

Social Planners in Service, Coordinating, and Planning Settings

INTRODUCTION TO PART II

A difference that makes no difference is no difference.
CHARLES PIERCE

The dogmas of a quiet past are inadequate to the stormy present. Let us disenthrall ourselves.
ABRAHAM LINCOLN

Professional social planners are found in a number of settings. They work under a variety of auspices, and their ideological commitments may vary from conservative to radical. Their training may have been in any of several dozen professional schools or academic disciplines. Despite this heterogeneity, their work shows considerable similarity when broken down into its operational components.

Nearly all social planners are engaged in such activities as (1) fact-finding and problem definition, (2) the building of communication or operating structures, (3) the selection and determination of social goals and policies in the design of action strategies, (4) some aspect of plan implementation, or (5) the monitoring of change and assessment of feedback information. Together, these activities may be considered the stages of a planning process. The planner may not be engaged in each. To the extent he is not, however, his influence and power to influence change may be diminished.

Planners are not free agents. They are employed on a regular or consultation basis by organizations and groups. What they actually do, and the problems they attune themselves towards, are very much the function of the auspices under which they work. In our interviews, we found planners in direct-service agencies, in coordinating and allocating

211

organizations, and in planning units at the local, state, regional, or national levels. Their social-planning concerns may have been comprehensive or limited to a particular social or functional sector.

Defining Social Planning

Definitions of planning are manifold and often contradictory. In contrast to organizers, planners have been highly self-conscious in their attempts to define the planning process. The planner's social position, and the frequently ambivalent nature of his occupational role, puts pressure on him to justify his reasons for being. Organizers are more likely (although, as our cases illustrate, not always) to have clear mandates from their sponsoring organizations or to seek them from the populations they are organizing. Their activities are located in an interpersonal arena. Personal relationships are paramount to the development of their occupational identities. Planners, on the other hand, operate in an interorganizational arena. They frequently play new and uncertain roles in well-established institutions. To be considered seriously, their organizational roles must be clearly defined and the domains well staked out.

A planner's objectives may vary according to the setting in which he finds himself, auspices under which his work is supported, the time span he takes into consideration, the geographic scope his efforts encompass, the problems to which he is attuned, and the organizational structure within which his activities take place.

Within these constraints, the planner may be further influenced by the nature of his ideological positions and value preferences, by his characteristic manner of looking at or defining problems, and by his political, interactional, technical, and analytic skills. These, in turn, may affect his definition of the planning process.

A sample of definitions may illustrate the diversity of viewpoints we have encountered among planners. Social planning has been defined to us as:

A way of concerting community influence towards achievement of a common goal.

A process that gives effect to the wishes of the community.

A rational method of problem solving.

A process in which policy, determined by a separate political process, is translated into a set of operational orders for the execution of that policy.

A systematic ordering of the near future; a designing of the future.

Rational, goal-directed behavior, seeking the optimum adaption of means and ends as guided by a limiting set of social values.

A process whereby the planner feeds more information into the decision-making system.

Program development based on a process of goal selection and the progressive overcoming of resistances to goal attainment.

A means of directing social change through some form of coordinated program in order to further social well-being by attacking social and community problems.

None of these definitions are fully satisfactory. They tend to express values or preferences. In general, definitions tend to be either too specific and hence limiting, or too general and therefore meaningless. Still, they do provide us with some insights into the planning process.

Emphases differ according to whether the focus of planning is on "process" or on "end," on "consensus" or "rationality," on "goals" or "means" selection, on "development" or "change," and finally on "policy determination" or "design of action."

A number of authors, Alfred Kahn the most recent among them, have attempted to integrate each of these foci in an all-encompassing definition. Their efforts suggest that no definition can be fully satisfactory. While definitions may include such elements as future orientation, problem solving, policy or goal determination, strategy formation, and means selection (plan-making), most definitions tend to be incomplete. They may stress the phases or stages in a planning process, the levels or locus of planning intervention, or the analytic and interactional components in the planner's task. Normative in nature, they tend to be prescriptive rather than descriptive.

Rather than attempt an all-encompassing definition, we prefer to describe and to discuss the kinds of social planning illustrated in this volume. We recognize this description to be time bound and limited to our own observations, based on our interviews with American social planners in the latter half of the 1960s. In the absence of any satisfactory theory of social planning, such descriptions and the accompanying analysis may be a helpful preliminary to understanding the nature of the planning process.

Analysis and Interaction in Social Planning

A number of practitioners have suggested to us that social planning is differentiated from community organization because of the planner's greater respect for rational means and careful analysis. We do not agree.

While we do observe that many organizers, under the press of action situations, are not sufficiently analytic or self-conscious about their practice, we have observed the same of many planners. Planners do, however, tend to use a number of analytic tools, such as program budgeting and information systems, to inform their practice, making it appear that their practice is rationally based. These planning tools and some of their limitations will be discussed in Chapter 13. While they contribute to rational analysis, they do not obviate the necessity for the planner to undertake interactional tasks. This point is amply illustrated in Chapter 12. Similarly, the fact that these tools are somewhat less useful to the organizer does not obviate the necessity for his being analytic. Planners and organizers must both use a variety of analytic as well as interactional skills in their practice.

At the point of *defining a problem* to be acted on, or on choosing an objective or intervention, for example, the planner will have to choose from among a number of competing goals. Such a choice will not be made on the basis of information about the problem or considerations of cause-effect relationships alone. The actual processes of problem definition and tentative goal selection are influenced by all those individuals with whom the planner interacts as he gathers information about the problem, as he elicits interpretations about it, and as he assesses the influence of those individuals and groups that maintain different perspectives on the problem situation.

The process of problem identification flows directly into *the establishment of a working structure* to deal with the problem. Planning, at this stage, is essentially an art of choosing and guiding coalition partners. The planner must concern himself with the establishment of communication and interactional patterns that will extend over time, long enough to accomplish some desired end.

Policy formulation and goal selection, too, is as much an interactional as an analytic process. The planner may bring to bear his insights based on former experience. He may utilize his understanding of the political process to assure selection of a feasible objective. He may allow situational logic to dictate the specifics of his plan and its objectives. He may also engage in an interactional process in which he elicits and examines the interests and preferences of fellow staff members, constituents, powerful community figures, target populations or organizations, and members of a sponsoring or auspice-providing organization.

Planning implementation may require a variety of organizational and interactional tasks. It also requires careful specification and detailing of the tasks to be performed at every step in the process. It may be particularly important for the planner, at this stage, to utilize his relationships with relevant actors so as to influence them towards actions that will not result in goal displacement. This too requires a careful reading of the consequences of every act.

The design of a *monitoring and feedback* system requires the receiving and elicitation of information based on the experiences of relevant actors, and the analysis of the consequences of plan implementation. The use of information systems is detailed in the final chapter of this section.

It should be clear from this discussion that planning is not social engineering; it is not simply a technical activity. While it involves the application of "know-how" within the limits of organizational and community capacities, planning is just as much a question of interest. The question is, *who* gets *what, when,* and *how?*

What differentiates planning from organizing, therefore, is not the relative weights given to analysis or interaction, to rationality or politics, or to technical or relationships skills. It is rather the target at which the practitioner's activities are directed. *Planners concern themselves with the modification, elimination, or creation of policies, services, programs, or resources in service systems.* Organizers direct their activities towards modifying the behavior of people in their roles as citizens, constituents, consumers, clients, members of organizations, or functionaries. Both organizers and planners, of course, may be concerned ultimately with similar structural changes. Certainly, the line between organizing and planning is a fine one. The practitioner may become engaged in both planning and organizing activities sequentially, or at the same time. A number of cases in Chapters 9 through 12 reflect this duality. Similarly, practitioners whose major organizational roles may be administrative or in the provision of a direct service, may also engage in planning or organizing activities so as to complement or enhance their primary functions.

PLANNING AS A CORRECTIVE IN THE SERVICE-DELIVERY SYSTEM

Most American social planning activities are directed towards creating changes in service organizations and in service systems. This is a crucial observation. It suggests that many American social planners do not aim their efforts directly at the amelioration or eradication of social problems and social ills. Instead, they attempt to deal with the effects of social problems by altering the processes of resource allocation, service delivery, and program development in those systems currently or potentially charged with supplying appropriate social provisions.

Social planning in the United States generally proceeds from the assumption that a service network is somehow deficient in its capability to serve the needs of an identifiable population. Five types of deficiencies may be acted on:

1. A quantitative lack of services or resources. This assumes that the means for dealing with actual or potential social problems are known.
2. Ineffective or inappropriate services or programs.
3. Inappropriate structuring of services and resources. This assumes that services are present, but are either too splintered or too centralized, or are offered under inappropriate auspices.
4. Lack of responsiveness to needs and wishes of some actual or potential consumer group.
5. Appropriate service, a responsive system, but an ineffective outreach to consumers.

It is important to distinguish between these deficiencies. We have observed that otherwise competent planners may apply unsuitable tactics in their efforts to produce changes in target organizations. An effective strategy aimed at a service organization that is inappropriately structured to deliver its services would be quite different from a strategy aimed at an unresponsive organization. Careful analysis of the presenting problem and its contextual elements is called for.

The planner attempts to bring rational means to play in the improvement of the conditions he finds at the outset of a planning process. We do not suggest that planning is fully rational. In all probability it will never be so. A planner, his constituents, and his sponsoring organization must make choices at every stage in the planning process. These choices are frequently made on the basis of preferences, value commitments, and available information. Preferences are expressions of wants. They can never be fully ordered. They are never fully satisfied. Values are by their nature too general to ever be fully realized. Information is rarely adequate. Successful accomplishment of planning goals may result in the recognition of new wants, the identification of different value commitments, and the reordering or uncovering of new information.

Whatever its limitations, rationality in social planning aims at producing the greatest return for the efforts expended. It chooses a middle ground between effectiveness, efficiency, and feasibility. It aims at what Simon and other administration theorists have termed "optimization" rather than "maximization." Much of a planner's success may be due to his ability to calculate a middle ground between goal attainment, reduction of costs, and the storing of credit for future projects.

The social planner's emphasis on planned change gives order to the otherwise purely technical or essentially political processes of attempting to influence social change. Creating a new birth-control device, a new fuel, a surgical technique, or a new data-processing system are examples of technological innovations that create social change. Quid pro quo agreements, the use of coercive power, or an appeal to public opinion are examples of political efforts to influence the direction of change. Planners certainly utilize technological innovations and political tactics. What distinguishes planning from other processes, however, is its attempt at a balanced ordering of feasible objectives and/or the use of analytic tools to determine the efficacy of various means to overcome resistance to desired change—that is, to replace the irrational forces of the market with rational, calculated change strategies.

Planning is not an entirely new or modern phenomenon. History is replete with attempts by men to concert their decision-making powers through cooperative efforts to deal with the consequences of social problems, or to anticipate the future and prepare for it. What distinguishes contemporary social-planning efforts from earlier models is the recognition that planning can encompass conflicts of interests and differences of opinion. Planners may engage in either collaborative or conflictful strategies. They may attempt to coordinate the activities of numerous parties, or they may attempt to negotiate between or on behalf of parties to a conflict. In contemporary social planning, cooperation and conflict are not mutually exclusive or antagonistic strategies. Elements of conflict and cooperation are combined with the planner's technical expertise to guide the process of change.

A number of critics as well as a number of proponents of social planning have equated planning with social harmony. But, as Pusic points out, differences of opinion are rarely resolved at the beginning of a planning process. There is no notion of perfectibility in the process of social planning. Planners do not aim their efforts at the achievement of some perfect and harmonious end-state. Planning activities may themselves create new sources of social conflict, even as plan targets are reached. The greatest source of problems, Eric Severaid once commented, is solutions.

Planning in the United States

There is very little planning at the societal level in this country. National planning would entail the selection and ranking of social goals, and the assessment of both cost and feasibility. Our brand of social planning is as much a spin-off of the crises born of governmental intervention as a method to direct that intervention. There are many social programs in this country. There is too little societal planning.

In the absence of a clear set of national social goals, planners have had to engage in remedial action. Planners frequently evidence a caretaker orientation, creating programs to serve those individuals who cannot meet their own needs, or who have been structurally or psychologically alienated and disenfranchised. The American planner's orientation towards creation or modification of service programs has been described as a "vacuum filing" process. Unfortunately, most service programs operate within a context of very limited resources. The vacuums remain large. While planning, by its very definition, is the opposite of laissez faire, it has frequently degenerated, as Alvin Schorr has pointed out, into a national program of "evitez faire" in which inadequate funds are poured into demonstration programs rather than into comprehensive, structurally oriented change efforts.

American social planning is by its very nature an attempt at ad hoc solutions to specific problems. Suffering from a lack of comprehensiveness, it serves primarily as a corrective device for a complex of welfare services. These services, in turn, evolved in order to compensate for the wastage and breakage of a competitive, industrial, urban society, in which individuals and groups are frequently cut adrift or left behind.

Planning is based on the assumption that the aggregate of individual and group activities does not adequately distribute resources or opportunities, and that preferable conditions may be brought about. Planners further assume that the absence of planning deprives man of freedom of choice.

In practice, American planners have neither the mandate nor the tools to influence or direct basic changes in the fabric of society. Their planning activities are generally aimed at (1) reexamination of the linkages between service agencies and between service systems and relevant community groups such as resource allocators, clients and consumers, and (2) provision of new or extended services to populations that have been rejected for service or that have never been appropriately served.

In the United States, planning has been largely an attempt to introduce order at the local or community level and in the midst of generally uncoordinated efforts to influence the direction of economic growth, physical and urban development, and income and power redistribution. Even in the American system, however, the tendency towards centralized decision-making at the extra-community level is increasingly evident.

For the moment, however, the location of authority for goal determination and resource allocation in the United States has been obscured. Despite a myth as to the countervailing power of the federal government, there is little evidence that federal power is adequate to redistribute goods, control that distribution, and guarantee adequate welfare for the citizenry.

National planning in this country is still more a myth and a mystique than an actual fact or serious endeavor. This stems only partially from the historic evolutionary and ideological commitments of the country. Our inability is also based on the inadequacies of planning theories and planning instruments. This is, itself, an accident of history. Scientific technology and physical engineering have progressed much more rapidly than knowledge in the social sciences or technology in social policy determination.

In part, however, the problem is in our unwillingness to specify national social priorities and in our reliance on the counterbalance of vested interests. This unwillingness is not accidental. It is the effect of these vested interests. It has been possible for the nation to harness scientific and technological know-how of gigantic proportions to reach the moon. Hundreds of professional specializations and scientific disciplines were coordinated in one of mankind's most spectacular collective achievements. It seems unlikely that similar resources or concentration of efforts will be directed at the resolution of urban problems. There is no project comparable to NASA in the fields of urban problems, social welfare, and social policy.

Until recently, central or national planning, if it existed at all in this country, was relegated to such instrumentalities as White House Conferences, Presidential task forces, and congressional investigatory and legislative committees. In the 1960s civil rights, mental health, housing, and antipoverty and social-security legislation gave some evidence of a shift towards national planning. Increasingly, too, pressures for the development of a national system of social accounts, for a Presidential Social State of the Union Message, and for policy recommendations from federal bureaucracies may shift the balance from the local to the national level, and from resource acquisition to resource utilization in accordance with national priorities.

Presently, however, most planners are employed by organizations with limited mandates and limited power to affect the course of social change and the arrangements of social institutions. Even venturesome organizations and social movements become institutionalized at the point at which they settle on the provision and maintenance of a service perspective. Planning organizations, like all other organizations, are dependent on exchanges with what Roland Warren calls "input" and "output" constituencies. Input constituencies provide them with legitimation, community support, staff, financial revenue, knowledge, and other resources. Output constituencies are those that are the recipients or beneficiaries of the planner's or planning organization's interventions.

Input constituencies generally exercise more control over the planner or the planning organization than do output constituencies. For this reason, planning efforts may be biased towards the provision of services and the establishment of programs aimed at changing individuals rather than changing the basic structural arrangements of society. It is easier to develop a job-training program or to experiment with new educational technologies than to attempt to intervene at the causal level of structural unemployment. It is also less risky.

The planner directing his efforts at more basic structural changes will threaten some of his more powerful input constituencies. Even apparently secure and independent sources of funding may dry up, if the planner appears to threaten entrenched and powerful institutions. The dismantling of the antipoverty program provides evidence of this fact, as do recent pressures put on the National Council of Churches following its support of Alinsky organizing efforts, or on the Ford Foundation following its support of controversial school decentralization in Ocean-Hill Brownsville. All too frequently, efforts aimed at changing the system or structure of institutional relationships shift so in orientation that the end result of a planning effort may be the provision of new or expanded services aimed at changing individuals.

This is the basic contradiction in most planning efforts. In the absence of clearly defined social objectives or a priority of national goals, even planning efforts aimed at reducing the fragmentation of social services and at restructuring the service network frequently end up with fragmented and palliative additions or correctives to the existent system. "A difference that makes no difference is no difference."

Planners, then, may act neither on the primary causes of social problems, nor on the primary consequences of social change. Many planning interventions may be said to be at the tertiary level. Planners intervene in the workings of those institutions that themselves act on the secondary consequences of social change (that is, inadequate housing, poor schooling, inaccessible medical services, unemployment, and the like) and accompanying social problems.

Planning Settings and Structures

Planning settings and structures in the United States vary according to whether they are under governmental or voluntary auspices, according to geographic scope, and according to the area of programmatic concern.

The best approximation of a fully comprehensive planning effort may be found at the regional level in the Tennessee Valley Authority (TVA). Other than the TVA, however, planning units generally can be distinguished on the basis of whether their concerns are (1) limited to certain sectors of the welfare system (for example, education, aging, delinquency, dependency, and child welfare), in which case they may practice within (a) a particular service agency or (b) a specialized coordinating or planning unit; or (2) intersectorial or more comprehensive either (a) at the local level or (b) beyond the local level.

SECTORIAL PLANNING

Sectorial planning takes place within a specialized problem or program arena. Such planning involves promotion of the interests of some target population, a service agency, or a service network organized on behalf of that population. Sectorial planning is frequently spurred by federal or voluntary appropriations or by the existing agencies to expand their domains, extend their effectiveness, or increase their efficiency. Much of the planning in this area, while nominally directed at expansion of resource allocation, is in reality engaged in resource acquisition.

THE DIRECT-SERVICE AGENCY

The planning that goes on within or on behalf of direct-service agencies is a case in point. Whether in social welfare, education, health or other sectors, these agencies grew in response to societal dysfunctions engendered by industrialization, urbanization, and bureaucratization. They deal with those individuals or groups that are the casualties of social and economic change. Their services, however useful and important, tend to be splintered, fragmentary, and limited in scope.

Direct-service agencies are dependent on external sources of financial support and good will. An agency's effectiveness is based in part on the skill and expertise of its practitioners and on the appropriateness of its services. Planners employed by direct-service agencies generally perform three functions: (1) they mobilize support for the agency's ideology, program, or financial needs; (2) they guide the process of interorganizational exchange of such resources as personnel, specialized expertise, facilities, funds and influence; and (3) they direct their efforts at changes in community resources and programs outside the direct jurisdiction of their agencies but necessary to the welfare of their clients and constituencies.

Mobilization of community support assures that the agency can maintain viable programs through (a) the winning of public acceptance, (b) the recruitment of clientele, and (c) the securing of adequate financing. If there is a lack of adequate support, the planner may seek to isolate or nullify external threats, or to reexamine the very nature of the agency's services with the view of rectifying inadequacies.

Just as agencies are dependent on external services, so they are looked upon for support by other organizations. Frequently, the planner in the direct service agency enters into (a) collaborative exchanges with other organizations through the coordination of services or responsibilities for mutual client systems or (b) joint-action efforts aimed at community education, the passage of new legislation, or the securing of new resources to be shared. Such exchanges depend on mutual (although not necessarily equal) sharing of benefits.

Agency planners may also attempt to change the directions of other service systems or influence the general direction of community resource allocation. Their efforts may result in the creation of new services that may be autonomous, jointly sponsored with other agencies, or in some cases developed within their own agencies. A number of such examples will be found in Chapter 10.

The planner's success will depend on the values attached to his efforts by his own and other existing service agencies. It will also depend on the administrative and other supports he receives within his own agency.

SECTORIAL PLANNING BEYOND THE SERVICE AGENCY

The press of ongoing administrative and maintenance responsibilities makes it unlikely that direct-service agencies can adequately plan for sectorial needs apart from their immediate clientele. Consequently, a variety of other sectorial planning bodies have been developed. In government, urban-renewal authorities, and city-planning commissions, statewide health, mental health or retardation planning councils, and commissions on human resources and human rights are examples of centralized planning bodies. Private foundations for the blind, for the handicapped, for the aged, and for the extension of family services play similar roles although generally without official public (governmental) sanction.

INTERSECTORIAL OR COMPREHENSIVE PLANNING

The proliferation of sectorial planning bodies and programs aimed at specific populations poses the problem of coordination and the need for more comprehensive approaches. Accordingly, a number of coordinating, allocating, and intersectorial planning bodies have grown up during the first two thirds of the 20th century.

COMPREHENSIVE PLANNING AT THE LOCAL LEVEL

At the local level, these have included welfare councils, sectarian federations, community-action agencies, model-cities boards, and human-resources commissions.

Welfare councils have received special attention in Chapter 9 of this volume because of their traditional relationship to social work and social welfare agencies. Their major contributions have been to further cooperative relationships between voluntary social agencies, to raise the standards of professional practice, and to stimulate the planning and coordination of new services.

Sectarian federations have played similar roles within ethnic or religious communities, notably among Catholics and Jews. In addition, "functional" federations, limited to particular fields, have coordinated and planned for other services. Examples are hospital associations, the National Federation of Settlements, the National Urban League, and nursery-school associations. Community-action agencies, funded by the Office of Economic Opportunity, were organized with the objective of stimulating existing agencies and councils to attempt innovative and necessary new programs, while providing a voice to the disenfranchised poor. CAAs also spawned a number of new direct-service programs, particularly in the area of youth services and job training. The human-resource commission (HRC) is still another form of service coordinating agency that emerged in the late 1960s. Generally under local governmental auspices, the typical Mayor's HRC is concerned with integration of governmental and private service networks.

COMPREHENSIVE PLANNING BEYOND THE LOCAL COMMUNITY

Attempts at comprehensive planning beyond the local community are still rare. Most recent attempts at comprehensive planning have been largely ad hoc in nature. Nevertheless, evidence abounds of new attempts to coordinate planning efforts at state and regional levels. State planning bodies and regional counterparts have developed in some 36 states. Their form may be that of the interdepartmental commission or the superdepartment of human services. While these are still in their infancy, it is likely that a new governmental emphasis on creative federalism, bringing together planners from federal, state and local levels, may spawn new and effective forms during the 1970s.

The Planner's Perspective

Much of the planning literature evidences concern with man's current inability to predict, shape, or control the effects of technological changes, and its repercussions for social values, social customs, and patterns of social interaction. Questions of consumer control or citizenship involvement vary according to whether the location of the planning unit is at the locality level or extracommunity in locus and scope. The planner at the community level, close to his clients or to the populations affected by his intervention, may give high priority to consumer choice and the problems of individual liberty. Planners at the extracommunity level may be more concerned with the establishment of overall goals and the "greatest good for the greatest number." In both situations, however, regardless of the planner's democratic ideal, there is in practice a tendency to shortcut processes, an impatience with delays, and an emphasis on efficiency.

While almost all planners adhere to the principle of citizen involvement, one is not hard put to identify at least two contradictory perspectives. Some planners envision planned change as emerging from the bottom and moving upwards. In their work, the general citizenry or a specific population may be involved in the process of both goal formation and task accomplishment. Planners of this persuasion may play advocacy roles or may concern themselves with the processes of community involvement more than with specific goal attainment. They may be found representing grass-roots organizations, or acting in coordinating capacities on welfare councils representing social agencies. In each case, their definitions of relevant constituencies may vary somewhat, but their conviction of the need to involve representatives of affected organizations and populations is similar.

Other planners may place greater emphasis on specific goal attainment, on "objective" central planning. Change emerging from the bottom up, they argue, is limited in perspective, fragmentary in objective, and divisive in effect. Comprehensive planning can only be done from a centralist position. Freedom, they argue, can best be guaranteed by planning for it, rather than by allowing the competition of the marketplace to distribute liberties inequitably. Planners who represent the interests of particular constituencies, they argue, may actually jeopardize the interests of the community as a whole.

This points up the central dilemma in planning. Opposition to planning in the name of freedom is self-defeating. Social change continues at an ever-accelerating rate regardless of planned intervention. Man's freedom of choice can only be preserved by choice. Without control over the direction of change, man is at the mercy of his social environment, much as, in an earlier day, he was the victim of a harsh physical environment. Nevertheless, complete centralization would undermine effective participation, and remove from the citizenry, control over the directions of their own lives.

The unanswerable, or perhaps multianswerable, question is, *how much and what planning is desirable?* The question becomes somewhat less intolerable when we accept the fact that the outcome of planning is not known. Planning as we know it today is still a system of interaction and adaptations whose outcome is never fully predictable. In practice, planning goals are never fully fixed, are never completely calculable, and are ever moving and changing.

Planning efforts may vary in accordance to the value placed on mutuality of goals and cooperative strategies, as against the utilization of contest and conflict strategies. This, however, may be neither a political nor an ideological consideration. Warren has observed that the successful utilization of various strategies may be more the effect of the social environment surrounding a planning effort than the planner's personal preferences of strategy. In an environment of consensus of goals and means, collaborative and cooperative strategies may be the most effective and efficient. In an issue environment where differences of opinion or plain indifference exists, the more effective strategy may be one of persuasion. Where differences of opinion are strong and where dissension as to either goals or means is present, contest or conflict strategies may be the most effective. The planner's analytic skills may determine both his understanding of the situation in which he finds himself and his selection of strategies.

Despite the influence of setting and environment and the constraints imposed by funding sources and other constituencies, much of what a planner chooses to do and how he goes about his work may be influenced by his characteristic manner of looking at problems. Cognitive styles may be as influential as ideological perspectives.

In our interviews, we have observed that a number of planners function in much the same manner that the "operationalist" does in the social sciences. In examining a presenting problem, the planner may begin with the following observations. "These are the skills I possess (for example, negotiating skills or the use of cost-benefit analysis) and these are the problems I observe that are within the scope or domain of my agency." He then asks himself, "Which of the problems I observe are amenable to intervention and what goals can I accomplish within the constraints of my organization and with the skills I have at my disposal?" Taken to the extreme, this position may suffer from what Abraham Kaplan calls "the law of the instrument." Give a small boy a hammer, and he may find that everything in sight needs pounding.

Other planners put implicit faith in the utilization of data and theory for the formation of goals. The gathering of relevant data and the analysis of facts become the guiding criteria for action. In positivist tradition, they may begin the planning process by asking themselves, "If this were so, what must I do?" They gauge the distance between some normative ideal and the observation and measurement of conditions as they perceive them to exist. There is a tendency for these planners to state objectives in terms of ideal goals, and to assume implicitly that by pursuing some immediate and measurable objective, movement towards the more distant objective has been demonstrated.

For still other planners, the meaning of current situations and observed social problems lie in their implications. In pragmatist fashion, they ask, "What difference does it make if this is so, and what difference would it make if it were altered in this manner or that?" Planners of this persuasion tend to be less selective about ends, and more apt to see the interconnectedness of ends and means. They aim toward optimization, and let their actions be dictated by their interpretations of what is and what is not feasible.

A number of students have suggested to us that a planner's occupational life is more secure than an organizer's. We do not agree. The planner or the organizer who does not take risks may face a secure if dull future. Many good planners do take risks. An experienced city planner confided to us that to be effective he stirs up so much trouble that he must move on every few years. "It's my job to open up the community. Other people can then come in to consolidate actions." One planner we interviewed called himself a "social-work bum," and another decried his position at the end of an "occupational yo-yo."

There is another side to this picture—one that is very difficult to illustrate but is expressed well in some of our case materials, notably those on grantsmanship in Chapter 11. Planning in this country is a relatively new field. Suddenly there is new money coming down the pike—not enough to really "solve" our massive social problems, but enough so that some people will make a good deal of money, and others can consolidate political power. All kinds of people are attracted to planning, many of them opportunists whose hidden agenda is their own political future. In such a free-wheeling situation, planners with a social-work or other professional background may suddenly find themselves working with people who play by different rules. This poses a serious problem and is of concern to all those practitioners who want to see their occupation legitimized and fully recognized.

PART II OF THIS VOLUME

We have said a great deal about planning and about planners. Lest we succumb to the temptation to write more, we refer the reader to the next five chapters. We will let the planners speak for themselves. In Chapter 9 we show examples of very good and very poor practice within welfare councils. In the next chapter, we examine the planner's roles as played out in direct-service agencies.

The next three chapters focus on the planner's skills and the manner in which he performs necessary tasks, rather than on his location. Chapter 11 explores the planner's skill in grantsmanship and proposal writing. Chapter 12 examines the interactional skill he must possess in order to successfully guide a plan. The last chapter focuses on the planner's use of newer planning tools, and his role as a technician.

The reader may wish to refer back to this chapter in order to pose questions in relation to the case materials. To what extent does the planning effort reinforce the existing state of power and resource distribution? Has an effort aimed at helping a target population ended up in serving an agency network? Do political considerations nullify technical knowledge? In a number of cases, the reader will observe similarities in approach among planners and between planners and organizers. What accounts for these similarities? How do planners and organizers differ?

Suggestions for Further Reading

Although many of these sources complement and give conceptual clarity to the case materials that follow, others go beyond this volume to discuss aspects of social planning for which case materials are not currently available.

A. BOOKS

Altshuler, Alan A., *The City Planning Process: A Political Analysis,* Cornell University Press, Ithaca, New York, 1965.

Braeback, David, and Charles E. Lindblom, *A Strategy of Decision: Policy Evaluation as a Social Process,* The Free Press of Glencoe, New York, 1963.

De Jouvenal, Bertrand (Ed.), *Futuribles,* Droz, Geneva, 1963.

Diesing, Paul, *Reason in Society: Five Types of Decisions and Their Social Consequences,* University of Illinois Press, Urbana, 1962.

Doxiadis, Constantinos, *Urban Renewal and the Future of the American City,* Public Administration Service, Chicago, 1966.

Gurin, Arnold, and Robert Perlman, *Community Organization and Social Planning,* Council on Social Work Education and John Wiley and Sons, Inc., New York, 1971.

Kahn, Alfred, *Studies in Social Policy and Planning,* Russell Sage Foundation, New York, 1969.

Kahn, Alfred, *Theory and Practice of Social Planning,* Russell Sage Foundation, New York, 1969.

Miller, S. M., and Frank Reissman, *Social Class and Social Policy,* Basic Books, Inc. New York, 1968.

Morris, Robert, and Robert H. Binstock, *Feasible Planning for Social Change*, Columbia University Press, New York, 1965.

Suchman, Edward A., *Evaluative Research: Principles and Practice in Public Service and Social Action Programs*, Russell Sage Foundation, New York, 1967.

B.   READERS, CASEBOOKS, AND INSTRUCTIONAL MATERIALS

Allen, Muriel I. (Ed.), *New Communities: Challenge for Today*, an AIP Task Force on New Communities Background Paper, AIP, Washington, D.C., 1968.

Anderson, Sanford (Ed.), *Planning for Diversity and Choice: Possible Futures and Their Relations to the Man-Controlled Environment*, The MIT Press, Cambridge, Massachusetts, 1968.

Annals of the American Academy of Political and Social Sciences, Parts I and II, May and September 1967, *Social Indicators*.

Bauer, Raymond A. (Ed.), *Social Indicators*, MIT Press, Cambridge Massachusetts, 1966 (paper).

Bell, Daniel (Ed.), "Toward the Year 2000: Work in Progress," *Daedalus*, Summer 1967.

Cornog, Geoffry Y., James B. Kenney, Ellis Scott, and John J. Crainelly (Eds.), *EDP Systems in Public Management*, Rand McNally and Company, Chicago, 1968.

Dorfman, Robert (Ed.), *Measuring Benefits of Government Investments*, The Brookings Institution, Washington, D.C., 1965.

Eldredge, H. Wentworth (Ed.), *Taming Megalopolis*, Anchor Books, Garden City, New York 1967, Volumes I and II (paper).

Ewald, William R., Jr. (Ed.), *Environment for Man: The Next Fifty Years*, Indiana University Press, Bloomington, 1967 (paper), based on paper commissioned by the American Institute of Planners.

———— (Ed.), *Environment and Change: The Next Fifty Years*, Indiana University Press, Bloomington, 1968 (paper).

———— (Ed.), *Environment and Policy: The Next Fifty Years*, Indiana University Press, Bloomington, 1968 (paper).

Frieden, Bernard J., and Robert Morris (Eds.), *Urban Planning and Social Policy*, Basic Books, New York, 1968.

Kahn, Alfred, *Studies in Social Policy and Planning*, Russell Sage Foundation, New York, 1969.

Morris, Robert (Ed.), *Centrally Planned Change: Prospects and Concepts*, NASW, New York, 1964.

PERT for CAA Planning: A Programmed Course of Instruction in PERT (a backward-chaining planning approach), prepared for Community Action Program, OEO Washington, D.C., 1968, by Policy Management Systems, Inc.

Planning and the Federal Establishment, Proceedings of the Fourth Biennial Government Relations and Planning Policy Conference of the American Institute of Planners, Washington, D.C., 1967.

Wilson, James Q. (Ed.), *Urban Renewal: The Research and the Controversy,* The MIT Press, Cambridge, Massachusetts, 1966.

C. ARTICLES AND PAPERS

Altschuler, Alan, "The Goals of Comprehensive Planning," *Journal of the American Institute of Planners,* August 1965.

Bateman, Worth, "Assessing Program Effectiveness: A Rating System For Identifying Relative Project Success," *Welfare in Review,* January/February 1968.

Bodarsky, C. J., "Comprehensive Planning for Community Mental Health Services: The Commonwealth of Pennsylvania," *Community Menal Health Journal,* Fall 1965, 1, No. 3.

Borko, H., "The Analysis and Design of Information Systems," System Development Corporation, Santa Monica, California, SP-2655, 1966.

Brooks, Michael P., and Michael A. Stegman, "Urban Social Policy, Race, and the Education of Planners," *Journal of the American Institute of Planners,* September 1968, 34.

Cavanagh, Jerome P., "Policy-Making in Large Cities," *Social Welfare Forum,* 1967.

Chetkow, Harold B., "The Planning of Social-Service Changes," *Public Administration Review,* May/June 1968, 29.

Dakin, John, "An Evaluation of the 'Choice' Theory of Planning," *Journal of the American Institute of Planners,* February 1963.

Davidoff, Paul, and Thomas A. Reiner, "A Choice Theory of Planning," *Journal of the American Institute of Planners,* May 1962.

Demone, Harold W., Jr., "The Limits of Rationality in Planning," *Community Mental Health Journal,* Winter 1965.

Doxiadis, Constantinos, "Report on the Human Community Project," *Ekistics,* July 1967.

Dror, Yehezkel, "Policy Analysts: A New Professional Role in Public Service," *Public Administration Review,* September 1967.

Duhl, Leonard J., "Planning and Predicting: Or What to Do When You Don't Know the Names of the Variables," *Daedalus,* Summer 1967.

Dumpson, James R., "Planning by Social Agencies," *Social Progress Through Social Planning,* Proceedings of the XIIth International Conference of Social Work, Athens, 1964.

Dyckman, John W., "Social Planning, Social Planners, and Planned Societies," *Journal of the American Institute of Planners*, January 1966.

Etzioni, Amitai, "Mixed-Scanning: A Third Approach to Decision Making," *Public Administration Review*, December 1967.

————, "Short Cuts to Social Change," *Public Interest*, Summer 1968.

Evan, William, "The Organization-Set: Toward A Theory of Interorganizational Relations," in James D. Thompson (Ed.), *Approaches of Organizational Design*, University of Pittsburgh Press, Pittsburgh, 1966.

Frieden, Bernard J., "The Changing Prospects for Social Planning," *Journal of the American Institute of Planners*, January 1967.

Friedman, John, "Conceptual Model for the Analysis of Planning Behavior," *Administrative Science Quarterly*, September 1967.

Gans, Herbert J., "Planning and City Planning for Mental Health," *Ekistics*, March 1965.

————, "Planning for Urban Renewal," *Transaction*, November 1963.

Greenhouse, Samuel, "The Planning-Programing Budget System: Rationale, Language, and Idea Relationships," *Public Administration Review*, December 1966, **26**, No. 4.

Gross, Bertram M., "National Planning: Findings and Fallacies," *Public Administration Review*, December 1965.

————, "The State of the Nation: A Social Systems Model," in Raymond A. Bauer (Ed.), *Social Indicators*, MIT Press, Cambridge, Massachusetts, 1966.

Gurin, Arnold, and Robert Perlman, "Current Conceptions of Planning and Their Implications for Public Welfare," in David G. French (Ed.), *Planning Responsibilities of State Departments of Public Welfare*, American Public Welfare Association, Chicago, 1967.

Herrmann, Cyril C., "Systems Approach to City Planning," *Harvard Business Review*, September/October 1966.

Kaplan, Marshall, "Advocacy and Urban Planning," *The Social Welfare Forum*, 1968.

Katz, Fred, "Social Participation and Social Structure," *Social Forces*, December 1966.

Keniston, Kenneth, "How Community Mental Health Stamped Out the Riots," *Transaction*, July/August 1968.

Levine, Abraham S., "Cost-Benefits Analysis for Social Welfare," *Welfare in Review*, February 1966.

Levine, Sol, and Paul White, "Exchange as a Conceptual Framework for the Study of Interorganizational Relationships," *Administrative Science Quarterly*, March 1961.

Lindblom, Charles, "Economics and the Administration of National Planning," *Public Administration Review*, December 1965.

————, "The Science of Muddling Through," *Public Administration Review*, Spring 1959.

Lindblom, Charles, et al., "Government Decision Making: A Symposium," *Public Administration Review*, September 1964.

Long, Norton E., "Citizenship or Consumership in Metropolitan Areas," *Journal of the American Institute of Planners*, February 1965.

Lubove, Roy, "A Community-Planning Approach to City Building," *Social Work*, April 1965.

Mansen, Willard B., "Metropolitan Planning and the New Comprehensiveness," *Journal of the American Institute of Planners*, September 1968.

Michael, Donald N., "Urban Policy in the Rationalized Society," *Journal of the American Institute of Planners*, November 1964, **31**, No. 4.

Morris, Robert, and Robert H. Binstock, "Comprehending the Social Planning Process: Towards a Theory of Social Planning," *Social Welfare Forum 1965*, Columbia University Press, New York, 1965.

Perlman, Robert, "Social Welfare Planning and Physical Planning," *Journal of American Institute of Planners*, July 1966.

Perlman, Robert, and Arnold Gurin, "Perspectives on Community Organization Practice," *The Social Welfare Forum 1968*, Columbia University Press, New York 1968.

Perloff, Harvey, "New Directions in Social Planning," *Journal of the American Institute of Planners*, November 1965.

Piven, Frances F., "Dilemmas in Social Planning: A Case Inquiry," *The Social Service Review*, June 1968, **42**, No. 2.

Pusic, Eugene, "The Development of Theories of Planning," University of Zagreb, Yugoslavia, 1966 (mimeo).

Rabinowitz, Francine F., "Politics, Personality and Planning," *Public Administration Review*, March 1967, **27**.

Reagan, Michael, "Toward Improving National Policy Planning," *Public Administration Review*, March 1963, **23**.

Reiner, Janet S., Everett Reimer, and Thomas A. Reiner, "Client Analysis and Development of Public Programs," *Journal of the American Institute of Planners*, November 1963.

Reissman, Frank, "The Myth of Saul Alinsky," *Dissent*, July/August 1967, **14**, No. 4.

Rossi, Peter, "Evaluation Social Action Programs," *Transaction*, June 1967, **4**, No. 7.

Schottland, Charles I., "The Future of State Planning for Public Welfare Programs," in David G. French (Ed.), *Planning Responsibilities of State Departments of Public Welfare*, Brandeis University, Waltham, Massachusetts, 1966.

Seeley, John R., "What is Planning? Definition and Strategy," *Journal of the American Institute of Planners*, May 1962.

Seider, Violet, "Organization the State Welfare Department for Community

Planning," in David B. French (Ed.), *Planning Responsibilities of State Departments of Public Welfare,* Brandeis University, Waltham, Massachusetts, 1966.

Spilhaus, Athelstan, "The Experimental City," *Daedalus,* Fall 1967.

Vickers, Sir Geoffrey, "Ecology, Planning, and the American Dream," in Leonard J. Duhl (Ed.), *The Urban Condition: People and Policy in the Metropolis,* Basic Books, Inc., 1963.

Warren, Roland, "Interaction of Community Decision Organizations: Some Basic Concepts and Needed Research," *Social Service Review,* 41, No. 3, September 1967.

Warren, Roland, "Model Cities First Round: Politics, Planning and Participation," *Journal of the American Institute of Planners,* July 1969.

Weidenbaum, Murray, "Government-Wide Budget Plannings," *Transaction,* March 1968.

Wildavsky, Aaron, "Aesthetic Power or the Triumph of the Sensitive Minority over the Vulgar Mass: A Political Analysis of the New Economics," *Daedalus,* Fall 1967.

————, "The Analysis of Issue-Context in the Study of Decision-Making," *Journal of Politics,* November 1962.

Winston, Ellen, "The Government's Role in Social Intervention," *Welfare in Review,* January 1967.

Wise, Harold, "Planning-Programming-Budgeting Systems and the Planning Role," *Planning and the Federal Establishment,* AIP, Washington, D.C., 1967.

Yarmolinsky, Adam, "Ideas into Programs," *Public Interest,* Winter 1966, No. 2.

Zald, Meyer N., "Organizations as Polities: An Analysis of Community Organization Agencies," *Social Work,* October 1966.

Zweig, Franklyn M., and Robert Morris, "The Social Planning Design Guide: Process and Proposal," *Social Work,* April 1966.

9

Welfare Councils—Planning or Coordinating

CASES AND ILLUSTRATIVE MATERIALS

Practitioners in welfare councils, in federations, and in other associations of voluntary health and welfare agencies are faced with underlying contradictions in their practice. They must on the one hand support, coordinate, and otherwise help to maintain their membership agencies that have banded together in partnership, while on the other hand, assume responsibilities to plan for social needs not currently being met by these agencies. While serving their member agencies, they must also establish and develop their own agency identifications and purposes. This underlying tension is present, to some degree, in each of the case materials and illustrations included in Chapter 9.

The very structure of federated agencies contributes to this conflict. The classic structural form was the Council on Social Agencies, purely an organization of agencies. While this form has been modified by the inclusion on boards and committees of "community leaders" who do not represent the interests of particular service agencies, the influence of delegated representatives is still felt either directly or indirectly.

The Havilland House case gives the most dramatic illustration of this dilemma. The Group Work and Recreation Division of a welfare council in a growing metropolitan area decided to raise the standards of practice for settlement houses. It found the staff at Havilland House out of tune with the times, and its services unrelated to pressing neighborhood needs.

234

The Council staff decided to make Havilland House a test case in order to show the Council's muscle to other agencies in the community. After a year of threats, counterthreats, and negotiations, the Council staff was successful neither in getting Havilland House to phase itself out of existence nor in radically improving its services. While the fault may lie either in the inexperience or lack of skill of the Council's staff or in the commitment of their consultant, the case also illustrates the ways in which "facts" and "values" become intertwined. Despite attempts to define issues in objective terms, issues continued to be defined in highly emotional value terms.

The staff members of the Welfare Council, who dealt with Mr. Salamanaca of the Association for Retarded Children, proved to be much more highly skilled and considerably more resourceful. The situation described here was even more emotion-laden than in Havilland House. Involved were parents of retarded children who had banded together for self-help purposes and for the provision of direct services to their afflicted children.

Despite the fact that Salamanaca and the Association Board approached the Welfare Council for help when a crisis almost split the Association, Salamanaca and his associates were so threatened by their perceptions of the Council's staff that they threatened in return to bring political pressure to bear on the Council. This case is most valuable for its detailed illustration of contingency planning and its description of rather typical Welfare Council strategies. These include (1) the use of studies for consultative and public-relations purposes, (2) the confrontation of differences, (3) the use of informal relationships, and (4) the creation of new structures of communication or new structural forms.

The latter strategy is rather well described in "Delinquent Girls Get a New Treatment." In this case, the executive of a Council takes the reader through the process of integrating some of the services of three member agencies and one nonmember agency that had applied for the first time for subsidization. Despite the fact that the administrator-planner accomplishes what he sets out to do, one wonders whether his viewpoint is not somewhat myopic. While the organizational changes he engendered made it possible to provide new services to delinquent girls, the question that was never fully raised was whether these services were really helpful or whether other programs were more beneficial.

The next case illustrates what happens when a Welfare Council does not anticipate the unanticipated. It also illustrates the frequent but muffled differences of opinion that may exist among Welfare Council members. This point is made dramatically in the case of the black social worker who finds himself torn between his professional and occupational commitments and his ethnic and racial identity. While the situation is described by a white worker, the internal conflict alluded to is not too different from the one described by a black community organizer in "Black Students Take Over" (Chapter 4).

These cases also hint at some of the limits of Welfare Councils in scope and concern. The solutions with which they seek to remedy social problems are always envisioned in terms of services, and invariably in terms of service agencies. Federated agencies are rather strongly bound by the service orientations of their affiliate agencies and by the definitions that these agencies give to the social problems with which they are concerned. The budgeting process of one federated agency is discussed in some detail. Note that the agencies actually define the terms by which the Federation Board will make its allocations. The process is long and involved. The decisions are consensual.

Finally, Mrs. Kaplan proves that the best laid plans of mice and men. . . .

*   *   *   *

P-1   SALAMANACA BUYS A STUDY FOR THE MENTALLY RETARDED[1]

RESEARCH AND CONSULTATION IN COMMUNITY PLANNING

A Cast of Characters

I am Irv Michaels, research director of the Health and Welfare Council. In some councils, research is kind of neutral. It is used for gathering data that might then be used for policy determination. We use research a little more actively. In some ways, it is one of our most important planning tools. When I get into a piece of research, I think of myself strictly in planning terms. As a matter of fact, I was a community organizer first. I only went back to school after I became convinced of the political importance of research in social planning. Let me give you an example.

A couple of years ago the Philanthropic Foundation granted the state-wide Association for Retarded Children a special allocation of $20,000. Ordinarily, the Foundation acts only on the basis of special applications.

---

[1] This case is an edited version of a study record by Franklin M. Zweig entitled "Research Consultation as Intervention in Community Planning for the Mentally Retarded." It appeared in its original form in Violet Sieder, *The Rehabilitation Agency and Community Work: A Source Book for Professional Training*, U.S. Dept. of Health, Education and Welfare, Washington, D.C., June 1965. Dr. Zweig is presently Dean at the School of Social Work, State College of New York at Buffalo.

That year, however, the Foundation's capital reserves had grown so large that it was advised by its legal counsel to increase its allocations. A President's Discretionary Fund was established by the Foundation's board of directors. Thus, at the discretion of the Foundation's president, an amount of money could be granted to any worthwhile civic, philanthropic, or charitable organization. Now, I can tell you that an organization does not have to have a budgetary deficit to be thrown into a crisis. When you're not used to planning ahead, and somebody throws $20,000 at you out of the blue, it can precipitate quite a ruckus.

But before I get to the details, let me introduce some of the characters in this little drama. John Franklin, the Foundation's president, is a very successful businessman and considered to be a very influential citizen in these parts. At the time, he was state chairman of the Republican Party. During the course of his tenure as president of the Foundation, Franklin had directed several grants to the Association for Retarded Children. All of these grants had been used for the establishment of direct services to retarded children. Franklin's interest in retardation was very real and very personal. One of his own kids had been retarded. She died as an adolescent some ten years ago.

The Association of Retarded Children was composed of 14 independent local associations with an overall board. Most of the statewide board members lived right here. Most of the important organizations in this state had their headquarters here. It's not only the biggest city in the state, but also the state capitol. The Association's president, Peter Salamanaca, also had a deep personal interest in retardation. One of his living children was severely retarded. I wouldn't say that Salamanaca is a wealthy man, but as manager of a large and successful business concern, he certainly is financially "comfortable." Salamanaca doesn't have nearly the influence Franklin has, but he's quite well known and highly respected in the Italian-American community. Last year, Salamanaca commanded a delegation to the state Republican Party Convention.

Franklin and Salamanaca had known each other through party politics, but really became acquainted by virtue of their mutual interest in retardation. As a matter of fact, Franklin had been active in the Association before he became chairman of the Republican State Committee or president of the Philanthropic Foundation.

The Health and Welfare Council is the third party to this drama. The whole staff and a lot of board members were involved, but I guess you might say that the three principal actors were Carl Norman, our director; Quincy Gregory, our board president; and myself. We have 14 professionals on the staff. About 75 percent of our budget comes from the United Fund and the other 25 percent comes from contracts with state or federal governmental agencies. On occasion, we get special grants for special projects like the one I'm about to describe, but these don't get reflected in our regular budget.

The First Act—The Association is Split

You might say that since its inception, the statewide Association for Retarded Children had been divided. One faction was adamant in its insistence that the organization should develop its own direct services for the children of members. Many of the local chapters, for example, had their own retraining centers and diagnostic and referral clinics. Pete Salamanaca was definitely the leader of this group. The second faction felt that the Association should not establish its own services, but should engage in social-action activities aimed at the tax-supported and voluntary agencies already vested with responsibility for rendering services. Members in this second faction felt that sufficient attention to retardation could only be obtained by mobilizing and employing resources outside the Association. The Association's board was equally split on this issue.

You can imagine the reaction when it was announced that the Philanthropic Foundation had made a grant from the President's Discretionary Fund of $20,000. A lot of people felt that it was a political payoff to Salamanaca, who had just the year earlier delivered a block of Italian-American voters to elect Franklin to the Republican Party chairmanship.

Somehow the pro-direct-services group didn't seem to be thrown off its guard nearly as much as the pro-social-action group. The Salamanaca crowd wanted to use the money to fulfill what it described as the most urgent need of all—the employment of a social group worker to organize leisure-time activities throughout the state. It took them a little longer to regain their balance, but the pro-social-action faction wanted the money devoted to the development of public-relations material to be used to pressure governmental agencies to greater recognition of the needs of the retarded.

The issue was discussed, debated, and fought over for 5 months. Things finally came to a head and it looked as though the Association would split down the middle into two separate organizations. In order to avert an actual separation, a temporary compromise was arranged. The board of the Association voted to request a study by the Capitol City Health and Welfare Council to determine how the money should be used. It wasn't unusual for organizations to come to us with requests for research or consultation. It was unusual, however, for the Association to come to us. Seven years earlier, the United Fund had asked us to conduct a study of the Association. That study was to be made in connection with the admission of the Association as a member of the United Fund. The request for the study was withdrawn, after Franklin intervened with influential lay leaders in the Fund. His position was that the Council took "too long to do things," but his real fear appeared to be that the Council would erect obstacles to his goals for the Association. The Association was admitted to the United Fund anyway, without the customary study.

I guess it's no overstatement to say that Pete Salamanaca was distrustful of the Council. He viewed us as the "hatchet-arm" of the United Fund and was certain that the submission of the request for study and consultation would open up a Pandora's box and yield him nothing but ill. Knowing of Franklin's intervention, vis-a-vis the United Fund request seven years earlier, he conferred with Franklin regarding strategy to be used with the Council.

Salamanaca had no previous personal contact with the Council. In various activities sponsored by the Council, either the Association was represented by a new board member or representation was not made. He did write the letter to Carl Norman requesting help from the Council, however. A few days later Salamanaca called Norman and made an appointment for a visit.

The visit was a cordial one. Salamanaca explained the Association's request in a little more detail. The meeting provided a good opportunity for both men to become acquainted. During the meeting, Salamanaca made his position very clear. He thought that the money should be used to add direct services to the Association; he was sure the Council would see it this way also. Norman listened to Salamanaca's statements and made no comment about either side of the issue. He indicated that the Council would take as objective a look as possible. Salamanaca agreed that an objective look was what was needed, but that, in conclusion, he was sure that the Council would see the need for direct services for the retarded. He also indicated that Franklin of the Industrial Philanthropic Foundation was very much interested in direct services by the Association. He was certain that "Mr. Franklin would be gratified" if the Council decided in favor of direct services in the spending of money.

Norman outlined what the Council's approach to the Association's request would be. A special subcommittee of the Council's board would be constituted as a subcommittee and devoted to the study of the Association's request. This prompt action, Norman was clear to point out, would be accorded in light of the threatened split of the Association's board around this issue. Salamanaca seemed appreciative of this special attention, and noted that he would establish a special subcommittee of the Association's statewide board of directors to meet with the Council's special subcommittee and to collaborate in arriving at a solution. Norman agreed with this approach, and told Salamanaca that the Council's president, Mr. Gregory, was in accord with this plan. Norman and Gregory had discussed the Council's request upon its receipt. The request was then discussed with all Council staff prior to submission and acceptance by the Council's board.

Act Two: First Two Meetings of the Joint Committee

The first meeting of the Council subcommittee and of the Association representatives was held two weeks later. Salamanaca had appointed six representatives from the Association to attend. Gregory, the Council president, had appointed four representatives from the board of directors, in addition to himself. Salamanaca's delegation included five members of the faction supporting his position and one member of the faction supporting the opposite side. Gregory had appointed four middle-range leaders who had no stake in the Association or in the outcome of the discussions. Gregory noted that this group was merely an exploratory panel that would be appropriately expanded if the matter warranted more study. I sat in as a Council staff member and took notes.

The first meeting was devoted to a presentation of the issues and proceeded smoothly for about an hour and a half. The Association representative holding the opinion of the second faction (favoring promotional programs) could not be present. One of the members of the Council's subcommittee suggested that the story of the second faction was underrepresented. At this suggestion, Salamanaca and one other close supporter commenced an emotion-filled denunciation of the perceived "attack" on him. He claimed that the Council was biased against the Association, particularly against the desire of the Association to develop a more comprehensive pattern of services for retarded children. He also claimed that the Council's exploratory committee was biased in its selection by not including someone who was close to the retardation situation. Salamanaca's close supporter expressed grave concern about the objectivity of the Council in approaching its task, stating baldly that it was well known that the Council was committed to a philosophy of depriving "the agencies" of adequate funds. The meeting ended in considerable confusion, but with a tentative agreement to meet again when tempers were cooled.

At the second meeting, the person representing the second faction in the Association made a brief presentation of the second faction's basic concerns. It was delivered rather sarcastically and haphazardly; apparently the guy had been influenced by what he had heard of the previous meeting. His position could not have been nearly as strong as it must have appeared in the long series of debates held by Association members during the preceding several months.

Soon after the opposing view was presented, Salamanaca proceeded to indict the Council for its "lack of concern about retardation." He said that it was the general impression of the Association that the Council was not sufficiently concerned and that there was agitation in the Association board from both factions to terminate the study by withdrawing the original request. Carl Norman and I had primed the Council representatives in advance for this kind of expression from the Association. They suggested that a four-week interim be declared, at the end of which the Council would present a plan to the Association. The plan would offer concrete steps toward the solution of the problem. Association representatives decried the need for delay, but accepted the proposal grudgingly.

The next day Carl Norman received a call from John Franklin, who said gravely that his call was to express his concern about the Council's behavior in dealing with the Association and his concern about future relationships between the Foundation and the Council if such "conditions" were to continue. Franklin also noted that State Senator Powers and state Representative Yardly had been contacted about the matter and would keep close contact with the situation. Franklin explained he had discussed the matter with them because he knew that they would not want the state to continue to authorize funds to support the Council if such conditions of conflict were the only results of the Council's work. Franklin said that he would like to have lunch with the Council Director and President "sometime," as he was sure that the matter could be satisfactorily worked out. Norman's response was an acceptance of a possible meeting and a note of his intent to relay Franklin's phone call to the president of the Council. Norman also told Franklin that the Council was working on a plan to be presented to the Association representatives in four weeks, and that this had been agreed on by the Council and the Association in the meeting the previous night. Franklin expressed his interest in seeing the plan when developed. The conversation ended.

Act Three (Scene 1): The Design of a Plan

That afternoon and evening a full staff seminar was held regarding the problem. The purpose of the seminar was to develop a plan—proposals and strategies—to be used by the Council after ratification by the Board subcommittee appointed to explore the issue.

Phase I (Primary Plan)

The Council would modify its study objectives and present a study program to the Association in another form. The form would be "research-consultation" to help the Association determine, for itself and the community, what the needs of the retarded actually were, the scope of those needs in the population, and the services and agencies currently devoting time and services to meeting those needs. The rationale for this, it would be explained to the Association, is that spending money for direct services or for promotional activities must be decided on the basis of a realistic assessment of the problems and needs of the retarded.

It would be proposed that the money allocated to the Association by the Philanthropic Foundation be considered "seed" money and be utilized in making an effective assessment of the needs of the retarded. This proposal would utilize the small Foundation grant for setting a pattern for the Association's functioning over a long period of time.

It would be proposed that the money be used for out-of-pocket expenses such as interviewers, data tabulation and analysis, and travel in connection with the study. A budget of $9000 would then be drawn up, with the recommendation that the remaining $11,000 be held by the Association to be used as seed money for implementation of the recommendations developed during the course of the study.

Moreover, the Council would act to establish an advisory committee for the study. The purpose of the advisory committee would be to draw representatives from each of the major statewide organizations having responsibility for the retarded, such as health, welfare, education, employment, and recreation organizations, both tax-supported and voluntary. The advisory committee would serve as a source of information on services and programming and would also provide a means by which the Association could reflect its concerns to the proper authorities. It would be explained that one of the primary difficulties of the Association was the distance it maintained from the major organizations rendering services; it would be suggested that a first step for the Association is to become familiar with the services, ideologies, and power relationships of such organizations.

First Alternative to Phase I. As an alternative, in case the primary plan was rejected by the Association, the Council would carry out such a study on the statewide needs of the retarded, and agreement would be reached to commence a one-year moratorium on any further discussion on the use of the $20,000.

Second Alternative to Phase I. The Council would withdraw from the study and not play a part in the decision-making at all, but would maintain an open-door policy so that the Association might again request the Council's help. In the light of the emotion-charged atmosphere characteristic of the first two encounters of the Association and the Council, the Council would rescind its offer to conduct the study. This action would be explained as forthrightly as possible with the statement that unless there could be some basic agreement between the Association and the Council, the time and effort spent in developing recommendations would be completely wasted.

Third Alternative to Phase I. The Council would formulate plans for a request to the statewide United Fund that a study be conducted (by the Council) of the relative responsibilities of the voluntary organizations, members of the Fund, that deal with retardation as an aspect of their program. This alternative, it was decided, would be suggested only after two meetings to be scheduled for consideration of the primary plan.

Phase II

The board of directors would invite the state's congressional delegation, seven U.S. congressmen and two U.S. senators, to a luncheon meeting within the next several weeks to discuss the needs of the retarded and the state situation with regard to the Association. If the Council's primary plan were accepted, the meeting would be delayed and staged jointly with the Association. The motivation for the attendance of the congressional representatives, split nearly equally by party, would be furnished by the vice president of the Council, who was the AFL-CIO president at the state level and a national officer of the AFL-CIO at the national level. This same labor leader had, at several previous points, acted in the Council's behalf. This invitation was intended to provide the Association with support for the development of services to the retarded as well as serving a safety function to the Council.

Phase III

A letter outlining the Council's primary plan would be sent to Franklin inviting his participation on the advisory committee to the study (should the Association accept the proposal).

To implement each of the three plans, a staff team was created placing me as the Council's research director, as team leader. I would be responsible for the implementation of the primary plan under the general direction of the executive director. Added to the team were the health secretary and the family-welfare secretary of the Council. The role of the health secretary would be to organize the advisory committee (Phase I, Primary Plan), while the role of the family-welfare secretary would be to handle the meetings scheduled with the state's congressional delegation (Phase II).

The plans were submitted to the special committee of the board and were accepted with few changes. A more careful strategy was developed with regard to the meeting with the congressional delegation and an additional stratagem was added: a meeting of the editorial chiefs of each of the major newspapers would be convened at a luncheon to discuss the problems of the retarded and to begin to develop support for state programming for the retarded. The resources and contacts for this would be arranged by a member of the board, a prominent newspaper and magazine publisher.

Act Three (Scene 2): Negotiating the Plan

Four weeks later the joint committee was convened again. Quincy Gregory, the Council's president, presided at this meeting, together with Pete Salamanaca, the Association's president. The cochairmanship had been worked out prior to the meeting by a telephone conversation between both men. Gregory presented the primary plan—the establishment of a study to determine needs of the retarded. The presentation was made at the outset of the meeting. Mimeographed copies of the proposal were distributed by my staff to each of the joint committee members. A copy of the proposal had been sent by special-delivery mail to John Franklin.

Association members were profoundly surprised. The Council president stimulated some questions and discussion, but most questions were very superficial, the Association representatives not having had an opportunity to digest the content of the proposal. Salamanaca remarked that he was very much impressed, that he had not known that the Council work could be so efficient and detailed. Salamanaca stated that the Association would give adequate consideration to the proposal, and that upon returning to the next meeting in two weeks, the Association would have a reaction. He said that he doubted that the Association would want to use the Foundation grant for such purposes, but that perhaps such a financial arrangement could be made in other ways.

Two weeks later the joint committee convened again. In the interim, Salamanaca had convened the Association board that had authorized its delegation to the joint committee to guardedly negotiate the proposal. The Association board found the proposal to be a tension-relief device in the light of the extreme tension generated in that agency by the original issue and the conflict with the Council that had developed out of that issue. We had hoped it would be just that. And that it would take the heat off us.

Having been given nearly a free hand to negotiate the proposal, Salamanaca spoke for the entire Association delegation to the next meeting of the joint committee. He agreed that a study of this scope was necessary, but that the Association should be the group responsible for conducting such a study. Having no prepared statement, Salmanaca spoke a bit on the importance of a parents' group conducting a study of this magnitude and the excellent experience possessed by the Association members in the light of their seeking out services throughout the state. He had discussed the proposal with Franklin, and the latter had agreed that such a study would be valuable. The problem was to decide who should do the study. Salamanaca could not see using $9000. He acknowledged that the Association did not have the trained research help necessary to analyze the data gathered in the course of the study, but that such help might not be necessary. After all, who was better prepared to make recommendations on the needs of the retarded than those who have retarded children themselves?

The Council president responded immediately. In a concise statement, he pointed out the technical difficulties in developing such a statewide study of needs and resources. He was certain that the Association had no idea of these difficulties and could not cope with them. Further, such a study, in order to be effective, must enlist those segments of the community that have responsibility for the provision of services for retarded— for example, the state departments of health and welfare, education, and employment. Finally, Gregory said that he did not understand the Association's position—did they have a proposal in return, and would they present it forthwith?

Salamanaca replied that the Association had no position, but that the Council would not take its responsibility away. At this point, several members of the joint committee, from both the Association and the Council, began to speak. Two Association members assured Salamanaca that the Council was not attempting to take the Association's responsibility away and that, in general, the position of the Association was that the Council's proposal was a sound one. Two members of the joint committee from the Council stated that cooperation in this matter was not only desirable, it was mandatory: what did the Association need to make such a working agreement stick? A long debate developed, considerably less heated than those that had characterized previous meetings, but still full of feeling. Salamanaca wanted to make sure that the autonomy and the freedom of the Association were protected. He was confident that using part of the grant from the Philanthropic Foundation to undertake the study would be endangering the Association's prerogatives. The Council's position, on the other hand, was that its usual practice was to charge fees for large-scale studies. The use of this money by the Association would be a wise investment. Out-of-pocket expense paid for by means of such funds in no way obligated or blocked the Association.

After nearly 3½ hours of debate, I proposed a compromise that was accepted by the joint committee. My proposal was that $4000 of the Philanthropic Foundation grant be used to finance a "preproject" and to serve as seed money to attract a federal grant to conduct a comprehensive research study. The Council would contribute one third of my time as Council Research Director, to carry out the preliminary study and to design a comprehensive study in detail for a one-year period, and this would be the Council's "seed" contribution. An application would be jointly made by the Council and the Association to the Social Rehabilitation Service (SRS) in HEW to finance a comprehensive study. It might include the employment of a social worker who would do the major data collecting from families on the needs of the retarded. The Council would collect preliminary data from organizations and the Association would collect preliminary data from its members. If I were to direct the study, I would need an advisory committee for it, which might consist of the following.

1. Two representatives of the Association for Retarded Children.
2. Two representatives of the Health and Welfare Council.
3. A representative of the Philanthropic Foundation.
4. A representative of the State Department of Education.
5. A representative of the Roman Catholic diocese concerned with parochial education.
6. A representative of the State Department of Health.
7. A representative of the State Department of Social Welfare.
8. A representative of the State Interdepartmental Committee on Mentally Retarded.
9. A representative of the State Department of Employment.

Needless to say, Carl Norman and I had thought this "compromise" out pretty carefully. The proposal was taken back to the two organizations and ratified, and two weeks later an agreement was consummated. In the meantime, the discussion with the editorial boards of newspapers was held and three influential newspapers came out with editorials favoring a new look at problems of the retarded in the state.

Act Four: Implementing the Modified Plan

Two weeks later, the joint committee hosted a luncheon of the state's congressional delegation. Franklin was invited to attend but declined. A member of the joint committee explained the need for a thorough study of the needs of the retarded. We received wholehearted endorsement by the congressional delegation with indications of support for any research grant application.

During the next month Bob Glick, the Health Secretary of the Council, convened the Advisory Committee. I developed a preliminary research design, and in a three-month period the information on resources for the retarded was collected. It showed that there were some 71 agencies offering services to the retarded in the form of some 212 specialized services. It also indicated that many of the services were duplicated in the same cities, even though they were paid for out of the same funding mechanism. For example, in one downstate city, one public and two private agencies offered the same type of counseling services to families with the retarded, and all were nonsectarian. The two private agencies both obtained monies from the local community chest. It was also discovered that resources were minimal in the outlying areas; that in these areas, schools had no provisions for retarded children. Diagnostic resources were sometimes as far as 80 miles away from families with retarded children.

The Advisory Committee met four times to consider the preliminary information. There was general agreement that the most important aspects of the study had disclosed the following.

1. The need for more decentralized diagnostic and referral services.
2. The possible need for traveling treatment teams for smaller towns and rural areas.
3. The need for statewide planning and coordination of services.

The most obvious and frightening aspect of the study was the disclosure that most agencies had very little idea of the social needs of the retarded. Most school systems, most recreational agencies, and most employment services did not consider the retarded to be in need of differentiation as a special group. Most leisure-time agencies were beginning to establish special programs for the retarded, but had little idea of the kinds of programs that would be useful. Most health officials treated retardation as a problem singularly limited to physical considerations.

The chairman of the Advisory Committee was Hank Porchek, the labor leader who had been instrumental in obtaining congressional delegation support for the Council's study process. Over a number of meetings, he had succeeded in gaining agreement on general priority areas from the Advisory Committee.

My staff and I presented the material in as succinct and visual a form as we could devise. We prepared the material in such a way that each representative to the Advisory Committee could take the information to his organization for study. The material had considerable impact on its own.

In the case of the Catholic diocese, for example, it became increasingly clear that the Catholic school system had no conception of the need for a special program for the retarded. Yet, proportionately, Catholic day schools had the highest number of retarded children in the elementary grades. The diocese was represented by the Bishop's delegate, Father Joseph, Secretary of the State Chancery Office. He had on two occasions convened his council of parish priests and his council of district lay representatives to unfold the story of retardation in the Catholic school system. Since there had been agreement by the Committee at its organizational meeting that no preliminary results would be shared with the press, Father Joseph was instructed by the Bishop to brief all relevant personnel in the diocese on the school-system situation. The diocese would prepare a position and a program in readiness for future press releases. Salamanaca's activity in the church was not an inconsiderable factor in moving the diocese. It was interesting that he had never considered pressing the Church for service programs in the past.

Some organizations had little reaction to the report. For example, the State Department of Employment indicated that it had never intended to develop a special program for the retarded. It took the position that it was constrained by law to develop broader programs, and, that while it considered the plight of the retarded to be an important problem, it could not see the need for developing special plans in this area. I guess you can't win them all.

One organization, the State Department of Education, claimed that the preliminary study was not accurate and did not reflect the true school situation. The representative of the Department was the Commissioner for Education, an appointee of the Governor. He claimed that his Department would develop a special study of the educational needs of the retarded, in conjunction with the Council's study process, and would withhold further judgments until such a study had been completed. Our follow-up with one of the state senators and the press assured that there would be a second study. We were able to exert the right pressure on the Governor's office.

Through all of this, I spent much time in interpreting the preliminary results of the study to Franklin and Salamanaca. I lunched with them three times, interpreted the preliminary data, discussed its ramifications for large public agencies, indicated possible directions for further study, and began to outline a broad series of action programs that might be considered by the Association for Retarded Children. On two other occasions, Hank Porchek, the Advisory Committee chairman, met with Franklin and with Salamanaca to discuss the progress of the study. On another occasion, Porchek, Norman, Gregory, Salamanaca, Franklin, and I met to discuss drafting a proposal for the demonstration and research study.

Subsequently, I prepared an application that we submitted to SRS four months later. A three-year study with some unique design aspects was funded and is currently in operation.

During this time, changes in the Association for Retarded Children became perceptible. By participating in the Advisory Committee, Association members began to notice those units that had primary responsibility for large-scale allocation of resources. At one informal meeting, Franklin and Salamanaca both admitted that the kind of needs that woud have to be met, given nearly 90,000 retarded persons in the state, could only be met through the massive application of public services.

Toward the end of the seven-month period, this information was brought back to the Association Board and the Association, with my help, began to prepare position statements on the needs of the retarded. These were circulated to the appropriate state and local, and, in some cases, federal agencies. The Association board had agreed that the preparation of carefully worded statements for circulation to other organizations and for release to the press could be an important tool in pressuring for the development of services.

When the State Catholic Bureau of Schools formulated a demonstration program in the upper third of the state for the screening and identification of retarded children, in response to a carefully prepared request by the Association, the board of the Association began to feel that it was functioning with greater unity than it had for several years. At the end of the year, which marked a moratorium on consideration of the Philanthropic grant, the Association, by majority vote, agreed to place the remaining $16,000 into the study as a local contribution for the research grant to be funded by the federal government. This change in procedure caused a major upheaval in the board of directors. Six of its forty-eight members resigned. The resignation was made amidst great publicity, but Salamanaca managed to maintain his leadership and to retain most of the important political support on the Board.

The Philanthropic Foundation, during the next year, granted the Association $36,000 more to be used for promotional and lobbying purposes. The Foundation also made available $16,000 to be used in a demonstration project for recreation for the retarded. The demonstration was to be conducted by an existing agency, contracted for service by the Association.

At the present time, the Association is in the process of developing an extensive lobbying program coupled with several demonstration projects in conjunction with existing agencies as part of the federally-funded project. I think we did all right. It's not so much how many facts you dig up with your research, it's how you use the process.

P-2   HAVILLAND HOUSE FIGHTS TO SURVIVE AND THE WELFARE COUNCIL SEEKS TO ESTABLISH ITS AUTHORITY AS A PLANNING BODY[1]

The trouble with most welfare councils is that they are so concerned with maintaining the support of their constituencies that they find it almost impossible to do any comprehensive planning. Raymond Davallos, the director of the Community Welfare Council (CWC), put it to me squarely when he asked me to consult on the Havilland House affair. "Look, the Welfare Council can't be everywhere, and we can't support every agency that lays a claim to us for money. We are supporting agencies in 16 suburbs now that didn't exist 10 years ago. The inner city has changed. The neighborhoods have changed. And the agencies that used to provide services may no longer be relevant to current needs. We have been interested in phasing out some of our support commitments for a long time. But we want to do it on some rational basis. It took us 3 years to hammer out a policy statement that we could use to examine whether an agency was really meeting a community's current needs, and whether its practices were sufficiently professional to warrant our support. Havilland House is our test case."

He then went on to give me the background to this caper. The CWC Group Work and Recreation Division had completed a lengthy study, a couple of years earlier, of the settlement houses in the community. The study committee had been made up of top-level lay and professional leaders. The study uncovered service duplication, vested interests, interagency rivalry, poorly structured programs, and an irrational pattern of United Fund commitments to supporting different settlement houses.

Alma Tetriakoff, the CWC staff person assigned to the Group Work and Recreation Division, had drawn up a set of guidelines by which each settlement house could conduct a self-appraisal, establish proof of economic and prudent stewardship, and evaluate the relevance of its programs in relationship to established community needs. Almost all the settlement houses welcomed the forms and condoned their own self-studies. Havilland House did not.

Havilland House has been around a long time. Its staff had always been small, very dedicated, but thoroughly inadequate in terms of training or professional competence. For years they had been running a

---

[1] This case was suggested by events documented by Harry D. Karpeles, D.S.W., while a student at the Florence Heller School for Advanced Studies in Social Welfare at Brandeis University. Dr. Karpeles is currently Assistant Chief, Regional Medical Program and Associate Professor, Temple University School of Medicine.

limited, recreation-type program while most of the other settlement houses had moved into civil rights, urban renewal, and antipoverty programs.

A year earlier the executive director had finally succeeded in making good her wish to retire. She was replaced by a manual-trade-school teacher who served part time as acting director. A few months later, the president of Havilland House's board of directors died. The board had been largely inactive, and its membership had dwindled dismally to a few "old-timers" whose interest was largely sentimental.

At about the same time, two letters by community people sharply criticizing the agency were sent to the Council. Alma Tetriakoff and one of the lay members of the Group Work and Recreation Division investigated. As Alma told me later, they found the agency "completely unacceptable in terms of professional standards and meaningful programs. We decided to make an example of Havilland House so that the other settlements would know that we meant business. Agencies were going to have to have good practices and meaningful programs, or else."

To substantiate their impressions, the Group Work and Recreation Division commissioned a confidential study by its Settlement Subcommittee. The committee also concluded that Havilland House's operation was professionally substandard in that its limited board membership raised the question of its constitution as a legal entity. The committee recommended that the operations of Havilland House be terminated, and that limited funds should be allocated in a closely supervised manner for a period not to exceed six months. Services could be terminated at any time. During that period, however, Havilland House was to be urged to show cause why, and in what manner, the agency could be revitalized and reestablished as a legal entity.

Tetriakoff and Davallos felt that this was a significant recommendation, because it was made by a Council subcommittee composed of settlement-house board members and professional staffs. The report was accepted by the group work and recreation division. It is at this point that the story gets interesting.

The Havilland House staff began scurrying around for some neighborhood support. Somehow they latched on to Rudolph Gernak, a young, aggressive, and highly successful businessman who operated two funeral houses and a furniture business in the area. Gernak relied on community contact for his business. He was already heavily involved in church, fraternal, and cancer-drive programs. When approached, Gernak accepted an invitation to become president of the Havilland House board. As he later put it to me, "I'm in favor of anything that's good for our neighbors." He immediately reconstituted a legitimate board of directors.

It was obvious then, and still is now, that Gernak knows little about settlement philosophy or social agency practices. But he is a go-getter.

Alma Tetriakoff sent the new president and his board an official letter describing what was expected of them if Havilland House was to demonstrate that it could function as a responsible agent of the community's fund. The effect of this letter was different from what had apparently been anticipated. Instead of acquiescing to the inevitability of the Council's decision to terminate the financial support, the new board reacted with great hostility. "We weren't going to serve to legitimate the Council's decision to terminate us," Gernak told me. His first action was to ask for a meeting of the settlement-house subcommittee of the Group Work and Recreation Division. Here he stated his case, pointing to the successful completion of one important requirement—the reestablishment of a responsible, functioning board of directors and officers. He agreed that professional direction was needed immediately for the house, but pointed out that funds were required if they were to demonstrate any capacity to provide a meaningful program. He said that he wanted to conduct a survey of social needs in the immediate neighborhood so that the settlement's program could be redirected to serve those needs. He admitted ignorance of the necessary procedures, and asked the subcommittee to appoint a consultant who could conduct a neighborhood need survey and subsequently advise his board on the kinds of staff and programming necessary. The subcommittee agreed to his request and offered to employ a good consultant. That's where I came in.

Alma Tetriakoff interviewed me for the job. I had had work experience in both welfare councils and settlement houses. She briefed me on the situation and made it very clear that she hoped my findings would be useful in making the original decisions stick. She pointed out the importance of the Welfare Council's demonstrating its ability to close down such an agency. The Council could not take a strong stand, "it could never do any comprehensive planning for all of the community's needs, if it could not make this stick," she told me.

I then met with Rudy Gernak in his home. Several other board members were there, including some old-timers. They couldn't understand why the Council had run a secret survey on them. Most of the people there were very angry with the council, but Gernak tried to keep the hostility toned down. "We hope you can help us," he told me, "to develop a really top-notch agency. As you can see, people in the community are resentful and don't want to be phased out. I hope you can help us find a way of staying in business. We are determined."

Consultation can be sticky business. It is rare that you just get called in to do fact finding or to give objective professional advice. I have rarely been called in to consult on an issue in which someone didn't have an axe to grind. Frequently it is the person who is hiring you. If you're going to keep your integrity, you have to walk a tight line. It is easy to get seduced by one side or another, especially by the people who are hiring you. In this particular case, the situation almost called for some form of arbitration or mediation. In a sense I was an arbitrator, called in to do some fact finding and to publish a report that, while not serving as a binding judgment, would be a major input into the decision about whether to kill Havilland House.

I had not yet decided to accept the job as consultant. I thought I knew some of the pitfalls that lay ahead. So I told Gernak that there was very little that I could do to be of help to him. I could survey the neighborhood's needs. If I found any that were amenable to intervention by a settlement house, I could point these out. I could also suggest a number of alternative approaches that a settlement house might take. Finally I could suggest a number of steps that Havilland House would have to undertake in order to be in a position to fulfill the neighborhood needs. There was no guarantee in advance, I told him, that I would find any relationship between community needs and settlement-house functions. In any event, I concluded that it would be necessary for the Havilland House board to accept the findings, then to agree to undertaking the changes needed to fulfill the taks required of them, and finally to make out as strong a case as possible in its petition to the Group Work and Recreation Division for reversal of its decision.

When it became apparent that Gernak and the other board members present were eager to have me undertake the survey, I suggested they write a formal letter to the Welfare Council to that effect.

Subsequently I asked for a meeting with Alma Tetriakoff, Ray Davallos, and some of the key lay people who were involved on the settlement's subcommittee. I put it to them bluntly. I would not be an instrument of their decision to eliminate Havilland House. After my study, I might conclude to that effect, but I was not ready to make any prejudgments. I suggested to them that they either offer Havilland House some funds to hire a part-time professional director with some extensive community-organization experience, or conceivably to give them someone on loan from the CO division of the Council itself. This guy might be able to accomplish the following things: orienting and educating the new board to settlement philosophy and new practice approaches; directing the current program and instilling some life into it; and finally, training them to participate in my survey and relating the findings of the study to the functions and roles of the settlement house as they now perceive them.

Davallos vetoed the idea outright. He said it was impractical in the light of the immediacy of the situation. Only four months were left of the original six allocated to the phase-out process. This is where I put my foot down. I told them that under those circumstances I could not conduct a survey or serve as a consultant to them. I am not averse to using a little coercion once in a while, and I pointed out not too subtly that it would make bad press for the Council if they did not try to do everything they could to save Havilland House before they cut if off. We finally compromised. The Council would send a community organizer to orient the Havilland House board. He would also help them to interpret my findings and to explore their capacities to fulfill my recommendations if this was appropriate. As for the ongoing program, the Council could not provide program staff for any of its member agencies. If I wanted to use any of the Havilland House board members in my survey, that was perfectly all right. It was to be my decision.

That's where I made my mistake. I should not have compromised. The Council did a very inadequate job of orienting the board. The Council staff person was looked on with suspicion. Board members were both resentful and fearful of his presence. They tried to be on their best behavior, but it was obvious that many of them resented his being there and "telling us what we should do with our agency." It was also obvious that most of the board members did not fully understand the purpose of my survey. Nor did they understand their responsibility. Almost every conversation I had with individual board members ended up in a question such as "Well do we or don't we stay in business?"

By this time, with some Havilland House staff support, the issue had become a hot one in the neighborhood. Several local politicians were looking for a cause. Gernak kept them quiet, asking them not to raise a stink until the end of the survey. He was certain that my report would be a means of upsetting the Group Work and Recreation Division's decision. My own time was limited, and I did not have time to do the kind of educational work that was required with the men. This was the Council's job and I felt they had really relinquished their responsibility.

When I had completed my survey and was ready to make my report, I showed it first to Rudy Gernak. He took my copy, promising to have it duplicated and to have it ready for an emergency board meeting he would call for next week. On the evening of the board meeting, only half the members showed. None of them had seen my report. Gernak had not duplicated it. Instead, he introduced me and asked me to discuss it with the members present.

I should have anticipated this, but I was thrown a bit. Sensing the total unpreparedness for a meaningful discussion, I first developed the entire story of how the survey had come to be. I could see they were restless and not listening. All they wanted to know was, "Will we or will we not stay in business?" I tried to summarize from my report. It included several sections:

1. The background and the negotiation leading to the request for a survey.

2. The letter outlining the proposed mode of procedure and limitations on scope of the survey.

3. The responsibilities of the board once they had heard the results of the survey.

4. Neighborhood statistical data related to various indices of social need.

5. A more subjective evaluation of local needs based on 30 interviews I had conducted.

6. A description of the kinds of social services that might be instituted to meet the needs we had identified.

7. An outline of the types of programs that a good settlement house would employ to contend with the problems seen.

8. A final section dealing with the implications of the study for Havilland House, stressing the alterations that would have to be made before they could hope to handle the problems found.

This kicked off a tremendous discussion. It lasted for four hours. It was full. It was positive. But it reflected a tragically low level of understanding of what was to be involved on their part. Repeatedly, while paying lip service to the thoroughness of my report, some of the members stated their personal opinions that "all theory aside" the House was doing a good job because it did so much for a few poor kids in its immediate vicinity. I felt in many ways I had struck out, and was blaming the Council for its irresponsibility and myself for my stupidity. Nevertheless the board endorsed my findings and presented it to the Group Work and Recreation Division.

The following week, on Gernak's request, I escorted him to a meeting with the settlement subcommittee. Everyone had a copy of the survey report in advance. As I had predicted, Gernak was questioned thoroughly on how he expected to use the report. He reiterated the claim that the decision to withdraw financial support to his agency had been made unilaterally and precipitously. It was obvious from the report that there were many local needs, and that a settlement house was indeed an appropriate instrument. He requested that the budget be reallocated so that the agency could demonstrate its capacity to meet the newly identified local needs.

Challenged by a committee member to detail his procedure for bringing about favorable changes if Havilland House were permitted to do so, Gernak had some difficulty in explaining what he would do beyond engaging a professional director. At this point, another committee member asked me if I had any additional suggestions to make. Since I had not been invited by the Council to be present at this meeting, I checked first to see whether it was all right for me to proceed. Everyone agreed. I suggested a series of steps that I thought might bridge the gap between the present inability of the Havilland House board to make promises about its future, and the unwillingness of the Subcommittee to retreat completely from its original decision to curtail and then eliminate its financial support of the Havilland House program. It was like blowing in the wind. Davallos, ignoring what I had said, turned to Gernak and asked him what he, as president of the Havilland House board, was prepared to do—not what the consultant was prepared to do. There was an obvious impasse, which was not resolved until the Subcommittee specifically requested that the Havilland House board put its request for reconsideration of the decision in writing. The request would be given to the Council's Budget Committee. They also suggested that the essence of my advice be incorporated in a covering letter from Gernak accompanying the report. Gernak agreed on this. The buck had been passed from one Council committee to another.

A week later the Budget Committee met. Not having been involved in the entire process, it could only look at the existing documents: the original confidential survey, the recommendations of the Group Work and Recreation Division, the subsequent Division and settlement's subcommittee minutes, and my report. The Budget Committee decided to allocate funds for the remainder of the six month phasing-out period. It also recommended to the board of the CWC that a committee be appointed to study proposals for a new program in the Havilland area. These were to be in keeping with my report. Such a committee should include members of the Havilland House board, community leaders, and members of the Council's CO division as well as representatives from the Poverty Program and the city's Urban Renewal Program.

A week later at the CWC regular board meeting, both Budget Committee proposals were accepted. I was asked to consult on call with the new committee.

The newly constituted Havilland Area Study Committee, after two weeks, suggested that the life of Havilland House be extended an additional six months. Any new developments in the neighborhood would have to have the continuing support of the Havilland House leadership. The new Area Study Committee also proposed that other settlements or the YMCA be contacted to see if they might be interested in extending CO services to the Havilland area. The settlements all declined the invitation, stating they were already overly committed. Obviously, there were jurisdictional and political considerations. The YMCA seemed receptive but indicated they would need additional budgeting from the United Fund. Gernak was against it. He reported that his entire Board was insulted by the suggestion. Again they were not being given the benefit of the doubt. Besides, the "Y" was a sectarian agency.

The Council board accepted the notion of the needed support from the Havilland area's only known leadership—members of Havilland House's board of directors. It agreed to extend funds but only to the end of the fiscal year, an additional two months. Shortly before the new termination date, Gernak announced that he had been able to recruit an able community organizer to be the new executor of the agency. The CO man, however, would not take the job unless he was assured of at least one year's job security. The Area Study Committee recommended an additional six months' extension, but the board of the Council turned the recommendation down. Until this moment, Gernak had been pressured by local politicians as well as newspapers to permit them to become involved in the situation. He had withstood this pressure, knowing full well that neither the politicians nor the press was sincerely committed to Havilland House. Both were eager to use the situation for their own reasons. But when the Council voted to terminate support, he concluded that he had nothing further to lose. The press made headline stories out of the United Fund's deprivation of support for local services. The Council prepared news releases giving its side which were duly printed in the press. However, editorial comments blasted the Council.

The pressure from the political front was even more severe. Ray Davallos, who had never been on particular good terms with the mayor, was called in to City Hall. The mayor wanted to know why Ray was creating a mess in the Havilland area. Ray wanted to know why the mayor was never in when the Welfare Council wanted his support on something, but always seemed to get involved in issues when the Council was on the defensive.

A special rump session of the Council's Executive Committee met and decided to reinstate Havilland House and to support it for one additional year. The support, however, would be limited, and would be accompanied by a requirement that Havilland House accept responsibility for local fund raising to augment its budget. At the end of the 12-month period its future would again be reviewed, and decisions made would be based entirely on an evaluation of its performance.

I guess I have to accept some credit for that decision. I was on good terms with the mayor and with the Council people. It was I who negotiated the settlement. I think I was helpful in this situation, but not as much as if I had had more time. When you're consulting, it's not just a matter of resolving a problem or bringing some facts to light. You have to educate the people with whom you're working, so the next time they face a similar problem they won't need a consultant. I should have pointed a number of things out to Davallos and to Alma Tetriakoff. It was their own stubbornness in trying to assert the Council's new toughness, after all, that precipitated much of the problem. They had not been fair to Havilland House from the beginning. Havilland House had been lousy for years—why pick on them all of a sudden just to prove a point?

I think I could have done a lot with Rudy Gernak. He was a reasonable man and ambitious—the kind of a guy who would have liked to be on the Council board. He was horribly naive about welfare matters, but could have learned with some guidance. Certainly someone should have spent more time with his board. All in all, I am not sorry I stepped into the picture. Still, I hate leaving a job feeling that I have not given it everything that it required.

*   *   *   *

P-3   DELINQUENT GIRLS GET A NEW TREATMENT

As executive of the Council, I personally examine every request for new or additional funds before I pass it on to the appropriate staff or board committee. It's interesting how realistic limitations and money for services can shape up a plan and dictate its outcome from the beginning.

Until this year, there were four small institutions for delinquent girls in this town. Each of them was independent of the other, and cared for ten to twenty girls. For several years, we have been dubious about the quality of the care offered by two of the institutions. Both were funded by us. A third one also funded by us seemed to be doing all right. This year all three were asking for additional funds. The final straw came when a fourth institution, one that we did not approve of at all, also requested funds.

All four of them came independently and all of them wanted professional services. There was no question in our minds that any institution dealing with delinquent behavior needs treatment capacities. So we could not argue with the need when these small agencies came to us for additional funds in order to utilize psychologists, case workers, group workers, and other professionals. On the other hand, we could not offer to put one professional of each category into each home. It's not merely too expensive; I also doubt that we could find the professionals willing to take such jobs.

While our funds are limited, federal funds are available for capital expenditures. I met with several members of my staff. At first we thought of developing a physical facility outside of town, but soon changed our minds. It would be foolish to take these girls ouside the inner city when, in fact, they needed to learn how to adapt to their present city environments.

Nevertheless, we sought to put the agencies together in some way, since we could not give sufficient money for them to operate effectively alone. Two of the institutions were affiliated with religious groups, one with a sorority, and one with a nonsectarian group. We were certain, therefore, right from the beginning, that a single agency would not be possible. We decided on a three-step course of action: (1) to study the need for the services; (2) to examine whether the agencies were sound from a professional point of view; and (3) to determine what professional services were needed.

In these first stages of the project, I recommended to my Budget Division that they set aside some money with no strings attached. I also consulted with a judge in the Juvenile Court, the Public Welfare Department, the Board of Education, and several others. I sought to get their point of view to make sure we were on the right track. It became evident to me that we would also need an expert as consultant to the study.

To implement the proposed steps, we set up a special study committee. It consisted of representatives of the four institutions and citizens of the larger community who comprised the majority. We felt that they, rather than the special-interest groups, should have the final say. We also hired an outside consultant.

By this time, I had transferred most of the work to members of my research and planning staff. I was involved in only a spotty fashion. I met with the consultant upon her arrival at the agency, to review the purposes of the study. As the administrator who must ultimately foot the bill, it is my role to insure the capabilities of the people we contract and to oversee the overall direction of the studies undertaken. I also attended the first meeting of the study committee. I spoke at some length, focusing attention on the goal of the study. I had already spoken with each of the members of my staff, the citizen representatives on the study committee, and the consultant about the goals of the project. However, the impact of selective perception cannot be minimized. I think that it is important at an initial meeting to clearly set forth the goals. All members should begin with the same assumptions.

The study was done entirely independent of me. I believe, although I'm not certain, that the consultant stayed in the city for two lengthy periods. After she had written up tentative recommendations, I joined with the staff in examining them. My contribution involved examining the implications of the recommendations, if implemented, on the community. We talked of the recommendations relative to other public, voluntary and sectarian agencies in the community. We also examined the recommendations' potential impact on community groups (that is, would it produce a row between rival factions? Would it upset the sectarian groups represented?). It is, of course, not our job to change the recommendations of an outside consultant. However, if we had detected flaws in the recommendations or in the areas omitted from consideration, we would have informed the committee of our views.

I was present at the consultant's first presentation to the study committee. I was vocal. It is part of my role to give the party line of the agency. An administrator can choose either to let his staff express agency views, or to go ready to speak. At this first meeting, I spent considerable time assuring the committee representatives that the recommendations seemed good for this community from a professional point of view. I also helped our consultant clarify her recommendations as they related specifically to our city. This involved guiding her emphasis and, in some cases, interpreting her language so that it could be understood by all present. Last, I attempted to give assurance to the agencies that we were not attempting to ram something down their throats. After all, we had considerable power over them, for three of them were depending on our funds. I tried to convey that these recommendations were simply something for them to chew on. I invited their honest reactions to the recommendations.

My involvement in a project such as this follows a pattern. I am heavily involved at the beginning when we first consider a problem before us. I'm also involved when we review the specific action steps recommended. In addition, I enter at the point where experts have reached some conclusions. However, I am most heavily involved when the project reaches the stage of implementation and recommendation. Perhaps 75 percent of my time on a project is spent here. It involves a CO process that is almost longer than the study itself.

The study committee proposed that each of the four small agencies continue to maintain its independence, but that they should form a federation with a central board that would provide for professional services. The recommendation made, our project was now at the implementation stage and I was ready to become involved again. My first act was to personally sell this plan to the Council's planning committee and to my board. I then helped the agency representatives from each of the girls' institutions to sell the plan to their boards. My board took no convincing. However, some of the agency boards did not want anything to do with the recommendations. In one, the agency's director was leaving and its board was frantically searching for a new director. I reminded the president of that agency's board that he had promised to examine the recommendations and urged him to give them careful consideration. A second agency was willing to accept the recommendations, but to tell you the truth, I don't think they understood them at all. I spent some time interpreting them to their board. The third agency that we had been funding was about to go out of business. They already leased their facility to the state for a halfway house for girls, but agreed to enter the federation because they wanted eventually to start another direct service project. The fourth agency agreed to the plan wholeheartedly. We had not been supporting them, and they were well aware that this was the only way in which they might get any funds from us to offer services.

At this point we were ready to appoint an implementation committee. I assigned our staff man in Family and Child Care to staff the committee. As my delegate, he asked each agency to select several of its members to work with the chairman of the study committee on the appointment of an implementing committee. I also asked several of the more active members on the original study committee to participate in the appointment of committee members. My Family and Child Care staff member and I made some suggestions. We did not dictate to anyone whom they should appoint to the new implementation committee.

I think a professional like myself has something to contribute because he knows a lot of people. On the other hand, if something is going to be a citizen's effort, decisions have to be made from citizen to citizen. If professionals want the community to do its own thinking, then we must let them. If we controlled all decisions we could kiss the CO process goodbye. Who are we to play God? The community must tell us their needs. They are the ones who must live with their decisions. Professionals come and go. You can't get the community's point of view if the professional selects all the committeemen.

An implementing committee was drawn up. It was not very different in composition from the original study committee. I entered discussions only at that point when the implementing committee decided to make some major changes over the original proposals. My staff man with the committee asked me to enter the discussion at this point. As the Council administrator, I only step in when original proposals are being questioned. Staff members can't do that. As executive of the Council, I have ultimate accountability to my board. I feel I'm in the best spot to understand everyone's position, and to try to bring everybody up to a mutual understanding.

The implementing committee selected a new board of directors. We had agreed to fund the new four-way federation of girls' agencies. The new board is looking for a part-time executive director who in turn will hire the professional staff to serve all four agencies.

Once the director of the federation has been chosen, we must get out of the picture. Our only function is to create distinctive and independent agencies. Of course I will be involved with the newly created federation in several ways. Certainly I will enter into all discussions on budgeting. Secondly, since they will be unsure about their professional standards for a while, I will probably be involved in a consulting capacity. Still, the more quickly the agency becomes independent, the happier we will be. Even after they do become independent, however, I still will keep my hand in the game. I intend to follow the activities of the juvenile-court judges in relation to this new agency. I want to insure that they follow through on their agreement to place delinquent girls in these four institutions.

* * * *

P-4 LEADERSHIP TRAINING FOR BOARD MEMBERS

As director of volunteer services for the Welfare Council, the business of training new board members for our affiliate agencies falls into my lap. Our Board Member Institutes have been in operation now for some 25 years. As long as anyone can remember, these Institutes have been held on one day at a big hotel downtown. They have been well attended, accompanied by a great deal of fanfare. We have 235 member agencies. We get between four and five hundred people to attend.

If I had to describe their objectives, I would say, for the record, that these Institutes were established to enable new board members to better understand the problems of their community, to give them some new insights into the problems of social welfare, and to train them to do their jobs as volunteers more effectively. Off the record, however, I would have to tell you that the whole thing has degenerated into a big public-relations affair—a way of bolstering a new board member's ego, and making it look to the community as if the Council is doing a job. Actually, I can tell you, not much learning goes on.

I would say the Institute we had two years ago was a total failure. A big luncheon in a swanky hotel doesn't cut the ice anymore. Boards have changed a great deal during the last five years. You don't think of a Board member arriving in a chauffer-driven car in a mink coat anymore. A lot of our agencies have become decentralized. Many of them are reaching people from minority groups. Neighborhood people and service recipients are finding their ways onto agency boards.

You might be able to bring four or five hundred people from all our agencies into a single room, but you certainly can't get them to hear the same things from the same speaker anymore. Their backgrounds and their perspectives have changed. That's how it should be. If welfare is going to be a community function, then policy making has to be shared with every sector of the community.

Our Institutes have always been planned by a lay group, a subcommittee of the board of directors for the Community Council. In addition, I have an advisory committee that works directly with me—these are board people from our member agencies who have particular interest in the whole question of volunteers. I have a lot of discretion in choosing the advisory committee. Over the past few years, I have recruited people who represent minority groups and neighborhoods that have never had any voice in giving direction to Council affairs. Last year, I decided to have my advisory group meet together with the subcommittee of the board to plan the Institute.

The planning process was educational in itself. The really different points of view expressed, reflected quite a range of socioeconomic backgrounds. If nothing else, everyone agreed that there was something wrong with the Institutes and that somehow they had to be made more pertinent. We couldn't resolve the issue of content, but we did reach unanimity on breaking down into smaller regional Institutes. We conducted four of them in four parts of town, giving us a chance to meet in smaller groups. We hoped for more opportunity for discussion and fuller participation.

The big decision we had to make was whether to assign new Board members to Institutes based on the proximity to the agencies they represented. In essence this would segregate people by neighborhood or sections of the city. We decided not to. Our purpose for having regional Institutes, we decided, was not to serve regional interests but to encourage more face-to-face interaction between board members from all our agencies. Don't think we didn't have some resistance from within the Council.

A lot of my colleagues thought I was being foolish. Several Council board members raised a big fuss. A lot of people wouldn't go to working-class neighborhoods. We lost some people (I guess you would call them the old guard), but we picked up a lot of new people. I had to push hard to get what I wanted, but I'm convinced it has been worth the effort. It actually worked out quite well. Board members related to each other not just as members of an audience but also as people who represented "community leadership," agency clientele, or constituencies such as neighborhood councils.

This year we decided to go the same route—regional Institutes. A good deal further along in our own consensus, we were able to think through some very imaginative program content. Before the Institutes actually took place, we had arranged field trips to poverty areas and to a variety of community agencies like the courts, a mental hospital, the welfare department, a family service agency, and the like. We wanted people to have a feel for what welfare was all about before they attended. But were we unprepared for what was to take place!

We planned a theme to focus on "urban problems." We wanted our members to understand and appreciate the need for public housing and good welfare programs, to understand why there seems to be an increasing movement towards decentralization of services and their control. We also wanted people to get a feel for the reasons behind the development of indigenous social movements.

At the first of our regional Board Institutes this year, a black participant stood up and challenged the main speaker. He said that white people did not understand the problems of blacks and that it was ludicrous for a white man to be standing at the podium talking about housing problems, poverty, and the need for better education, when in fact all we were doing was perpetuating our racist society with handout programs and palliative efforts that made no dent on the social structure. He was obviously intelligent and very articulate. He asked that we take a one-hour break in order for the black participants to caucus. The chairman opened up the issue to the floor. There were some heated feelings pro and con, mostly among the white members, for about 15 minutes. Finally someone said, "If the black participants want to have a black caucus, then let's have a white caucus."

I met with the white group. There seemed to be a lot of sympathy for the black perspective, but a good deal of uneasiness as well. Since no one was altogether sure what the black caucus was discussing, the white board members could do very little but share their confusions, air their guilt, or give verbal support to the needs of blacks for self-determination. I must tell you, I was not sure how to play my own role. I was hoping that Charles Patterson, a black member of our staff who went to the black caucus, was having less difficulty than I. It was a futile hope.

The black members decided to develop their own association within the Council. Without deciding on the name, they decided to elect temporary officers and to contact black board members from all the other agencies in town. They wanted to elect Charles as secretary because of his position as a staff member on a council, but he declined on the same grounds, although he later told me that he was really torn. He felt the blacks should have their own association. He told me that he felt he "belonged" to them, and that he felt he should be their staff person.

At the end of the hour, the black caucus issued a statement accusing the Welfare Council and the welfare agencies in this community of being racist and against the interests of black people. They demanded one third representation on the Council board (roughly the same proportion as there are blacks in the central city). They also called for a stoppage of all Board Member Institutes not planned with black people, or not in the interests of black people. Apologizing for the disruption, but explaining that it was long overdue, they marched out of the Institute, which they said was not for them.

The whites who were left discussed the issue for about two hours. It was a good discussion in that it cleared the air and opened up a lot of feelings. It was a poor discussion in that there were no blacks to whom we could relate.

All this happened three weeks ago. I'm not sure where we go next.

* * * *

P-5 THE FEDERATION MAKES A BUDGET

When I arrived on staff four years ago, our method of deciding on the agencies to fund was confused and did not sufficiently involve the community. As the staff person assigned to the Community Relations Division, I set out to correct this. I presumed that successful action on my part would result in changes in the other three divisions of the Jewish Welfare Federation as well.

Before I can coherently describe my activities in the project, I must briefly describe the organization of the situation that I found there. The budget is in the hands of the Board of Governors of the Jewish Welfare Federation. Every segment of the Jewish community is represented on this board. The board allocates the funds raised by the Allied Jewish Campaign and the United Jewish Appeal.

All four divisions report to the board, recommending the nature and size of allocations to local and national Jewish agencies, and to Jewish

Welfare Projects abroad. The President of the Jewish Welfare Federation appoints each division chairman, although we on the staff have veto power.

When I arrived on the scene, Saul Kayser had already been appointed chairman of the Community Relations Division. I inherited a gem. He knew the community, and was on good terms with political figures and with community leaders of other factions and ethnic groups. He had been active at the national level in the Anti-Defamation League of B'nai B'rith. Locally, he had been involved in the public school study, the art institute, the Police-Community Relations Board, and others. Because of these activities and his position as owner of a large department store in town, he is in a wonderful position to give expression to the consensus of the Jewish community. He is also in a key spot to inform us of events in the community. And besides, how many businessmen would meet with a professional social worker at 7 in the morning or 5:30 in the evening? Maybe part of it is my magic touch; I tried to arrange things so that my volunteers can devote their full efforts to their personal jobs.

Kayser, my staff, and I, jointly decided on who should be appointed to the Division and its subcommittees (one for every two or three agencies under our jurisdiction). We have a master file in which community members active in fund raising, budgeting and planning, campaigning and so on, are listed. Once a year, we examine each person's attendance. Sometimes we strike out members due to lack of participation. Sometimes we add members if there is an expressed interest on their part. We also add members of the community that are of potential leadership capacities. In selecting members from this list, we try to avoid representation without taxation. It is not that we select only the richest; we expect generosity and interest according to their capacities. Ability, talent, and knowledge are of greatest importance in our selections. We try to get those who can learn from their experiences and go on to further contribute to the community in leadership capacity.

One of my goals is to develop leadership for both the Jewish Welfare Federation and the larger Jewish community of the city and nation. The lay people selected were from every walk of life. Each is talented and committed.

Unfortunately, our people don't know a damned thing about goals or planning or budgeting. Many know little beyond drum banging and slogans. In an attempt to educate the lay people and to evaluate the agencies for our annual budgeting, I drew up a set of questions related to program priorities and the like. In the process, I consulted personally with the professional staffs of two national institutions: the Large City

Budgeting Conference, and the Budget Research Department of the Council of Jewish Federation and Welfare Fund and Company.

My draft was not, and is never, final. My method of working on something like this generally involves four steps. I discussed my draft with the Assistant Director responsible for planning and with the Executive Director. Second, I discussed it with the Chairman of the Division and with the Assistant Chairman. Numerous modifications were made here. Third, I discussed it with the Steering Committee. Finally, I discussed it with all the division subcommittee chairmen and members. There were modifications at each step.

This general procedural pattern is always followed. This is the way it should be and it heavily invests the participants; in this case it made them want to find the answers to the questions. Too often, in my opinion, the lay people end up as mouthpieces of the professionals. Frequently, they do not know what they are doing. It is best to have the fullest possible efforts of both the lay and professionals. Where the power base is in the professionals, relying on the professionals' personal influence over the lay people, it is like building a structure on a shaky foundation. It is best to have cooperation between professionals and committed and informed lay people. As professionals we develop the basic facts and point the direction. This direction setting is not analogous to direction giving. As professionals we point the way to the possibility of action in several different directions. It is an open and conscious process involving joint efforts.

After my original draft of questions had been thoroughly revised, it was reproduced and sent to all the agencies. I then spent much time helping the agency professionals clearly answer the questions. We didn't want public-relations answers. We had to make certain that the agencies knew what we were seeking. For example, in one case a layman in a local agency took all of the data on his vacation and submitted a book-length paper to me. This was, of course, useless, since priorities could not be extracted from the welter of detail. I typically meet with the director of the agency four or five times and then meet with the director and the lay people several times more. In addition to clarifying questions, I give some of the agencies advice on what aspects to highlight.

As each agency submitted their essay answers to the questions, I set about reducing them to concise, vivid statements. I then carefully checked back with the agencies, made revisions, reproduced the result, and then distributed it to the subcommittee members and the agencies.

The agencies then met with the subcommittees. I felt I should allow the professionals and lay people of the agencies to tell their own story to the subcommittees. I did not bias subcommittee members. They made their own decisions about the agencies' quality. My task was to schedule the meetings. After numerous sessions with the agencies, the subcommittees met alone. I participated to give them the information they needed, helping them to concentrate on the program validity of the agencies, and answering technical questions as they arose. After the subcommittee meetings we held several full division meetings out of which came a four-page final report.

I can best illustrate the intricacies of this process through my involvement with the American Jewish Committee (AJC). After the AJC had submitted their revised report to the subcommittee, I scheduled a meeting between their agency and the subcommittee at which they were requested to verbally expand on the report. A lay leader, who also happens to be a national officer, talked. During the course of the meeting, several issues beyond those on which he had been requested to elaborate arose; for example, the validity of expanding overseas programs, the duplication of services with other agencies, the future direction of the agency, the local involvement with their national organization, and the percentage of funds raised by their own activities. After three or four meetings I drafted a summary of the proceedings. The subcommittee then met alone and revised my draft. The recommendations of the final draft were then presented to the full division by the subcommittee chairman. No dollar amounts were fixed; only "less," "the same," or "more" money was recommended.

After the full division had been given a chance to mull these recommendations over, the agency was given a chance for final appeal before the full division. The full division then reviewed all the facts available on the agencies, and in light of community priorities, decided on a dollar amount. I then summarized these proceedings. Mr. Kayser then read and revised my report. He presented it to the Federation's Executive Committee and to its Board of Governors. Copies of the report were shared with all the agencies involved and also with the Large City Budgeting Conference and the Budget Research Department of the Council of Jewish Federations and Welfare Fund and Company.

The ramifications of this project are substantial. All the agencies have taken a hard look at their program activities, at budgeting, and at priorities. Many have discarded the attitude of "Well, let's go ahead with it. We'll get the money later." Now, many of them will examine priorities first. The educational upgrading of the lay leadership has also had an influence on parent bodies; the ongoing relationship between the national and local agencies in many cities has improved and we have avoided the duplication of manpower. Some of our lay leaders have even pushed their new thinking to the national level. In some cases they have just joined a national trend, but in other cases I think they have helped to stimulate national trends. The project certainly influenced the leadership of the Community Relations Division of the Federation. The members are in a much better position to evaluate thoroughly the agencies of the community. I think the group has also gained a glimpse into the professional's and the layman's role in the agency. They have also learned how the two groups of people can work together effectively.

There has developed some sense of community and a desire to co-ordinate efforts. The agencies certainly have more confidence in the validity of our evaluation of them. We have communicated to the agencies that we are concerned about their success. The personal involvement of the project participants has also added a plus, I think, to our funding activities.

The basic method of study, diagnosis, and treatment illustrated here is universally applicable. It involves professional thinking, lay reaction to that thinking, joint consideration of the issue through intensive involvement of all people, and a communitywide consensus. The biggest failures in community organization come when there is not full participation. Projects must be partnerships. A professional without a point of view is worthless. But he plays his role behind the scenes.

*   *   *   *

P-6 MRS. KAPLAN SPEAKS UP

As a planner for the Welfare Council, I work with a lot of city agencies. Because of my interest and my background, I have a lot of dealings with the school system and with the Parks and Recreation Department. For some time we had been concerned with the fact that so many senior citizens would hang around the downtown area aimlessly, with almost nothing to do. The small park near the Civic Center was full of older people. The Recreation Department offered a fairly good program, and the school system conducted a variety of evening adult-education courses in the area. Still, most of these people needed other kinds of professional services. A lot of the people who filled the park looked pretty desolate and lonely. I met with people from the school system and Recreation Department, and while both groups seemed interested, neither felt that they could commit additional funds or that they really had the jurisdiction to provide the kind of counseling services that were needed. People from both departments were willing to help me organize some other kind of service, however. I called a lot of the clergymen in the area and asked them if they had noticed the older people looking hopeless and helpless in the park. Most of them agreed that they had been troubled by this fact for some time. I invited those interested to become part of a group that might perhaps be able to set up a store front with all kinds of professional help for the senior citizens who lived or frequented the downtown area.

At an initial discussion meeting, we pulled together 25 or 26 people to talk about the issues. I invited Professor Clark and Dean Nosechal of the School of Social Work. Both had made studies of the needs of senior adults in this city, and had concluded that one of the top priorities was the development of a multiservice center for older people in the downtown area. Professor Clark talked to the group about his findings. Now get this scene.

Everything is going along well. I am beginning to get a nice glow of satisfaction. Professor Clark is really detailed in his recommendations, and the clergymen and some of the downtown business people there are nodding in agreement that something needs to be done. Then Mrs. Kaplan, a senior citizen who had heard about the meeting, gets up and starts talking.

She looks at me and she says, "Mr. Melan, I don't want to hurt your feelings. You spent a lot of time getting this group together and it's wonderful. But, you do not need a downtown center for older people in this city. What you do need are small neighborhood centers where a lot of older people live and which they can walk to. Those people who need the care the most do not have transportation money and do not come downtown. What's more, these people do not come out in bad weather and you do not see them hanging around the park in the winter. Where are they to go? The people in the park come down here two months out of the year. True, a few of us live downtown, but most of the people who come downtown are not the people who need services. These senior citizens come downtown to shop or go to the theater and they're not going to use the storefront that you're talking about."

You know I'll never forget how I felt. My first reaction was to be angry at her because the experts, I mean everything I had based the calling of this group together on, had been leading us to designing a new program downtown. Then here in the flash of a pan and out of the mouth of a person who was not a professional, who had not been working as a volunteer for years, and who had never conducted a study of senior adults, the rug was pulled straight out from under my feet. I think I was speechless for a moment, but I did a lot of quick thinking. I said, "You know you're absolutely right. You're absolutely right. I think I've been wrong and I am grateful to you for this suggestion." I wasn't even sure exactly what I was going to say until I said it.

You know, as a result of her comments, we gave up the idea of a downtown center. We are now working very closely with the city redevelopment authority, with each of the major Protestant churches, and with one of the local Catholic parishes. It didn't take us long to find out that there were hundreds of people on Old Age Assistance or on Social Security and that there were few agencies serving the neighborhoods in which they lived.

We are in the process now of trying to get funded to set up a couple of pilot demonstration projects in three of the census tracts. Now the easiest thing to do would be just to get the money, find some buildings, and open up some storefronts. But that's not the way we are going to go about doing it. I think Mrs. Kaplan taught me something. We are going to go about it the long, hard way. We are going to talk to senior adults in each of the neighborhoods, and find out what they really think they need. Then we're going to go out and find a top-notch administrator to head up the program. If possible, we are going to find a retired person who can do the job, and get him to train some other older people as neighborhood aides to locate those in trouble and in need of help. What we're talking about is a senior adult service center made up of senior adults and for senior adults. I have a feeling we are going to not only find people in need, but also lots of people with things to offer and no outlet. Why just think of senior adults as people who have nothing but "needs"? After all, they weren't senior adults all their lives.

10

Community Workers in Direct-Service Agencies

CASES AND ILLUSTRATIVE MATERIALS

P-7　A SETTLEMENT-HOUSE STAFF LOSES ITS BUILDING

P-8　BUILDING IT, KILLING IT, AND MAKING IT: THE EVOLUTION OF A NARCOTICS PROGRAM

P-9　A UNION WINS MENTAL HEALTH

P-10　THE INDIGENOUS SUBPROFESSIONAL: TO EMPLOY OR NOT TO EMPLOY?

P-11　MY CLIENTS ARE THE SLUMLORDS

Increasingly, administrators and practitioners in direct-service agencies are finding themselves involved in community work essential to agency survival and expansion, and necessary for fulfillment of their service objectives. Welfare agencies are enmeshed in a complex of social institutions. They are increasingly beset by conflicting pressures from both input and output constituencies.

The social and organizational environments in which agencies find themselves may be supportive or hostile to their missions. New sources of funding, largely unstable, put pressure on agencies to establish broad bases of support. The increasing militancy of clients and community people that demand a voice in determining policies and procedures of service agencies, frequently puts agencies on the defensive and creates serious internal organizational problems and staff imbalances.

All too often, agencies do not engage in planning processes until beset by a crisis or facing a problem that demands immediate action. The reader will recall the Havilland House case from the preceding chapter. A threatened cut in funding should have initiated a thorough planning process. Unfortunately, with the exceptions of a part-time consultant, no one was prepared to plan on a Havilland House's behalf. Almost dramatically different is the way in which the administrator of a Settlement House reacted when his agency was forced to respond to a threat. What distinguishes him is his willingness to reexamine all the assumptions on which he and his staff had based their practice over a number of years. In this sense, he functions in a way similar to the practitioner in the next case.

The administrator-planner who describes the evolution of a narcotics program traces its history from its inception by a group of interested citizens. They are motivated by a combination of public interest and the glamor of being related to narcotics users inhabiting an illicit world. He details the development of a new service organization, its eventual conversion from service to education and hence to social action, and its transference from private to governmental auspices. What makes this case particularly intriguing is the planner's particularization of the way he approaches the hiring interview, and his analysis of the effects of his presence on the volunteers originally responsible for bringing him on the scene. The manner in which this worker manipulates people suggests a very astute political sense and a rather powerful urge towards self-preservation. It also suggests a degree of opportunism under the guise of practice principles. Is he more analytic when it comes to means selection than he is with regard to policy formation and goal determination? This is one of the few cases in our observation in which an administrator of a direct-service agency actually chose to phase out direct services. What were the reasons he deliberately set out to kill citizen participation?

Both these cases depict the overriding concern of the direct-service agency and its staff with the issue of an organizational domain, its sphere of influence or activity. The reader will notice that in both cases, the agency was able to shift its domain in terms of (1) the social problem covered, (2) the populations served, and (3) the services rendered. Not all agencies are capable of such flexibility.

One might suspect that the agency concerned with the use of "The Indigenous Subprofessional" might be having some difficulty in this regard. Since we have chosen to simply present an issue here (along with a variety of staff perspectives on it) rather than to flesh out a case, the reader will have to uncover the complexities for himself. We suggest that this material be used for role playing in a classroom, staff meeting, educational seminar, or other appropriate setting.

This material also dramatizes the frequent inappropriateness of staff functions and professional training apropos the provision of services to clients. Planners often concern themselves only with interorganizational relationships, whereas a more appropriate locus of attention, if one wishes to change the nature of an agency's services, may be internal. The pattern of organizational relationships and of staff interaction of assignment of responsibility may be the critical variable in an organization's effectiveness or efficiency. Defensiveness and entrenched interest, or just plain ignorance and incompetence, may block possibilities for important changes.

In "A Union Wins Mental Health," the planner describes how he overcomes interorganizational obstacles and sources of resistance. Charged with the responsibility of creating a mental-health service program within an industry, he finds that neither management nor the union is fully certain about how a mental-health insurance program can benefit either side. The planner recognizes that each party is accustomed to dealing with the other around issues of self-interest, and that each will be looking at the development of the new program from the perspective of its own advantage. He knows that each fears that the other party may benefit more. He enters the field by playing a familiar role recognized by both parties— that of negotiator or mediator.

Negotiating and mediating skills are increasingly important, as agencies compete with each other for resources and as clients and community groups present demands to formal organizations within the service network. At the locality level, certainly, the ability to balance interests, to compromise, and to emerge from negotiated settlements with victories for all sides is a skill that planners will increasingly be expected to perform.

While service agencies are at the forefront of confrontation with social ills and with the victims of inequitable social conditions, they have little power to influence the direction of social change or to deal with the structural conditions leading to the need for remedial service. The coordinator of a Service Center for the Housing and Redevelopment Board of a major city has allowed her service orientation to completely engulf and negate her planning role. Instead of concentrating her efforts on creating structural changes in the housing field, she develops a new service for slumlords.

This experience is not atypical. The closer the planner is to the people who may be directly affected by his interventions, the more he will be influenced by their perspectives and by their needs.

Question: Where does planning end and service begin?

* * * *

P-7　A SETTLEMENT-HOUSE STAFF LOSES ITS BUILDING

I was faced with a crisis. I had recently been notified by the church group that supports our settlement house that they were interested in continued support of our services, but not of the building. We were free to take over the building and finance it ourselves, or redirect our services in some other manner. In either case, the church would continue to provide us with staff funding. To be honest with you, I regarded the letter as a mixed blessing. The settlement house had been operating in this neighborhood for 40 years. The problems had changed and the traditional program that we still conducted seemed a far cry from the community's needs. There had been three police-community confrontations within the month and one bombing of a local retail merchant's store. The schools are bad and the whole area is very tense. Urban Renewal has never considered it a target. For some reason it's become a forgotten area.

My first response to the letter was, "Hell, they're giving these people the shaft again. We're going to stay in the building." When I cooled down, I realized that we had been too tied to the building, and that we had done too little in terms of moving out and handling real community problems. I shared the letter and my feelings with the board of directors. Of course, I first discussed it with a number of key board people, especially the chairman of the program committee. When the board met, they told me to do three things: (1) determine the problems in the area, (2) determine those services that were critically needed and suggest how we ought to be involved in meeting those needs, and (3) answer the question about whether we needed the building to offer our services.

Now when I say that the board delegated this authority to me, I don't mean to imply I'm a passive guy. The program chairman and I thought these issues through pretty carefully. And I certainly wasn't going to do all the work. We involved all the board members, for example, in meetings with community and neighborhood groups. As most of the board people are not from the local area, I wanted them to get a feel for what the real problems were. We set up different kinds of meetings. We involved the "respectable" community leaders, the agency people, and some of the political leaders. We also asked to be invited to regular meetings of other community groups: neighborhood councils, welfare-rights organizations, churches, and so on. Some of them didn't even know we existed. But in each case, I told them of our dilemma, and that we wanted to find out what people thought the community's real needs were and if any of them could be met with the settlement-house program in the building. Or I would ask if our staff could be helpful in some other ways.

The board members present took good notes at each of these meetings. The program-committee chairman and I had developed an inventory of things to look for. So when a board person took minutes, he only recorded those things that were significant.

After nine or ten of these meetings, we found certain themes emerging. People in the community needed (1) recreation and social services, (2) day care and preschool services, and (3) expert help in running organizations and all the processes that are involved in community organization. We shared these findings with our board and set up three task forces.

I worked with the CO task force. We tried to figure out how our staff could be helpful in pulling this community together. Several alternatives presented themselves.

Were we to form an organization of citizens or residents ourselves, or were to help other groups get organized for whatever purpose they had in mind? Should we develop a community council of all the other organizations in the community, or should we hire ourselves out as consultants to groups and individuals that wanted to engage in social action on behalf of the community?

I had really thought hard about these issues. My model in working with my community is to be as articulate and to the point as I can. I don't necessarily throw out all the ideas. My people wouldn't stand for that. But I do say that if we are going to do this or that, then the consequences for us are that we are going to have to be willing to commit this or that other thing. In other words, I want them to see the consequences of their decisions. I am not one of these guys who holds off, cool and aloof.

My affiliation with the task force on day care and preschool services was primarily as supervisor of another staff member. After documenting needs for day care, they began negotiating with the antipoverty agency for a demonstration project. Our hope was that if we could get something started in this neighborhood, it could spread to a citywide project. Even if Head Start or the antipoverty programs couldn't fund us, we might at least start a citywide "mothers for day care" organization.

The recreation and social-services task force visited every local agency. The most important thing they found out was that services were fragmented, and that someone had to take the initiative in pulling services together in some integrated manner.

It's interesting how all three task forces pointed to the need for CO expertise. The board examined the findings of each of the three task forces and voted to accept eviction. It was a historic meeting. We decided that night to stop being a settlement house and to become an action agency. Our feedback from the church that supported us was positive. We knew we would have their continued support. We had some question about the welfare council, however. They provide us with 50 percent of our budget. I wondered what they might think of our becoming an action agency, concerned with organizing and planning. The council has been very jealous about its planning function. But they can't get down to the neighborhood level, and we were right there. It might take a little effort, but I was sure we could convince them that we were on the right track.

As a community organizer, I am very verbal and very honest about the way I feel about things. I guess I possess a certain charisma in the way I function. Once I get started, I can easily move a whole group. I usually see a direction in which I want to move and I can convince people that this is the way they ought to want to move as well. I know that this may not be good "process." It's just like "Mr. Charlie" walking into a neighborhood and telling the people how to function. But I try to listen and sense what people are feeling, and then I respond to what they feel. I guess I am manipulative, but I'm not sure whether being manipulative is good or bad. I can really listen to people, but unlike the caseworker, I become an extremely active and emotional participant in the whole process. I have feelings about what transpires and frequently express anger when I feel it. I have none of the professional reserve and scientific objectivity advocated by the profession. And people are candid in the way in which they express their thoughts to me. They can get angry at me and I can take it without hating them for it. I think it's healthy.

*   *   *   *

P-8   BUILDING IT, KILLING IT, AND MAKING IT: THE EVOLUTION OF A NARCOTICS PROGRAM

NARCAD[1] Gives Birth to a Narcotics Center

I think what happened with NARCAD is typical of what happens when a community-service group brings in a professional. It's the death of the group because the membership roles have been taken over. They have brought professional competence to the scene, and they can't compete with it. Oh, it might work differently in parents' groups, like those for the mentally retarded, for example, where they want a real good service for their kids. The parents step out of giving direct services and turn this over to the professionals, or if they stay with it, they let the professionals supervise them. But if the community group is not personally involved, or if their status depends on giving direct services, then when the professionals move in, it's death.

Eight years ago, a black lawyer in town named Fred Dinton organized a group of local citizens to do something about narcotics. The press in Los Angeles had been giving narcotics a big play. *Life* did an article on

---

[1] NARCAD is a fictitious acronym. As in many cases in this volume we have disguised names and localities.

narcotics in suburbia, especially among teens. This town was close enough to Los Angeles and similar enough to the *Life* magazine article to give the issue sex appeal.

Dinton's group was pretty heterogeneous. It had M.D.'s, cops, lawyers, a high-school counselor, some local mental-health practitioners, a state narcotics official, and a mixed bunch of interested citizens, mostly house-wives. I don't think any of them had ever been on dope, or really knew much about narcotics except maybe the state narco-man and one of the doctors. They were motivated by a mixture of genuine concern for the addict—especially the young addict—and a sexual-type fascination with the addict's world. It was like an adventure for many of them, sort of "peeping tomish"—you know, looking in on something forbidden. For Dinton, it was different. For him, it was a chance to build a reputation for social commitment and community leadership. Oh, hell. I don't want to paint these guys as being a bunch of frauds. They're not. They're typical of any community group. People let all kinds of things motivate them to do good things. And NARCAD tried to do good.

The group had the notion that they could help addicts by using volunteer workers. They set up an office and staffed it 12 hours a day. They passed out cards saying, "If you have a friend using H, call this number." If an addict arrived, or if kids came in to talk, they were told of the legal consequences, the moral issues. Addicts were sent to the hospital for detoxification. The NARCAD group would get the ex-addict a job after his stay in the hospital, or help kids catch up in school. Usually, the addict went back on H quickly.

NARCAD was not a professional operation. That's why Dinton and some of the others tried to recruit many professionals from related fields to their group of volunteers. That's why they got Chuck McCormick, the guy from the state narcotics commission, and Ted Barker, from the welfare council.

After a couple of years, it was getting hard to staff the office with volunteers, and some of the professional people in the organization were saying that NARCAD's services were not adequate. I would guess that Dinton must have been pretty defensive about this, but that it was hard for him to argue against better practice standards. Barker and McCormick wrote up a proposal to set up a Narcotics Center, complete with pro-fessional staff, rehabilitation programs, and the like. Dinton gave it his OK. They submitted it to NIMH[2] and got a very quick response. NIMH liked it because of the existent involvement of citizens, but since

---

2 National Institute of Mental Health.

NARCAD was not an organized board with extensive experience in fiscal management, NIMH stipulated that the $350,000 grant would have to be managed through the Welfare Council. The Council would be the official recipient of the cash.

The Council accepted and they set up a subcommittee of its board to be the board of the new Narcotics Center. They invited several NARCAD members to be on the Center board. Dinton was invited but he was not elected president. The new president was Shirley Amherst, a very attractive, light-skinned black pediatrician. Dinton continued as president of NARCAD. There was some confusion at this point over what NARCAD would do, and what the new board would do. According to the proposal, NARCAD members would continue to staff the program —but under the direction of the executive of the Center and his professional staff. That's where I came in. I was approached by Carl Brenner of Baker's staff to see if I would be interested in the directorship.

I Look Over the Organization, Decide to Take The Job

I was intrigued with the project for three reasons: First, it had been pushed by the community rather than by professionals. Second, it was a free-swinging setup for a CO worker. I figured that I would probably be able to work as independently here as would ever be possible. And third, I felt that I had something to offer. I could repattern the formal setup including staffing and budgeting. They needed someone who could think beyond a formal agency outline.

As far as I'm concerned, the community organization and planning processes start with the first job interview. I began the process even though I was not sure that I wanted the job. From talking with Brenner and from familiarity with the proposal I had feelings about the project. I knew that the structure, including NARCAD, was antagonistic to the desired function. The structure was clearly defined, yet no one was sure of the functions to be performed. But such difficulties are to be expected. A planner never expects a perfect situation. I guess that all he can expect is that the citizens will bring their concerns to him.

I began the planning process by listening. Ted Barker invited me out to lunch. He had already sent me the project proposal. It was a long lunch. Barker filled me in on the intricacies of the proposal's development; he told me things it would have taken me months to find out. He was straight with me. But as I listened, I was discovering things that Barker wasn't aware of because of his closeness to the situation. As I listened about the project and the people, all the time I was assessing Barker. As director of the Welfare Council, he would, in effect, be my boss. He had the funds and he had influence in selecting my board. So the planning process began with my assessment of his strengths and weaknesses, and the nature of his relationship to the board.

I probed gently for a number of things—Ted's relationship to McCormick, his perceptions of Dinton and Amherst, the relationship between those two. I figure if you can't work with the people who are initiating a project, you might as well not start. No planner or community organizer walking into a situation cold is going to be able to muster the clout to get a program off the ground. He might have lots of knowledge and lots of expertise, but it's all useless without the right kinds of community support.

As it turned out, Ted was an honest and open individual who confessed his own failings and mistakes. I knew that he would not have to be handled as a layman but could be treated as a professional with whom I could plan. So the first step turned into planning with Ted. I added my own perceptions, and got his reactions to things.

Each of us was learning the other's style. Among other things, I explored with Ted the persons on the subcommittee of the board, that is, how he would see an effective approach to them. I did so without violating Ted's professional role. I didn't seek what the board members wanted in a professional; I sought to know what breed of people they were—what they had on their minds. I knew that my interview with the personnel committee would determine whether I wanted to go ahead with the project.

When I go for a job interview, I figure if the people are interested enough to invite me, I owe them something in return. Whether I decide to take the job or not, I try to help them see the broader ramifications of their work, the possible pitfalls, and the like. If I decide a job is a "no go" for me, I usually ask the hiring committee if they want my suggestions on hiring someone else for the job. I asked Ted what he thought of my doing this with the personnel committee. He relished it.

I was really direct with Ted throughout our luncheon. He was comfortable and open. But I would have asked the same questions and gone after the same information regardless of how open he was. I just wouldn't have been as blunt. For example, I said to him: "Look, Ted, you're not Jewish. I am. And there aren't many Jews in your town. How will I be accepted? My staff will contain many people from minority groups—if they are talented. I intend to hire people on the basis of competence alone. Will I find any constraints to this policy?" I went into a lot of other issues. I told him I believed in horizontal rather than vertical administration. I would give my staff wide swing. I would hire all the staff, but I would expect all my staff to attend board meetings. If the board didn't like my choices, they could fire me, not my staff.

Ted, in turn, also told me that the personnel committee included one psychologist to check out the prospective director's stability. I figured this showed their insecurity. But when Ted told me that if the personnel committee liked me, I would also have to appear before the entire board, and that subsequently the recommendation would have to go from the Narcotics Center board to the board of the Welfare Council, I told him to forget it. I wasn't going to have anything to do with two appearances or with a board that couldn't hire its own director. Ted said he could do something about not having to bump the decision-making process up beyond the Center board even though it was officially a subcommittee of the Council board, but that he would not do anything about the meeting between me and the Center board if I got past the personnel committee. I would have to make that pitch myself.

As it turned out in a telephone conversation later on, the caper was that the personnel committee had planned to select the two top contenders for the job and invite both to attend the Center board meeting on the same night. I guess they expected the poor slobs to slug it out. I put it to them this way: "If you think I'm the best guy for the job, then I'll come to your board meeting. But if you think I'm second best, or if you have plans to bring anybody else in, forget it. You accept me or reject me on my own merits, and you give your personnel committee the responsibility it ought to have." There is just no sense in having a group assigned to making recommendations if they can't make recommendations. And there is no sense in having a decision-making body if it can't make decisions. If they could neither delegate nor assume responsibility, I reasoned, how could they transfer any to an executive and his staff?

At the meeting with the personnel committee, I went over the same things that I had gone over with Ted. Ted had educated them to the point that, at the end of the meeting, they asked me if I had any questions. I not only asked questions that were on my mind, but asked them for clarifications and implications of questions which they had asked me. For example, I asked them point blank, "What do you think the project will do?" They responded that the answer was in the project proposal. I said that was not what I wanted. I stated that I wanted their own views. I also asked them what type of person they wanted for their executive and why they wanted such a man. We explored this in detail. They learned that they wanted a CO person. They talked around this issue during the session but I nailed it down for them. "Since you are dealing with the community as a whole, you need a community organizer and not a caseworker. He must be involved with the people and with agencies in the community." I tried to leave the situation with more knowledge than when I entered it. I also explored how the members of the personnel committee saw their relationship with NARCAD. I didn't tip them off to the difficulties that I saw with NARCAD. They had, incidentally, brought NARCAD people to the meeting.

After I had driven home from the meeting I phoned Ted and reviewed the meeting with him. I didn't probe about whether they had been impressed with me. Ted volunteered that they were shaken by me. He volunteered it, I did not request it. I quickly moved on and searched to see how much they had caught and how much of what I had said seemed meaningful. I knew that if they were all cement heads, there was no point in my taking the position. This personnel committee was a microcosm of the board. Because the project was experimental and unstructured, I wanted to know if they had clout in the community, if they had any muscle. I wanted to know if they had perception, and if they had a workable conception of their eventual relationship with the executive director. During this phone call I was still on my research tack. I had mixed reactions to the whole thing, yet in general my reactions were positive.

Still, in the back of my mind I thought that a change in the functions of the board might be necessary. When one sets up a research project in the physical sciences he does not restrict the scientist. By the nature of things, the scientist must make his own decision as to the most fruitful direction of the research. In this case, the situation was such that there were simply no decisions left for the board. The budget had been set by the Council in conjunction with the federal government. The goals had been stated clearly in the proposal. There was simply nothing left for them to do in an official sense except meddle in the intricacies of the research.

On the other hand, I did need a means to contact the community and a means to get feedback from the community. I needed two-way communication with the community, dissemination of information into the community and assessment of the community. Yet, since these functions are normally peripheral to the function of the board, I knew that there had to be a change.

This conviction was accentuated by the ridiculous formal structure already set up. A board that was responsible for an agency (the Narcotics Center) was to be a subcommittee of another board (the Welfare Council board), which was in turn the parent organization of the narcotics project. My fears were further accentuated by the fact that no single agency was willing to take full responsibility for this project. The welfare council had brought in many area people to share the blame for the resulting project. The board of the Welfare Council had also copped out by delegating authority to a subcommittee. The subcommittee had in turn copped out when they felt that they could turn to the board for a final decision on the executive director. I knew that I would definitely have to take a firm stand some time in the future. I discussed all this openly with Ted. I had in Ted a professional ally who was committed to making things move ahead.

During the next weeks the personnel committee interviewed more people. I had no contact with Ted after the phone call; we had assessed each other and had reached the point of closure. It was up to them to call me. After a few weeks Ted called and asked me if I was ready to meet with the board. He told me that the only other strong candidate had withdrawn.

This information gave me a powerful weapon that I did not intend to use. I knew that the board was in desperate straits. They had received funds two months previously. Nothing had happened and I knew that more and more anxiety must have been building. I could have written my own ticket. I could have squeezed them dry. It became an issue of self-interest versus professional integrity. Some of my professional colleagues urged me to go for broke. However, I refrained. In the long run, it would have cost me needed support.

The informal gathering immediately prior to the official board meeting would have confirmed, for any candidate, that he was the only choice. In a voice loud enough to be heard by anyone in the next room, a board member asked the president of the Center board, "Where are the other candidates?" The president responded with something like "He is the only one we've got."

In the official meeting with the Center board I used the same approach as I had used with the personnel committee (whose membership sat before me). After considerable discussion, they asked me to leave the room while they decided. I suggested that we could convene in a week and thus give them more time to deliberate. However, they insisted. To my surprise, Ted left the room with me. I asked him about this. He simply said that this is the way they normally do it. I did not pursue the issue at this point because I did not feel that it was appropriate. However, this told me that I would have to face squarely, and soon, the issue of the relationship between a lay board and their professional staff. At any rate, the Council board called us back into the room and hired me with a handshake. I still wish that they had taken a week to make the decision, because the anxiety level was just too high.

There comes a time when boards must simply be educated. They must understand that although they hired their executives it does not mean that their executives are their employees. The professional works *with* the board and *for* the community. The responsibility for policy decisions inevitably overlaps between the executive and the board. The situation can work only in what I call a gentleman's agreement. It makes no sense to keep the professional in the dark on policy issues or to exclude him from the decision-making process.

We Decide to Kill NARCAD

A week later I went to my first NARCAD meeting. I met intense hostility there. Unknown to me, a card sent to all NARCAD members made me the focus of the meeting. The card had stated that I would present the Center goals. I walked innocently into the meeting to take the role of a passive, learning, listening individual who sought love and wanted to join their group. I had planned to go all out to give NARCAD status and an active role in the Center. However, the minute I walked past the door I met intense hostility. Dinton said that I was going to tell the group about the program of the Center. I asked him after a bit if he would voice NARCAD's opinion on the matter. He did not bite. As I talked I believe I removed the fears of some of the group. After the meeting, they enthusiastically came to me with comments and suggestions.

However, my talk only served to intensify the hostility of other members. The hostility derived from many sources. One source centered about their insecurity in performing assistance functions for addicts. The fact that they had felt a need to call in professionals reflected their felt inadequacy. Their meetings were completely unstructured. They took no attendance rolls. I think they were afraid to face the fact that the vast majority of their membership rarely attended more than one meeting.

Personal rivalry between Dinton and the president of my board also played a role. Dinton's personal insecurity prompted hostility. Personal incidents that had occurred between individuals on the board of the Narcotics Center and those in NARCAD also produced hostility. The removal of NARCAD's function in dealing with addicts prompted both hostility and insecurity. Many of the NARCAD members considered themselves the experts.

I had anticipated some of the hostility, but not even Ted Barker knew of its intensity and extensiveness. Neither of us could really anticipate NARCAD's reaction until he had met the executive in question. It is rare that a group can move from planning to working directly with the targets. In most cases, as I said, difficulties can be anticipated when professionals come upon the scene.

I pulled out all the stops in an attempt to construct a viable relationship between NARCAD and the Center. I suggested community education, volunteer roles, visits with the addict, and many others. At one point

Ted and I got together with Dinton and asked in essence, "What do you want, Fred?" He talked in phrases such as "when addicts come, you turn on." When we asked him for suggestions, he merely said, "You're a professional. You suggest a role." It was hopeless.

When the first black came on the staff I got him to ask Dinton for suggestions. He approached Dinton casually and as a friend. Fred ignored him. NARCAD members were not serving as volunteers or doing anything at the Center. In fact, there was no connection. Still, in the eyes of the public and in the eyes of the addicts, we were all the same. It was an impossible situation. We had no control over NARCAD, and yet by doing irresponsible things, they could discredit us. We were the professionals, after all, and they were the amateurs. They refused to listen to us, yet they could always claim that we had not helped them do their jobs.

Ted and I finally decided that we simply had to break the connection. We did it by having our staff stop attending NARCAD meetings. With our staff not around, NARCAD simply faded away. The combat had kept them alive. There was no one around to be stimulating or aggravating. And most of the direct service was being handled by professionals at the Center.

For some time, NARCAD ran a rival program by taking addicts to the hospital for detoxication. However, after a time, they simply fell apart. It was sad to be put in the position where we had to kill NARCAD, because they began the program, they pushed, and they knew the addicts. However, there was nothing we could do.

I Decide to Change the Board Structure

The board of the Welfare Council would get stuck legally if the Center did something wrong. The whole setup with the Center board being a subcommittee of the Council board was ridiculous. At first, I was able to keep the Center board cowed. For example, I was able to tell the board that I would indeed hire my own staff. I had several aces in the hole. I could overwhelm them with intellect. I could overwhelm them with problems they could not handle and of course, if worst came to worst, I could always threaten them with leaving, for I knew they had no one else.

One day, several of the board ladies came and stated that they did not like the way I had run a meeting. "After all," they said, "you work for us." One heller in control of the board was a particular thorn in my side. I decided at this point that it was time to do something about the ridiculous structure. I contacted an industrial psychologist and a clinical psychologist who were personal friends. I asked them to do a study of the board's relation to its executive. I told them that I wanted the board eliminated. Specifically, I told them that I wanted its main function to be relations with the community, that is, education. I also said that the board must be enlarged. The psychologist looked at me and told me that I was crooked. I replied that indeed I was crooked. Democracy a la the Constitution can produce a dictatorship. It depends on the intent of the people in power. Power plays are OK if the person has a clean heart. I made it clear that I didn't want any study at all if they were not willing to come up with my specifications. They agreed.

I knew that the board would like, and be impressed by, the whole idea of research. Research is liked in this town. My two psychologists did a beautiful job. They conducted depth interviews with board members in whom they planted the idea of change. After they had conducted the research, they made an unbelievably complex line-and-staff presentation to the Center board and to the chairman of the Community Council board. After they had finished, the board asked the psychologists for their opinion. However, the psychologists successfully turned it around to say to the board, "It is your choice." The Center board became an Advisory Committee. The Welfare Council board became the sole body to which I was responsible.

We Change the Function of the Center

Finally, we were unencumbered by groups that were incapable or unwilling to assume responsibility for the program. I did not anticipate that we would be able to achieve miraculous things in this town. I said to myself that I would give it the old college try to see if the intervention of an agency could do something about addiction in a suburban community. I knew that it had not in Los Angeles. I thought that suburbia might be different, but I found that it is not—the problem of addiction in suburbia is no different from the problems of addiction in Los Angeles.

About two and a half years after the project started we had done nothing to stem the tide of addiction. We were forced to ask ourselves what we should do. The attempt to assist the addict through an agency was doomed to failure. We had two alternatives. One was to continue as we were doing—assuring salaries to our staff. The other was to close out the agency. We almost did. I felt that we should not use public funds to maintain staff. I felt that we were bound to close out the agency unless we could make a valid case in its defense. We were just patching up a few people at tremendous cost.

At this point we called in two top people from the New York Medical Center to advise us. They pointed out that there were important things that had to be done. They identified for us how the community was creating addiction. It is a long story. Suffice it to say that it's true. If a great deal of the social fabric is not changed, including the legal structure, you won't get any place with addiction. Even though I'm a community organizer, I had become so involved in directing an agency that I failed to realize that addiction was not a problem of the addict. It was a problem *for* the addict, and *of* society.

OK, the experts helped us see that. But we did not know what to do about it. One possibility was to document the structural and social causes of addiction. If we could do that, at least this community might be able to recognize how it was creating the problem. An effective study and follow-up program might have big payoff for other communities as well.

I wasn't sure where to start until I thought of Betty Vendeaux, a reporter and sometimes T.V. commentator on health and welfare problems. I had met her when I first came to town. Five other people and I had given panel presentations on the problems of addiction, and she approached me with the thought that the whole show was worth a story. I didn't go for it. I like to work behind the scenes. I hate big spreads that promise more than you can produce. Besides, the newspapers usually give a very bad press to volatile issues like drug addiction. At that time, I had completely avoided her.

Now I called her, and asked if she was still interested in addiction. I reminded her that she had wanted to do a story once, and told her I was glad she didn't. We had not been very successful. Now, I told her, we were moving into a project that would document the origins of addiction but would only be successful if it included community education. She was still interested. I told her I would let her do the story, if she underwent an educational program. We had recently instituted a six-session community-education program on narcotics. She agreed. Then I told Betty that she would have to let me see the final copy on everything to be released. I especially wanted her to concentrate on narcotics and addiction. I wanted very little in the papers about the Narcotics Center. Community education, not agency publicity, was the issue. Again, she agreed.

After she had undergone the training program and had several talks with me, she arranged an interview with the mayor. The mayor actually wound up interviewing her. He literally peppered her with questions about what was going on in addiction. She emphasized that he should contact the Center. "After all," she said, "it is here."

Then she urged me repeatedly to go talk with the mayor. I didn't want to get involved in politics. Political involvement is what destroyed treatment of addiction in Los Angeles. I saw no reason to play this game of frivolities in this city.

Finally, I did speak with him and found him to be a completely different breed of guy. In effect, he said that he would like to do something with what we had learned. In no uncertain terms, he stated that we could have the weight of his office if we would advise him on how we wanted it used. Frankly, I would have liked to not get involved—I would have liked to just sit back and write a book. Obviously, as a professional, I could not do that—I had to take the opportunity before me.

The completely accidental focus of the mayor's interest permitted us to do more than merely articulate the variables that caused addiction. A health-oriented mayor who agrees to keep it out of politics and spearhead a task force—you simply can't walk away from it. It is a very big undertaking. From a selfish viewpoint I would have preferred to quietly sit back, but the fact that we could do something with our research was the point at which I knew the project could move.

At this time, we had a pretty good advisory committee going. You remember, this is what had become of the original Center board. The advisory committee was broken up into several viable subgroups. They were each made up of different types: school personnel, public health workers, employers and personnel managers, social-agency types, and the like. All these people entered training programs. Once the professionals were trained, we trained lay people and added them to the subcommittees. At first, we had expected the training and establishment of semi-autonomous subunits by function or field to be an end in itself. Each one could use its new knowledge to effectuate changes in its own field.

This approach worked for a while. Then came the pressure from the mayor's office. He wanted us to set up task forces to study and recommend programs for the elimination of addiction or for its treatment on a central and coordinated basis. I felt that the opportunity was great. But we did not have the manpower to keep up our work with the function-field subcommittees of our advisory committee and to staff the mayor's task forces at the same time. We had to make a choice. Something had to give. We decided to let the advisory committee and its functional-field subcommittees go. It was a hard decision. When you are a community organizer, you hate to let a viable structure fall apart.

Working with the mayor, we changed our approach somewhat. We focussed only on the people who had enough influence to change the community's posture towards addiction. Some were people we identified as well-known community influentials. Others were the key administrators or decision-makers in the relevant organizations. Actually, our work with the advisory committee and our educational efforts and training programs bore fruit at this point. We were well known and had already been in contact with many of the people we were now trying to influence anew.

We aimed our efforts at the following:

1. The coordinating agencies, such as the welfare council in the voluntary arena and city and state governments in the public arena.

2. The relevant caretaker services, such as the welfare department, vocational rehabilitation, family-service agencies, recreation, or group-service groups.

3. Community leadership (the power structure)—often we involved the wives of powerful men, knowing that their family names committed the husbands.

4. The general community—in essence we said that if you want to combat the problem, you have to be sympathetic, patient and understanding—like bring an addict home for supper—I mean it.

5. The schools.

6. T.V., the newspapers, the local radio station—Betty took charge of this.

It is hard to tell, but I think we are on our way to something important.

Looking Back

Often, CO projects develop from completely accidental events. Often the only credit that community organizers can take is that they saw a hot opportunity go by and grabbed it. Many of the neat reports of community organizers do not reflect this; they make it appear calculated. However, more often than not, the CO worker moves with a situation rather than having control over it.

In this project, we started out with an attempt to help the addict through an agency. After a few years we were ready to quit. Then we aimed toward research and extensive documentation of the fact that addiction is an adaption to the environment. From here we moved to the formation of an educational task force from the structure of the advisory committee (previously the Center board). This educational task force was seen at the time to be an end goal in itself, and then, completely by accident, the mayor came along and in effect asked us if we wanted to get action on our new-found knowledge.

I think I like the way things are going. I can't take credit for them. I didn't plan way in advance for things to turn out this way. I guess you could say my staff and I set the stage for certain things to happen. The good community organizer is the guy who can spot an opportunity and take it. He has to be willing to give up a pet project, or even something he has invested a lot of himself in. You've got to take yourself seriously as a professional, but you can't be too concerned about yourself personally. Ego has no part in this business. Sometimes you just have to know how to admit failure. Lots of times you can't do a thing right. You have to know when to stay and when to get out.

*   *   *   *

P-9   A UNION WINS MENTAL HEALTH

I have no confidence in demonstration projects. When I go in to do a job, I go in to do a job. Unless there is an audience lined up who will use your demonstration and implement it, what's the use? So when the union and industry called me in to talk about setting up a new mental-health program, I asked myself, "What's in it for them? What are they going to be willing to give? What am I going to have to offer each of them in order to make sure the program is going to work?"

I knew it wasn't going to be easy. One of the really big unions started a national mental-health program a few years back. They won a contract with the industry to subsidize every worker and his immediate family for mental-health services. It was like a health-insurance plan. But it didn't work well. The foremen weren't pushing the program because it cost the industry money. The union men and shop stewards weren't pushing it, because they didn't understand it. As a matter of fact, after two years of the operation, the union I am talking about conducted a survey. Eighty percent of their members knew nothing about the mental-health coverage. Of the 20 percent that were aware of it, the majority wouldn't have been able to spot a mental-health problem. Some of the workers were down on mental health because it was a "communist conspiracy." And the few that would have used the plan didn't know how to go about looking for help. Getting a doctor or going down to the local clinic when you have a health problem is easy. But if you've never tangled with agencies, finding the right one or locating a psychiatrist can be quite difficult. So the program was failing. Before taking the job that was being offered me, I decided to fully explore the reasons for the failure of the mental-health program in the other union.

It wasn't hard to find out. The reasons were blatantly obvious. Management never liked the program, because it cost them money everytime a worker collected insurance premiums. The union, always looking for a new political issue, had negotiated the mental-health contract as much for public relations as for anything else. Having won the contract, and having interpreted the victory to their members, they found nothing but apathy. The program no longer had any political significance for them, so they lost interest.

The contract in the industry that approached me was a little bit different. Management and labor (that is the industry and the union) were each to contribute equally to the program. But it was obvious to me that the same problem would manifest itself here as in the programs I had just studied, unless I could do something about it. I agreed to take the job on the condition that the union and management set up a policy board made up of high-ranking officials. They agreed. I should tell you about the atmosphere at that first meeting. We had the same labor and management people there that had negotiated over the bargaining table many times before. They knew each other well, but suspected each other's every move, listening to every innuendo. I came in as a technician, a foreigner with a set of demands that neither of them fully understood. I was an outsider who played by another set of rules. If anything could have united them, it was their distrust of me. I sure as hell wasn't going to fall into that trap.

I spent my first day listening, trying not to answer too many questions, and asking a good many more. I didn't want them to think I was a soft-hearted intellectual coming to tug away at their bleeding hearts, or pushing some impractical program that nobody wanted. At the end of the meeting I said "It seems to me, from what I've heard around the room, that the mental-health program may not be needed after all. Maybe the whole project should be dropped."

It was a ploy. No matter what their reaction, I had the next move figured. If they were apathetic, or agreed with me, I could say that I wanted to meet separately with union people and with management so as to figure out a way in which we could redesign the program or they could extricate themselves with grace. Management then would have been afraid that the union was getting away with something, and vice versa. If, on the other hand, they protested my remarks, as in fact they did, I had a similar ace in the hole. I told them that it was obvious that the program as currently designed seemed to have little potential payoff to either the industry or the workers. I would be willing, I told them, to meet with each side so as to figure out a way in which it might have a much greater payoff. What I was doing was very simple. I was taking the heat and the potential hostility off me. Instead, I was playing a role that was quite familiar to both sides, that of the "mediator." I was going to help each side figure out a way of solving a problem that otherwise would have led to an impasse.

My strategy with the union was very simple. The mental-health program had to become a major organizational goal or we could forget it. Unless it could be turned into political capital for the union leaders, it would never work. I built my arguments with them around the issue of prestige, a favorable national press, and a potential success that could set a precedent for all other labor-management negotiations around mental-health issues for the next ten years. I had some good contacts in Washington, and told them I thought we could get some support monies from the National Institute of Mental Health. I had some friends in the Labor Department contact the union leadership and congratulate them on getting the program off the ground. I contacted all the labor intellectuals in town, those who advised the union, and those who worked for it. I got their support. I talked with the people at the National Institute of Rehabilitation and Health Services. That's a labor lobby located in Washington. They promised to give me support and to encourage the union leadership.

When I met with the industry people, it wasn't that easy. I don't believe in all that baloney that success of the industry depends on the mental health of its employees. We see too many compulsive workers who can really produce. On the other hand, I was able to pull together some recent studies that gave dramatic evidence to the prevalence of mental illness in the industry. The employers were shocked. I also arranged meetings between the executives of the social agencies in which some of the industry leaders were board members. We had a couple of freewheeling luncheons, in which the agency people showed some real enthusiasm for the industry's leadership in this matter. I think the clincher in my case was my documentation of the extent to which absenteeism from the job was related to mental-health problems—either the employee's or those in his family. There is a shortage of certain skills in industry, and manufacturers were most interested in keeping good men working. I had the issues pretty well identified. Management could congratulate itself on increasing efficiency, and the union could win a political victory and gain national recognition.

In setting up our services, we didn't try to blanket the entire industry all at once. We made a few mistakes at first. We tried to run our own service center, and found that all our staff time was spent in direct practice and in clinical work. We had almost no time for education or for research and evaluation. It was a classical bind, and we had to extricate ourselves.

Our pattern now is very simple. We pick a union local in a certain community. A team of advance men go out. It includes some of my staff, myself, and some union leaders. I usually go to the social agencies in town and interpret the program. I meet with the agency heads and offer them staff-development programs aimed at providing services to blue-collar workers. A big selling point is the innovativeness of this program, as well as the fee-for-service approach. The union and management pay a standard amount for everyone who gets mental-health services from an agency or from a private clinician.

In the meantime, the union leaders and my staff have been meeting with the shop stewards. They explain the provisions of the new contract and get the shop stewards to describe cases of bizarre behavior or crack-ups that they have witnessed. Then the union leaders give them a pitch about how they want this to be a model plan. My staff shows some movies and explain a little bit about how the program will work. Then they arrange for a tour of the plant.

They then spend a few days circulating around the plant, meeting with the workers during coffee and cigarette breaks, interpreting the program, and doing a little bit of case finding right on the spot. At the end of a week, I assign a man to intake, referral, and emergency service. If he doesn't get enough business quickly, he circulates around the plant some more. It's also his job to make sure the social agencies are prepared to deal properly with the union members when they apply for service.

We don't neglect management either. We set up special workshops for the foremen and pay them to attend. We introduce them to our intake-and-referral man and role play a couple of situations. In one, a worker has a personal problem that affects his productivity. The foreman has been unsuccessful in dealing with it until he realizes that the problem has subconscious origins. We then role play the whole referral process. We give the foreman a feeling of being an important partner in the entire process.

We have been doing this for about six months now, and preliminary studies indicate that our ratio of success to failure has been satisfactory. Our biggest victory has been with the union itself. We are no longer looked at with suspicion. They see us as a welcome house guest. They openly share secrets with us and I think that's a good indicator of intimacy. We have open communications and can make demands on each other. Our biggest problem, of course, has been what union members think about mental health. But last month there were three articles in the union newspaper by individual workers who discussed their experience with the insurance program. When workers will talk openly about their mental illness in the union newspaper, it's clear that there has been some shifts in the norms.

*   *   *   *

P-10   THE INDIGENOUS SUBPROFESSIONAL

To Employ or Not to Employ?

Background

In the process of gathering materials for this volume, one of the authors was invited to attend a staff meeting in a multiservice center operated under voluntary auspices. Eleven professional staff members and one "indigenous community leader" were present. The discussion illustrated many of the factors that must be taken into consideration in making decisions about staff patterns and manpower allocations.

Rather than reproduce the discussion as we observed it, we have chosen to describe the position and perspective of each of the actors in the drama. We suggest that a class or staff group use the following materials in order to role play a similar staff meeting. We think this may have more benefit than a more standard case presentation.

The Scene

A regular agency staff meeting convened by the executive director. The major item on the agenda calls for exploring the possibility of employing indigenous subprofessional staff members from the immediate community. The possibility has been knocked around informally, but never discussed openly with the entire staff. When the center was opened two years earlier, the emphasis had been on delivery of high-quality professional service to a much-neglected neighborhood.

The Actors

No. 1. As the *director of the multiservice agency,* you are in a constant bind over the lack of available funds and the pressure to expand service. The biggest item in your budget is personnel. The need for program staff (group workers, caseworkers, nurses, community organizers, lawyers, and the like) is so great that you have understaffed them with the necessary clerical and maintenance supports.

You are plagued by the notion that somehow the division of labor is not very logical. A recent study on how your staff utilize their time was very disturbing. Less than 30 hours per month per caseworker, for example, was actually spent in client interviews. Organizers tended to spend twice as much time on a telephone as they spent on the street or at meetings.

You are not convinced that the introduction of neighborhood people on the staff would markedly reduce this inefficient use of time, but you would be willing to consider it. You are concerned about the politics of the situation, however. You know your budget will not be increased, and the addition of every two nonprofessionals might have to be made at the expense of one professional position.

No. 2. As the *program director,* you are *responsible for staff development.* Try as you may, you have been unable to move the staff as a whole to consider a number of issues. Professional socialization, you have concluded, does indeed lead to a trained incapacity. It is not that the staff is professionally incompetent, it is just that they tend to regard procedure and methodology as more important than accomplishment. Of course they would never admit this, if accused of it. If you could only balance the staff out with some indigenous nonprofessional personnel, you might be better able to keep everybody honest.

On the other hand, if you are having difficulty with staff development now, how much more difficult might you reasonably expect it to be, if the staff were made up of people without any kind of training, and with tremendous educational deficits?

No. 3. As *associate director of the multiservice center,* you take a keen interest in the public image of the agency—in particular within the community it serves. You know that, despite all efforts to the contrary, the agency is still seen by some neighborhood people as a middle-class and predominantly white intrusion into a lower-class community made up largely of blacks and Spanish Americans.

Unfortunately, there are few trained blacks or Spanish Americans in the professions. The neighborhood is 72 percent black and 20 percent are Spanish Americans, but only 3 of the 18 professionals on the staff are black. Only the clerical and maintenance staffs tend to be from the community. An activist in civil rights, you are very sensitive to charges of colonialism and irrelevance. You feel that as long as the staff of the Center does not reflect the cultural backgrounds of the community, it will continue to be perceived as a foreign outpost in a hostile environment. Is this any way to run a service agency? Somehow local people must be trained to assume service functions. But even if they could be trained, how will the agency assure that they will remain on their jobs? Is the cost of recruitment and training such that it would actually be more expensive to put indigenous people on the staff than to recruit professionally trained people? After all, governmental agencies and the universities are now bearing the brunt of professional training costs. How adequate a training program could you provide? You bring these concerns to the staff meeting.

No. 4. As *coordinator of the intake and referral services of the agency,* you are concerned with your staff's ineffectiveness in reaching community people, in interpreting your agency services, or in helping people take advantage of these services and those of other agencies.

You feel that much of the problem has to do with a "cultural gap" between the staff of the agencies and the residents in the neighborhood. The staff have some notions of how service ought properly to be dispensed, and of the appropriate procedures for dispensing them. Community people are befuddled, angered, or just turned off by much of what they perceive to be "getting the runaround," when they ask for service.

You feel that the employment of indigenous nonprofessionals will aid the professional staff in understanding the styles and needs of people in the community, that they can serve as interpreters of the agency to the community, and that they might very well perform many of the tasks currently performed by professional workers.

Whatever else transpires during the course of the meeting, you will not waiver from this position.

No. 5. As an *active member in NASW*[1] you have consistently opposed the inclusion of subprofessionals and BA people in the Association. It is not that you don't think that they deserve an occupational association or need one, it is just that you don't think they ought to be considered credentialed social workers, or even to use the title "social worker" at all.

You do not oppose the use of indigenous nonprofessionals on the agency staff. As a caseworker, you might welcome the relief from some of the humdrum duties you are required to perform daily. You could see employing a few on a trial basis—as case aides.

No. 6. As an *organizer for the community council program of the agency,* you have run into an amazingly talented bunch of local people. Many of the most active in your block organizations are unemployed or underemployed. Many have superb natural interpersonal skills.

You have frequently considered the advantages of finding them salaried positions within the agency, but have rejected the idea. If they were to become overly identified with the agency, they might lose their abilities to truly reflect neighborhood sentiment, especially when it was in conflict with the agency. If they were to become too much involved in the agency's service functions, they might find themselves disinclined to commit themselves to action programs.

No. 7. You are a *member of the neighborhood council,* and president of one of the block clubs. Active in the community for a long time, and a staunch supporter of the service center, you have strong feelings about the use of indigenous people on the staff. You were invited to share your impressions at the staff meeting.

You are dead set against it. You want professional skill, not neighborly help when you come to this agency. You don't want to risk someone's sharing confidences all over the block. You try, but not too successfully, to hide the fact that you would be very jealous if some people of whom you did not approve were hired. Because you have no particular interest in a job at the agency, you would find your position as a lay person in the organization threatened if other people on the block held powerful staff positions.

---

[1] National Association of Social Workers.

No. 8.   As a *student from the School of Social Work,* you have a *field assignment in the agency.* This semester you helped the executive conduct a time study to determine how staff people allocated their time. This convinced you that the agency is really set up to serve the occupational and career interests of the staff rather than the neighborhood itself. As you listen to today's discussion, you are smoldering inside. You want to blurt out your feelings, but instead, jot down notes on what is being said and on the key points from your time study. When the right moment presents itself, you ask for the floor and give what you feel is a supremely rational presentation. But you are still smoldering inside. Some of this heat shows.

No. 9.   You are a *casework supervisor with 15 years of experience* in this and similar agencies. You have your MSW and your ACSW. You attend continuing-education summer institutes every year at the University. You also enroll in a variety of seminars and institutes during the year.

You feel strongly that professional competence is based on knowledge and skill. You are keenly aware that therapists from other professions such as psychiatry and psychology tend to look down on social workers. You feel the status issue strongly, but your real concerns are with the quality of service.

No. 10.   As a *planning consultant to the agency,* you are accustomed to beginning any consultation with an attempt to get the staff or the administration to look at the problem, to define it, and to examine alternative ways of resolving it. You try to be logical and rational in your approach. You insist that the staff look at various alternative solutions to any problem.

It becomes obvious to you, at this meeting, that there are quite a few agendas on the table. There are more than just a few ways in which the staff problem is being defined. And there are a number of solutions being offered even before there is agreement on whether there is really a problem, or what that problem might be. You try to help the staff examine the issues rationally.

No. 11.   You are a *group worker,* and you like being a group worker. But you do not feel qualified to run all the recreational programs that group workers are expected to have skill in. You do well with dramatic and crafts activities, but badly with sports and games. Even in crafts, you find yourself spending inordinate amounts of time ordering, storing, laying out, or replenishing supplies.

A time study showed that you spend less than eight hours a week in actual contact with clients. The rest of the time is devoted to planning and to administrative or clerical responsibilities. You feel that the latter are beneath you and that they do not utilize your skills and your training. You are being used inefficiently, you resent it, and you find yourself bored with much of your work.

A cadre of neighborhood people, who could pick up some of your work that does not require professional skill, would not only make you happier at your work, but would assure the maximum use of your competence. You may agree or disagree with other things discussed today, but you will remain convinced of this position.

No. 12. As a *caseworker in the agency,* you feel overtrained. Much of what you must do in the course of an interview—help people write up a budget and help them figure out how to get to the unemployment office and how to organize a weekly menu—could be done by someone with less diagnostic skill than you have, but with more particular skill in the specific area of concern—marketing, budgeting, employment, and the like.

If you could work with a team of community people, each with specialized training, you could refer each of your clients to the appropriate person, thereby seeing a greater number of people. Whatever else transpires at today's meeting, you will remain convinced that this is the soundest way to go.

*   *   *   *

P-11 MY CLIENTS ARE THE SLUMLORDS

Organizing tenants' or renters' associations to put pressure on landlords makes sense, if your objective is to build some kind of grassroots organization for other purposes. If your main concern is to get the landlord to change his policies and improve conditions, then a tenants' association is risky business. First of all, it takes a long time and a lot of energy. Second, if the landlord has more than one holding, a victory in one will have little impact on another. In the third place, I don't think that we social workers have any business playing with people's lives. Renters are the ones who take the real risks in tenant-action programs. And they are the ones who usually get evicted.

You want to know my approach? I approach a landlord as a human being. I heard Joan Baez talk about it on TV one night. When the Nazis occupied Denmark, the Danes refused to treat them as soldiers or as beasts. I have seen the same approach used with policemen in this country. It works an awful lot better than calling them pigs or assaulting them with either words or missiles. But I don't mean to be talking here in terms of political strategy alone.

I also concern myself with the landlord's selfish motivations, and with his personal needs. These too, after all, are expressions of his humanity.

At least one concern a landlord is going to have is in maximizing profits. I never forget that. Another will be in enhancing his public image. And I don't put altruism down either. Everyone likes to feel he's making some kind of contribution, especially if it's not costing him much.

Now I don't mean to be spouting out clichés; I have worked with lots of landlords for whom no rational approach is workable. There are lots of sick and neurotic people around, landlords not the least of them. That's why I tend to treat landlords as clients.

When I became coordinator of one of the City's Service Centers under the auspices of the Housing and Redevelopment Board, I set up two parallel services. One is aimed at helping tenants, hearing their complaints, and trying to obtain a redress of their grievances. The other is aimed at treating landlords. Frequently, in the process of serving clients we uncover the facts that lead to another service aimed at the landlord. It works the other way around too.

We had gotten a number of complaints from tenants in a particular building. Out of 20 units only 9 were occupied. The apartments were in terrible disrepair. A half-empty building like this is dangerous. Bums get in and start fires. The tenants had legitimate grievances. The building inspectors had already cited the building for 6 violations. The owner, Samuel Plotnick, had already shelled out over $400 in fines.

I reasoned he couldn't afford much more. Certainly he couldn't be making any money on a building that stood half empty. I could have reported the building to the Welfare Department. Since he had not corrected his code violations, the welfare people could refuse to pay rent for those tenants on welfare. Eight of the nine remaining tenants were on ADC.

I called Plotnick immediately after learning that half the building was empty. He cried over the phone and said that I was persecuting him. I tried to get through to him, but the man was obviously paranoid. I made an appointment to see him in my office, telling him that I was concerned not only that half the building was empty, but also that, unless we could figure out some plan together, he might lose the rest of his tenants. I hadn't put it as a threat, but I knew that in his state of mind he would view it as such.

There's no sense in my going into all the details. I said to him that if he made some improvements, I would refer new tenants to the building. I suggested that we go look at the building. We did. It was in a terrible state of disrepair. Plotnick agreed, but then began whining about his bills and his financial status. I told him I was concerned about this and wondered if I could help. I had some suggestions. We sat down and we looked over some of his financial statements for the building itself.

We examined several alternatives. One was that Plotnick could do nothing, in which case things would probably stay much as they were or they could get worse. The Welfare Department might refuse to pay rents for their clients. The city inspectors could heap on additional fines. The remainder of the renters might move out.

A second alternative was that he sell the apartment building, since he claimed it was too expensive to repair and keep in good shape. A third alternative was that we figure out a way for him to apply for a redevelopment loan. This would allow him to rebuild the interior units and do some face-lifting on the outside. I suggested that it might be much easier to get tenants to move back in if he knocked down a number of the flimsy partitions he had erected when he first purchased the building in order to enlarge the number of available apartments. Larger apartments would attract families that might stay longer and keep them in better shape. The last alternative was that he just make the necessary improvements to keep up the code. In relationship to any of the last three alternatives, it might be good, I suggested, for him to meet with the current tenants and indicate to them his good will. It might be tough, as they might shower him with a lot of abuse, since they felt that he didn't care much about them all these years. I said I'd be happy to work with the tenants and prepare them for a meeting at which both sides could try to figure out how the building might be made livable and yet profitable for the owner.

I must tell you that this approach has worked innumerable times with more rational landlords. With Plotnick, it fell on deaf ears. The man was completely irrational, and just didn't respond to reality. When I found out that Plotnick had a partner, I went to talk to him. This man was not only interested in my suggestions, he also shared with me his concern for Plotnick's stability. With the partner's support, the three of us were able to map out a plan for the building. The partner, we agreed, would meet with the tenants. Interpersonal relationships were not Plotnick's forte. You might be interested in knowing that some time later, Plotnick's wife approached me about his irrationality, and I was able to refer her to a family-service agency.

11

The Planner as Grantsman

CASES AND ILLUSTRATIVE MATERIALS

An essential ingredient in the planning process is the drawing up of a plan, or at least a "plan for planning." A plan is a design for the solution to a problem. Frequently, plans are made explicit during the process of proposal writing. A number of planners use the proposal-writing or grant-application process as a means of testing out their own deliberate, rational schemata for intervention. Planners may slant their proposals to specific audiences. Or they may hint tentatively at one direction or another, probing for support or resistance to their ideas.

Planners have different styles. What they do with proposals and with grant applications is highly idiosyncratic. While one of our interviewees specifies his proposed plan of action in great detail, another tends to roll with the punches and to concern himself more with the political process of seeing an application through than with the specification of details.

One planner described his approach to us as follows:

"I think of proposal writing as being like pursuing a woman. You never explicate your intentions at the beginning. When I want to get a project started, I call up or arrange to bump into the relevant people 'accidentally.' I never disclose what I have in mind. I say something ambiguous, like 'I heard some of your county directors are uptight about the welfare rights confrontations.' The guy I'm speaking to knows I've got something on my mind. He can turn me off simply by replying that 'it will pass over.' Or he can say something ambiguous to get me to commit myself further.

"After a bit, we know whether we want to talk with each other about a project. Progressively, I test out my ideas with the people who will have a lot to say about whether my project goes or not. The proposal then writes itself.

"It's pretty much like dating. You don't ask a girl right out what she is willing to commit. You work yourself towards a mutuality of perspective gradually."

We cannot express this approach more vividly. Not all planners are as suave or as "seductive" as the gentleman quoted above. Easton and Bennett, administrators of a community action agency, were clearly neither skillful nor planful in their approach to grantsmanship. They were harried. If money is abundant, planners do have a tendency to say "Let's get the money. We can always turn it down later." We do not recommend this approach. It is of questionable integrity, and in the long run may be self-defeating. Yet it is typical of new programs that are under pressure to expand rapidly. How would the reader have reacted under similar circumstances?

The planner who views "Grantsmanship as a Political Art" evidences great thoughtfulness and attention to detail despite the fact that he is assured of being refunded. He gives his attention to pursuing the prososal through every step of the review process.

We recommend careful reading of the vignette entitled "Grantsmanship as a Technical Art." The speaker, obviously experienced in the art of proposal writing, takes the reader through a careful detailing of every stage in his design or plan for planning. His use of both fact and theory is very instructive. The reader may wish to develop a proposal-writing model of his own, based on the approaches outlined.

P-12   GRANTSMANSHIP WITHOUT SANCTION[1,2]

or "Let's Get the Money. We Can Always Turn It Down Later."

Members of the Riverside lower-middle-income cooperative-housing project and other residents of the neighborhood requested a meeting with

---

[1] Note: The authors have used this case as a "script" for presentation in class. Students have played the roles of Bennett, Gray, Easton, Barnes, Davis, the Comptroller, and a narrator. The results were highly informative.

[2] Authorship unknown.

Tom Easton, Executive Director of HOPE, Inc., the community action agency. Knowing that the group wanted to get OEO money for a day care center, Easton asked his assistant director for program development, Irving Bennett, to sit in on the meeting.

The meeting went smoothly. Easton and Bennett both wanted to start a day-care program in that neighborhood—it was the only neighborhood without one. They knew and trusted the group that had formed to ask HOPE to apply for the OEO funds.

"What we'd like to do," Ed Gray, the group's spokesman said, "is hold the program in the Co-op itself. If we can enroll young children from the Co-op—who are from low-middle-income families—and low-income children from the neighborhood, we will have more social and economic integration than if we keep it just for low-income children."

Easton asked Gray if the group expected that the OEO would pay for day care for children from non-low-income families.

"We'd charge fees on a sliding scale according to income," Gray answered. "The poor kids would go free and the children from the Co-op would pay according to income."

Bennett, HOPE's assistant director for program development, suggested that "The fees can probably make up our local 10 percent and even more, which we can apply as matching funds."

Ed Gray went on to explain that the neighborhood needed a full-time day-care center even though it had a Head Start program, since Head Start didn't last enough hours per day to accommodate the special needs of working mothers. He also said that the Co-op would donate space for the day-care center free of charge and that the mothers and fathers in the Co-op would volunteer to help out with parent counseling and maintenance of the space.

Easton asked, "Have you written up your program and made out a budget?" "No, Gray said. "We thought we would let you do that since you're the experts at grantsmanship."

"OK," Easton said, "Mr. Bennett will get right to work on it with you and any other members of your committee you suggest. We'll have to hurry to get it prepared for our citizens' advisory committee and our board to approve this month. The next committee meeting is in four days and the board meets in eight more days. The committee has to clear it first, assuming that your Neighborhood Council is behind it."

"Most of the Neighborhood Council members are on our committee for this program," Gray said, "so that's no problem."

"Fine," Easton said to the group as it left, "we'll do the best we can. I should warn you now that these things take time even after they clear our local approval process. We generally count on the OEO taking anywhere from four to eight months to act on them. So don't get your hopes too high too soon."

When they left, Bennett told Easton he would want a little time to do some further research on day care. He needed to consult with some experts. The day-care centers in the other neighborhoods didn't seem to be working too well. He wasn't sure of the reasons. Some things should probably be done differently in the proposed new center.

But Easton wouldn't have any delays. "You don't need more research," he snapped at Bennett. "It's just the people running the other centers that are the problem. We'll get better ones for the Riverside program. Let's not waste any time—Ed Gray is an important ally and friend. He's helped our programs in many ways. I'd like to deliver this for him as soon as we can."

The next day Bennett and Gray met at lunch to draw up a budget. Bennett explained that this was the most important part, and that the work program could be dashed off in a few spare moments or at night. "We're not experts at day care," Bennett said, "so the best we can do on the work program is sketch out what we want. Anyway, everybody knows what day care is. We haven't got time to write up an elaborate work program anyway, even if we wanted to. The residents in your area want day care badly, and it's HOPE's job to get them their program."

"Fine," Ed Gray replied. "Let's get this budget drawn up. I have to be finished and back to work in an hour."

Bennett and Gray decided that they should serve 50 children in the program—30 from low-income families and 20 from the Co-op. This would require a supervisor at $8000, 3 head teachers at $6500, 3 assistant teachers at $5500, 3 non-professional aides at $4500, a Secretary at $4000, and a part-time cook/housekeeper at $3000. Fringe benefits, they estimated, would cost about 10 percent of salaries. The center would probably need about $5000 worth of equipment ("I'll have to back into that figure through itemization later," Bennett thought), $2000 worth of consumable supplies, $6500 for hot lunches (50¢ per child per day), and $2000 for insurance, laundry, and contingency costs.

"What about telephone?" Gray asked.

"We'd better throw in $600 for that," Bennett said. He added up the figures. "This gives us a grand total of $85,700 or $1715 per child per year. That's funny—the other centers come out about $1450."

"Well," Gray added, "this is our center and we want it to meet the needs of our neighborhood. What the other neighborhoods do is their business. Isn't that OEO policy?"

"Yes and no," Bennett replied. "When it comes to money, that can be another thing. But I'll see what I can do."

Bennett then asked how Gray was going to set the fee schedule and what space and services the Co-op would donate as local share.

"Why don't we say that each of the 20 Co-op kids will pay an average of $15 per week or about $750 per year, and the 30 other kids from the rest of the neighborhood will go free?"

"OK" Bennett said, "but will the Co-op families buy it at that price?"

"I'll check and let you know," Gray said.

"Now," Bennett continued, "How much space and what services will the Co-op donate?"

"Let me see," Gray said. "About 2500 square feet of space; fathers will do the custodial work, and mothers will do some counseling."

"How much is all that worth?" Bennett asked.

"I guess the space would go for $4.50 per square foot, the fathers' time is worth at least $4 per hour and the mothers' worth $3 per hour. Let's say that the mothers and fathers together will give 50 hours each week. How's that?" Gray said.

"The OEO won't allow but $3.50 per square foot for space or more than $1.50 per hour for volunteer services. But don't you worry about that— it's my problem to work this out. Thanks for coming in—I'll be in touch," Bennett concluded.

Bennett couldn't get back to the job until that night. At home he figured that the space would be worth $8750 and the volunteer services (he had decided he could only get away with claiming a total of 30 hours per week) worth $2250. This, combined with fee income, cut the Federal share down to $59,200, with $26,500 for the local share.

"That will leave me a nice $18,000 local cushion to apply against other projects," he thought. "I need right now about $12,000 against remedial reading and tutoring. If I can pull this off, my other matching problems will be solved."

Next, Bennett itemized $5000 worth of equipment using the GSA Catalogue. The latest edition he could get was 1962, but he had to use GSA price quotes. He didn't really know that much about day-care equipment, but he had to make a list.

After that, he wrote the work program. "These things go much easier now," he thought. "Ten months ago it would have taken me six hours instead of two to write this up."

The next day at the office, Bennett put the finishing touches on the budget and gave it and the work program to a typist. Then he filled out the CAP forms and sent them to Gray to sign. One problem was whom to designate as the delegate agency—there was only a committee now in existence. He couldn't reach Gray, so he decided to say that it would be the Riverside Co-op Day Care Center. Then he made a mental note to call HOPE's lawyer to see whether the group would have to incorporate to receive the grant when it came through.

The program application cleared the citizens' advisory committee and the board with little trouble. One problem raised by the other neighborhoods was why the Riverside program would cost more than theirs. Bennett got over this difficulty by pointing out that about one third of the cost of the Riverside program would come from fees and in-kind contributions.

The day following the Board meeting, Bennett had Tom Easton sign the covering letter for HOPE, and mailed the original and five copies of the application to the regional office of the OEO, with a copy to the state OEO director. In the covering letter Bennett drafted for Easton, he took pains to point out that this application had the full support of the CAP area residents and had, in fact, been initiated by the residents of the Riverside area.

Bennett was careful this time to make sure that HOPE's comptroller and contract officer got copies of the application. They would have to understand the grant and interpret it when it came through.

A few days after the application was mailed to the regional office, HOPE got a standard letter acknowledging receipt. About six more weeks went by and HOPE heard no more from the regional office about it. Bennett went in to see Easton. Easton got on the phone to Carl Barnes, the OEO staff person who handled most of HOPE, Inc.'s applications.

"Where are we with our Riverside Co-op day care program?" Easton asked Barnes. "We filed the application six weeks ago."

"Yes, we've got that," Barnes answered. "We're still working on a couple of your refunding applications, though. Do you want us to drop those and do the day care first?"

Easton recalled that the refunding had to be made in two weeks or some people would have to go off the payroll. "No," he said, "go ahead with the refunding but please hurry. We've only got two weeks to go or we're in serious trouble. When will we have that package?"

Barnes said he couldn't make any promises on it. The OEO regional office was understaffed and had a heavy workload. "Besides," he said, "we're all trying to get out the Project ENABLE grant by December as a Christmas present. It looks like all of us here will be assigned full time to processing those soon."

Easton told him that about 25 people would have to go off the payroll in two weeks if the HOPE, Inc., package were not approved in time.

Barnes said he understood the problem but didn't know what he could do about it. "A lot of people in Washington are pushing this ENABLE project pretty hard."

After he hung up, Easton asked Bennett to keep him informed on the status of the refunding application. "Call Barnes every day if you have to," Easton said, "and tell the comptroller to stand by for a funding crisis and find out what we can do to keep from putting people off the payroll. And from now on don't let things go this far without alerting me."

As Bennett was on his way back to see HOPE's comptroller about this, he got a call from Ed Gray. "Where is our program?" Gray wanted to know. "The neighborhood residents are getting anxious about it."

Bennett decided not to go into the details of the problems of refunding and ENABLE. "It just takes time with the OEO," he explained to Gray. "We told you it would be four to eight months when we first met, and it's only been about two months now."

"I don't understand why Riverside keeps getting shortchanged," Gray said impatiently. "The other neighborhoods have more programs than we do. I'm trying to work out some programs here to take the edge off the trouble that's brewing around redevelopment and racial imbalance in the school. I need help."

Bennett said he was doing all he could. This is true, he reassured himself, in light of the other problems HOPE, Inc. faced on funding.

Bennett then went to see his comptroller about the impending funding crisis. "Can we move some money around," Bennett asked, "from some other components to these so that we won't have to lay off people?"

"I don't know, Irv," the comptroller replied, "we have a 10 percent rule according to the CAP Guide Volume II. An auditor would raise hell over anything more."

"But it's either that or laying off able, dedicated staff, most of them poor people we've employed to work in the neighborhoods."

"Take your choice—layoffs or we all go to jail."

Bennett wondered if OEO would allow them to move enough money over to get through the interim between old and new grants. He asked his comptroller if he could give him an exact figure on how much money was left and how much it would take for a 4-week period.

"We'd have to do all that by hand," the comptroller said. "My staff is already working overtime getting out the payroll and we're two months behind in the treasurer's report for the board and two months behind on our auditor's statements to OEO."

"I guess I'll have to make an estimate, then," Bennett concluded.

Back in his office, Bennett placed a call to Barnes at OEO. He was on another line but would call back. Then Bennett made some calculations that showed that HOPE, Inc., would need to take a total of $6000 from other CAP components to meet two interim payrolls on the refunding applications. They would have to get the landlord to wait for his rent payments and their suppliers to wait for other bills. Then he drafted a letter to the OEO explaining the potential problem and asking permission to move the $6000 from other components. He didn't know where HOPE would move it from, and the comptroller was too much over his head to tell him now. "We'll just have to leave that problem until we have to face it," he thought.

When Barnes called back from the OEO, at 5:45 that afternoon, Bennett explained the situation and told him about the letter he had just drafted.

"I'll see if I can get that through down here," Barnes said. "Send us a revised budget for all components that are affected, including the ones you're taking the money from."

Bennett decided not to tell Barnes about his problem with the comptroller's time. "That will take a little while to get to you. Can't you give us the green light on the basis of the letter?"

"I'll see," Barnes said and then had to hang up to take another call.

The next day Bennett mailed the letter and the budget estimates for the refunding projects. "I'll have to see when the comptroller can get around to fixing up revised budgets," he thought.

Later that day Easton asked Bennett for a report on where things stood. When Bennett told him he'd mailed the request, Easton asked why he hadn't gotten it hand-carried or at least special delivery. "With the Christmas rush on mail, it might never get there."

The next 10 days were tense ones around HOPE, Inc. The day-care committee was calling every day. Finally, Bennett had to refuse to take their calls. He was too busy reassuring the three delegate agencies with grants about to expire that all would be OK with them. Barnes at the OEO was unreachable until 24 hours before the grants were to expire. HOPE, Inc., had gotten no authorization to transfer funds. Barnes apologized, explaining that between ENABLE and traveling around the region he hadn't gotten to anything on his desk.

"What'll we do?" Bennett asked.

"It's up to you, if I can speak off the record," Barnes said. "It's you that will have to face the auditors later."

Bennett went in to see Easton, and explained the situation. Easton considered all the factors for a moment, then called the comptroller into his office.

"Advance these projects the money Irv Bennett says they need," he directed.

"I'm not sure where we can take it from," the comptroller replied, "and what's more we haven't got any authorization from OEO to do this."

"You and Irv fix it up—right away," Easton snapped.

Bennett and the comptroller managed to work it out. Checks were made out from the bank account. The comptroller said he would figure out later what components to take the money from for bookkeeping purposes.

Irv Bennett didn't call Barnes at OEO for another two weeks. In the meantime, Ed Gray and his committee were calling everyone in Porterfield—including the mayor and members of HOPE, Inc.'s board—to find out why they couldn't get their day-care program. There was no satisfactory answer.

At last, five months after the day-care application had been filed, Carl Barnes called Irv Bennett and was ready to negotiate. "I've got five days left to do this," Barnes said, "before I go on vacation. I need a lot of information and material from you.

"Shoot," Bennett answered.

"OK. In the first place, our Head Start staff here has looked at your program and thinks it should be Head Start. We've got a new policy on this—no more day care, and only Head Start, unless there are unusual circumstances."

"The answer to that," Bennett said, "is that this is a full-day program. Head Start is only half a day. Another factor is that the Board of Education does Head Start, and the Riverside group is in a fight with them on the imbalance issue and doesn't want to get involved with professional educators. This will be very much a neighborhood program with lots of nonprofessionals hired."

"They are going to get pretty good pay for nonprofessionals," Barnes remarked. "Why didn't you say these things in your work program to begin with?"

"All right, I'll send you an amendment and lower the pay scales some," Bennett said. He hoped this would be all right with the committee, but there wasn't time to check it out now. He had to hold Barnes while he had him.

"The next thing," Barnes went on, "is this business of fees and non-low-income children. We've got a policy against these. We can support programs only for low-income kids, and 90 percent of the enrollment has to be low-income. All we can give you is money for the 30 low-income kids."

Bennett felt he had to make commitments then and there to keep the ball rolling. Otherwise they might have to wait another three months for the program. "OK," he said.

"Will the Co-op still want to sponsor the program now that the kids that live there can't attend?" Barnes asked.

"Yes," Bennett said.

"The next item is the in-kind local share. We won't allow fees, I've already told you. We wonder whether that space is really worth $3.50 per square foot. And how about the federal subsidy involved through Section 221-d-3 of the Housing Act for the Co-op in the first place. How can you claim it all as local?"

Bennett told him that he thought $3.50 was reasonable. He had no idea how to prorate local and federal shares of the cost of building the Co-op.

"Well, I'll need a letter from the Co-op detailing the space to be used, the facilities, the values, and all that," Barnes said. "And I'll need an itemization of the volunteer services to be contributed. Give me names and addresses of the people who will do maintenance and counseling work, exactly what they will do, how many hours, their qualifications, etc."

"OK," Bennett replied, making notes rapidly.

Barnes went on. "I'll also need a new CAP Form 1. The original was unsigned. And I need to know exactly who will subcontract for the grant. As I understand it, this is only a committee so far."

"Do they have to incorporate?" Bennett asked. "I really don't know," Barnes said. "HOPE, Inc., can subcontract only with *bona fide* groups that are accountable for the funds. You work it out."

Bennett asked if there was anything else.

"Yes," Barnes replied. "I need a fuller explanation of the parent involvement and counseling activities. The Head Start staff will never sign off on the basis of what you have now."

"Right," Bennett said.

"That's it," Barnes concluded. "Get it to me in three days and I'll get it through before I leave."

As soon as he hung up with Barnes, Bennett called Ed Gray's office to fill him in and get him to make some decisions on the basis of the new information. He learned that Gray was out of town and wouldn't be back until the following week. Bennett then tried other committee members and finally reached Mrs. Adele Davis, a Co-op resident. He explained the situation to her as briefly as he could and then asked if the committee would be willing to go through with the plan now that the Co-op children had been eliminated.

"I really can't speak for the committee," she said.

"What shall I tell the OEO?" Bennett asked.

"I don't know," Mrs. Davis responded.

"Well, I think we'll go ahead and get the grant. You can always turn it down," Bennett said.

"All right," Mrs. Davis said. "Is there anything else? My children are crying for their lunch."

"I need some information on the legal status-to-be of your group, and a breakdown on the space you'll use and the volunteers you'll have. Can you write this up for me today?"

"Oh goodness, I wouldn't know what to do and, besides, I'm loaded down with things to do today and tonight," Mrs. Davis explained. "Can't you do it for us?"

"If you'll trust me, I'll do the best I can," Bennett said. "But just give me some names and addresses of people who will volunteer."

"All right, Mr. Bennett." Mrs. Davis then named eight mothers and eight fathers who might help in the counseling and maintenance work. "Just let us know when the money comes in, Mr. Bennett," she concluded.

Irving Bennett picked up a pencil and started to write.

*   *   *   *

P-13   GRANTSMANSHIP AS A POLITICAL ART

I write the grant proposals around here. If it is for renewal of a current project, I just go through the files, abstract from old proposals, add some progress reports, and the like. If it is for a new project, I check around to see what the funding agency wants, and what other groups have gotten funding for. I usually talk to the staff men at the funding agency before I begin writing. I get to know them and what they expect. They also get to know me. The way they are going to handle my application will have a lot to do with what they think of me. Getting the grant requires very little technical activity. It is a political art.

When I submitted a proposal for renewal of our job training program, Ron Petrini, the field representative for the Labor Department, suggested that I increase the age range of the people to be trained from 17 to 22 to 17 to 30. He explained that the market was bigger for older people. Our outfit is concerned mostly with youth, but we were not going to jeopardize the program for a few years of age. The change was made.

I try to move a grant through the various channels as fast as I can. If a grant is delayed, as they often are, we lose money. Our staff has to get paid whether the grant funds come in on time or not. Red tape is usually the reason for slowdowns. I didn't leave the proposal in Petrini's office for more than a week without following up.

I called Ron. I've known him personally—otherwise calling him might have been pushy. You have to be subtle. I invited him to lunch. Of course, he knew what I was after. That's when he suggested we change the age range. I told him it would take us about three days to get the necessary approvals from staff and board committees to make the changes. Could he move it as quickly up the line? He gave me some excuses about being very busy, bogged down with all kinds of work. But he would see what he could do. I asked him to call me about whether he liked the "rewrite" after I got it back to him.

He called me the day after he got it. He said the proposal was now in the hands of Ed Wickendon, the assistant regional director. From there, it goes to Washington, where it is checked against current policy. Then it goes back here to the state director of the Labor Department. He checks to see if there is a shortage in the market for the type of workers we are proposing to train. At this point, a perfect proposal can get fractured. When a proposal has to pass from the regional guys to the feds, and back to the state boys, all kinds of conflicts of interest arise. Those are the ones I look out for. That's where the hang-ups take place.

In order to speed the process through the office of the regional director that determines the labor shortage, I made some additions to my report. I attached a copy of the latest Department of Labor *Newsletter,* which had an article on the shortage of skills in the production area we were training for in this very city. Our project proposes to train the handicapped. I also clipped out of a Sunday Times the advertising pages for skilled personnel in this area. This got the point across.

As I said, the proposal was now in the hands of the assistant regional director. It still had to go to Washington. I wanted to contact him, but I couldn't go over Ron's head. This was the beginning of August. I called Ron and casually found out when he was going on vacation. Then when Ron was not in the office, I telephoned the assistant regional director. I told him that I was getting pressure from my board about the grant.

In the course of the last few years, I've taken the occasion to have the important federal and state bureaucrats attend my board meetings. So now, when I talk about my board, they know the men about whom I'm talking and the positions they hold in the community.

The assistant regional director, Ed Wickendon, told me that he had just sent the grant request off to Washington. Now, Washington is a wild jungle. You never know what's happening to these grants. I decided to call a meeting of our committee on government relations. I told them that I'd like to get this grant out of Washington and back into state channels as soon as possible. One of the board members said that he knew Senator Harvey and would contact him. I don't know what happened after that—but in a few days I got a personal letter from the Senator saying that all is moving again. The same day, I got a call from Ed: "What the hell are you getting Senator Harvey down on our necks for?!"

I told him that it was not my fault; the matter got out of my hands and into those of my board of directors. I said I was sorry if it caused any embarrassment.

I have established a close rapport with the regional director's office. Last year one of the Labor staff was being transferred to a location he didn't like. Ed called me and told me about this. They know we have an influential board and I said that I'd do my best. At the next board meeting I presented the situation. One of the board members is a close associate and friend of the Secretary of Labor. He said he'd take care of it. And he did. The staff member at the regional office wasn't transferred. They appreciated this. Our board has helped them and we expect considerations in return.

Since Senator Harvey had moved the grant request out of Washington, it had to be in the hands of the assistant regional director. So I gave Ed a week and then called. Ron was still on vacation. Ed said that the request was now in the State Capitol. He promised me they wouldn't keep it there long. "How long?" I asked. He said two to three weeks. One of his men had made an error in calculations on our funding request and this would hang up the grant for a while. He was very apologetic. There was nothing I could do about this. It's one of those things that you can't help. But when a guy makes a mistake and screws something up, he owes you one, the next go-round.

On his return, I called Ron. The request, he said, had been tied up in handling. He promised me that he'd speak to his boss and get it moving.

I had not heard from the assistant regional director's office, so I telephoned Ed. I told him that I had a board meeting this afternoon and "they will cut my head off if I don't have something substantial to give them. The board will want to know what is going on." As it turned out, I got a telephone call during the board meeting. It was from Ed. He told me that the grant had definitely been approved. As a matter of formality, the Senator had to sign the grant. He did so in a week's time.

I have since learned that both Ron and Ed are due for promotions. I have put in a good word for them with the Senator. I'm sure that the next time we have to go through these same channels, the grant process will be even faster and smoother.

*   *   *   *

P-14 GRANTSMANSHIP AS A TECHNICAL ART

I know there are people in this profession who regard proposal writing with utter cynicism. For some, it's "who you know" that determines "what you get." People holding that point of view are usually motivated exclusively by self-interest. I'm not so contemptuous of people that I resort to such stratagems.

My own approach is to be very specific and very concrete about what I will produce and about those areas about which I am unsure. I don't ignore the grantor's requirements as to content or form, but I am much more concerned with the integrity of my design.

I have been on both sides. I have applied for grants, and I have been on foundation and government panels determining the fate of other people's applications. Proposal writers have different styles. There is one school of thought that recommends that you write proposals in the most general of terms. People in this school hold that since you can never fully adequately design a plan in advance, you should lay open a number of contingencies. Once they have written the proposals and received the funds, they then move on to operationalizing the design. Frequently, their activities and their end results are considerably different from what one would have anticipated from reading the original grant proposals. I have heard some of my colleagues on the grant panels espouse the opinion that "It is not so much what a proposal says, as the reputation of the proposal writer and project director." I suppose, in a sense that is true. Some men do have the reputation for fulfilling their obligations. Given the choice, I would award a grant to a man whose proposal is loosely written but who I know from experience will do a thorough and honest job. I would not be as likely to award a grant to a man whose proposal is beautifully and concretely written, but whose reputation for producing leaves something to be desired.

Still, I do represent the school that espouses that a proposal should be as clear and as precise about intentions as is humanly possible. I do not view a proposal as a precursor to a design or to a plan of action. The proposal should be operational. That is, if funds are granted, the planners should not then sit back and ask themselves what they should do next. The next steps should be quite clear.

To me, a proposal is a "plan for planning." It is a deliberate, rational design for social intervention. I don't mean to suggest that planning is a rational process. Of course it is not. It has its rational elements, but these have to do with the way in which one analyzes one's political situation. It is precisely this analytic aspect, which is foremost in the planning design, that I feel ought to be found in all proposals.

A proposal should make very clear what the problem is that the planner is addressing himself to. Proposal writing is a precise art. To be useful beyond merely "getting the money," it has to include an explanation of the problem; an assessment of its severity or its effect on someone; a set of objectives that can be translated into an ameliorative or preventative program; a listing of alternative and preferred means by which these objectives are to be met; and a method of evaluating the impact or effectiveness of each of these means, and ultimately of the overall impact of the program.

I have developed a style of proposal writing that I have found quite effective. It helps me, it helps the granting agency, and it helps my board, my staff, and frequently my constituency or target population to understand precisely what I am about. In less than a page, at the beginning of a proposal, I state the problem. I outline *what* the situation is that concerns me, and *why* it is a problem. I indicate *who* is directly affected by the problem, and who is indirectly affected by it. I hint at how the affected parties stand to benefit by some intervention. I say something about who else might recognize the problem or be aware of it. In a sentence or two I say something about *where* the problem is located, at least for this project.

I then write a very simple statement of objectives. It is a contrast between the situation that exists at present and the situation that I hope to achieve by the termination of the project. This is something of a preamble statement. It does not suggest the sequence of action that I intend to follow to get from the current to the future state.

Next, I outline some conceptual framework that will inform the remainder of my design, and much of my subsequent action. I'm not suggesting here, anything as grand as a theory of causation. There are few enough theories in the social sciences. Social problems are situationally specific. Theories are abstractions from the specific. It is difficult to develop theories sufficiently broad and yet sufficiently specific to inform all the stages of a planning process. "Opportunity theory" was an attempt to build first a local program (Mobilization for Youth) and then a national effort (The War on Poverty) out of a theory. It was only partially successful. Overly close adherence to a theory may blind you to important empirical realities. My own notion is to be less hung up with the comprehensiveness of theory, and more pragmatic about it. I search my memory and the literature for any concepts, conceptual schemes, or bits of theory that might be used to explain the etiology of a problem, or to show the relationships between the social variables that I will try to affect. Anything might be useful. For example, I might go to Morris and Binstock for their notions of "pathways to influence." There are more descriptions than conceptual schemes, but useful. Or I might go to Etzioni for his notions on the difference between "real" and "stated" goals or the notion of "compliance" as a major organization variable.

I then use these conceptual notions as a background against which I redefine the problem in operational terms. It is now possible for me to list alternative modes of intervention, and to select from among them a particular course or several courses of action. I make it very clear why I select one course of action over another. I don't like to see proposals that suggest that only one course of action is open to the solution of a problem. I feel that the writer of that proposal is being intellectually dishonest. I give reasons why I have selected one mode of intervention over others. It may be because of the strength of a particular theory, but more likely the reasons will have to do with feasibility—that is, with what is accomplishable considering the availability of resources, the time that we have to accomplish our objectives, and the political or sociological constraints limiting our interventions.

At this point, I usually go back to my original statement of the problem. And I include here necessary information about the population I hope to serve, or the organizations that will be the target of my intervention. If I want to get the school system to develop a bilingual educational program to serve Spanish Americans, for example, I will include all the pertinent data about the Spanish-American population in the community affected. I then will describe the efforts in this direction already attempted by the school system, its limitation in resources, and the blocks I anticipate prior to achievement of my objective.

Having done this, I overview, in inventory form, my contemplated action. Now, it's at this point that I may not be as specific as I would like. This is, after all, simply a plan for planning, and not an after-the-fact report. I can specify the people to be helped, the target population, the auspices or structure within which I will operate, and the hoped-for future state. I can also list the budget, the categories and quantity of personnel, the time plan I hope to use, and I can specify some of the intermediate steps or goals leading to my expected overall outcome.

On the other hand, I cannot specify every action I will take, and it is this section that, in some respects, remains very general. As I have indicated, however, where I can be specific, I am so.

Finally, I describe the built-in evaluation measures that I will employ. These may include descriptive studies, impact studies, cost-benefit analyses of different stages of the process, the use of information loops, and so on.

This section of the proposal is very important. It signifies to the grantors that you are serious about what you propose. It also promises them that you will keep them regularly informed about your progress, and that you will be constantly on the lookout to improve your own performance. After all, when you're in the business of planning social change, you must act responsibly and you must be accountable to someone other than yourself.

CHAPTER 12

The Planner
As Concert Master

BUILDING AND MAINTAINING SUPPORT

CASES AND ILLUSTRATIVE MATERIALS

We cannot stress too strongly the importance of the planner's maintaining and building support for his programs. Planned-change efforts do not sell themselves, nor do they follow a carefully plotted straight line. There are always potential sources of conflict between the planner and those who provide him with funding, with auspice, and with legitimacy. There are, almost invariably, groups in the community who will suspect the planner's motives or actively resist his efforts. Even where no active opposition exists, the transiency or disinterest of community groups or influentials can shatter the planner's good intentions.

Planned social intervention requires action at several levels to produce change. Frequently public support, for example, must be achieved prior to efforts to create legislative changes or new services. No matter how progressive a planning unit or how enlightened an agency staff or legislative body, the quality and scope of social services will not vary much from the values placed on them by the general public. This point is illustrated in the efforts of a planner to debrief influentials after subjecting them to a sensitivity and empathic experience in public welfare.

In "A Planning Project That Failed," a young sociologist documents how the lack of social-agency supports and his administrator's lack of responsiveness to the feelings of those who should have been his greatest allies, resulted in project failure. Disputed issues were never made clear. The parties involved could not enter into accommodative or collaborative efforts to deal comprehensively with problems of juvenile delinquency. This case also points to the shortcomings of many short-lived demonstration projects in which programs are expected to sell themselves despite the fact that the community is not really ready for a major onslaught on the social problem.

The worker who helped create a program of "Mental Health for the Poor" in a city housing project, on the other hand, displayed great sensitivity to the interests and concerns of agency representatives. His mode of social interaction varied during the process of selecting a goal, in accordance with how he perceived each person who might have influenced development of the plan. Was he involving others, or, as he put it, "selling them" on a program?

Attention to the interests and potential contributions of those individuals on a mayor's list of possible appointees to a model cities board is the subject of still another vignette. One almost gets the feeling that the narrator is attempting to orchestrate a symphony by the manner in which he plays off the strength of one actor against the other. This material also illustrates the dilemma faced by both planners and funding agencies that fear that community involvement may be disruptive and end in abortive and stalemated efforts.

There are a number of important points in this case. Although the program calls for concerted community action, each agency lives to a great extent in a world of its own and has relatively little capacity to put energy into a cooperative effort. Similarly, professional staffs are limited by their agency commitments and accustomed ways of doing things, just as community people consider their own careers and political considerations paramount. It is difficult to find leadership that is both dedicated and capable. The pitfalls of minority group leadership are cooptation on the one hand and demagoguery on the other.

Relationships with the city's mayor are the subject of "Protecting the Mayor" and "Quiet Diplomacy." In the former, a consultant on job training effectively ransoms an $800,000 work-training program that was being held up by the intransiency of a bureaucrat in city government. Attention to the mayor's self interest suggested the appropriate political response. In contrast, the administrator-planner who practices quiet diplomacy, allowed a work training program to lie dormant for six months because of his desire to put pressure on the schools to desegregate. He also describes his approach to maintaining a relationship to a mayor who is very much opposed to the actions of his antipoverty agency.

The state planner concerned with comprehensive mental-health programs gives a clear accounting of the way planners modify their objectives in the light of political feasibility. The narrator illustrates the coordination of a specialized planning team by a generalist uncommitted to any treatment discipline or service agency. He also shows how a developing program takes advantage of the available opportunities by couching proposals for money in a fashion to meet the requirements of granting agencies. With considerable candor, he discusses the quid pro quo manner in which he exchanges influence.

In "Paving the Way for Medicare," a public-health official takes the reader through the committee and task-force process through which much of our current social legislation is written, and through which administrative policy decisions are subsequently made. Those familiar with the legislative process may know that laws are often written in general terms, and that they may contain contradictory components. Legislation is frequently a compromise, emerging from the influences of many disparate interests. Without the work of staff committees such as the one described herein, most of our legislation would be inoperable.

We think a further word is in order. Whatever the dangers, latent or apparent, of governmental intervention, there is no question that it will continue to be an increasingly potent force for social change. The location of the planning unit within the political structure and its proximity to the recipients of the services it is attempting to create or to modify, will be a major factor in the planner's success. Planning units under governmental auspice are under a variety of pressures to effectuate meaningful changes in the delivery of social service.

A number of critics have charged that such services are palliative and serve to maintain the system as it is, rather than to allow for more radical changes aimed at the roots of social problems. Others charge that many governmental or privately sponsored social services are in essence political socialization programs aimed at colonizing and controlling the citizenry. There is a good deal of merit to both of these arguments. But just as there are no simplistic solutions to social problems, there are no simplistic and satisfactory explanations either.

In each of these vignettes, the object of planning was to get something accomplished. We have observed, however, that so many variables enter the planning process that goal displacement and failure are not uncommon. Community decision making is subject to the interaction of many actors interested in different things and subjected to different influences. The planner who does not engage in an entrepreneurial activity to build support and to maintain it, may end up with a batting average of zero.

The power to prevent the emergence of organized change efforts is located in many places. Conversely, the power to initiate and guide projects toward accomplishment is also diverse.

*   *   *   *

P-15   PROTECTING THE MAYOR

As a consultant on community affairs for a nonprofit firm specializing in new approaches to job training, I get to travel a great deal. One of the cities with which we had a contract was in trouble. The new careers program, operated through the city schools but funded by the Office of Economic Opportunity, was facing a budget crisis. Federal regulations stipulated that funds could only be allocated to programs in which trainees were guaranteed jobs upon completion of their work training. A few months earlier I had helped Ralph Lemsky, director of the city's program, write an $800,000 three-year proposal to train paraprofessionals and lay assistants for the schools, for hospitals, for the police, and for social agencies. It was predicated on the willingness of private and public organizations to help train and then to hire the trainees. Where the public agencies were concerned, however, there was a hitch. Civil-service requirements had to be lowered so that our trainees, many without high-school diplomas, could qualify.

When I arrived at the airport, Lemsky was waiting for me, in a panic. "The feds just called again. If we can't get Riley (the Civil Service Commissioner) to ease up on these requirements, and if we can't guarantee jobs for all our trainees, we lose the money to Metrotown (a large city in another state). I've only got two weeks." "Hang on, Ralph," I said. "That *is* a problem, but let's see if we can 'psych' it out."

"O.K., I have been thinking about it," he replied more calmly. "I know that bastard Riley, and he wouldn't give you the time of day. But Hank Kaminsky, his third in command, is a reasonable guy. If we can convince him, maybe he can bring Connor, the Deputy Commissioner, along, and the two of them can talk it up with Riley. That way, if I don't get anywhere with Kaminsky first, I can still take my chances with Connor and then with Riley. If I go to Riley first and get turned down, I'm finished."

"Sounds reasonable," I agreed, "but too 'if-y.'" We tried on several other ideas for size. I didn't really believe that any of them were too good, but I didn't want to jump the gun or tell him what to do right away. If I was wrong, he would lose the grant and we would lose the contract. I tried to get him to think up the answer himself, but he was just too anxious, thinking in circles. Finally, I said, "What if you went directly to the mayor?" "Can't do that," he replied. "The mayor would think I'm really incompetent if I went running to him every time I ran into some trouble."

"The hell he would," I jumped back at him. "You would be protecting him, and he would end up owing you a political favor." My reasoning went something like this. This was a normally Democratic town with a new, young Republican mayor. Metrotown had a Democrat as mayor. I figured that the reason the feds were being so helpful in telling Lemsky what he had to do to get the proposal funded was because the feds didn't want to have to award the money to a Democratic mayor. Nixon was in enough trouble with his party. It would be an embarrassment to a political ally and a hell of a way to ensure political allegiance if the money were to go to Metrotown.

I explained all this to Lemsky, and then said, "Look. You call up the mayor, and you tell him that some bastard in the Civil Service Commission is holding up an $800,000 grant. Tell him that the money will go to Metrotown if we can't put the screws on Riley right away (after all, he was a political appointee), and that you just wanted him to know so that he could decide what to do. You didn't want him to be embarrassed later." Well he did it. He called the mayor that afternoon. The mayor did a little arm twisting, and we got the jobs and the money. Glad I wasn't consulting with Metrotown too.

*   *   *   *

P-16   QUIET DIPLOMACY

When you're running a poverty program in a small Southwestern city, you have to keep your lines of communication open to everybody. Our board is made up mostly of power-structure people, but we manage to encourage plenty of social action at the neighborhood level. This takes quite a bit of sidestepping and tight-rope walking. Our neighborhood people have encouraged rent strikes, welfare rights sit-ins, merchant boycotts, and the like. We get away with it because I keep things out of the press.

Much of the time, I don't want to know what our neighborhood-center directors are doing, because it will only make me worry. What I do impress on them is the need to work through existing organizations of neighborhood people. We may advise them and encourage them, but our staff stays out of the picture when direct actions or confrontations take place.

Perhaps much of my success stems directly from my background. After receiving my MSW I worked for several years as assistant director of a planning council. I came to this city about five years ago as director of the local health-and-welfare council. I am a native Southerner. I think that because I've been associated, employed, and identified with the established power-structure agencies before becoming the poverty-program director, I am much less suspect than I would have been had I been an outsider. On the other hand, some people did not want to see me become poverty director because they feared I had too much of a commitment to the value orientations one would usually associate with the director of a health-and-welfare council. In any case the agencies accepted me, and didn't cause a fuss when I pushed them to move in new directions. If they didn't move fast enough, I often set up experimental or demonstration projects. I made sure to inform people at every step along the way, and if a project went well, I got one of the agencies to cosponsor it with us, thereby giving them credit for the success.

Of course, things don't always go so well. The city government is very conservative. One day the mayor decided to resign from the board of the Community Action Program, because he disagreed with our "liberal" policies. Although the mayor had been one of the founders of the CAP, he didn't come to executive committee or board meetings for about six months. He objected to the involvement of indigenous neighborhood leaders on the board. He also didn't like the fact that we had so many Chicano employees, or that we paid $1.75 an hour as minimum wage for the Neighborhood Youth Corps workers.

Instead of trying to change our policies, he stopped attending meetings. We had just selected a new chairman of the board and he arranged to have board meetings on the night that he knew the mayor was free. The mayor was now put on the spot, and he no longer could use other commitments as an excuse for not attending meetings. He came to one executive committee meeting and made a big issue over the $1.75-an-hour minimum wage. Not one person there supported the mayor's position. The mayor left very upset. That night he wrote out his resignation from the board and the executive committee, sent it to the new president, and the next morning left for Las Vegas.

As you can imagine, our executive committee was quite upset and so was I. Still, his going off to Las Vegas left everyone with some time to cool off and to plan a strategy. Fortunately, the mayor had not made a public announcement of his resignation. He had simply sent a letter to the president of the board. I met with the president and the next day we decided to visit the mayor's closest friend, who was also on the board, and who was very much concerned with civil rights, fair employment, and so on. We knew he was on our side even though he was close to the mayor. We asked him for his advice. The board member in question said he felt the mayor would withdraw his resignation, as he suspected it had been made in haste. He advised our board president to call the mayor at his vacation place and to say how surprised the executive committee was, how much they needed him, and how much they would like to talk to him before the resignation became effective. On his return, the mayor met with the executive committee for two hours and asked the president of the board to hold the letter of resignation in abeyance until we heard from him again. I interpreted this to mean that the mayor had withdrawn his resignation.

In the meantime, I had checked with several members of the Chamber of Commerce. Most of them were very much concerned with improving labor relations and getting wage increases for the city. I felt that the Mayor was on shaky ground, and that it would make a lot of sense for some of these important business leaders to tell him so. A number of them did so informally. The mayor then withdrew his objections, but could no longer resign from the board without losing face.

I find this way of working behind the scenes most effective. Let me give you another example. When we originally applied for the Neighborhood Youth Corps grant, the Office of Education wouldn't approve it because the teaching staffs of the local school system were not integrated. Because of political pressure, however, the school system did get a tentative approval from the OEO to resubmit the Neighborhood Youth Corps proposal. This really bugged me.

I did some quick behind-the-scenes dealing that nobody knows about. I saw to it that the schools would not get the Neighborhood Youth programs because they would not integrate. The OEO people did not tell the schools why their proposals had not been granted, but told them instead that they had submitted them too late. Privately, however, I found some subtle ways to let the school people know that the integration problem is what got them in trouble. Without being the bad guy in this case, I tried to demonstrate to the school people that their unwillingness to integrate may have more pronounced effects than they realize.

I realize that I sacrificed at least six months of job opportunity for some kids who really need it by killing the project, but I think there are broader issues at stake here. It wasn't easy to come to this point of view. A few years earlier I would have pushed to get the program no matter what the consequences, because I would have felt that the people were in need and that we ought to be servicing them. Now I have changed my perspective and I firmly believe in the way I'm operating. I really don't know how much of this kind of stuff I can get away with, but I am willing to sacrifice my job and my position to push for structural changes in this town as far as I can. I try to be politically astute. I don't mind the risks.

*   *   *   *

P-17   A PLANNING PROJECT THAT FAILED[1]

One of my first experiences in community planning was as research director of a project to plan programs to combat juvenile delinquency. The funds had been granted by the President's Committee on Juvenile Delinquency to the mayor of our city. We were one of 17 cities selected. Only half would be funded for operations at the end of a two-year planning period.

Even with 20-20 hindsight, I cannot be sure of the reasons for the mayor's selection of his first director. It had been widely rumored that the appointment was political. The man was a probation officer who, some social agency personnel believed, had worked hard in the mayor's campaign for election. At the same time a "community organization coordinator" was appointed. The latter was a political hanger-on, reinforcing the communitywide notion that the directorship itself was now a political position.

These appointments were ill-advised. They provided hostile City Council members with a new weapon; they antagonized—even infuriated—local social agencies; they were unacceptable to the few community leaders in the local area where action was to have been directed. From this point forward, whatever support the project had developed was lost. It was a political boondoggle—but the appointments stood. The director tried to hire other staff members: a research coordinator, a program coordinator, an agency service analyst, and a person to serve as a liaison officer with the schools. After a year, he failed to fill even one of these positions. Locally, no one would accept a position. A broader national search proved ineffective because the positions were only temporary ones. The first year on a two-year planning grant was lost. Local people, believing the project doomed to failure, withheld needed support. The project failed—a massive self-fulfilling prophecy.

Then the feds stepped in. It was an election year, and they did not want a fizzle-out. After a considerable amount of cajoling and persuasion, the mayor announced that the present director of the project would

---

[1] This case was abstracted from Michael Schwartz, "The Sociologist in an Unsuccessful Delinquency Prevention Planning Project," in Arthur B. Shostack (Ed.), *Sociology in Action*, Dorsey Press, Homewood, Illinois, 1966.

become the administrative director and that a new executive director would be hired. The mayor asked a search committee to locate a new director. The man chosen appeared a good choice. The new director had no political ties; he was a professor of education, well respected in his field; he knew many local agency heads, at least casually. While the first director was white, the new one was a black. He did not live in the city, but took a leave of absence from the university and moved to town.

The new director seemed equal to the task. Resistance was higher than it had been in the past, but some of the personal hostility toward the first director had abated. There was a wait-and-see attitude everywhere. The new director immediately began to locate and appoint personnel. The new staff were all quite good. They represented schools, the juvenile court, and psychiatric social work. I was appointed research director. It was another month or two before all staff members were on the job. What had been a two-year planning project was now left with about nine months. That meant working seven days a week and evenings. We believed that we would move, and we knew our progress was being observed carefully.

My job as a research coordinator was clear. It involved locating a "target area" of the city—an area with the highest rates of delinquency, adult crime, welfare cases, unemployment, and the like. These data were readily available. A block of contiguous census tracts was defined as the target area. The next step was to assess the variety and extent of social services available to people in that area, to determine the manner in which those services were delivered, and to estimate the degree to which people were not being served and the reasons for that lack.

This task proved nearly impossible. In the first place, agency data were either inadequate or were not made available to us. Second, the social worker who was to aid me in this work simply refused at one point to do so, claiming that she was a casework specialist and found the legwork of such data-gathering to be demeaning. Her psychoanalytic orientation caused her to oppose practically every bit of research and planning to be done. Five months later, she was fired.

The "target area" research task was never adequately completed. Time was short. A research staff of one man was ludicrous. The best I could do was analyze the vast complexity of the network of interrelating agencies, indicating, for example, that clients often had to travel long distances by bus to reach agencies that then sent them back across town to other agencies. Even from such a simple analysis, some reasonably fruitful ideas for programs did emerge. For example, we were able to propose a central service agency for the target area. That was to have been one building with at least one representative from every relevant agency located in it.

It was to have included facilities for central record-keeping and training of new personnel, and most important, it was to be open 24 hours a day, 7 days a week. It was designed to untangle the web of services, make data on families immediately available to concerned agencies, and make access to service more open.

This work was extraordinarily frustrating. The most difficult problem was my lack of access to data in the agencies. No amount of pleading with the project director was sufficient to get him to intervene. I assumed, at that point, that he was willing to sacrifice the adequacy of the research in order to preserve the good will of the agencies for later negotiations with them over new programs. But since those programs would depend heavily on research, his attitude seemed self-defeating.

Three more research tasks of major concern were undertaken. First, I conducted extended interviews with adolescents in the target area. This was necessary in order to plan programs to meet the self-perceived needs of the adolescents. The research went very well, and the interview data were transcribed, coded, and analyzed in about five months. The interviews provided some first-rate insights into the problems that adolescents perceived, and gave us some clues to the kinds of programming most needed and most likely to succeed. In a second way, this was very satisfying work. While our main research concern was with providing interview-based data useful for programming, I was additionally able to examine some of Albert Cohen's propositions on working-class delinquency, and some of Walter Miller's as well. This may seem to be a trivial point, but one of my major personal problems was my transition from academic preoccupation with theoretical and methodological issues to an atmosphere of practical, applied research demanded on schedule. This bit of research experience was gratifying.

The third study I conducted was also rewarding. The goal here was to determine differences in family structure, mobility, and employment patterns between the blacks and the Southern white migrants in the target area. Our purpose was to determine the extent to which different patterns of social organization and subcultural phenomena might require different program approaches. We learned, for example, that the position of the southern white in the labor market seemed to be a fair equivalent to that of the blacks. We also found evidence that the southern whites were underrepresented on welfare and relief rolls and that blacks were overrepresented.

We located two important and related pieces of data. First, the Southern whites returned to the South when they were "broke," more often than not. Second, they often developed patterns of exchanging interfamilial economic aid when some were unemployed. These factors kept them off the relief rolls, and supported the impression that the Southern whites maintained an ethic of independence and did not easily become urbanized. These were most important observations for our planning.

Armed with such data, members of our advisory committee met with several social-agency heads. This was one of the greatest frustrations of the entire experience. I argued that our observations indicated that delivering services to Southern whites in the same manner as to blacks would likely prove unsuccessful, or if "successful," could mean increasing the dependency of the people served. There is the possibility that the presentation of our data was not very tactful. But I had resolved to make my point as strongly and as logically as possible. I concluded by asking the agencies to consider alternatives to their usual approaches; I wanted the agencies to become part of the planning process and to develop some commitment to the project on their own. Their response was unimpressive. Follow-up phone calls usually produced no results, and we began to find fewer and fewer people "in."

Much later, after the program had collapsed, some agency people explained to me that they had found the data significant. The data backed up many of their own hunches. They had not been responding to the data in a hostile way at all, but to something quite different. For nearly 18 months the agencies had been ignored as a source of planning ideas. Their interpretation of the meeting was that we were in a bind and could not understand an issue that was a social-work problem because we were not social workers. Now it was their turn to let us "sweat a bit." At this point, the new project director should have mollified the agencies and persuaded them to participate, and he did not. He was too busy.

The director gave an average of three or four public speeches a week. He had moved to a very high-status area of the city. His prestige in the middle-class black community was soaring and he seemed to enjoy it. The building and maintaining of that prestige consumed much of his time and ours, at a period when time was the one fixed variable in the situation. Negotiating with agencies also required much time and energy, but this received less and less of the director's time each week. While he possessed the requisite skills for negotiation, he apparently perceived his position as that of a figurehead occupying an honorific position. He seemed to think of himself as the "company black" on display. The innumerable invitations to speaking and social engagements reinforced that image. Agency heads began to think of him in this way also. This all helped lead to the ultimate collapse of the project.

Only two of us were left to carry out the crucial agency negotiations: the research coordinator (me) and the program coordinator. As negotiators, we were unsatisfactory substitutes for the director: neither of us was a social worker; neither was over 30; and neither was widely known in the community. We both were clearly defined as staff people, well down on the status hierarchy. Nevertheless the negotiations were added to our already enormous work loads.

Heads of agencies did not expect to be asked to discuss such critical issues with people in lower administrative positions, and they began to withdraw all support. It was futile to continue in this way. We halted our efforts. The end of the road had been reached. Only a rapid shift in the behavior of the director could have salvaged the project. We were quite unable to bring it about. Time was too short for the feds to intervene again in our local affairs.

By this time the planning period had ended. Committee members and staff were going through the motions of completing reports and compiling them in book form. As research coordinator, I went through the motions of designing evaluation research projects for programs of action that clearly would never come into being. It became an intellectual challenge, but there was always a feeling of futility about the work. And somehow, sociologist or not, I kept hoping for an accident to occur—some unexpected, low-probability event that would get us to the action stage. It did not occur. Our staff flew to Washington for a review of our work. It was all very polite—and the project was finished.

There remains the real frustration of having seen the outcome in advance and having been powerless to alter it. I would not like to believe that I had defined the situation as a failure in advance and then aided in causing that failure to occur. The structural and social-psychological constraints on success were so strong that little could have happened to alter the events. I could have resigned when the realities became apparent but I elected to stay on. Leaving might have damaged the project still further. The feeling of defeat is only strengthened by the fact that there are about 80,000 children and adolescents who are, after all, the victims of such a failure. Their lives might not have been made easier by the proposed action programs, but there would have been at least some chance for them.

The death of such programs only rarely is accorded a full-fledged funeral. In this case, to permit public awareness of the defeat would have been gross political stupidity. A most convenient "out" was at hand. The city was planning an antipoverty program. The newspapers carried a story indicating that the Delinquency Prevention Planning Program was to be absorbed by the antipoverty program. Many of the programs planned by our committee were most suitable for inclusion in a "war on poverty" program. The community never understood what had happened. The project appeared to be involved in bureaucratic reorganization at the point at which it disappeared from public view. It seemed a logical precursor of the antipoverty program, but none of our recommendations were ever enacted.

*   *   *   *

P-18 MENTAL HEALTH FOR THE POOR

Most mental-health programs in this city are geared to middle-class whites. Our project will be aimed specifically at the poor black, and hopefully will involve the indigenous poor as staff technicians and organizers.

About one year ago, we first began to articulate the needs for a comprehensive mental-health program in the ghetto. Our proposals are designed to provide individual and group therapy, and intensive short-term care. We've decided to provide these services to residents in a public housing project. We hope to work with the police so as to familiarize them with the problems of the community. If we can equip them with techniques and skills, perhaps they will be able to establish a more positive relationship with the community's residents. We plan to use the indigenous poor, backed by a team of psychiatrists, psychologists, CO people, and so on, as an important "link" group between the new center and the residents.

The notions behind this project actually originated three years ago, when the State Department of Social Welfare asked my agency to help them upgrade their AFDC services. They needed program changes to meet new legal requirements. At the same time, the Department of Social Welfare in the city expressed some interest in exploring problems related to poverty in the city. We set up a Program Advisory Committee with representatives from all of the relevant agencies and from existent resident groups. We undertook an intensive analysis of the area's problems and of the services needed. Our objective quickly shifted from upgrading the AFDC program to breaking the web of dependency.

My involvement was most intensive at the outset of the planning process. I'm on a lot of community groups as a representative of my agency. I see my role as helping to get ideas articulated and getting a planning machinery off the ground. I'm a "doer" and people expect me to play that role. At first, there was a reluctance on the part of the Program Advisory Committee to look in depth at existing community needs, because such a study implied that they and the staffs of the service agencies had not been sensitive to the needs of the poor, nor had they provided them with adequate services. It took a major selling job on my part to convince the agencies' representatives that identifying unmet needs was not an indictment of them personally nor of their agencies. I talked of the opportunity to do something pioneering and significant. I talked about the possibility of experimental programs. I suppose my selling job involved firing up the representatives and injecting a note of charisma.

The nature of my selling job depended entirely on the personal qualities of the people with whom I interacted. For some of those with a superior intellectual ability, I used a very direct and open approach. We talked about the community, about its needs, about potential services, and so on. For other representatives, the selling job involved selling myself, so that they had confidence in my suggestions. Discussions with these people were more characterized by my taking them out to lunch, buying them a drink, and participating in social engagements. In some instances, where I could not persuade or entice the representatives to genuinely examine the issues, I went to their superiors. I have a close personal and professional relationship with most of the agency executives. I approached these men with a sensitive interpretation of the situation, in an attempt to win them as allies. They decided whether they could persuade their agency's representative or whether it would be necessary to replace him.

After some time, members of the Committee all agreed that mental-health programs for the poor had first priority. Group pressure probably played some part in bringing about this unanimity. I think the strain of our meetings wore people down. They were glad to be able to agree on something. I did not steer the consensus to mental health, but once that became the issue, I did suggest that it would be interesting to develop a comprehensive mental-health program in a housing project.

My agency has three recreation and small-group service programs in housing projects, and I was well aware of the need for mental-health services. The emotional strains that accompany tenancy in public housing are sufficient to destroy the healthiest individual.

We drew up some tentative proposals. I volunteered to put them in order and to resubmit them at our next meeting. I find that rambling discussions and chronological minutes result in poor recall. People always remember what they want to, anyway. You can have more influence on a group by keeping your mouth closed but taking the minutes and recording them in some logical fashion.

I then worked to open communication channels with the target population in the housing projects. Some time ago, I appeared before a tenants' board soliciting their support and reactions to the proposals. In the weeks preceding and following this meeting, I personally talked with 22 tenant leaders in an attempt to accurately interpret the proposals. I have a close relationship with many of these people from our other agency activities. Many of my staff also have close relationships with certain tenants. These relationships helped to insure support and to maintain support when one aspect or another of the program proposed was beyond their grasp.

I think people in CO have an inclination to take short cuts and to otherwise take advantage of their strong personal relationships. I believe that it is necessary to engage in explanation to the extent of my ability and my listener's ability to comprehend. If this is not done, we risk instituting a project without the basic agreement of the community. Failure to maintain an adequate dialogue with the community is also inexcusable because community people know existing needs better than we do. I carefully explained the total program goals to many of the local leaders. Of course, certain aspects of the program have special appeal; much of our conversation centered about the points that appealed most to their self-interest, such as the use of the indigenous poor as planners and paid participants. Others dealt with physical improvements in the community, and opportunities for children.

I have also been in contact with other relevant community leaders. The new director of the City Mental Health Planning Board called me. He wanted to discuss the proposals. I wanted his advice and his support. He made several suggestions that we were careful to follow. The psychiatric director of a mental-health center also called. He asked whether it would be possible to work out a cooperative arrangement for training between his center and the new program. I said yes, because such a plan would greatly benefit the project once implemented and because it would increase our support.

We revised the proposals frequently; they have bounced back and forth like a ping-pong ball between the various representatives. The results involved the best recommendations of all concerned. We currently seek funding from the State Department of Mental Health. We are requesting $365,000 per year to operate the program.

After my intensive participation in the initial stages of the project, I found myself slowly withdrawing. I have recently found myself more heavily engaged again. I had to get involved in order to maintain the momentum of the proposals. The specific points at which I enter depend entirely upon the circumstances of the situation. I pull in and out as my relationships with the community representatives demand. I intervene primarily at the upper levels. I frequently join with agency heads and also with the community representatives. Most of the community organization work in the housing project itself has been done by staff people.

Sponsorship of the project continues to be a problem. Our organization is not classified as a mental-health agency. There is some question about whether we should sponsor it. I have talked with officials of numerous mental-health agencies about sponsorship. The proposals, which call for hiring many nonprofessionals, are threatening to them. We do not seek the sponsorship because community acceptance and funding would be easier to obtain if a legitimate mental-health agency is playing the key role. If we went after the money ourselves, we would only be accused of Machiavellism by the other agencies. We need good relationships for future projects.

* * * *

P-19 DEBRIEFING FOR INFLUENTIALS

This is my third year as chairman of the State Council of NASW.[1] I have lived in this state all of my life and I know a fair share of politicians and community leaders. Whenever possible, the Council tries to take a public stand on relevant issues before the legislature. I can't say we're always successful in winning people over to our point of view. The biggest problem is ignorance. The point really struck home during the legislative hearing on the budget for the State Department of Social Welfare. It really was apparent that legislators and a number of rather distinguished community leaders from around the state who appeared as witnesses knew nothing of the welfare system, its objectives, operations, or its clientele. People were full of misconceptions.

I felt that something had to be done. I knew the welfare department was going to come out hurting this year. Money is tight this year and that, combined with some backlash, made it a foregone conclusion. I attended all the hearings, but despite the fact that I was on close personal terms with a lot of the community people there, I had very little influence.

At these hearings, I met Joe April, a reporter who won a Pulitzer Prize for a series of articles on welfare back in 1960. One day, over lunch, I said to him, "Why don't we expose these people to what welfare is about?" Joe agreed and we began to think about the project.

A new and radical approach to the public had to be tried. Public welfare itself had been too defensive about its program, yielding to suspicions that it had something to hide. While some county administrator dealt with the press and the other news media effectively, the vast majority had neither the skill not the staff help available to do the kind of job that obviously needed to be done.

---

[1] National Association of Social Workers.

Even those voluntary agency executives who worked intimately with public welfare in their own communities did not feel sufficiently related to public-welfare programs to publicly defend principles of welfare administration and services as sound. Their boards generally seemed to have limited knowledge of public welfare. Most voluntary agency executives showed no interest in the public-welfare programs. Public-welfare personnel were spending more time in convincing the converted than in informing the skeptics and critics.

ADC, as usual, came up looking the worst. Why wouldn't the mothers work? Didn't they have babies just to get more relief? What about the fathers? I had an idea that we should take the power-structure people in each community who were against public welfare and see if they could be converted to a positive attitude through exposure to Aid to Dependent Children (ADC) cases. Power-structure people have no conception about what poverty is like. What if we invited 10 to 12 community leaders to take part in an afternoon and evening program whereby they would go to the welfare office and see the work that the caseworker does? Then each of them could visit an ADC home with the worker in the afternoon. A meeting could be held at night with the local commissioner, which would be closed to the press. We didn't want any publicity, as I was afraid we would be accused of "gimmicking" or "brainwashing." The evening session would serve as a debriefing period.

It made sense for Joe April to be the director. He had many contacts with newspaper editors, welfare commissioners, and community leaders and a knowledge of the public-welfare field. We decided that no preselection of cases or workers would be permitted, and that we would limit the visits to ADC and Home Relief cases—the most controversial welfare programs. We also decided that no effort would be made to convert any visitor to any point of view on public welfare. The visitors should observe and draw their own conclusions. Families to be visited would not be advised in advance of the visit. We did not want anyone to think that we rigged the visit in any way.

I contacted the counsel to the State Department of Social Welfare to find out whether these visits violated the social-welfare law. As they didn't, we then wrestled with the problem of confidentiality. There would be no breach of confidentiality if the welfare recipient would be able to turn down a visitor if he wanted to. But I knew that if I did not get the right kinds of clearance, I would be accused of breach of confidentiality.

I then drew up a list of all the agency contacts necessary for our project clearance. I decided to keep certain people in the state informed as to our progress. This was a political consideration to protect them from embarrassment if our project backfired or if we got into trouble.

I talked about my plans for the project several months before I actually initiated any official action on them. I had lunch several times with the State Commissioner of Welfare, whom I've known for fifteen years, and felt him out on the project. Since he gave favorable signs, I spoke to members of the NASW State Council, as I needed their support to get the project going. They were very enthusiastic. They made no changes and decided to present the proposal to the full board.

Before this meeting, I discussed the proposal with several key people on the board. Everyone was very excited. They agreed to sponsor the project. I then went before the Executive Committee of the Public Welfare Association, the statewide organization of public-welfare commissioners, and they agreed on the plan. By this time, the State Commissioner, the Secretary of the Executive Committee, the Secretary of the State Senate and I had met and lobbied, before the Executive Committee of the Public Welfare Association met.

I also presented the plan to the State Department of Social Welfare and the State Board of Social Welfare and got approval from both of them. Finally, I discussed the plans with leaders of the State Association of Councils and Chests and got their approval. I went to each of these groups, as any one of them could have killed the project by not approving our plan.

I immediately prepared an application for funds and applied to the Jones Foundation. I spoke to Mr. Jones himself. He was a great business success and, one day, he just cast aside all of his golf and everything and became interested in public welfare. We had met at the welfare hearings. As it happens, I also have lunch regularly with the director of the Foundation and have had long-time connections with him. I also flew out to Chicago with Joe April to speak to the president of the American Public Welfare Association, who is an old friend of mine and is very close to the Foundation. I really worked to get those funds.

At a Foundation hearing, I was asked who was for and who was against my plan. Since I was ready with all the clearances I had been working on, we were funded. The endorsement from the American Public Welfare Association had come just prior to this. I kept the Foundation informed from then on as to what was happening in the project. I was told by the Foundation director that if the project failed at any point, I was to inform him, and return the unused moneys. Another factor that helped our funding was Joe April's request that the Foundation give him time and money to write a book, which they did. The Foundation later got credit for its sponsorship.

I decided that if the reaction in the first two or three communities turned out to be essentially negative, I would discontinue the program. I got leave from my own agency for about two months to engage in groundwork. Thereafter, I stayed with it one day per week until its completion.

Joe April did the actual field work for the project, while I offered general supervision, wrote progress reports based on my weekly communications with Joe, and conducted an attitude study. I got approval from my agency board to use part of our research staff to record the reactions of the power-structure people who participated in the program. I'm the executive of a welfare council.

The chairman of the State Board of Social Welfare and the State Commissioner of Social Welfare asked me to keep them informed on how the project was going. I also got the same request from several state legislators, and as I was good friends with them and we frequently had lunch together, I filled them in on the progress of the program. This was a sound political means to keep them interested. I forgot to mention that before I asked the Foundation to fund us, I contacted and got the endorsement of a high official in the U.S. Health, Education, and Welfare Department, as his approval carried great weight in favor of any project. I also had known him for many years.

Before we went ahead, Joe April and I agreed on the counties to be involved in the project. I called the local welfare commissioners to inform them that we were coming in and to prepare them. Several were very uneasy by the time we arrived, but everything went well. I decided to move ahead slowly and to test the project in one upstate county as a sort of trial run. Joe did the actual recruiting of community people. He is very able and knew the power structure. I wanted to get at the "Establishment-type" people, that is, newspaper publishers and editors, bankers, members of the League of Women Voters, ministers, and prominent businessmen. I suggested to Joe that he contact the County Board of Supervisors for leads to the power structure. He did this and felt his way around from there. As I had contacts in the Governor's office, I kept them informed on the project.

At about this time, some social-work agencies were calling and complaining that our project was violating caseworker-recipient confidentiality. I decided to ignore their complaints as I had already cleared this issue with everyone of influence.

Our first experience was an overwhelming success. The community people's reactions were very positive and the whole day's events had a great effect on their views on welfare, poverty, and the like. Newspaper editorials "spontaneously" appeared praising the project and citing the need for public welfare. Of course, Joe helped the spontaneity along.

Very favorable newspaper coverage of social welfare news began. One executive with a bakery company sent coffee and doughnuts for the caseworkers to their office, as he was most impressed with the job "his caseworker" was doing. One prominent businessman offered a caseworker a job because he was so impressed with his abilities.

I attended several of the evening "debriefing" sessions with Joe. They were very exciting. Most of the participants showed real empathy for both the welfare recipient and the welfare worker. At one meeting in Coopersville, a county commissioner felt that they were getting too much of the perspective of the caseworker. Joe picked up on this, and several of the community influentials decided to apply for welfare in a nearby county where they were not known. The empathy experience was terrific, but the staff of the welfare office in the other county were up in arms. We had to drop this approach or take a chance on losing the entire program.

Of course, I was overjoyed and passed this initial success on to all the people I mentioned before. I spoke to the chairman of the State Board of Social Welfare, urging him to institute the project as a function of the State Board. As I saw it, this was an appropriate request, as public education was one of their duties under the law. Besides, there is a need for constant stimulation and follow-up to reinforce these people's changed attitudes towards public welfare.

Joe is currently working on his book. I think it will be a great success. As for me, I learned a good deal about the defensiveness and intransigency of some welfare workers and county directors. I am working on the start of a second project now. It's based on something I read about in the papers when I was in San Francisco on vacation last summer. Apparently, San Francisco Community College invited 30 or 40 community college teachers from around the county for one month of empathy training in the ghetto. They lived in the ghetto with "teacher-guides" who tried to sensitize them to ghetto life. They were subjected to a constant bombardment of hostility aimed at breaking down their prejudices and resistances to real empathic understanding. I think we ought to try something like that for the public-welfare staff. Most of them can't possibly understand the real meaning of poverty no matter how well-intentioned they might be. Somehow, working in an agency, no matter what its purposes nor one's own motivations, desensitizes you to real feelings. You compartmentalize them. What you often call professional detachment is really nothing more than bureaucratic coldness.

I'm not sure exactly how to get this new project off the ground. A lot of it has to do with timing. I can't emphasize enough how important timing is. You might have all the good intentions and well laid out plans in the world, and you might have a great bunch of contacts around the state, the way I do; but without the right timing, you won't get any place. We need some kind of issue that either gets a lot of public play in the press or somehow shakes up the welfare department internally. When the right issue comes up, I'll be ready for it.

*   *   *   *

P-20   STATE PLANNING FOR COMPREHENSIVE MENTAL HEALTH

I am a social planner. I am a generalist, and certainly no expert in mental health. That's my great advantage. Not being trained in one of the mental-health disciplines, nor being an employee of a mental-health agency, I can look at mental-health problems from a more objective perspective. Most of us in Social Research Associates are like that. We are specialists in certain skills, like social planning, government administration, statistical research, and so on, but generalists in terms of a subject area like mental health, poverty, or delinquency. I guess you might call us a "think tank." We are a nonprofit organization, and get most of our funds by contracting our services. We bring together a lot of disciplines and a lot of skills when we look at a problem.

The particular assignment I am on now involves a three-year contract with the state to redesign the relationships between all state-supported mental health programs. The impetus for the new design came from federal legislation calling for comprehensive mental health care. The state stood to lose money if the legislature couldn't design an acceptable integrated and comprehensive program.

I think state planning of this sort is an inevitability. First of all, the multiplicity of federal programs alone makes it essential. Someone has to integrate them. Secondly, the federal government itself is encouraging planning by providing states with large planning grants. The relationships between federal, state, county, and local governments have become so complex that without some form of planning, it becomes impossible to monitor programs. Many of them compete with and contradict each other. And it becomes too easy to pass the buck and to say the other guy should be doing something when large segments of the public are being ill-served. The way we look at it in the Association, the biggest challenge is to find ways in which planning can assure greater coordination between voluntary agencies and the increasingly complex governmental programs.

When the state contracted with our Association, a number of leading politicians from the Governor's office made it quite clear that they wanted us to define a comprehensive and implementable state program with the full gamut of services required to properly cover the mental-health needs in communities throughout the state. The Governor's staff is made up of sharp young men who tend to look at their work with professional detachment. They selected us to develop the plan because they wanted a professional job done. It was our task to develop legislative proposals that would redesign the state's approach to mental health. Actually, I took it to mean more than that. There is no straight line in planning.

There would have been no sense in our developing some rational design only to have it fail to meet federal guidelines, or to be otherwise unworkable because of political considerations at the state level. We are not in the business of planning utopias—we are trying to effectuate some changes that will benefit our clients.

I pointed out to the Governor's men that talking about a comprehensive plan is really talking in incomprehensive terms. "Comprehensive" is really a misnomer, in view of the practical impossibility of covering everything, which the term implies. What were we to include in our assignment, I asked the Governor's people. Should we focus on developing comprehensive mental-health centers at the county level? Should we attempt to redesign the staffing of mental hospitals and institutions? Should we focus on relationships between hospitals and agencies in the community?

Our first three months were used just to shake down such questions and to identfiy some more specific goals that could be subsumed under our general objectives of redesigning the state's mental-health program.

I put together a staff team of five others, each with relevant knowledge and skill. The first thing we did was look toward federal-government resources and guidelines for hints. Then we looked at innovative programs we were aware of in other states. We then met with the heads of various state agencies to ascertain their interest and intentions, and to identify their resistance to change. We also set up the outline for a statewide study of mental-health needs. We met with a number of experts from agencies, from universities, and from private practice. We also did a great deal of reading in the literature on mental health.

My staff and I met on a weekly basis in order to digest and share this information. We were slowly beginning to formulate impressions of what was possible and what was not, considering the time, budgetary, and staff limitations imposed on our operation. We also tried to identify those projects that would under no circumstances be feasible in this state because of political considerations and the entrenched resistance of mental-health practitioners in some rather high places.

I guess you could say that we are a combination of pragmatists and idealists in the ways in which we select areas on which to focus and develop our program recommendations. In all of our contacts, we continually asked what the pressing needs were of the agencies and practitioners, and of general public. We tried to convey our concerns and our interests in what people were doing. We did not want to antagonize people early in the game. If our recommendations were going to pass through the legislature, they would have to be supported by the mental-health practitioners in the state. In our questioning and interviewing, we sought to find working consensus of needed changes. Where no consensus existed about the direction our planning should follow, we sought to develop it.

At the end of three months we sat down with the Governor and his aides to discuss our progress and to lay out the general guidelines for our subsequent efforts. I guess you could say that we used our first three months to "set up a plan for planning."

This is the start of the process. It's not a question of designing the best plan for comprehensive mental health care, but of designing the best *possible* plan. We see our function as much more than information gathering and program designing. What makes us unique among consulting firms is that we take an interest in public, professional, and organizational concerns. We try to stimulate them, to open up new channels of communication, and to stimulate a cooperative spirit. Let me clarify what I mean by "cooperation." I visualize the various agencies potentially responsible for mental-health programming as providing the social supports needed by the mentally ill and the potentially mentally ill. Only by having truly cooperative efforts at the local level can the whole person be served. If we were to develop a program at the state level that resulted in conflicts or competition at the local level, we would only be doing a disservice to those people who we were supposed to be helping through the development of our plan.

The project is currently in its second year. Like anything else, when you first begin looking at an issue, you see its surface dimensions. We have since uncovered a whole range of new interests. Unfortunately, our contract with the state has not called for going into detail on some of these interests. Accordingly, we have applied to two different funding sources for money in order to undertake some side efforts in research. Our first application to OEO has been turned down. We have submitted a second application now to NIMH. In applying to different funding sources, we write up the problem and research project in terms of the orientation and interest of the potentially sponsoring agency. For example, whereas the proposal to OEO emphasized the ways that might be found to maximize the potential for employment and independent living of former mental patients, the proposal to NIMH focused on the relationships between the ex-mental patient and the network of community agencies. If we were to submit a proposal to the Department of Labor, we would focus on jobs again.

Don't get the impression that planning is a smooth operation. At the present time we are confronted with a whole host of difficulties involving conflicts between the official agencies concerned with mental health in this state. Each has its own parochial interests. Few can even take an interdepartmental perspective, much less a perspective of state needs. We are constantly cognizant that the recommendations of our planning task force might alienate one or more of the major departments in the state. Even in the framing of the questions that we ask, we have to be constantly aware of political implications.

In a way, our project may also be involved in "biting the hand that feeds it." The Governor's office originally contracted with us because of a concern that the state might lose money from federal sources if a comprehensive plan were not developed. It now looks as if even our most modest plans might actually cost the state a good deal of money. We will just have to handle each issue as it arises. One of the hardest things about this job is that it is like operating in a fishbowl. We will be in the public eye constantly until our job is completed. My guess is that our working relationships with some of the older state departments and local agencies may become increasingly problematic as we get closer to our recommendations.

In order to nullify the potential sources of resistance, we have attempted to develop close personal relationships in some of the agencies that might feel alienated by our final report. Of course it would be easier just to satisfy the agencies and give them each a little bit of what they wanted. But this course would be contrary to our professional goals as a staff and would destroy the integrity of our firm.

Still, we do swap favors. For example, the director of one of the mental hospitals in this state has opened up several doors for me and has just agreed not to block one of our proposals even though it will take certain responsibilities out of the mental hospitals and place them in countywide community mental-health agencies. In return, I reciprocated by making it possible for him to communicate with other persons in the state without his having to initiate those contacts. Sometimes you're in a much better bartering position if someone else contacts you even though they were aware that you wanted the contact. This same hospital director depends on me to interpret the attitudes of the other persons towards him. Insofar as he perceives me as a neutral planner with a social-science background, he feels free to interpret the structure of his hospital and the problems he is facing in its administration. So while he's using me as a consultant, I am learning a good deal about the operating difficulties of mental hospitals. He also protects me from a very powerful state senator with whom he has good relationships, but who does not look on any efforts initiated by the government's office with any favor. I hope that when we are ready to make our recommendations, the hospital director will be able to get the state senator to accept them. At the same time, I must admit that we have decided not to expose some of the malpractice that we have uncovered in mental hospitals. Exposing it would open up a hornet's nest and put the focus on current practices instead of on future plans.

If I were to sum it all up, I would say that I look at my responsibility as one of maximizing the public responsibility for the mentally ill. I don't think of myself as a crusader, although from time to time I would welcome the emergence of a crusade here or there. Seeing as much hypocrisy, dishonesty, and malpractice as I do, I am often tempted to make crusader-type public releases, myself. But of course I don't. It would destroy our effectiveness.

*   *   *   *

P-21 PAVING THE WAY FOR MEDICARE

The politicians won the battle on Medicare. We don't set policy in the bureaucracy, but we have a lot to do with making sure that policy can be operationalized. Congress may make the laws, but staff men in federal offices often write the laws and then interpret them. The way we public-health officials cooperated with other federal agencies is a good example.

In March of 1965 everybody knew that the Health Insurance Program would be enacted by Congress. Interbranch departments were set up before the law was passed. In addition, staff working groups were set up. My chief appointed me to chair one. My committee dealt with conditions of hospitals and nursing homes. It included representatives from social security, welfare, and the public health service. The goal of the committee was preset; it was to develop one draft of the conditions of participation for hospitals and another draft for extended-care facilities. The goal didn't change. As chairman, I contacted other divisions for their advice, such as the Hospital and Medical Facilities Division, the Division of Hospitals, the Nursing Division, and the NIMH. I delegated responsibilities to the individual members. The committee met weekly for about 6 months.

My ongoing responsibilities were to ascertain that the committee had the information it needed; to see that necessary materials were duplicated and forwarded to each of the members before the meetings; to set up the agenda for each meeting; and to coordinate the meetings and schedule the next one. I also had to make sure that the writing got done. The members of my staff were doing the actual writing. I did a lot of editing of the final drafts.

The entire committee worked well together. Among the difficulties I encountered was the pressure of time. There was less than one year to get the job done. I had to check if anything the committee did would have any effects on current or future legislation. We needed to develop standards for independent labs and to work on these rapidly. This was especially difficult, since this field had no standardized procedures. I handled this through outside consultation. I called in lab experts from the Public Health Service's Communicable Disease Center in Atlanta. I formed an ad hoc committee with the chief of that branch and we worked on it together.

There are always problems with agencies that will not qualify under the law to serve patients. The law required, for example, that a registered nurse be on duty round the clock in an extended care facility. Many nursing homes employed only practical nurses. I spoke with my chief about this and we compromised by requiring that the practical nurse, who is substituted for the registered nurse, be licensed by an approved school. There have been questions arising over this requirement, but I have continued to maintain it. All kinds of pressures are put on us daily.

I met with various outside consultants and representatives—nurses and physicians—for their advice. These meetings were initiated by the Welfare Administration and were attended by representatives of Social Security and Welfare. After these meetings I would make changes in the draft to meet their requirements. The next level of review was with the Health Insurance Benefits Advisory Council, which consists of (expert) members outside the government who advise on policy. The draft would have to conform to their requirements, too.

After the council reviewed it, it went through a course of clearance via the departments involved, such as the Public Health Service, the Bureau of Health Insurance, the Commissioner of Social Security, and finally the Undersecretary and Secretary of the Department of Health and Welfare. If at any point along this line a change was suggested, they would contact me and a person at Social Security. If the change was minor there would be an informal exchange between Social Security and my office. If the change meant an alteration in policy, then I would set up a more formal meeting with those concerned.

The law went into effect on July 1, 1966. If questions of policy still arise, I have staff members in each of nine regional offices who deal with them. My staff members work along with Social Security people and in the state agencies as interpreters of policy and procedure. Depending on the problem, Social Security or one of my regional officers will make a draft of the issue. A copy will be sent to me and another to Social Security. A representative of Social Security and I will then get together to make recommendations to our chiefs.

Since there are few facilities available and a great demand for them, there is pressure to approve as many facilities as possible. However, I abide by the law and have learned to say no. I say it at least once daily.

There are other problems. How firmly are the standards to be applied? Which ones are flexible? What steps are to be taken in case of deficiencies? I review all related materials and make the decisions. Being an administrator of a program I have helped plan gives me an edge, but I am also very much aware of the contingencies.

One of the positive side effects of working with the Social Security people was that it enabled the Public Health Service staff and the Social Security staff to understand each other's philosophies. The competencies and principal motivations of the staff of both agencies are different. The Social Security Administration, for example, has always had a deep conviction of the rights of beneficiaries. They usually bend over backward to see that beneficiaries get what they should. The concern of my department is with quality of care. This can lead to conflict unless there's modification on both sides. Social Security could have said they wanted every facility to be certified—I could have said "no." But we compromised. Where there's need for care, my office will agree to give short-term certification. My office will then take precautions to ensure that the agency continues to improve the quality of its services and facilities. If we had not engaged in the planning together, I doubt that we could have worked so amicably with Social Security.

*   *   *   *

P-22 SELECTING A MODEL CITIES BOARD
or How not to "Stack the Deck"

The Mayor Wants a Program

"Look, Phil," the mayor said to me, "I want these 14 people on the Model Cities Board." He handed me a list. It looked pretty well balanced—maybe a little bit heavy on establishment types, but with enough representatives of the black community and enough critics of the Establishment to balance it off. "What do you want me to do with this list?" I asked. "I want you to talk to each of these people and find out what it would take to get them to serve on the board without creating all kinds of havoc and obstruction. I want a Model Cities grant."

"Very simple," I said to myself. The mayor wants a Model Cities program. He knows he can't get it without community involvement. At the same time he doesn't want to turn the program over to the neighborhood. He wants to take some credit for the program himself and keep control. Besides, he wouldn't get money from Washington if he turned over control to a group of militants anyway.

I know that for a fact. I was in Washington a couple of months ago and spoke to some officials pretty high up in the Model Cities hierarchy. They don't want another community-action program with a lot of disruption at the local level. The question was, could I bring together the people on the mayor's list so that they would collaborate on the writing of a Model Cities proposal? Looking over the list, I knew it wasn't going to be done without some conflict. There's a lot of jockeying around for power and influence in this town. I know the mayor wouldn't want this board to set the stage for a series of power plays. But the way he picked his fourteen people, it looked like trouble. You can't put a guy like Griffith Wilkinson on the same committee with Carl Colbert without expecting some kind of fireworks.

As the mayor's staff man on social welfare, I knew a lot of these people pretty well. I took the list back to my office and looked it over. I made a mental note about each one on it.

1. *Griffith Wilkinson* is a very controversial, flamboyant *black doctor* who has been a consistent critic of the Community Action Program. Although he was on the CAP board, I knew that last week he had flown to Washington with Willis Thomas to support Thomas's efforts to get a job-training program funded by OEO outside the community-action agency.

2. *Carl Colbert* is the *Director of the Poverty Program.* Colbert had worked for the Governor's Council on Retardation and had been in the mental health field before he took over the poverty program. His major concern is service delivery, and I know that in the past he has been critical of the federal government's emphasis on using poverty programs for civil-rights objectives. I have often heard him say that it is more important to get blacks jobs than to put them on his boards.

3. *Willis Thomas* is minister of the all-black Presbyterian church. I know that Thomas and some of his church people have been pressing for job-training programs for some time. Thomas had asked me for some help some months back in drawing up the outlines of a proposal. He

later submitted it to Colbert, who apparently told him it needed a lot of rewriting. That's when Thomas got mad and got Wilkinson to accompany him to Washington.

4. *Roosevelt Carleson* is an *economics instructor at the community college*. He is black and very close to a number of the black-power militant leaders in the ghetto.

5. *Robert Boemus* is a well established *black businessman* who has served on the Chamber of Commerce and on the City Council. He has made his pile, and lately has become interested in helping establish housing and purchasing co-operatives within the ghetto. Boemus and Carleson have an interesting relationship. They agree with each other on the need for co-ops, but disagree on almost everything else.

6. *Rafe Rocha* represents the *AFL-CIO*. I was glad to see him on the list. He could play a crucial role. He is white, but he gets along well with everybody. I made a mental note to use him as a mediator in case there was danger of an open fight once the board was constituted.

7. *Ray Woody* was also a member of the union, although his selection by the mayor was obviously in reference to his leadership of the Committee for Action Now. CAN was pressing for more security and for rapid promotions for black union members.

8. *Marshall Spaniard* is *director of the local office of the State Employment Service*. I haven't talked to him lately, but I knew that he had had some interesting notions on restructuring and redirecting the program of the employment service.

9. *Jim Colliss* is *director of the City Planning Commission* and has a national reputation among planners and architects.

10. *Leon Gottkind* is the *Assistant Superintendent of Schools for Program Development*. Gottkind has been a strong supporter of community control.

11. *Dorothy Sola* is a *community psychiatrist*. As director of the community mental-health center, she has been instrumental in pressing voluntary and state agencies to increase their services to the ghetto.

12. *Dr. Rebecca Kantrowitz* is kind of an innocuous old-timer. As *County Public Health Officer,* she has made few enemies and managed to keep out of the public eye. She knows the community well and has a lot of influence in the medical community.

13. *Stephanie Fowler* is *director of a neighborhood center* funded by the poverty program. I knew she was close to Carl Colbert, but she has a lot of support in the black community. I don't think Wilkinson or Thomas, for example, would openly take her on.

14. *Hector O'Rourk* is *Director of the County Welfare Department,* a conservative, defensive, punitive sonofabitch if I ever saw one.

I figured that my best strategy was to talk to each of these people individually. I decided not to say anything about the mayor's wanting them to serve on the Model Cities board. I would leave that up to him. But I would find out what they thought about Model Cities and try and figure what serving on the board might have in it for each of them.

Interview With Carl Colbert

I decided to talk to Colbert first. I knew Carl well and I knew we couldn't design a Model Cities program without his help. I explained to him that the mayor was interested in applying for a Model Cities grant and asked him what he thought of the idea. Colbert was enthusiastic. One of his first efforts in the community program had been to establish a health component. He had gotten plenty of support from Dr. Rebecca Kantrowitz of the *county* public health department, but ran into some other difficulties. The *city* health department director was a pretty difficult guy, a "prima donna," Colbert explained. He detailed the difficulties he had had in trying to get the city to set up a neighborhood program, and then the additional difficulties he had had in getting the health-department staff to work out of the neighborhood centers. It would have been easier, he told me, if Griffith Wilkinson had been on his side. Since Wilkinson was a member of the community-action board and a leading physician, Colbert had expected him to support his efforts. But Wilkinson was interested only in himself.

Wilkinson didn't give a damn about local conditions, Colbert continued. All he wanted was to use local issues to make a national name for himself as a black leader. If he could do it better by criticizing the Community Action Program, then that's the way he would go. Colbert thought he was a rank opportunist. "That's why he went to Washington with Willis Thomas last week," he explained. "As a member of my board you would have expected him to talk to me first. Instead he takes off to Washington without saying anything to me and tells them up there that we are not tuned in to community needs. He comes off as a real hero, and we're the bad guys." I made a mental note that having Colbert and Wilkinson on the same board might not be an easy thing to handle. Still, when I pressed Colbert, I found a willingness on his part to work with Wilkinson.

"A Model Cities Program would be good," he said. "The Community Action Program has stirred up too much controversy. If we are going to get anything done about health and jobs in this community, maybe we ought to try to do it under a new agency. You can count on our cooperation."

I tried to get his feelings about other community leaders. Carl was very down on the United Fund. He felt that the Fund and the Welfare Council might block the development of a Model Cities Program. I knew what he was alluding to. I know people at the Fund quite well. They like to think they can control all social-welfare activities in the city. Their executive director slowed down the antipoverty program by dragging his feet and by stalling when the City was applying for OEO funds five years ago. The poverty program, of course, has been a threat to the Fund. Private agencies have applied to OEO for funds, making them somewhat more independent of the Fund. At this stage, with OEO phasing out, I could see where the United Fund people would be fearful of a Model Cities Program. It dawned on me why the mayor hadn't included any of them on his list. He was a pretty astute guy, after all.

Interview With Dr. Rebecca Kantrowitz, County Public Health Department

Dr. Kantrowitz is really a remarkable character. She has been involved in the planning stages of almost every new health program developed in the area. She was instrumental in getting Colbert to focus on health programs when the poverty program first started up here. I found her a little bit more outspoken than I anticipated. She told me she had been thinking about Model Cities ever since the legislation had been described in the press, but she would not want a Model Cities program to be as fouled up as the poverty program. "The poverty-program people know less about community organization than anyone in the field," she told me. "Look who they employ." She said Colbert was a nice man with some good experience in mental health, but with no training in community organization. He had a few gifted people on his staff, but the community-action technicians and some of the health technicians were absolutely hopeless. "I haven't the foggiest notion who trained them." The trouble with the poverty people, she continued, is that they think the private agencies have never done anything. The private-agency people resent them as "Johnny-come-latelys," and they show it. Of course it causes a reaction, and then you develop competition and retaliation. "The same goes for the more militant leaders in the black community."

"The biggest problem," she told me, "is getting health services to the community. It's got to be made readily accessible and easy to get to for everybody. The second problem is to get preventative health-care programs to the community. This means education. The best place to start is in the school system. But the people in the community don't trust the schools. If the people had some control over their schools, you could bet they would have an investment in a health program. That's why I like that fellow Leon Gottkind over at the board of education. He wants to decentralize."

I questioned Dr. Kantrowitz some more about the support of black physicians, dentists, and nurses in the area. "The problem is Griffith Wilkinson," she said. "Wilkinson wants to make all the decisions. When they put Negroes on the antipoverty board, he said they weren't representative. When he was put on the antipoverty board, he sabotaged it at every turn by going off to Washington whenever he wanted something for personal gain. Still, you can't get a Model Cities program or a new health program in this city without Wilkinson. I've got a notion that you can't get one *with* Wilkinson either."

Interview With Hector O'Rourk, County Director of Public Welfare

I saw O'Rourk the same day. His office was in the same building as Kantrowitz's. In O'Rourk's office was Clarence Ropa, chief social worker; Paul Patrick, staff development supervisor; and Sylvia Tivoli, supervisor of ADC. It was kink of weird. Apparently O'Rourk and the other three had met for two or three hours the previous afternoon to prepare for their meeting with me. But during the two hours that I was there, almost no one did any talking besides O'Rourk. It was an impossible two hours, like almost any two hours with O'Rourk are apt to be. Under no circumstances could I get him to venture an opinion on any other agency or any other actor on my list. He absolutely avoided any discussion of what our future Model Cities program might look like.

What he did say is that "what are we much concerned about are black militants and Alinsky organizers. They encourage anarchy and revolutionary processes and extremes. This 'welfare rights' just doesn't help the mothers and the kids who are left holding the bag. And I don't go for this talk about separating welfare from services either. It's not easy for poor people to take advantage of the resources available to them, but no amount of financing or putting money in the hands of poor people will work without a social-casework approach."

I tried to get O'Rourk to talk about public health needs, but he kept on steering the conversation back to his pet project—birth control and family planning. He described a time when he had wanted to get Rebecca Kantrowitz to develop a birth control clinic and she hedged. He went to the director of the city health department, and quietly instituted a clinic within a two-week period. "I could have gone to all the power people in the community like the community organizers would do," he said "but that would have killed the project. I just went and did it." He went on to describe how he had been influential in getting sterilization legislation through the state legislature three years earlier.

When I pressed him about Model Cities, he said that if you're going to have that kind of program, it's "got to be planned from the top down. You give poor people the power to make decisions, and all you are going to do is antagonize the real-estate and business interests. These people will then throw roadblocks in front of the program and nothing will get done."

Interview With Marshall Spaniard, State Employment Service

Spaniard got right to the point. You could pour millions in welfare, medical services, and education into the ghetto, but it would make not a single bit of difference if you couldn't provide jobs for the residents. Nevertheless, job-training programs, he thought, were on the wrong track. He felt that a number of the efforts by poverty people or by well-intentioned citizens, like Willis Thomas and members of his congregation, were all on the wrong track. "Job training is no good if there are no jobs. What we need is a massive statewide program of matching jobs to skills. If they don't match, then you have a choice of doing one of two things: training people to get the necessary skills, or creating new jobs. We have been doing the first. We ought to be doing the latter."

As far as Spaniard was concerned, unless jobs were offered to residents, there would be "violence in the neighborhoods." "People have skills, regardless of whether they have had formal training or accreditation. The trouble is that we don't find out from a guy whether he can cut hair (almost every married man with kids who walks in here has cut his son's hair at one time or another) and then try to find him a job using that skill. Instead, we look at the jobs first, then try to find a way of processing a guy to meet the employer's needs. It's all ass-backwards."

Spaniard told me he had come a long way in his thinking. Previously, he had never cared to become engaged in political action. But his every attempt to make major changes in the department have been met with frustration. "If you can't change it from the top down," he said "maybe you can change it from the bottom up." He feels that the only way blacks are going to get jobs is if they demand them, if they organize and put pressure on the power structure. His immediate strategy is to open up a number of unemployment centers through the ghetto. He would then embark on a campaign to register the unemployed. If you can get enough of them registered and talking to each other, they are going to start pressing for changes. He felt that without that kind of pressure, he was totally ineffectual in opening up new jobs in business and industry. He needed the backup of the black masses, but he couldn't be caught organizing them himself.

Like some of the other people I had spoken to, Spaniard was really angry at Wilkinson. He saw Wilkinson as an opportunist, and sent a letter to Washington as soon as he heard of the Wilkinson-Thomas trip. His letter indicated that no one represented all the blacks in town and that any appropriations should be held up until there was a thorough investigation. Spaniard is a pretty straight guy, and I appreciated his sharing this confidence with me. Somehow I have managed to keep good personal relationships open with most of the key people in the welfare system in town. I am not for myself, and I'm not seen exclusively as the mayor's man. So people do talk to me.

Interview With Dr. Griffith Wilkinson

So many of the people with whom I was talking were pointing their fingers at Wilkinson, that I felt I ought to see him next. I think I agreed with everyone. Wilkinson is a rank opportunist playing to a national audience. By making enough noise at the local scene and claiming to speak for the blacks and the poor, he is looking for a federal appointment of some sort. Wilkinson has a silver plated Cadillac, air-conditioned with electric windows. It's difficult to pin this guy down. He complaints a lot about what everybody else isn't doing. But it is very hard to get him to commit himself to a plan of action or a series of tactics. He was interested in Model Cities but couldn't make any real suggestions about how the Mayor ought to proceed if we were going to apply for funds. "It better not be the same as the poverty program," he said. "The trouble is that the poverty people have devised a program whereby to delay and control black aspirations. They only do what is minimum. They pit the poor whites and the blacks against each other. The ghetto has no faith in the white power structure. The mayor can call himself a good guy, but the police pumped 17 bullets into my house as a result of my activity in voter registration drives. I have reported this to the police and to the mayor, but never heard a word from either of them."

Wilkinson went on to complain that most of the poverty funds have been seized by the private voluntary agencies for support of their programs and if a Model Cities program were going to do the same thing he would oppose it. As far as he was concerned, he told me, the only way civil-rights leaders could get anywhere was to "raise hell." And if the Model Cities program weren't in the hands of black leadership, that's exactly what he would do. Listening to him talk, you would be under the impression that nobody in town was concerned about education, jobs, or medical care for the ghetto. And yet I had just spoken to four people who were very much concerned. I wondered if he were trying to set me up with a hard line that he would later use for negotiating purposes.

I get the feeling every time I talk to this guy that he speaks purely in *symbolic* terms. He may be talking about jobs, but he's really talking about equal rights and a redefinition of the position of the black man. On the other hand, the guy is very ambitious and it's just awfully difficult to be able to anticipate his next move. I don't know how widespread his support is in the ghetto, but I do know he has a number of influential friends in the state capitol and in Congress.

Other Interviews

I have only met with five of the key people on the mayor's list so far —there are nine to go. Somethings are becoming quite clear. The people on the list were not going to all work amicably together, not without a good deal of arm twisting and behind-the-scenes pressuring. The two major issues that I have uncovered so far are jobs and health care. It is possible that we might be able to get these people to agree at least on some general objectives, if not on a strategy, to achieve any set of goals.

I could see getting Wilkinson and Colbert in the same room together. They might not agree. They might even hate each other. On the other hand, they could understand each other and have some empathy for each other's positions. That's the first step if you are going to negotiate a solution to a problem or to an impasse. I didn't know what the hell I would do with a character like O'Rourk. Probably the best thing to do would be to keep him on the board but to nullify him, neutralize him, or block him off in a corner somehow. I would have to think through the political pressures we could apply to him. Rebecca Kantrowitz was all right. She was prejudiced as hell, but based on previous experiences she would probably handle herself pretty well on a planning board. Spaniard, I made a mental note, was just a good man to have around.

At this point I began thinking through my assignment again. It would sure as hell be easier to drop some of the people from the mayor's list. If it was to be as representative as he made it, nothing would get done. Still, we couldn't keep community people out. Without guys like Wilkinson and Thomas, for example, we would have to contend with neighborhood people. The poverty program didn't have these kinds of troubles when it started, but four years of a community-action program made the neighborhood people pretty sore. We needed Wilkinson to keep them cool. But would it be to his advantage to do so?

Would it be to the mayor's advantage to try to coopt Wilkinson, or would the guy just use his new post to his political advantage?

Too many agendas, I thought to myself. Even if we got some consensus at the local level, by the time we got around to writing up proposals to meet the guidelines of every federal agency that HUD is trying to coordinate, we would wind up with a program that would be unrecognizable to our community people anyway. I would hate to be the planner in that kind of a squeeze.

Wonder if the mayor knows what he is letting himself in for?

I called the other people on my list and made appointments.

13

The Planner
as a Technician

CASES AND ILLUSTRATIVE MATERIALS

During the last 20 years, a number of new planning tools have been developed by experts in management science, in military planning, and in social economics. Social planners are indebted to all of these. Recently developed military planning tools such as program budgeting and the use of strategic games, for example, have already been transformed into social-planning tools. However, while most planners are aware of the utility of these tools, we have not encountered many competent planners who are skilled in their use. Even those experts in the use of planning tools are very cautious about claims for their usefulness. Unlike military planning, which is simplified by relatively identifiable and clear objectives, the goals of social planning are much more diffuse and difficult to operationalize. Many of these tools may be useful in dealing with logistical problems, but are ineffective in helping to make political and strategic policy decisions.

Further, to continue the comparison, the centralization of authority within the military makes it relatively easy to deploy large forces or to direct action. Social planners have little of the clearly defined and institutionalized authority of military planners and strategists. Nevertheless, social planners continue to borrow from the military. Advocate planners, for example, have given increasing attention to the coordination of large masses of people and to the imperatives of situational factors.

They act to bring people into situations where it becomes difficult to avoid certain actions. At this juncture many of their activities may resemble those of the organizer.

Military emphasis on logistics, and the careful calculations of time, events, and actions have also affected social planning. Design tools such as PERT are good examples.

Recently, one of the authors was challenged by a student who felt that reliance on tools developed for and by the military, denied social planning of any social legitimacy. This is, in our opinion, a specious argument. The caveman's club may have been invented for aggressive and violent purposes, but no one would deny that the modern hammer can be a useful tool for constructive purposes. Of course, it can also destroy. It is not where a tool originated that is important, but how it is used and to what purpose. The same may be said of those tools borrowed or adopted from the economists.

Economic planning has early origins. The Bible speaks of Joseph in Egypt and the preparation for seven lean years after seven years of plenty. Marxian theories have had a major impact on socialist countries that attempted to achieve regulation of economic processes by consciously selecting social policies and using regulatory means. More recently, Keynesian economics opened up a new mode of planning, heretofore impossible. Based on the creation and availability of new measurement and forecasting tools—notably national income statistics—economic planners have been able to anticipate trends and to predict the impact of various alternative economic policies. A strong case is being made for the development of similar tools in social planning and for the development of a comprehensive system of social accounts.

A planner discusses the need for such social indicators as the basis for "An Information System for State Planning." He documents the handicap most planners function under, due to an "intelligence gap" based on one-sided, missing, distorted, misinterpreted, or unusable information. In the absence of an adequate information system, clearly visible and easily accessible, any planner, policy maker, or demagogue can make almost any assertion, basing it on partial or fragmentary information. A similar point is made by a systems analyst who talks of "Designing an Information System" for an agency. The computerization of management-science techniques are discussed in some detail. The planner gives attention to the purposes of an information system and to the interpersonal and political considerations that must accompany the planning process.

The economist who describes his method of "Costing Out a Tuberculosis Screening Program," gives equal attention to technical details, but suggests that the decisions made at the end of a cost-benefits analysis, may still be based on primarily political considerations. If this is so, how might the planner have ensured support for his conclusions? This vignette demonstrates the disadvantages of the planner's playing the single role of a technical expert. What other roles might he have played?

The use of a rather simple tool like PERT, suggests how the combination of analytic and interactional elements must be logistically combined to assure consideration of each detail at every step in the planning process.

Client analysis, a tool borrowed from market and consumer analysis, is described in the next vignette. In the absence of a market mechanism and a freedom of choice of social services, analytic tools such as this one are useful in predicting service need and service utilization. Too little work has been done in this area. The reader may wish to speculate on how client analysis might be used to ensure responsiveness to consumer preferences.

In a Public-health program aimed at American Indians, we examine how the development of a survey instrument may be useful in gathering data upon which to base legislative proposals. Using his position in Washington, the health planner demonstrates the usefulness of new medical approaches to physicians at the local level. Why is he not fully successful?

Finally, a planner describes the utility of PPBS as a planning tool and its limitations in social planning. Although some planners view it as a complete planning system, we regard program planning and budgeting systems as useful in developing programs in light of a predetermined policy and the testing out of the probability of that policy's success. We do not feel that PPBS is an adequate tool by which to fully determine policy.

There are, of course, a great variety of other planning tools—input-output analysis, the use of impact studies, and the like—that we have not documented in this volume. Many of these tools are still in very primitive stages of design. Their current utility, however, suggests greater use in the future.

*   *   *   *

P-23 AN INFORMATION SYSTEM FOR STATE PLANNING

The Governor is talking about setting up regional councils like those in Oregon, Minnesota, Wisconsin, Vermont, and Georgia. We have been pushing him in this direction, but didn't want to move until the value of our own state planning commission was established. Regional councils can't survive without state support. With our own past successes, however, and with the new federalism as national policy, we are expecting to have new monies made available. In July 1969, for instance, Arkansas appropriated $30,000 to each of its planning districts. This year, our legislature also passed enabling legislation for the establishment of 15 regional COG's (Councils of Government) as devices for solving area-wide problems.

As the state planning agency, we view it as our job to give the COG's technical assistance and policy direction. We have just applied for a block grant from the Department of Housing and Urban Development for state and regional planning assistance. This would bring us up to par with states like Minnesota and Colorado. Our grant calls for setting up a number of statewide task forces with regional COG counterparts. The task forces are in transportation, health, mental health (tied in with our recent comprehensive mental-health legislation), welfare, housing, education, corrections, and law enforcement.

One of our first aims is to give social problems more visibility. Our second objective is to make it possible to evaluate the effects of public programs. Subsequently, of course, we will become involved in the coordination of programs and in the planning for new legislation and new statewide programs.

Actually, we've already been involved in all three functions. Last year we began, for the first time, trying to rationalize some of our law-enforcement procedures. With our help, the state police have provided a good deal of training and staff-development help to local and county police departments. Much of the highway, education, mental-health, and health planning has for some time been conducted at the state level. Our emergence on the scene three years ago made it possible, for the first time, to begin coordinating efforts in all of these areas of public service. The Governor is now talking about elevating the planning commission to cabinet status.

My immediate concern is with the development of a statewide information system. Most of our statistics are useless. The national census comes only once every ten years. We could use one every two years. Large-scale migrations and the growth of new industries and births of new towns, make the census less than helpful after three years, and obsolete after five. The biggest problem, of course, is not how *often* you gather the information, but *what* information you gather and its comparability.

Police records show, for example, that there has been an increase in theft in almost every community in the state. But they don't show that people are wealthier and have more items to steal, and that they are more apt to insure their belongings. When something you have insured is stolen, you're going to report it. You might not if you didn't have the insurance. As it also happens, our population has grown considerably during the last five years. I can't prove it, because we have no statistics that account for these variables, but I would be willing to bet that our increases in theft are directly related to the increase in the population and to the increased sale of theft insurance.

Recently, our morning paper in the state capital carried a series on auto thefts. True, they've gone up astronomically. But what does it all mean? In the 1940s and early 1950s, auto thefts were well organized. Stolen cars were repainted, taken across the state lines, and resold. Today most auto thefts are by kids for joy rides. Let's face it: there are a lot more kids, there are a lot more kids in the city, and there are a lot more cars to be stolen.

Most of our available statistics show increases of one sort or another. They show an increase in the number of people who have finished secondary school, the number of people who have gone on to junior college, and the number who finished four years or more of higher education. But we have twice as many people of college age today than we had in 1955. In 1955 we had three junior colleges. Now we have the beginning of a network of 22 community colleges. We also have statistics on job training conducted under federal, state, or local auspices. But we have no information on how many of our citizens received technical training while in the armed services, through mail-order courses, through in-service training, and so on. So what do our statistics mean?

We have had an increase in mental illness in this state. But we're not sure it's a real increase. My guess is that the statistical increase is due to an increase in hospital admissions, and in out-patient care and more readily accessible diagnostic services through our community mental-health programs. Our admissions procedures in state mental hospitals are ludicrous. What is considered admission in one hospital is considered out-patient care in another.

We have almost no information on things like civil liberties, discrimination, political radicalization, citizen participation in community life, social breakdown, and so on. The intelligence gap is almost staggering. Information is one-sided, distorted, missing, misinterpreted, or just plain useless. The result is that anybody can come up here to the state capital and quote the statistics that he likes. You can prove anything. Politicians can appeal to their constituencies on the basis of fear, ignorance, and prejudice.

We are in the process of trying to lay out the social sectors within which information is needed. It's a long process. In a way, our efforts may be premature. The HEW report that came out in January 1969, "Towards a Social Report," points the way for a national system of social accounts.

If we could, we would wait for a national system, and then design our own to be comparable. But we can't wait. We have to have our own data now. Without them, state planning can be as arbitrary as political pressure. The purpose of having more and the right kind of information is that it would enable us to act more rationally. It would make possible coordinated action on the state level. I read something by Daniel Bell once about man shaping his future. The question is, will we do it blindly or consciously?

*   *   *   *

P-24   DESIGNING AN INFORMATION SYSTEM

I'm a systems analyst. Although I've moved out of the field and into an academic setting, I still like to keep my hand in some action. I've done some work with program budgeting and planning systems, but lately I've devoted most of my time to exploring how the use of information systems can lead to more efficient organizational operations and more effective planning.

I know most data men consider information systems only in terms of their utility for program effectiveness or operational efficiency. I have a slightly different point of view. I think that the kinds of data you collect and the way you interpret them are a major input in the process of goal selection and policy determination.

I make this very clear to administrators who call on me to help them develop information systems. The first thing I tell them is that if they are really serious about looking at their information needs, they must also be serious in their willingness to examine their programs and their program objectives. A simple test usually helps me decide whether a policy maker is really open to change.

I always ask them for some quantitative indication of a programmatic success. I then tell them that their indicator suggests to me that they have either failed in their programmatic objective, or that their objective was inappropriate. I then wait for the reaction. I'll give you an example.

A psychiatrist, the director of a community mental-health center, showed me his annual report. In it, as an indicator of his agency's success, he pointed to the fact that his staff had been instrumental in getting the local high school to double the number of counselors and counseling hours available to students with learning and social difficulties. "I would suggest," I said to him, "that this is an indicator of your agency's failure. Success might better be measured by your cutting the number of counseling hours in half." Of course he looked incredulous. I went on to explain that the reason students needed counseling might better be found in the system rather than in the students. What was there in the system of the high school that made it impossible for some students to learn? Was there something in the way in which teachers comported themselves that resulted in lack of control and acting out on the part of students? "Perhaps," I suggested "you ought really to have focused on the structural causes of poor learning and acting out. If you can work with the teachers and the curriculum, you may find that you can reduce and almost eliminate the need for counseling hours."

Now, admittedly, this is pretty tough medicine for an administrator, even a psychiatrist, to take. I can usually tell at this point whether I should continue with my consultation.

Let's assume for the moment that the agency I'm consulting with wants to set up an electronic data processing system. An EDP system is a rather complex entity and requires a great deal of clear thinking. It begins with an awareness of information needs. Let me run you through the series of steps that we might take together if I were consulting with you.

Step 1. Becoming Aware of the Need

We might begin by examining the reasons for your dissatisfaction with the current data being used. Does the pressure for change come from a management that has become aware of the potentialities for an expanded information system? Or does the pressure come from the outside—from a legislative group, for example, or from a funding agency or a client group that wants additional information that the agency cannot provide? Typical problems that an agency with an inadequate information system might suffer from might include the following.

(a) Misuse of professional staff time in recording useless data.

(b) Loss of information as it moves from the intake worker through a secretary through a caseworker to a supervisor, and the like.

(c) Just plain lack of necessary information.

(d) No automatic feedback on change or effectiveness of program.

(e) No possibility of doing a cost-effectiveness study or a cost analysis because the data are unavailable or improperly recorded.

(f) No possibility of comparing the data from this organization with that from other agencies.

There are some other problems too. Partial information, which is what most of us have to work with most of the time, can be misleading and can lead us up blind alleys. You also get something that Simon calls the "absorption of bad news." Nobody wants to admit that his operation isn't working too well or that he's got problems. No underling is going to willfully be the bearer of bad news to his superior. Only good news gets bumped upwards, and because a lot of people can block information at any point in the system, policy makers never really know what's going on. Now an efficient, open, and available data system gives access to information to everyone—including, incidentally, clients. A good information system, therefore, redistributes power. You have to know that, and the people with whom you're consulting have to know that, or you may be wasting several months of hard work to set up an ideal system that no one will use.

Step 2. Putting Together a Planning Unit to Pursue the Development of an Information System

Next, the policy makers have to be willing to assign a committee that will have major responsibility for planning the new system. I generally suggest to the administrator that he take into consideration political factors within his own organization. The representative of the opposition, for example, might be included in the planning. The planning group should also involve those people who will be using the information, who will be feeding it into the machine, and who will run the system. In any case, assignment to the planning group must carry some weight. Other administrative and programmatic responsibilities should be reduced—otherwise you wind up with a committee that diddles around and complains about overwork. The result is often an information system that looks like one of Dr. Seuss' animals!

Step 3. Conducting an Information Survey

This is an equally crucial step and it is the basis for all the remaining steps. You get your planning group to review all the reports and records of the last year or two. To whom did they go? For what reason were they prepared?

You check out all your administrative relationships. To what other organization is your agency related? What do others need to know of you and what do they actually know of you? How are your ongoing recording procedures used for service or administrative purposes? Are these being gathered ritualistically or are they really usable?

Here's a simple one.

Is payroll information used for planning purposes? Are salaries in your agency compared to salaries elsewhere?

And you begin to ask yourself some additional questions. You begin to think through what kind of information you're gathering, now that you can do without. You begin to identify what's inaccurate and what is not up to date. And you try to identify how your current agency practices are limited by the nonavailability of still other data.

Step 4. Examine Your Information Survey, Evaluate the Available Information, and Set Priorities

By now your committee is ready to think through what it wants the system to do or to be. It can begin to think through whether the agency would really benefit by a change or whether the current system is adequate with some minor modifications. It might also be possible at this stage to attach a cost figure to the current system and think in terms of the convergence of the current expenditures into the new system. Would a new budget line have to be set up? Will the initial cost be so prohibitive that a major change is unfeasible even though over the long run (say five years) you might increase agency efficiency considerably? What kind of personnel do you need to run the new system and what kind of personnel do you have currently available?

It's at this stage that your committee develops an information policy statement describing the future state of affairs, and projects the events and procedures for getting to that future state. I guess you might say that this is the establishment of a plan. If at this point your committee should decide not to proceed but only to make some minor modifications, then your information policy statement might be usable at some future date for comparative purposes. If, however, your committee decides to recommend a major change, you then go on to Step 5.

Step 5. Setting Up a Series of Meetings with Hardware Consultants

I'm no computer expert. At this point I generally suggest that a hardware consultant be called in. "Consultant" is a euphemism for "salesman." Here is a tip. I usually start with small companies first. They often have very good machinery and are liable to offer you a very good deal. Because they are small, they don't intimidate your people. It's after you've met with a couple of small-company people that you call in IBM.

When your hardware consultants have been called in, you sit down with your committee and try to help them sort out their impressions as to cost, utility, and usefulness. The trouble with a lot of agencies is they start with Step 5. They don't go through the other four steps first. So any hardware salesman can come in and sell them a bill of goods. They wind up with a piece of costly electronic machinery with no idea of what information they are going to feed into it. Often the hardware salesman suggests the kinds of information that ought to go into the system, based on what his machinery can do. On occasion, I have been called in to consult at this stage. I can tell you it's a mess. The agency has already committed so many resources, and the staff are so disillusioned, that it is sometimes impossible to pick up the pieces and redesign an effective information system at this point. Assuming, however, that the preceding steps have been followed and that all goes well, you can move on to the next stage.

Step 6. Selecting Tentative Hardware

After having gotten competitive bids and learning something about how easy or difficult it is to use each of the machines, and knowing something about their cost, your committee makes a choice. Up until now, your choice of hardware has been dependent on your resources and your software development. Software, of course, includes all the components other than the hardware—the information you want, the forms you may be using, your objectives, the staff relationships developed in the planning process, and so on. From now on, however, your software components will be dependent on your tentative choice of hardware.

Step 7. Developing Your Software Components

Having decided what information you want and what information you don't, you develop forms for recording. Forms should be simple. It's best if all the data, like those on an intake sheet, can be placed on one side of the page. It reduces boredom and fatigue.

Of course what you ask is more important than the form on which you ask it. Garbage in, garbage out. Still, you want your staff to fill out the forms willingly, and you want the information to go easily into the computer. It may be possible to save a number of in-between steps at this point. For example, data might come directly from the client onto the form and into the computer rather than from the client to the staff member and then onto the form.

Equally as important as the design of the recording form is the design of the printout form. How do you want the computer to give you back information? What kinds of information sheets do you want? Do you want a closed TV screen?

It's important, in designing your first EDP[1] system, to be certain that your agency workers can get instantaneous feedback on their recording. No committee should design an initial system that will take months to get working. The machine should be used like a toy—simply at first. It should prove its utility through instantaneous feedback. If you try to do too much at first, (like creating long information forms), you wind up

---

[1] Electronic data processing.

with ill-will from the staff, and you'll probably have to change your information forms later on, anyway.

Step 8. Installing The System

Now that you have developed your software components, install your system. I must tell you of one agency that did not think through the location of their computer very carefully. They wound up paying rent on it (which can be very costly) for six months, until they were able to locate the right room and get the proper ventilation for the machine. There are some very simple kinds of questions to ask, like how much electricity will you need and who is going to run the equipment? Or, how conveniently or centrally is it to be located?

Step 9. Feedback and Evaluation

If the software is properly developed, it should not be difficult for your committee to regularize feedback on whether information needs are being properly met. By this time, you might assume that the agency staff is considerably more sophisticated about its information needs and its usages. As awareness and sophistication continue to increase, new information needs will be identified. If the information system is developed in a self-corrective manner, your people may start all over again at Step 1, "Becoming Aware of the Need."

Some Tips on Working With the Planning Committee

The biggest problem at any step in the process is the resistance you might engender within the agency's administrative hierarchy or among the line staff members themselves. It's critical, therefore, that your planning committee be composed of important people. It's also critical that they develop the information system themselves. If things go wrong, or if they get discouraged or hit on one block or another, it's always easy to blame the consultant. I use a very simple formula.

I never tell people what to do or what they need. By the same token, I don't assume that they know what they need, either. If I know something about the organization or the agency with which I am consulting, I put together a reading list of some 15 or 20 articles and illustrations on how information systems have been used by similar agencies or organizations in similar circumstances. Now, I preselect these articles pretty carefully. I know that if I ask my committee members to read them, and suggest several things for them to look for, they are bound to come up with a program quite similar to the one I might have suggested. If they have not identified some of their needs properly, or if they have suggested some things too impractical to consider, I point these out and engage in a discussion with the committee. In this way, they feel they are really doing the planning and utilizing me only as an expert consultant. When the plan is finally developed, it's theirs, not mine. When it is presented to the agency's policy makers, it has the weight of their investment and the support of my expert testimony. The planning committee gets the credit or the blame.

*   *   *   *

P-25   COSTING OUT A TUBERCULOSIS SCREENING PROGRAM

Let's face it. Most of the time we don't know whether we're saving or losing money in our public programs. Let me give you an example.

A few years ago I did a benefit-cost analysis for the State Department of Public Health. I evaluated the utility and efficiency of a traveling TB detection center. In that year, a single mobile unit owned by the state was able to screen about 300,000 people in 32 communities. The cost was roughly $150,000, or about 50¢ per person. That year, they discovered 50 new active source cases. You can see that it cost roughly $3000 to spot each person before his tuberculosis got so severe he would be incapacitated and hospitalized. None of these people knew they had tuberculosis before the screening showed up the disease. The question I was asked to answer was whether it was worth $150,000 to catch only 50 people in the early stages of the disease.

My first step was to identify the benefits of early detection. These included (1) direct benefits such as a reduction in hospital and other treatment costs by early detection, while freeing those resources for other programs; (2) the indirect benefit of reducing the cost of other programs such as welfare or unemployment benefits, which would be necessary to maintain the sick person or his family and thereby reducing the level of aggregate productivity; and finally (3) the external benefit, which might be a reduction of contagion among the contacts of the 50 active source cases.

It's easiest, of course, to measure economic return for a program by using only direct benefits. The economic return for this public investment, for example, would be the difference between economic losses attributable to these 50 cases (if they had not been detected), as against the cost of screening and preventative care. As it turned out, the cost to the state in hospital and other treatment programs would have been roughly $300,000, or about $60,000 per person. The actual cost based on early detection was $100,000 for early treatment plus the $150,000 to run the mobile screening unit around the state. It's obvious, therefore, that there was an investment benefit here. If you figure the investment benefit to equal the "without-program cost" minus the "with-program cost," you get a total investment benefit of $50,000. In a sense these benefits are re-distributive. Some people in the community who do not benefit directly from the program are willing to provide the services for others who do benefit from them. Such redistributive benefits are not measurable. I wish they could be. If they were we would have normative welfare criteria in quantifiable form. Unfortunately, there was no way in which we could cost out these benefits in our analysis. Of course there are other benefits not costed out in this analysis as well. These include benefits to the consumer, future benefits from the continued existence of this program (like total elimination of TB), and values to people in the community based on the continued maintenance of this program. About all we could do with our analysis was to focus on the efficiency benefits to whomever they accrued.

Remember, the total investment benefit was $50,000. I could have left it at that, and the Public Health Department might have been quite satisfied that they were spending the money wisely. This would not have told the entire truth.

I decided to examine the locations in which TB cases were detected, and the populations most adversely affected. I found that half the screenings had been conducted in Detroit. The other half were conducted in smaller cities throughout the state. In Detroit, they located approximately 40 cases. The trick now is to calculate a total investment benefit for Detroit as against the total investment benefits for running the mobile unit across the remainder of the state. The calculations are rather complicated, but for simplicity's sake let's say that the "without-program cost" to 40 people in Detroit would have been roughly $4/5$ of the total cost of the 50 people across the state. The "without-program cost" is therefore $240,000. The "with-program costs" are $1/2$ of the $150,000 that it cost to run the unit across the state ($75,000) plus $4/5$ of the $100,000 for all 50 people across the state ($80,000). The total investment benefits for Detroit, therefore, are equal to the "without-program cost" ($240,000) minus the "with-program cost" ($155,000) or $85,000.

Now, if you run the same calculation for all the communities outside of Detroit, you get a total investment benefit of minus $35,000. In other words, if you did not run the mobile unit outside of Detroit, you would have $35,000. In dollars and cents, spending $75,000 throughout the state and losing $35,000 is certainly a poor investment.

When I presented my findings to the State Public Health Commission, I recommended that they drop the screening program outside the Detroit area. You can imagine the reaction I got. One physician asked me if I was so crass as to put a dollar value on human life. How could I sacrifice the 10 people whose tuberculosis was caught early enough outside the Detroit area? The answer of course was rather simple. It could be made in humanistic rather than in dollars and cents terms. If the expenditure of $75,000 in Detroit was adequate enough to locate 40 new active source cases, why should we spend another $75,000 to locate only 10 source cases outside the metropolitan area? That second $75,000 could be redirected to screening additional persons in Detroit. I recommended that for the next year, at least on a trial basis, the mobile screening unit be kept in the Detroit metropolitan area. If in screening 300,000 people, it would now detect 80 new active source cases, then we could make decisions based not only on cost effectiveness, but on the basis of the most humane criteria. True, we might be sacrificing 10 people from outside the metropolitan area, but on the other hand we would be finding 40 new people within Detroit. Should we sacrifice those 40 people?

There was another question that I could not answer. A man from the governor's staff asked me, "How are you going to satisfy the people in Port Huron and Grand Rapids? Their congressmen have to vote for the TB detection program, and if that mobile unit isn't traveling around the state, we're not going to have funds for Detroit either." As I said earlier, benefits-cost analysis doesn't answer every question.

*　　*　　*　　*

P-26 PERKING UP WITH PERT

I have been a field instructor ever since the School of Social Work started its CO program back in 1962. The biggest problem I have found with CO students is that they are lousy administrators; they are no good on details.

I had one student last year who could not be beaten when it comes to insight, the ability to relate, and charisma. He could work with a neighborhood council like nobody's business. The trouble was that he had so much "faith in the people" that he never anticipated their difficulties. He would tell people they should make phone calls in order to have large turnouts for a meeting. But he never thought through who should make the phone calls, exactly what they should say, from where the phone call ought to be made, or when they should be made so as to have the maximum effectiveness. If he had a lousy turnout, it wasn't because the issue was unimportant or the people weren't interested, it was because he was always two or three steps ahead of himself.

A lot of students know exactly where they want to go with a program. They don't have any difficulty in setting goals for themselves. But they are always worrying about time. They are always complaining that two days a week in the field or an 8-month-long assignment isn't adequate to achieve their objectives. Half the time, they wait around for something (a process) to take place. It's amazing how busy they get during their last month of field work.

For a while, I was thinking of giving up field instruction. It was too much of a drain on my time and emotional energy. And it seemed to have little payoff for the agency. Then, a short time ago, I got hold of the PERT manual used for training purposes in the Community Action Program. Now, PERT is no panacea for problem solving. It doesn't tell you want to do or why to do it. But once you have selected your goal, it does force you to specify the details of implementation.

I now teach all my new students and new workers how to develop a PERT model of their activities. The model includes estimates of time, resources, people, and equipment necessary to accomplish a sequence of interdependent activities. A PERT model makes it possible to figure out what you have to do and when, while also specifying what someone else has to do and when, in order for an objective to be reached. PERT isn't helpful in determining whether your plan is the right one to eliminate a problem, but it can be helpful in assuring that a plan is logical in sequence, and that it's the most efficient way to achieve a particular objective.

How does PERT work? It's simple. Let's say you are assigned to developing a staff-development institute for representatives of 10 agencies in a particular neighborhood. Suppose it's October and you want to run your institute in December. The first thing you do is lay out a calendar with all the in-between dates. Then you think through the events that must precede a successful institute. The events might include establishment of an advisory or planning committee and a series of meetings for that committee. It might include publicity. It would undoubtedly include review of semifinal plans by the agencies involved. It might involve the creation of a temporary bank account, and so on. You lay these *events* out in a string across your calendar, so that you have an idea of where you should be at every stage in the planning process.

Having done that, you now lay out a series of *activities* that will lead to the success of each event along your path to the final objective (the staff-development institute). In planning publicity, for example, the activities might include a first letter to agencies, contacting newspapermen, arranging publicity releases, the purchasing of paper for mimeographing, running the mimeograph, stuffing and stamping envelopes, and so on. For each of these activities, you decide who is going to do it and when.

If you lay out a chart of this type in advance, you not only have a detailed guide for your activities, but you also have a way of monitoring your progress. At every stage in the planning process you can see whether you have done what was necessary. If something goes wrong, you can always correct it by deciding on some other event or modifying your activities.

I guess you might say PERT is a frame of mind and a discipline.

* * * *

P-27 THE NEW FEDERALISM AND CLIENT ANALYSIS

The Nixon Administration's new push toward federalism is going to put planning more squarely in the hands of state officials. Ten years ago you wouldn't have found any planners like myself in state departments of public welfare. Five years ago there were only a handful of people talking about state planning for public welfare. Now every state is going to have to have a planning capacity of its own. It has only been a week since Nixon announced the national income floor and abolishment of ADC. But let's not kid ourselves. ADC and the welfare system are not going to be dismantled so soon. Still, we are going to have to change our way of looking at things. The welfare system is going to find itself increasingly called upon to plan and coordinate services at the state and regional levels when Congress passes welfare reform.

Let's take this ADC business, for example. The new legislation is going to double the number of people getting income assistance. In an urban-industrial state like ours, the state and the counties are going to have to supplement the federal payments considerably. We are going to be giving welfare checks not only to our current clientele, but also to close to a million people not currently served. Who are these people? The federal guidelines, when they come out, may be helpful in determining the client population, but legislation is written to please a lot of legislators and their constituencies. It's going to be written in general terms, and it will be our job to redefine the law in operational terms. It would be nice if we could wait until the federal guidelines came in, but we don't have that kind of luxury. Once the "feds" tell us what we are going to get and how we should spend it, we'll probably only have a few weeks left to set up our procedures. I've been in even worse situations. Once I was told to start spending money on July 1st, but did not receive the federal guidelines on how it was to be spent until the middle of September. Under those kinds of circumstances, you can't wait. You have to anticipate. You have to think through the alternative contingencies, and figure out what you will have to do under each one.

Take the client population as an example. You have to figure out who you now serve, and who you'll potentially be serving when the new legislation comes through. You go through a number of steps.

First you anticipate what the proposed legislation might call for. This is not too difficult. The President's message has made that quite clear. Current income will be the major determining variable. We have enough census and other data to estimate the number of families earning, say, less than $2400 for a family of four. We can calculate the number of families earning less than $2000 or $3600, too. These calculations give us some notion of what our potential population might be, that is, the total number of people who might qualify or be eligible for supplemental income from the Department of Public Welfare.

Comparing this potential population to the clients we now are serving, will give us some notion of the similarities and differences in income and in need. At the very least, it will give us the gross figures on the people we are currently serving, as against the maximum number we might serve under the new laws.

At present, we pay a family of four about $3100 on ADC. The difference between $2400 and $3100 is $700. How much would the state have to put in if the federal government contributed 35 percent of the supplemental welfare grant of $8700? Or 55 percent? Or 75 percent? Or more?

If we take our share of the contribution and multiply it by the number of people that we anticipate will be falling into that particular category of income or family size, we can figure how much state revenue we will need to mount the program.

We can do several other things as well. We can look at the potential effect of job placement and job training. We can also anticipate the needs for new child-care centers. How many will we need if a certain percentage of mothers on welfare become wage earners? How much will we need in terms of new recreation facilities and programs? Are there enough buildings for child-care centers or shall we, as Senator Percy has suggested, write new state legislation altering the building-code requirements for child-care centers so that church buildings that are licensed for Sunday schools can also be licensed as child-care centers?

These are just the first steps in planning—thinking through the issues. We are going to have to go after the hard data and make lots of hard decisions. How many people will we be able to serve during the initial few months of the new federal program? How many after six months? How many after a year? New legislation at the state level is going to require more than simple federal guidelines. It will require a receptive public and a well-informed legislature. We've got to start our citizen-education process right now. We've got to prepare the state representatives and senators with an understanding of what the new legislation will mean for us at the state level and at the county and local levels. It's no easy job, but that's what planning is all about.

* * * *

P-28 A HEALTH STUDY FOR AMERICAN INDIANS

I had a mandate from Congress to determine the health status of the Indian population and what could be done about it.

The responsibility of providing public health services had been transferred from the Department of the Interior to the Public Health Service (PHS). The reason for the shift revolved around the serious health problems of Indians—they were 40 years behind the rest of the American population in terms of death rates. The health leadership in this country, and the health officers, felt that the PHS, being health oriented and having a larger staff, would be a better base than the Interior Department for doing the job.

What you do is a question of philosophy. Is it better to preserve a separate Indian culture or is it more desirable to integrate Indians into the American stream of life? The way you answer that question determines whether you set up specialized health programs or relate them to general health services. Several points of view were represented in the Bureau of Indian Affairs: (1) the Indian culture is unique, like the whooping cranes, so you have to preserve it from extinction and encourage them to stay on reservations; (2) it's impossible to preserve their cultural patterns and you have to integrate them into American culture; and (3) (the middle position) it should be made possible for them to reach a reasonable standard of living and maintain some kind of cultural pattern.

My personal view is that, except for the very large tribes, you could not preserve their original cultural patterns, for they were largely destroyed already. But if we could improve their economic resources and education, we would at the same time improve their health status. The government should be building up health services for everyone in the country, for Indians and non-Indians alike.

When Congress passed the law transferring health programs to the PHS, they requested a comprehensive survey of the Indians' health needs and how their health could be improved. The PHS had to set up a study group to carry out the mandate. About six people were chosen from various spots in the PHS and were assigned the survey as their full-time worry. I was one of them. This group was given funds and assigned staff. We had 18 months to present a report to Congress.

I was made assistant director of the project and a senior medical officer was assigned as director. No one member of the core staff of six had major responsibility. Responsibility and decisions were shared. One of the other members was a competent statistician and another was an anthropologist from the Bureau of Indian Affairs who knew and understood the Indians. I'm a physician with a social-work and public-health background.

The first problem was a logical one. What information did we need (for example, demographic data such as birth and death rates and economic levels)? What information was available from existing sources? What reservations were to be studied on a sampling basis? After discussions among us, we decided to do an interview survey getting at the illness experience on a sample of 11 reservations. We tried to make the sample as representative as possible as to geographic location, income level, degree of acculturation, and the like. Final approval was given by our chief in the Surgeon General's Office—we only made recommendations. In deciding on the reservations to be sampled, we used the help of two statisticians from the Bureau of Census.

Next, an interview schedule had to be developed. The committee decided to interview heads of the households at all 11 reservations (most had a population of 5000 or less). On 5 of these reservations, it was decided to do medical examinations to test the relationships of what was reported in the interviews and what actually existed. The 5 most representative reservations had to be determined. As the physician of the group, I was placed in charge of the medical exams. I had to decide on the examination procedures (for example, X ray or cardiogram) on the number of tests, and on the record forms.

My next task was to find a temporary staff to do the examinations— two or three physicians and nurses and an X-ray and lab technician (a staff of about eight). I had to have at least two local people on the team to help with language problems. I also decided to use, for the most part, the same team on each reservation, to avoid retraining and bias. Although I was in charge, I consulted with others as to the mechanical problems such as the types of machines and instruments to use, the problem of unreliable electric power, language barriers, and the like. The anthropologist, who was in charge of the interview, and I decided to do the interview and medical examination simultaneously so as to help eliminate any time effects. There were also nonmedical problems such as the weather—at one reservation, winter set in earlier than we expected.

In most of the cases, I went to the reservation ahead of time to look over the facilities. I checked on sources of electric power and where we could set up. First I'd talk with the superintendent of the reservation. Sometimes the anthropologist and I would go together for the initial talk with the superintendent and the tribal council (a formal organization designated by the Interior Department). I had to be sure the superintendent and the Indians would cooperate. I also met with whomever was responsible for the existing health program on the reservation, usually the physician in charge of the hospital there. I'd talk to him so that he'd understand what we were doing. I also discussed with him the possibility of using his staff—although I didn't press him because of his lack of facilities and understaffing, and because I wanted to keep bias to a minimum.

Although I didn't conduct the examinations, I'd usually arrive with the team and help with the procedures. If someone on the team didn't show up, I'd take his place. I'd try to spend at least the first few days with the team on every reservation so as to iron out any difficulties. When I was back at my office I had reports and records that were coming in from the study to look over. I had to set up procedures for tabulating information, editing, interpreting, and coding of the doctors' comments and diagnoses. I had a clerical staff to help me with the transferral of information onto cards. Statistical problems came up. I was responsible for drafting a description of the medical-exam survey for the final report. I also reviewed and commented on the narrative and conclusions of the health survey, and gave my comments on the chapter dealing with the history of Indian health services.

In looking back over my work, I think the approach used was a good one. I might have liked to have done the study on more reservations and gotten a larger representative sample. I'm not so sure we needed all the tests we gave. Some of the lab people were research oriented and wanted a lot of material, such as stool specimens; I'm not sure it contributed to the end result. I'd also question the electrocardiogram's worth.

I'd want to handle findings on individual patients differently by having a follow-up with the local health service, especially with the eye diseases such as trachoma. Trachoma is a chronic, severe eye disease that can lead to blindness; it is spread by flies and found where there is poor sanitation. I found that a large percentage of children had it. Although this was reported to the local health service, we never had any chance to follow up on our findings. The local people had to provide the services.

It's quite possible that a local chief of Indian health in the PHS was resentful that an independent team had come in, rather than his own, and he thus took no action. I do think that they had problems such as understaffing. There needed to be strong leadership from the top to push new health programs. We were able to do research but could not force local groups to do anything.

Still, I think we accomplished a great deal. The group got out a report that contributed to the interest of the congressional committee. I would like to think that, as a result of the survey, the PHS gave Indian health a higher priority than did the Department of Interior. In most government operating units, each unit competes for funds and the funds are relocated to departments. In the PHS, the amount for Indian health was doubled.

Personally, I learned a lot about the dynamics of community relations, and about how careful you have to be when involving the cooperation of sizable groups of people. One should get the best advice available from the people who have the know-how. I learned that you can't work faster than the situation allows you to. There are things, like behavior, that you can't control, but you can try to influence it. You can't issue a decree and then expect behavior to change as a result. Working on the reservations was an experience in working on a local level. Every bureaucrat should have it.

Our doing the study involved an inherent dilemma—if the health people on the reservation had done it they might have gotten different results because of their bias. But, it's hard to tell. They may sweep our findings under the rug, but then again, maybe they'll do something about them. Would they have done more if they had uncovered the same problems through their own studies?

*   *   *   *

P-29   PPBS[1]—THE POLITICS OF RATIONALITY AND THE RATIONALIZATION OF POLITICS

Limits and Constraints of Program Budgeting

I read something by Jacques Ellul once, to the effect that politics is increasingly becoming a battlefield between competing technologies. I believe that this is true. And I'm convinced that a tool like PPBS gives us an effective weaponry that combines software (ideas and approaches) with hardware (computers and mechanical equipment). There is no question of quantifying or mechanizing human values here. That's nonsense! PPBS provides the planner with an opportunity to optimize values. This is a point not fully understood by planners of the more traditional mode who do not think in systemic terms. I'll tell you what PPBS is not.

---

1 Program Planning and Budgeting Systems.

It is not

—an accounting process
—a system of administrative control by budget
—some mystical computer magic
—an activity conducted by experts alone
—a full-blown planning system

Certainly, program budgeting has a long way to go before its applicability to urban problems approaches its current usefulness for space or military planning. Without national guidelines or clear consensuses on goals, little of what the boys at the Urban Institute concoct is apt to have any major impact. It is not just that PPBS is still a primitive tool—it is that we are unschooled in its utility, or nonpurposive in its applicability.

One of McNamara's whiz kids once explained to me that "in Strategic Air Command where the goals are very precise, you can cost everything out in terms of reaching a target, reducing losses, or making advantageous trade-offs (absolute number of megadeaths versus sustained industrial capacity, for example). You can computerize an effectiveness scale and monitor your operation at every step." He had this image of Curtis Le-May getting feedback on error from his computers and, "Zeus-like," sending out a thunderbolt to make an instantaneous correction.

This guy had come out of the Rand Corporation and done a stint in the Department of Defense and another in the Budget Bureau. He's now with Mayor Lindsay's staff in New York. Well, political strategy is not yet like military strategy. LeMay wasn't casting out any effective thunderbolts in the 1968 presidential campaign. And Lindsay can hardly be said to be in control of his troops or to command the couple of thousand semi-autonomous governmental units in New York. When you operate in a system with a mixture of goals that are rarely specified, and in which consensus on positive objectives is almost impossible to achieve, no planning system is going to provide all the answers. Last year, my friend was having some serious doubts about the efficacy of using any systems approach whatever. I'm not plagued by such overwhelming doubt, but then I was never that convinced about the universalism of program budgeting to start with, only about its utility as a competing technology.

Look, PPBS *is* primitive! In dealing with social problems, it is almost impossible to assign fixed values to either ends or means. Nevertheless, the program-budget system depends on some ordering of values. It can be a long, drawn-out process, whereas administrative decisions may have to be made quickly in the light of immediate demands. Ultimately, PPBS can be a money saver, but it costs a lot to convert to it.

I would say that the biggest problem in using the program-budgeting approach is that it threatens the hell out of administrators, bureaucrats, and politicians. Any system that will force you into a public evaluation of either your objectives or your means is going to put a crimp in your traditional ways of operating. I've never seen a PPBS introduced into local government, for example, where a significant shift in power was not the result.

The notion behind PPBS is very simple. Considerations of effectiveness (goal attainment) and cost (resource allocation) are fed into the goal-setting process. These considerations don't determine goals, but they do act as a corrective, when goals are unrealistic or poorly specified, by focusing on the functions to be discharged by every unit in the system.

Steps in Program Budgeting

In program budgeting, (1) you start off by appraising the contributions of every unit within an organization in terms of the organization's objectives. (2) You then determine how those objectives could be reached with a minimal expenditure of resources. Here you try to account for estimates of fiscal constraints and projections of future program needs. (3) The third step is to look at your program alternatives and project them over time. (4) Once having selected a program, you create an ongoing process of program and budget review. (5) The system is not complete without a continuous monitoring and evaluation of program effects in light of experience and changing circumstances.

Social workers and mental-health people have the hardest time with Step 1. The most difficult thing to get them to do is specify activities by outputs instead of by administrative units. In a multiservice center, for example, I found each service unit defensively and jealously guarding its domain instead of specifying how its activities contributed to the agency's overall objectives. The first step in PPBS is to specify and then to categorize all organizational activities leading to goal achievement and to show the interrelationships between them. This gives you a kind of program structure that may differ considerably from the old administrative structure. It puts the emphasis on goal achievement and gets the agency's staff to begin an examination of their real tasks and contributions.

Once you've set the stage with this kind of analysis, you move on to Step 2—identification of the range of fiscal and other resources (manpower, expertise, good-will, and the like) currently or potentially helpful in achieving the stated objectives. You look for budget distortions in which money spent for one objective is actually accomplishing another.

Now, thinking with reference to both short-term and long-range programs, examine the alternative ways of achieving your predetermined objectives. This third step requires a good bit of technical expertise and a substantial amount of data. You must have indices of effectiveness (for example, the number of successful job placements in an employment service center) and efficiency (for instance, the costs per person placed and the success of placement by duration of employment).

A cost-benefits analysis of this sort is most effective when you can compare the efficiency of one means with the efficiency of another, or when you can compare the effectiveness of one program with the effectiveness of another. Some systems analysts leave off right here. They neglect to take into account shifts in the environment resultant from the impact of each program alternative, and so neglect to identify and quantify all discoverable costs and benefits. This can be a fatal negligence. Assuming that the goal is fairly clear and that choices are to be made between alternative means, you now make your decision, based on some reasonable estimate of effectiveness and efficiency. The process is called "optimizing."

The fourth step is to list target dates for the achievement of programmatic objectives and subgoals, figuring your costs over time. This makes up your plan. It serves as both a guide to action and a guide to ongoing evaluation.

Finally, you design an information system to supply you with the data that you will need on program effectiveness and program costs. The system should be able to identify blocks to accomplishment.

I'm speaking in ideal terms. There really is no single model for PPBS. The most important thing is to have wide participation right from the start, involving a combination of policy and technical staff throughout the process. Choice of indicators and identification of objectives is not a technical matter.

The most obvious advantage of this kind of systems analysis is the re-education of staff and the technical guidance to policy makers.

Interview
Guide

This guide is similar to those used by the interviewers who gathered materials for this volume. It may be used by students, researchers, and practitioners interested in gathering additional illustrations of practice.

1. Can you first give me a thumbnail sketch of the project or program activities in which you have been personally involved in the last few months? (CLEARLY DISTINGUISH DISCRETE "PROJECTS" IF POSSIBLE. SHARPEN THE IDENTITY OF ONE OR TWO FOR LATER ELABORATION)

2. Are you presently involved in any of these projects? (IF THERE ARE SEVERAL, PICK THE ONE IN WHICH HE SEEMS MOST PERSONALLY INVOLVED EVEN IF RECENTLY COMPLETED. AVOID A VERY NEW ONE FOR PURPOSES OF DETAILED EXPLANATION.)

   How did the project begin?

   How did the *idea* for the project arise?

      (PROBE FOR: Individual initiation

                   Degree of information available

                   Felt need

                   Decision regarding plans to proceed

                   Decision regarding organization of formal project)

3. What was the stated project goal at that time? How was the goal determined? By whom? Were alternatives considered? Why were they rejected?

4. What were the first steps that you personally took in the project? (PROBE FOR PURPOSES THAT PROMPTED HIM TO TAKE THE ACTION HE DID.)

5. What kind of things did you do in the weeks that followed to develop the project further?
   (PROBE FOR: What happened at each stage
   Developments within each stage
   Why each action was taken
   What influenced him to take such action
   What factors were involved in his decisions)

6. In what ways do you continue to be involved in the project?
   (PROBE FOR: Policy making
   Program planning
   Program implementation
   Degree of responsibility)
   (SELECT THE AREA OR EVENT OF GREATEST INTEREST TO THE RESPONDENT.) Can you tell me in detail just what happened? (PROBE FOR ACTIONS TAKEN, PURPOSES FOR ACTIONS.)

7. Where do you see the project going from here? How would you characterize the present goals of the projects? Why are they different from the original?

8. What are some of the difficulties that consistently confronted you in working on this project? How did you resolve these? Which ones did you not resolve? How satisfied are you with the way these difficulties were handled?

9. If you had a chance to work your way through the complexity of the whole project again, how would you alter your involvement? What would you do differently? What other supports would you need?